P9-DFJ-070

CONTENTS

CONTENTS

RELIGIOUS WRITERS MARKET-PLACE

*All-new Fourth Edition,
Completely Revised
and Updated*

WILLIAM H. GENTZ
SANDRA H. BROOKS

Abingdon Press
Nashville

RELIGIOUS WRITERS MARKETPLACE

This book is printed on acid-free, recycled paper.

Library of Congress Cataloging-in-Publication Data

Gentz, William H.
    Religious writers marketplace / William H. Gentz, Sandra H. Brooks. —
    All-new 4th ed., completely rev. and updated.
        p. cm.
    Includes bibliographical references and indexes.
    ISBN 0-687-36052-8 (alk. paper)
    1. Religious literature—Publication and distribution—United States—Directories. 2. Religious
literature—Publication and distribution—Canada—Directories. 3. Religious newspapers and periodicals—
United States—Directories. 4. Religious newspapers and periodicals—Canada—Directories. 5. Religious
literature—Authorship—Marketing—Directories. I. Brooks, Sandra H. II. Title.
Z479.G46 1993
070.5'0973—dc20   93-22587
                                                                                                              CIP

93 94 95 96 97 98 99 00 01 02—10 9 8 7 6 5 4 3 2 1

MANUFACTURED IN THE UNITED STATES OF AMERICA

FOREWORD

Twenty-five years ago when I entered the field of writing for religious periodicals, there was a rule of thumb that everyone in publishing used as a marketing guide: "Whatever is a hot topic in the secular market today will be a hot topic in the religious market ten years from now."

And there was evidence to prove that: Romance novels became hot items in the 1960s; so by the 1970s, there were "Christian" romances. Self-help books flooded the market in the 1970s; so by the 1980s, the religious market had "recovery" books. Countless other parallels.

Today, however, there is no such lag time. The 1990s have found families eager for instantaneous news. Homes today have telephones, fax machines, radios, televisions, VCR's, and computers with "electronic mail" bulletin boards. By the time the daily newspaper thumps the front porch each evening, most households have already heard about the day's events. As such, the so-called *news*paper now serves more as a record of that day's history.

The print media (newspapers, magazines, newsletters), realizing that they cannot match the speed of the electronic media (TV, radio, fax, E-mail), have been forced to redefine their functions. Since a newspaper is too slow a vehicle to *break* a story, it instead will now *analyze* a story. It will take the 20-second "sound byte" item from radio and give it a history, a social evaluation, a psychological profile, and a political interpretation.

Similarly, since television has created the "visual magazine" with programs such as "20/20" and "Entertainment Tonight" that offer everything from personality profiles to forums for political debates, magazines have had to redefine their function, too. Borrowing from the visual impact of TV, magazines now run many more photographs than a decade ago. Borrowing the importance of "flash news" from radio, magazines now print dozens of short items rather than six or eight long features. Borrowing from the speed of satellite communications, magazines now go a step farther by giving the news of the future (a review of next week's TV special, or a review of a book or movie set for release next month).

Each of these significant changes in format, function, and lead time is of great importance to the free-lance writer. That is why a market guide such as *Religious Writers Marketplace* is essential to every contemporary writer's reference library. Within these pages you will find not only the basic data about all the current religious markets, but also insider information on how markets are changing, how editorial needs are being redefined, and how religious publishers are making an effort to match the secular market in timeliness yet retain a God-honoring perspective.

William Gentz has a strong background in free-lance writing, market compiling, book and newsletter editing, and workshop teaching. Sandra Brooks has been a columnist, feature writer, editor, and guest instructor at writers' conferences. They have pooled their talent and experience in producing this in-depth volume of marketing information. As writers themselves, they know the kind of specific data free-lancers need in order to approach new markets. As editors, they are able to anticipate the questions free-lancers have about aspects of writing and marketing. They've included appropriate answers to those questions.

This book will provide you with a world of opportunities: (1) It will show you ways to share your life experiences, personal testimonies, and individual interests with thousands of readers; (2) it will show you how to earn a second or primary income for yourself as a writer; and (3) it will take whatever skills you have already developed in writing and enhance and improve on them.

If you are smart, you will read and dog-ear these pages every day. This book is a tool. Use it.

Dennis E. Hensley
Fort Wayne, Indiana

Dennis E. Hensley has written 26 books and 2,400 articles in the last twenty-five years, many of them in the religious field or as helps with the craft of writing. He has also written columns for leading magazines including *Writer's Digest*. In recent years he has instructed or spoken on 125 occasions at 48 conferences and workshops for writers.

AN INVITATION
TO READERS

We've taken extraordinary measures to make this edition of *Religious Writers Marketplace* the best ever! We've made it as accurate and current as possible—even revising the last proofs sent to the publisher. The publishing industry has always been in a continual state of change, but in the last few years, the frequency of those changes has radically escalated. Periodicals and book publishers have come and gone. Continuing change in editorial leadership and publishing house ownership has become commonplace. On a smaller scale, local writer's groups have dissolved, new ones have begun. Resources and services for religious writers have proliferated. We welcome your assistance in helping us stay abreast of these changes. In the meantime, keep track of continuing changes through the "MarketLines" column in *Cross & Quill, The Christian Writers Newsletter.* For more information on *Cross & Quill,* see the section entitled, "Writers Magazines and Newsletters" in chapter 6.

As we prepare for the fifth edition of *Religious Writers Marketplace,* we'd deeply appreciate any corrections, additions, and suggestions that will help us serve you better. Write to William H. Gentz, 300 East 34th Street (9C), New York, NY 10016, or Sandra H. Brooks, Rt. 3 Box 1635, Clinton, SC 29325.

ACKNOWLEDGMENTS

We are indebted to the hundreds of editors, publishers, and editorial staff members who have contributed information about the periodicals and books listed in this volume.

Special acknowledgment goes to those who made significant contributions of time and knowledge: Laura Sue Mordoff, who researched information on scholarly journals for chapter 2; Lion Koppman, who supervised the gathering of information and writing of entries in chapter 4; Dennis E. Hensley, who wrote the foreword; Audrey Dorsch, who contributed information on Canadian markets from her recently published *Canadian Christian Publishing Guide.*

We also thank the seventeen persons who contributed material from their expertise to the last three chapters of the book. For chapter 5: Don M. Aycock, Fannie Houck, Larry Neagle, Maynard Head, Nan Duerling, Geri Hess Mitsch, Cynthia Ann Wachner,

Mary Ann Diorio, and Dennis E. Hensley; for chapter 6: Norman B. Rohrer, Gayle Roper, Norma Jean Lutz, and Mary Harwell Sayler; for chapter 7: Aggie Villanueva, Marlene Bagnull, Connie Soth, and Albertine Phaneuf Wicher.

In addition, we are grateful to Abingdon Press for agreeing to publish this fourth edition of *Religious Writers Marketplace* and to Jack Keller, reference books editor, for supervising the process and making it all come together and reach writers for whom the book is intended.

W. H. G. and S. H. B.

A NOTE ON ALPHABETIZING

Our listings follow strict letter-by-letter alphabetizing for the names of publishers and periodicals—with one exception: When the name of a publisher is a person's name, we alphabetize by last name as followed by *Literary Market Place* and other reference guides—as if the entry were a name in the telephone directory. For example, you'll find Thomas Nelson Publishers listed under N and Harold Shaw Publishers under S. When in doubt use the indexes at the back of the book.

* ONE *

How to Use This Book

This isn't a book on *why* you should write for the religious marketplace. Perhaps more than in any other writing field, religious authors need inspiration for their task. They write for the religious market because they feel compelled to write, to tell a story, to relay truths about God's world as they see them. Although you may be inspired by the sheer numbers of opportunities profiled in this book, inspiration for becoming a religious writer comes primarily from sources other than books of this kind.

Nor is it a guidebook about *how* to write. Although a careful study of the material gives much information on how to find help in improving your writing skills, the book's basic premise is to tell you how to *market* your writing. Like its three predecessors, this fourth edition of *Religious Writers Marketplace* is about *who, where,* and *what.* Who are the publishers? Where can you find them? What are they looking for? With whom can you make contact for help in improving your writing skills? Where can you go for help? What do you need to know about the business end of writing in order to market successfully? Writers, religious authors no less, want to be published. Except for the therapeutic benefits, it's scarcely worth the effort to put words on paper unless someone reads what you write in a book, magazine, journal, or newspaper. That's our purpose in writing this book—to give you timely, detailed information about existing markets so that someone, somewhere can be instructed or inspired by the words you put on paper.

Religious writing is a burgeoning field. The sheer numbers of religious books and magazines printed each year stagger the mind. To gather information for the first edition of *Religious Writers Marketplace,* we sent questionnaires to more than 1,000 outlets for religious writing. With each new edition, we've added new features and hundreds of new sources to the book. We believe this fourth edition is the most valuable and user-friendly ever.

Your challenge is to learn to use the book well. Let's look briefly at what the book contains and how to find and use the information you need.

We devoted the greatest portion of this book—chapters 2, 3, and 4—to publishers and publications with which you need to acquaint yourself. Note, first, the construction of the entries. Except for the brief ones, each entry consists of three paragraphs.

1. *The first paragraph* gives important statistical information: the name, address, and telephone and fax number (where available) of the periodical or publisher; the chief editor's name and others to whom manuscripts can be sent; the name of the

9

sponsoring group or church, if this information is relevant. A brief characterization of the publisher follows along with circulation in the case of the periodical and number of books per year in the case of a book publisher.

2. *The second paragraph* contains detailed information about the publisher or publication. It identifies the target audience, the publisher's purpose in printing the book or magazine, the theological position, and the kind of material being sought. Sentences and phrases quoted directly from the publisher or editor are placed in quotation marks.

3. *The third paragraph* gives the mechanics of submitting material to a particular publisher. How long is the average article or book? Does the publisher prefer queries or finished manuscripts? Are sample copies and author's guidelines available? What other special instructions does the publisher have for authors? If you're approaching a magazine, what is the payment rate? Is payment made on acceptance or on publication? Is the magazine purchasing first, reprint, or all rights to your work? If you're approaching a book publisher, do they offer outright purchases or do they pay royalty? If they pay royalty, what percentage will you receive? Is that percentage based on the wholesale or retail price? Does the publisher offer an advance? If so, how much? What is the average reporting time?

Browsing through the entries will give you many ideas on where to submit the material you write, but we suggest that you study the indexes in the back of the book first. There you'll find publishers and periodicals listed according to publishing or denominational affiliations. You will also find a list of the kinds of material publishers accept. If you are a poet, for example, you'll find it easier to look up "poetry" in the index than to go through the pages of entries looking for poetry publishers. The indexes can become your best friend as you consult them for specific marketing needs.

When you're more familiar with the markets, customize the entries to meet your specific needs. Use colored highlighters to draw your attention to a particular type of writing within the entry. For instance, use one color to draw your eye to the word "poetry." Use a different color to tell you at a glance whether a market pays on acceptance or on publication. If you're a children's writer, highlight juvenile market entries in a designated color. Juvenile writers can cut research time still further by using separate colors for different age groups: young children, older children, and teens.

Now let's look more closely at the specific marketing needs that this book fills.

In chapter 2 you'll find Christian periodicals—all varieties: slick four-color magazines, Sunday school take-home papers, scholarly journals, and many others. In addition, you'll find most theological positions: mainline Protestant, evangelical, Roman Catholic, and nondenominational audiences. Under subheadings to these categories, you'll find publications that have an orthodox, fundamentalist, charismatic, ecumenical, or liberal slant. Some periodicals have all these emphases among their readers.

Chapter 3 lists religious book publishers, most of them specifically Christian. You'll find publishing houses that target denominational, nondenominational, and Roman Catholic audiences with an orthodox, evangelical, charismatic, ecumenical, or liberal slant. The entries give you clues to the emphasis of each.

Chapter 4 is one of several unique features in *Religious Writers Marketplace,* in that it lists periodicals and publishers of Judaica. Because of the special needs, interests, and terminology of Jewish periodicals and book publishers, we designed a special questionnaire. Lion Koppman, former director of public information for the Jewish Community Centers Association of North America (JCC) and an author of several books, supervised the handling of the entries. Again the emphasis of each publisher, such as orthodox, conservative, or reform, is explained on the basis of information submitted.

Increasingly, publishers for the Christian marketplace are adding books of Jewish interest to their lists. What is more, some periodicals appeal to both Christian and Jewish readers. Accordingly, we have entered their names in both chapters 3 and 4.

Once you have learned to use the indexes and market entries well, you'll want to acquaint yourself with chapters 5, 6, and 7. This portion of the book has been greatly expanded in this edition. Some sections have been rewritten.

Chapter 5, entitled "Branching Out," profiles specialized kinds of writing such as poetry, greeting cards, juvenile, newspaper, drama, script, and many others. Please note that in this fourth edition we have expanded information under our curriculum and music sections. We have also added sections on writing devotionals, writing for crossover markets, and entering contests.

Chapter 6, entitled "Getting Help," tells you where to find the help you need to acquire and improve your writing skills: correspondence courses, books on writing, audio and video teaching cassettes, conferences and workshops, newsletters and magazines, and critique groups.

Here's a word to the wise. Repeatedly editors and publishers have told us through our questionnaires that many writers still fail to follow basic submission rules and etiquette, such as including the SASE (self-addressed stamped envelope), preparing the manuscript in proper manuscript form, and so forth. To find this information, study books on basic writing and follow the guidelines.

Chapter 7, entitled "Minding Your Writing Business," gives valuable tips on keeping track of where your manuscripts are, how long they've been there, bookkeeping and taxes, agents, and self-publishing. Each of these sections has been rewritten and expanded. A new section in this chapter on writing on a computer includes valuable information on word processing, databases, and other resources that computer technology has made available to writers. This knowledge and information is essential in marketing writing today.

Some markets that you've seen in *Religious Writers Marketplace* in the past may not be listed in this fourth edition. The reasons are varied: Some have asked to be omitted because they take little free-lance material or because they're receiving too many unprofessional submissions; others have reorganized and no longer take free-lance; some no longer publish religious books or materials; many no longer exist.

You may also find that information you would like to have about a particular publisher is not listed. We went the extra mile to list everything the publishers asked us to, but we also respected their wishes, if they requested it, to withhold information, such as their telephone number.

This book contains more than 1,000 names and addresses of publishers, publications, agencies, conferences, workshops, newsletters—all waiting for you to pursue your dream of becoming a *well-published* religious writer. We bid you Godspeed!

TWO

Writing for Christian Periodicals

This chapter lists publishers of Christian periodicals including magazines (weekly, biweekly, monthly, or bimonthly), journals (mostly quarterlies), yearbooks, newspapers, newsletters, take-home papers, and others with formats difficult to categorize.

We have reported from every periodical questionnaire returned to us. You'll find a wide variety from which to choose. They range from general magazines with a circulation of more than a million, to specialized markets with only a few hundred subscribers. Some opted for no listing since they accept no free-lance material.

You'll find that some publications pay well. Others pay little, and some pay only in copies. Consider the payment policy of periodicals you intend to approach. A pay-on-acceptance market issues the check for your manuscript soon after acceptance. A pay-on-publication market issues your check after your manuscript goes into print. For newspapers that may mean a week, but for magazines it may mean three years or more! Another area you'll need to consider is the doctrinal and theological emphasis of periodicals that interest you. Christian periodicals as a whole break easily into two categories: Roman Catholic and Protestant. These two categories break into several sub-categories with different emphases: conservative, fundamentalist, evangelical, liberal, mainline, charismatic, ecumenical, and so forth. Although publishers often disagree on the exact definition of these terms, using the terms gives guidance to the theological emphasis of the publication. Please note that some publications address more than one category or sub-category. To simplify the task of choosing markets that best suit your theological position, we stated the periodical's emphasis whenever the editor indicated it to us.

Knowing the target audience of a periodical helps in choosing the markets best suited to you and your field of writing. While the audience of some publications is broad and general, many others are limited and highly specialized. For instance, some periodicals address the needs and concerns of adults; others address children, young readers, or senior adults; many address the needs and concerns of all ages and interests. It's improbable that you'll want to write for a parenting magazine if you aren't a parent. You wouldn't want to write an article on teaching if you've never taught a class.

Another aspect of determining audience is whether a denominational or nondenominational house produces the material. This is important because denominational houses publish materials that reflect the doctrinal position and needs of members in their denomination. In most cases, however, and unless they so state in their entry, this does not mean that they will accept material only from members of their denomination. Periodicals produced by independent houses cross doctrinal and denominational lines. A few publications cross faith lines and serve both Christian and Jewish readers. In such cases, we have listed the publication both in this chapter and in chapter 4, "Writing for the Jewish Market." Publication titles listed in this chapter are in strict alphabetical order. Leaf through it to get an overview of the available markets. If you have a specific kind of article or market in mind, consult the indexes. There you'll find publications listed under their sponsorship (i.e., Roman Catholic, Southern Baptist, United Methodist, etc.) as well as under the kinds of material they print—fiction, nonfiction, poetry, photographs, and so on.

To discover the best possible markets for your material, request sample copies of publications and author's guidelines. Studied carefully, these help immeasurably in determining where to send which kind of writing. As you do personal market research, keep three principal questions in mind: (1) Who is this publication's primary audience? Consider things like: age group, gender, ethnicity, faith status (i.e., Christian or non-Christian), level of education, and profession. (2) Which viewpoint appears most often among the articles: first, second, or third-person singular or plural? (3) What is the overarching purpose of this magazine? By that we mean, What is the editor or publisher trying to convey through the selections offered in the magazine? What kinds of material (i.e., personal experience, self-help, short stories, poetry, etc.) have they used to accomplish their purpose? To develop your market savvy further, stay abreast of market trends by reading magazines, journals, and newsletters written especially for writers. We compiled an exhaustive list of publications to help you with that task. Find them listed under "Writers Magazines and Newsletters" in chapter 6.

Keeping a file or notebook on markets you've researched is a necessity. If you need help with recordkeeping, follow the suggestions under "Keeping Track of It All" in chapter 7.

Computers can play a significant role in helping you to warehouse market information. Using a filer program, you can easily create a database of market information. Computer submissions call for special handling.

Find out which software the publishers or publication desires: IBM compatible or Mac compatible. Or ask the editor about submitting your manuscript as an ASCII file.

- Find out what disk size the editor needs: a 3.5" or 5.25" floppy.
- Avoid using high density disks. Many computers cannot read them.
- Protect your disk before mailing to guard against data damage by magnetic fields it may come in contact with during transit. For instance, disks exposed to ringing telephones, radios, or X-ray machines can easily be erased. Protect data by covering the notch on 5.25" disks or closing the slot on 3.5" disks.
- Include a hard copy (printout) of the manuscript in case problems arise with your disk. Doing so may save you the time, money, and frustration of preparing and mailing another parcel.
- Mail disks in containers that will protect them from breakage during transit.

For more information on how computers serve writers and editors, see "Computers: The High Tech Muse" in chapter 7.

When submitting material, keep in mind that much material is seasonal in nature. Since periodicals are planned well in advance, submit seasonal material six months to a year before the season for which you're writing.

Many requests made by the editors who responded to our questionnaire are basic submission rules and etiquette:

- Use a good grade of white bond paper (20 lb.), 8.5 × 11.
- Do not use erasable bond.
- Type all manuscripts double-spaced, on one side of the paper only, black ribbon only. If you use a computer, use your printer's letter quality fonts.
- Leave at least one-inch margins on all edges.
- If you need to insert corrections on a typewritten manuscript, make them in ordinary lead pencil—not in ink.
- Be accurate and consistent in spelling, punctuation, capitalization, and other rules of style and grammar. Computer users will find grammar and spelling checkers extremely helpful in pinpointing trouble spots.
- Consult a good style book, such as the *Chicago Manual of Style, A Christian Writer's Manual of Style,* or *Words Into Type* and follow the standard rules as closely as possible.
- Be accurate and complete in citations, bibliographies, and permissions lists. Check all quotations against the original source (especially Bible quotations) before submitting the manuscript.
- In a brief cover letter, give a few facts about yourself and your qualifications for writing the manuscript.
- Enclose a SASE (self-addressed stamped envelope) for return of the manuscript in case it is rejected and when requesting free materials such as sample copies of a magazine or author's guidelines.

Do everything possible to present yourself as a professional—in writing style and mechanics, in submitting manuscripts to editors and publishers. But don't let the structure and demands of periodical publishing intimidate you. Despite human failings and unwitting errors, editors are eager to hear from you. In fact, they depend on you to provide the material they need. Read on and acquaint yourself with the many editors and publishers waiting to hear from you.

ADVANCE, 1445 Boonville Avenue, Springfield, MO 65802. (417) 862-2781, 4095. Fax: (417) 862-8558. Harris Jensen, editor. A 40- to 48-page monthly magazine published by General Council of the Assemblies of God. Circulation 30,000.

☐ *Advance* addresses a clergy and laity audience with an Assemblies of God background. "Serves as a vehicle of communication between national headquarters departments and local church, consolidating in one unit promotional and program." Needs articles on preaching, doctrine practice, how-to features for ministers and church leaders. Sermon illustrations. Original material only.

Article length 1,000 to 1,500 words. Prefers a complete manuscript. Buys first, reprint rights. Guidelines for SASE. Pays up to 6 cents per word on acceptance.

ADVENT CHRISTIAN WITNESS, P.O. Box 23152, 14601 Albemarle Road, Charlotte, NC 28212. (704) 545-6161. Fax: (704) 573-0712. Robert J. Mayer, editor. A 20-page monthly magazine published by Advent Christian Conference. Circulation 4,000.

☐ *Advent Christian Witness* addresses an Evangelical audience of clergy, laity, and scholars with an Advent Christian Church background. Needs personal experiences, devotional articles, articles on current issues and inspirational topics. Assigns material for columns on current issues and theology. Uses photographs.

Article length from 750 to 1,200 words. Columns run 500 words. Requires model release with B&W glossies. Prefers a complete manuscript. Buys one-time and simultaneous rights. Guidelines and sample copy for $2. Pays $15 to $25 on publication.

THE ADVOCATE, Box 12609, Oklahoma City, OK 74157. (405) 787-7110. Fax: (405) 789-3957. Shirley Spencer, editor. A 20-page monthly magazine published by the Pentecostal Holiness Church International. Circulation 35,000.

☐ *The Advocate* serves an Evangelical audience of laity and church leadership with a Pentecostal Holiness background. Needs personal experiences and articles on current issues and theological topics. Also uses poetry (traditional), column material (on current issues), fillers (devotions and meditations), and photographs.

Articles run 1,000 to 1,200 words. Limit poetry to three poems per envelope. Model release required with B&W glossies. Prefers a complete manuscript. Buys all rights. Guidelines and sample copy for SASE. Lead time three months. Pays $10 to $25 on publication.

AGAIN MAGAZINE, P.O. Box 106, Mt. Hermon, CA 95014. (408) 336-5118. Fax: (408) 336-8882. Weldon M. Hardenbrook, editor. A 32-page quarterly magazine published by the Antiochian Evangelical Orthodox Mission. Circulation 4,000.

☐ *Again Magazine* serves a Conservative, Evangelical audience of laity and clergy with a mainline Protestant background. A thematic magazine which needs articles on current issues and theological topics in saints' lives. Meditations, "excerpts from Church Fathers or writings of the saints."

Article length 1,500 to 2,000 words, meditations 500 to 1,500 words. Prefers a query. Accepts computer submissions. Macintosh compatible, any format but MacWrite preferred. Buys all rights. Guidelines and theme list free for SASE, sample copy for $3.50 including postage and handling. Reports in one month. Pays on publication, but most nonpaid.

ALIVE! A MAGAZINE FOR CHRISTIAN SENIOR ADULTS, P.O. Box 46464, Cincinnati, OH 45246-0464. (513) 825-3681. J. David Lang, editor. Submit to A. June Lang, office editor. A 12-page bimonthly magazine published by Christian Seniors Fellowship. Circulation 10,000.

☐ *Alive!* addresses a nondenominational audience of senior adults, clergy, scholars, and laity with an Evangelical background. Needs personal experiences, interviews, and articles on current issues for senior adults. Also uses fiction (adventure, mystery, romance, humor), an occasional poem, fillers (humor), and photographs.

Articles and fiction 600 to 1,200 words, fillers to 100 words. Limit poems to 3 per envelope. Model release required for B&W glossies. Prefers a complete manuscript. Accepts photocopies and simultaneous submissions. Buys first, reprint, and one-time rights. Guidelines for SASE, sample copy for SASE with 2 first-class stamps or 75 cents for mailing and handling. Reports in 6 to 8 weeks. Lead time 4 months. Pays $18 to $75 on publication.

ALIVE NOW! P.O. Box 189, Nashville, TN 37202. (615) 340-7218. Fax: (615) 340-7006. George Graham, editor. A 64-page bimonthly magazine published by The Upper Room. Circulation 65,000.

☐ *Alive Now!* serves an Ecumenical audience, 40 percent of whom are clergy; the majority of readers are 30-59 years of age. Needs prose articles (meditations, theme-based fiction), poetry, Scripture, and worship resources that reflect on spiritual themes.

Article length 250 words for nonfiction, 250 to 750 words for fiction. Complete manuscripts accepted. Guidelines and theme list available for SASE. Lead time is approximately 6 months. Newspaper and periodical rights. Payment on publication.

THE A.M.E. CHRISTIAN RECORDER, 500 Eighth Avenue, South, Nashville, TN 37203. (615) 256-8548. Dr. R. H. Reid, Jr., editor. A 16- to 24-page biweekly newspaper published by A.M.E. Church.

☐ *The A.M.E. Christian Recorder* addresses an African Methodist Episcopal audience of clergy and laity, with an Evangelical background.

AME CHURCH REVIEW, 500 Eighth Avenue S, Nashville, TN 37203. (615) 256-7020. Dr. Paulette Coleman, editor. An 84-page quarterly journal published by the African Methodist Episcopal Church. Circulation 3,400.

☐ *AME Church Review* addresses an adult audience, primarily male, with an AME background. Needs articles on current issues, theology, sermons, and addresses. Also uses column material on Federal legislation and book reviews. Filler needs include letters to the editor and historical vignettes. Also buys photographs.

Article, column, and filler length not specified. Photograph needs are for B&W glossies. Prefers complete manuscript. Guidelines and sample copy for SASE. Generally no payment.

AMERICA, 106 West 56th Street, New York, NY 10019. (212) 581-4640. Fax: (212) 399-3596. Rev. George W. Hunt, S.J., editor. A 24- to 32-page weekly magazine with a circulation of 40,000.

☐ *America* serves a clergy, laity, and leadership audience with a Roman Catholic background. Needs articles on current political and social issues, poetry, and column material.

Article length 2,000 words. Limit poems to 3 per envelope. Columns appear in the op-ed format and run about 750 words. Accepts complete manuscript and electronic submissions. No simultaneous submissions. Buys first rights. Guidelines and sample copy for SASE. Reports in 7 to 10 days. Pays $50 to $100 on acceptance.

THE AMERICAN BENEDICTINE REVIEW, Box A, Assumption Abbey, Richardson, ND 56852. (701) 974-3315. Father Terrence Kardong, editor. A 110-page quarterly journal with a circulation of 1,000.

☐ *The American Benedictine Review* serves an audience of scholars and clergy with a Roman Catholic background. Needs articles on theological topics.

Article length about 20 double-spaced pages. Accepts complete manuscripts and computer submissions that are IBM compatible. Buys all rights. Guidelines and sample copy for SASE. Reports in 3 months. No payment.

AMERICAN BIBLE SOCIETY RECORD, 1865 Broadway, New York, NY 10023. (212) 408-1480. Fax: (212) 408-1456. Clifford P. Macdonald, editor. A 32-page monthly magazine published by the American Bible Society. Circulation 275,000.

☐ *American Bible Society Record* serves a Roman Catholic and mainline Protestant audience of adults and senior adults with either an Evangelical or a Liberal background. Needs personal experiences and articles on current issues. "Magazine prints only articles directly concerned with the work and mission of American Bible Society." Also buys photographs.

Article length not specified. Model release required for color prints. Prefers a query. Buys all rights. Guidelines not available. Pays on acceptance. Rate not stated.

THE AMERICAN ORGANIST, 475 Riverside Drive, Suite 1260, New York, NY 10115. (212) 870-2310. Fax: (212) 870-2163. Anthony Baglivi, editor. A 96-page monthly magazine published by the American Guild of Organists. Circulation 25,000.

☐ *The American Organist* serves an audience of laity, clergy, and scholars, both Evangelical and Liberal, with a Roman Catholic or mainline Protestant background. Needs articles on organ, choral, and sacred music. They also need photographs.

Article length not stated. Photographic needs are for B&W glossies. Must query. Accepts computer submissions. Buys all rights. Guidelines and sample copy for SASE. Reports in 2 months. Lead time 2 months. No payment.

AMERICAN PRESBYTERIANS, 425 Lombard Street, Philadelphia, PA 19147-1516. (215) 627-1852. Fax: (215) 627-0509. James H. Smylie, editor. A 72-page quarterly journal published by the Presbyterian Historical Society. Circulation 1,200.

☐ *American Presbyterians* addresses an audience of scholars, clergy, and laity with a Presbyterian background. Needs nonfiction articles on Presbyterian history and photographs.

Article length is 25 double-spaced manuscript pages. No model release required with B&W glossies. Prefers a complete manuscript. Accepts computer disks and electronic submissions in most PC and Mac programs. Guidelines free for SASE. No payment.

THE ANGLICAN, P.O. Box 94, Somers, NY 10589. (914) 277-3122. David L. James, editor. A 12-page quarterly magazine published by The Anglican Society. Circulation is 2,000.

☐ *The Anglican* addresses a clergy and laity audience with an Episcopal background. Needs personal experiences, articles on current issues and theological topics. Also needs traditional poetry, meditations, and photographs.

Article length is 5 to 8 double-spaced pages. Limit poems to 3 per envelope. Meditations are 3 to 5 double-spaced pages. No model release required for B&W glossies. Prefers a complete manuscript. Accepts photocopies, computer disks. Requests one-time rights. Guidelines free for SASE. Reports in 2 weeks. No payment.

ANGLICAN JOURNAL, 600 Jarvis Street, Toronto, ON, M4Y 2J6 Canada. (416) 924-9192. Fax: (416) 921-4452. Carolyn Purden, editor. Submit to Vianney Carriere. A 20- to 24-page newspaper published by General Synod of the Anglican Church. Circulation 272,000.

☐ *Anglican Journal* serves an adult and senior adult audience with a Canadian Anglican background. The magazine's purpose is to "inform Canadian Anglicans about the church at home/overseas, activities in other denominations/faiths, reports issues that affect its readership." Uses news, profiles, theology, doctrine on the arts, church education, education, environment, evangelism, feminism, health, media, missions, stewardship, natives, politics, seniors, social issues. Also buys book reviews and photographs.

Articles and book reviews 200 to 800 words. Prefers a query. Accepts computer disks, but no simultaneous submissions or photocopies. Buys first and reprint rights. Free guidelines for SASE. Lead time 6 weeks. Pays $50 to $500 on publication.

ANGLICAN THEOLOGICAL REVIEW, 600 Haven Street, Evanston, IL 60201. (708) 864-6024. Fax: (708) 328-9624. James E. Griffis, editor. Submit poetry to Robert Cooper, book reviews to Donald Winslow. A 130-page quarterly journal published by the Episcopal and Anglican Seminaries of the United States and Canada. Circulation 1,500.

☐ *Anglican Theological Review* serves an audience of clergy and scholars with an Anglican, Episcopal background. Needs articles on theology.

Article length unspecified. Prefers a complete manuscript. No guidelines or sample copies available. No payment.

THE ANNALS OF ST. ANNE DE BEAUPRE, P.O. Box 1000, St. Anne de Beaupre, Quebec G0A 3C0, Canada. (418) 827-4538. Roch Achard, editor. A monthly magazine published by the Redemptorist Fathers. Circulation 45,000.

☐ *The Annals of St. Anne de Beaupre* addresses an adult audience with a Roman Catholic background. The magazine "promotes Christian family values." Needs fiction, nonfiction, and traditional poetry.

Articles on family related topics run 500 to 1,200 words. Short stories run 500 to 1,200 words. Poetry length 12 to 20 lines. Limit poems to 6 per envelope. Prefers a complete manuscript. Accepts simultaneous submissions and photocopies. Buys first rights. Guidelines for SASE. Lead time 2 to 3 months. Pays 3 to 4 cents per word for fiction and nonfiction, $5 to $8 for poems on acceptance.

THE ASBURY HERALD, Asbury Theological Seminary, Wilmore, KY 40390. (606) 858-3581. Fax: Same as phone. Robert Bridges, editor. Submit to Scott Burson, managing editor. A 16-page quarterly magazine published by the Asbury Theological Seminary. Circulation 26,000.

☐ *The Asbury Herald* addresses an Evangelical audience of scholars, clergy, and laity from a Wesleyan Methodist background. A thematic magazine needing personal experiences, interviews, and devotional articles on current issues and theology. Also uses columns (on theology), fillers (devotionals, meditations, and anecdotes), and photographs.

Article length 1,500 words, columns and fillers 500 words. No model release required for B&W glossies and color slides. Prefers a complete manuscript. Accepts electronic submissions in WordPerfect and Microsoft Word. Call about other software. Guidelines and theme list available, sample copy not available. No payment.

THE ASSOCIATE REFORMED PRESBYTERIAN, One Cleveland Street, Greenville, SC 29601. (803) 232-8297. Ben Johnston, editor. A 40-page monthly magazine published by the General Synod, Associate Reformed Presbyterians. Circulation 6,200.

☐ *The Associate Reformed Presbyterian* addresses an Evangelical audience of children, youth, adults, and senior adults. Adult readers are clergy, laity with an Associate Reformed Presbyterian background. Needs personal experiences, devotional articles, and articles on current issues and theological topics. Uses photographs.

Article length 500 to 2,000 words. Model release required for B&W glossies and color slides. Prefers query. Accepts photocopies, simultaneous and computer submissions. Buys first, reprint, and one-time rights. Guidelines for SASE and $1.50. Reports in 1 month. Pays $50 maximum for articles, $25 maximum for photographs on acceptance.

AT EASE, 1445 Boonville Avenue, Springfield, MO 65802. (417) 862-2781, ext. 3270. Fax: (417) 862-8558. Lemuel D. McElyea, editor. A 4-page bimonthly newspaper published by the Chaplaincy Department of the General Council of the Assemblies of God. Circulation 27,000.

☐ *At Ease* serves an Evangelical audience in the military of clergy and laity with an Assemblies of God background. Needs personal experiences, interviews, devotional articles, and column material (current issues and theology). Also needs traditional poetry, fillers (devotions, meditations, anecdotes and humor), and photographs.

Article length 400 to 600 words, column material 400 to 500, fillers 25 to 100, poems 25 to 75. Model release required with B&W glossies and color slides. Prefers a complete manuscript. Buys first rights. Guidelines and sample copies not available. Reports in 6 weeks. Lead time 6 months. Pays 3 cents per word for prose, $10 for poems, $10 for fillers on publication.

ATTENTION PLEASE! 2106 3rd Avenue, N, Seattle, WA 98109. (206) 284-2733. Lois Ludwig, editor. A 14-page mini-magazine with a circulation of 300.

☐ *Attention Please!* addresses a "secular audience with a Christian mission for children and teens with attention deficit disorder. The audience is also interfaith." Readers are children, teens, and adults. The adults are support group coordinators, educators, and medical professionals for individuals with attention deficit disorder. Needs interviews with ADD adults, fiction (adventure and mystery), puzzles as fillers.

Article length 500 to 700 words. Fiction is for children ages 6 to 8 and runs 350 words. Puzzles fit a 5" × 3.75" space and have to do with ADD or learning disability. Prefers a complete manuscript. Accepts photocopies, simultaneous submissions, and computer submissions. Buys first rights. Guidelines and sample copy for 6 × 9 envelope with 52 cents postage. Reports in 2 weeks. Lead time 4 months. Pays in 3 copies.

AXIOS, 806 South Euclid Street, Fullerton, CA 92632. (714) 526-4952. Fax: (714) 526-2387. Daniel John Gorham, editor. A 32-page bimonthly journal with a circulation of 10,000.

☐ *Axios* serves an audience of clergy and laity with an Orthodox Christian Church background. Needs interviews and articles on current issues, theology, and lives of the saints. Also needs traditional poetry.

Article length 1,000 to 3,000 words. Limit poems to 4 per envelope. Prefers query. Buys first rights. Guidelines and sample copy for 9 × 12 SASE and $2. Reports in 1 month. Lead time 4 months. Pays 4 cents per word upon publication.

THE BAPTIST BEACON, RR #1, Watterford, ON, N0E 1Y0 Canada. (519) 443-8525. Rev. Sterling Clark, editor. A 20-page magazine published 11 times yearly by the Fundamental Baptist Mission. Circulation 300.

☐ *The Baptist Beacon* serves an adult audience with a Fundamental Baptist background. Article needs are for Bible studies, devotions, meditations, personal experiences on topics like Bible teaching, evangelism, prophecy, and inspiration, theology and doctrine, sermons on Christian living, evangelism, family, and leadership. Prefers Fundamental Baptist writers.

Article length unspecified. Prefers query but accepts complete manuscript. Accepts simultaneous submissions, photocopies, but no computer disks. Buys first rights. Guidelines and sample copy not available. Reports in 4 weeks. Lead time 3 months. Pays on acceptance. Rate not stated.

BAPTIST HERALD, One South 210 Summit Avenue, Oakbrook Terrace, IL 60181. (708) 495-2000. Fax: (708) 495-3301. Barbara J. Binder, editor. A 32-page magazine published 10 times yearly by the North American Baptist Conference. Circulation 8,000.

☐ *Baptist Herald* serves an Evangelical audience of American Baptist laity. Needs personal experiences, interviews, and articles on current issues. Also needs photographs.

Article length 500 to 1,000 words. Model release required for B&W glossies. Prefers a query. Pays on publication.

BAPTIST LEADER, P.O. Box 851, Valley Forge, PA 19482-0581. (215) 768-2153. Fax: (215) 768-2056. Linda Isham, editor. A 32-page quarterly magazine published by Educational Ministries of American Baptist Church. Circulation 6,000.

☐ *Baptist Leader* addresses an audience of lay leaders, pastors, and Christian education staff with an American Baptist background. The magazine's purpose is to "support the teaching ministry and leader development of the church. We use inclusive language and illustrations." Needs practical how-to's on church education topics. Also uses fillers (anecdotes and cartoons).

Article length 1,300 to 2,000 words. Prefers a complete manuscript. Buys first rights. Guidelines and sample copy for $1.50. Reports in 1 to 6 months. Lead time 1 year. Pays $25 to $100 on acceptance.

THE B.C. CATHOLIC, 150 Robson Street, Vancouver, BC, V6B 2A7 Canada. (604) 683-0281. Fax: (604) 683-8117. Rev. Vincent Hawkswell, editor. A 16-page newspaper published 47 times yearly with a circulation of 20,000.

☐ *The B.C. Catholic* serves an adult, Roman Catholic audience. Its purpose is to report Roman Catholic news. Needs news articles, opinion, commentary, personal experience, theology, doctrine on Christian living, church education, family, health, missions, seniors, social issues. Prefers Roman Catholic writers.

Article length 400 to 500 words. Prefers query. Accepts simultaneous submissions, computer disks. Buys first and reprint rights. Guidelines and sample copy not available. Reports in 4 weeks. Pays on publication. Rate not stated.

THE BEACON, #200, 20316-56 Avenue, Langley, BC, V3A 3Y7 Canada. (604) 530-2292. Lillian Whitmore, editor. A 20-page quarterly magazine published by Evangelical Free Church of Canada.

☐ *The Beacon* serves an adult audience with a Canadian Evangelical Free Church background. The magazine's purpose is "to educate, promote vision and encourage our churches to reach their communities for Christ and to network with other churches in our denomination." Article needs are humor, opinion, commentary, personal experience, and profiles on theology, doctrine on Christian living, church education, evangelism, family, leadership, missions, money management/stewardship, music, social issues. Also uses photographs. Prefers Evangelical Free writers.

Article length 500 to 700 words. Prefers query. Accepts simultaneous submissions, photocopies, or computer submissions. Buys first and reprint rights. Guidelines and sample copy not available. Reporting time not specified. No payment.

BEGINNER LOOK & LISTEN PAPER, 1445 Boonville Avenue, Springfield, MO 65802-1894. Gary L. Leggett, editor. Submit to Dawn N. Hartman, Early Childhood editor. A 4-page weekly take-home paper published by Gospel Publishing House. Circulation 93,000.

☐ *Beginner Look & Listen Paper* serves a preschool children's audience from an Assemblies of God background. "Because the take-home paper correlates closely with lesson materials, all materials are done on assignment basis only. Writers must be approved, with Assemblies of God background. The material is recycled and is currently not in the writing stage."

A BETTER TOMORROW, 5301 Wisconsin Avenue, NW, Suite 620, Washington, DC 20015. (202) 364-8000. Fax: (202) 364-8910. Dale Hanson Bourke, editor. Submit to Cathy Constant, assistant editor. A 110-page quarterly magazine published by Thomas Nelson Publishers. Circulation 100,000.

☐ *A Better Tomorrow* serves an Evangelical audience of senior adult women from a mainline Protestant background. Needs personal experiences, interviews, devotional articles, and articles on current issues. Also needs fiction, poetry (traditional and free verse), column material (advice, health and fitness), fillers (devotions, anecdotes, and humor), and photographs.

Article and short story length 1,500 words, column material 1,000 to 1,500 words. Filler length varies. Photographic needs are for color slides. Must query before submitting complete manuscript. Accepts computer submissions in IBM WordPerfect. Buys reprint and one-time rights. Guidelines and sample copy for SASE. Pays $100 to $200 on publication.

THE BIBLE ADVOCATE, P.O. Box 33677, Denver, CO 80233. (303) 452-7973. Fax: (303) 452-0657. Roy Marrs, editor. Submit to Sherri Langston, assistant editor. A 20-page monthly magazine published by the Church of God (Seventh Day). Circulation 16,000.
☐ *The Bible Advocate* serves an audience of clergy and laity with a Church of God (Seventh Day) background. Needs articles on current issues, theology, exposition of a Bible passage, Christian living, and so forth. Uses traditional and free verse poetry, meditations as fillers, and photographs.

Article length 1,000 to 2,000 words. Limit poems to 5 per envelope. Meditations run 200 to 500 words. Prefers a complete manuscript. Accepts simultaneous and computer submissions in Microsoft Word 4.0 or 5.0. Buys first, reprint, and simultaneous rights. Guidelines and sample copy for SASE with 3 postage stamps. "Please become familiar with the doctrines of the Church of God (Seventh Day) before you submit. We will send out the doctrinal beliefs booklet with the guidelines and sample if you request it." Reports in 1 to 2 months. Pays an honorarium on publication. Does not pay for photographs.

BIBLE REVIEW, 3000 Connecticut Avenue, NW Washington, DC 20008. (202) 387-8888. Fax: (202) 483-3423. Hershel Shanks, editor. Submit to Editorial Department. A 60-page bimonthly magazine published by the Biblical Archaeology Society. Circulation 40,000.
☐ *Bible Review* serves a popular audience of laypersons and clergy with Evangelical, Liberal, mainline Protestant, and Roman Catholic backgrounds. Needs articles on exegesis, column material on theology and Bible trivia, and photographs.

Article length varies. No model release required for photographs. Must query before submitting. Guidelines and sample copy not available. Pays $75 to $150 on publication.

BIBLE-SCIENCE NEWS, P.O. Box 32457, Minneapolis, MN 55432. (612) 755-8606. Paul A. Bartz, editor. A 20-page magazine published every 6 weeks by the Bible-Science Association. Circulation 8,000.
☐ *Bible-Science News* serves a nondenominational audience of scholars, laity, and clergy with a Protestant, Evangelical background. Needs interviews and articles on current issues, column materials on current issues and theology. "We anticipate purchasing a maximum of 4 articles over the coming year. A close familiarity with our publication is a must! So is a query!"

Article length 1,200 words, column material to 750 words. Prefers a query. Buys all rights. Guidelines and sample copy for 9 × 12 SASE with 4 stamps. Reports in 30 days. Lead time approximately 2 months. Pays $100 per final production page on publication.

BIBLE TIME FOR 4'S AND 5'S, P.O. Box 632, Glen Ellyn, IL 60138. (708) 668-6000. A weekly take-home paper published by Scripture Press.
☐ *Bible Time* serves an Evangelical audience of children ages 4 to 5. A thematic magazine needing real-life stories. No retold Bible stories. Also needs conduct stories illustrating spiritual truths.

Story length 220 to 225 words. Accepts complete manuscript. Buys all rights. Guidelines and sample copy for SASE. Pays $20 to $30 on acceptance.

THE BIBLE TODAY, 5401 South Cornell Avenue, Chicago, IL 60615. (312) 324-8000. Fax: (312) 752-7540. Rev. Leslie J. Hoppe, editor. A 53-page bimonthly magazine published by the Liturgical Press with a circulation of 11,000.

☐ *The Bible Today* serves an adult audience of laity and clergy with a Liberal, Roman Catholic background. Needs articles on biblical studies.

Article length is 2,000 words. Accepts complete manuscript and computer submissions in WordPerfect. Buys all rights. Guidelines and sample copy for SASE. Reports in 1 year. Lead time 3 months. Pays in a gift subscription.

BIBLICAL ARCHAEOLOGY REVIEW, 3000 Connecticut Avenue, NW #300, Washington, DC 20008. (202) 387-8888. Fax: (202) 483-3423. Hershel Shanks, editor. Submit to "Editorial Office." An 88-page bimonthly magazine published by the Biblical Archaeology Society. Circulation 180,000.

☐ *Biblical Archaeology Review* is a popular magazine dealing with the archaeology of the Old Testament, New Testament, and the biblical era. Articles are written by biblical and archaeological scholars and are intended for the interested lay audience. "We hardly ever publish unsolicited manuscripts and photographs. All manuscripts and pictures must include a SASE, otherwise they will not be returned."

Prefers a query. Guidelines and sample copy for $4.50. Pays on publication.

BIBLICAL ILLUSTRATOR, 127 Ninth Avenue N, Nashville, TN 37234. (615) 251-3649. Fax: (615) 251-3866. James D. McLemore, editor. An 82-page quarterly magazine published by the Baptist Sunday School Board.

☐ *Biblical Illustrator* addresses an Evangelical audience of church leaders and laity with a Southern Baptist background. Uses nonfiction articles in all areas of biblical history and backgrounds. "Articles are assigned by invitation of the design editor. Please send vital information to the editor. Include church membership information."

Articles run 1,200 to 2,000 words. Must query first. Buys all rights. Lead time 3 to 6 months. Pays 5 cents per word on acceptance.

BIBLICAL LITERACY TODAY, 290 South Hull Street, Athens, GA 30605. (404) 353-1448. Roger N. Carstensen, editor. A 16-page quarterly magazine published by The Mission for Biblical Literacy. Circulation is 5,000.

☐ *Biblical Literacy Today* "is published to help open today's Bible responsibly to the laity, to help close the breach between pulpit and pew, and to help equip the whole Church to the ministry of the Word."

Article length 500 to 1,200 words. Prefers query. Sample copy to prospective writers upon request. Payment in copies of the magazine.

BOOKSTORE JOURNAL, P.O. Box 200, Colorado Springs, CO 80901. (719) 576-7880. Fax: (719) 675-0795. Todd Hafer, editor. A 170-page monthly magazine published by Christian Booksellers Association. Circulation 7,200.

☐ *Bookstore Journal* addresses an Evangelical audience of retailers. This thematic magazine's purpose is to "help Christian retailers and suppliers have more effective ministries by providing them how-to articles, product information, and relevant industry news." Leading articles cover financial management, retail business management and procedures, and marketing to consumers. Feature articles covering specific Christian retail stores, supplier companies, authors, and artists appear regularly.

Article length 1,500 words. Prefers a complete manuscript. Accepts photocopies and simultaneous submissions. Accepts computer and electronic submissions in WordPerfect and ASCII. Buys all rights. Guidelines, theme list, and sample copy for $7.50. Reports in 60 days. Lead time 2 months prior to issue date. Pays a minimum of $4 per column inch on publication.

THE BRANCH, Box 911, Barrie, ON, L4M 4Y6 Canada. (705) 726-8439. Ted Maxwell, editor. A 40-page digest published 3 times yearly by Women Alive!

☐ *The Branch* serves an interdenominational audience of donors, alumni, and organization members with a mainline Protestant background. "Style is informative, good biblical content, motivational, encouraging, challenging." Needs devotions, meditations, opinion, commentary, personal experience, and profiles on theology, doctrine on Christian living, evangelism, family, leadership, media, missions, money management, stewardship, and social issues. Also buys book reviews, poetry, and photographs.

Article length 300 to 900 words. Accepts queries or complete manuscripts: simultaneous submissions, computer disks, but no photocopies. Buys first and reprint rights. Guidelines and sample copy not available. Reports in 4 months. No payment.

BREAD FOR GOD'S CHILDREN, Bread Ministries Incorporated, P.O. Box 1017, Arcadia, FL 33821. (813) 494-6214. Anna Lee Carlton, editor. A 28-page monthly newspaper with a circulation of 10,000.

☐ *Bread for God's Children* serves an Evangelical audience of families (children ages 5 to 10, teens ages 11 to 15) from a nondenominational perspective. Needs personal experiences, fiction (adventure), and column material (current issues).

Article length 600 to 800 words, fiction 600 words for young children, 1,000 to 1,500 words for teens. Column material runs 600 to 800 words. Prefers a complete manuscript. Buys first rights. Will consider reprint rights depending on where it was published. Guidelines and sample copy for 9 × 12 SASE with enough postage for 3 28-page magazines. Reports in 1 month on rejections, indefinite time on acceptances. Pays $40 for teen stories, $30 for child's stories, $20 to $30 for articles on publication.

BREAKAWAY, 420 North Cascade Avenue, Colorado Springs, CO 80903. (719) 531-3400. Fax: (719) 531-3499. Greg Johnson, editor. A 24- to 32-page monthly magazine published by Focus on the Family. Circulation 95,000.

☐ *Breakaway* serves a nondenominational audience of boys ages 12 to 15 with an Evangelical background. Needs personal experiences, interviews, and devotions with humor where appropriate. Also uses fiction (adventure and mystery) and photographs (color slides and prints). Column material written in-house.

Article length is 700 to 2,000 words. Fiction is 1,200 to 2,500 words. Model release is required with photographs. Prefers query, but accepts complete manuscript. Accepts photocopies and computer submissions in WordPerfect 4.2 or 5.1. Buys first rights. Guidelines, theme list, and sample copy free for SASE. Reports in 2 to 4 weeks. Lead time 5 months. Pays 15 cents per word on acceptance.

BREAKTHROUGH! MAGAZINE, 204 Millbank Drive, SW, Calgary, AB, T2Y 2H9 Canada. (403) 256-4639. J. Alvin Speers, editor. A 200-page quarterly magazine published by Aardvark Enterprises.

☐ *Breakthrough! Magazine* serves an interdenominational audience with a mainline Protestant background. The magazine's purpose is to showcase prose and poetry. "Submit upbeat, no uncouth, material." Needs comics, how-to, humor, news, opinion, commentary, personal experience, and profiles on the arts, Christian living, education, family, health, history, leadership, stewardship, politics, seniors, social issues, and travel. Also uses book/film/video reviews, poetry, illustrations, and photographs.

Article length 2,000 words. Accepts photocopies and simultaneous submissions from subscribers only. Buys first and reprint rights. Guidelines for SASE, sample copy for $5. Lead time 6 months. No payment.

BRETHREN LIFE AND THOUGHT, Elizabethtown College, One Alpha Drive, Elizabethtown, PA 17022-2298. (717) 361-1182. Christina Bucher, editor. A 64-page quarterly journal published by Brethren Journal Association. Circulation 750.

☐ *Brethren Life and Thought* serves an academic audience of laity and clergy with a Church of the Brethren background. Needs personal experiences, devotional articles, and articles on current issues, theology, and other topics of interest to the Church of the Brethren such as Anabaptism, Radical Reformation, Pietism, and so on. Also uses poetry (traditional, free verse, and haiku).

Article length 10 to 20 double-spaced pages. Prefers a complete manuscript. Accepts computer submissions in WordPerfect 5.0 or 5.1, or ASCII. Guidelines available for SASE. No payment.

BRIGADE LEADER, P.O. Box 150, Wheaton, IL 60189. (708) 665-0630. Fax: (708) 665-0372. Submit to Deborah Christensen, managing editor. A 16-page quarterly magazine published by the Christian Service Brigade. Circulation 9,000.

☐ *Brigade Leader* serves an interdenominational audience of men with an Evangelical background. "I'm looking for experts in various fields to write articles on assignment. I use very little straight freelance—it's 99% assigned." Needs personal experiences, interviews, and articles on current issues. "Most features done on assignment." Also needs B&W glossies.

Article length 1,500 words. No model release required for photographs. Prefers query. Buys first and reprint rights. Guidelines and sample copy for $1.50. Reports in 1 week. Lead time 2 months. Pays 5 to 10 cents per word on publication. Offers $35 kill fee.

BRIO, 420 North Cascade Avenue, Colorado Springs, CO 80903. (719) 531-3400. Susie Shellenberger, editor. A 16-page monthly magazine published by Focus on the Family. Circulation 80,000.

☐ *Brio* serves an interdenominational audience of girls, ages 13 to 15, with an Evangelical background. Needs articles and short stories related to the issues faced by today's young teenage girls. Also uses fillers (humor, cartoons, anecdotes).

Article and story length 800 to 1,500 words. Prefers complete manuscript. Buys first and reprint rights. Guidelines and sample copy for SASE. Reports in 4 to 6 weeks. Lead time 9 months. Pays 8 to 15 cents per word on acceptance.

BROKEN STREETS, 57 Morningside Drive, East, Bristol, CT 06010. (203) 582-2493. Ron Grossman, editor. A 50-page quarterly journal with a circulation of 750.

☐ *Broken Streets* serves an adult audience of laity with an Evangelical background. Needs personal experiences and devotional articles. Also uses poetry and fillers (devotions, meditations, journal entries, and anecdotes).

Article length one-half page maximum. Poetry any style 5 to 50 lines, limit 5 per envelope. Prefers a complete manuscript. Accepts photocopies, computer, electronic, and simultaneous submissions. Buys one-time rights. Guidelines for $1, sample copy for $2.50. Reports in 1 week. Pays in copies.

BUILDER, 616 Walnut Avenue, Scottdale, PA 15683. David Hiebert, editor. A 16-page monthly journal with a circulation of 10,000.

☐ *Builder* serves an audience of congregational leaders with a Mennonite background. Uses articles that relate to church education and leadership. Also uses book reviews.

Article length 500 to 1,000 words, book reviews 500 words. Query first. Accepts simultaneous submissions. Buys first, reprint, and one-time rights. Guidelines and sample copy for SASE. Lead time 12 months. Pays about $45 per article on publication.

CALVIN THEOLOGICAL JOURNAL, 3233 Burton Street, SE, Grand Rapids, MI 49546. (616) 957-6144. Fax: (616) 957-8621. John Bolt, editor. A 300-page semiannual journal published by Calvin Theological Seminary. Circulation 3,000.

☐ *Calvin Theological Journal* addresses an audience of clergy and scholars with a Christian Reformed background. Needs articles on theological topics.

Article length is 25 double-spaced pages. Prefers a complete manuscript. Requires all rights. No payment.

CAMPUS LIFE MAGAZINE, 465 Gundersen Drive, Carol Stream, IL 60188. (708) 260-6200. James Long, editor. Submit to Chris Lutes, senior editor. A 76-page monthly magazine published by Christianity Today, Incorporated. Circulation 120,000.

☐ *Campus Life Magazine* is a nondenominational magazine and addresses a youth audience of high school and early college students with a Protestant, Evangelical background. Needs personal experience articles and fiction on contemporary teen themes. Also uses free verse poetry, column material on health and fitness, humorous fillers, and photographs.

Articles and fiction 2,500 to 3,500 words, column material 50 to 250 words, fillers 250 to 500 words. Requires model release on B&W glossies and color slides. Must query. Accepts computer submissions. Buys first rights. Guidelines and sample copy for $2. Reports in 6 weeks. Lead time 3 months. Pays 10 to 20 cents per word for articles and fiction, $25 to $75 for fillers, $25 to $100 for poems on acceptance. Offers a kill fee.

CANADA LUTHERAN, 1512 St. James Street, Winnipeg, MB, R3H 0L2 Canada. (204) 786-6707. Fax: (204) 783-7548. Kenn Ward, editor. A 48-page magazine published 11 times yearly by the Evangelical Lutheran Church in Canada. Circulation 30,000.

☐ *Canada Lutheran* addresses an adult audience with an Evangelical Lutheran Church in Canada background. The magazine's purpose is to "provide material for ELCIC members that informs, inspires, investigates, and analyzes." Article needs are for news, opinion, commentary, personal experience, and profiles on theology and doctrine, the arts, Christian living, drama, environment, evangelism, feminism, health, leadership, media, missions, stewardship, natives, and social issues. Also needs book, music, film, video, and television reviews.

Article length 1,000 to 2,500 words. Prefers query. Accepts computer disks, but no simultaneous submissions or photocopies. Buys first rights and reprints. Guidelines and sample copy for SASE. Lead time 12 months. Pays $25 to $100 on publication.

CANADIAN BAPTIST, 217 St. George Street, Toronto, ON, M5R 2M2 Canada. (416) 922-5163. Fax: (416) 922-4369. Larry Matthews, editor. A 6-page bimonthly magazine published by the Baptist Convention of Ontario, Quebec, and the Baptist Union of Western Canada.

☐ *Canadian Baptist* addresses an adult audience with a Canadian Baptist background. The magazine's purpose is to "document and encourage the life and ministry of the churches and people of the BCOQ and the BUWC and to act as an agent of consensus among them." Article needs are for humor, news, opinion, commentary, personal experience, and profiles on theology, doctrine, the arts, Christian living, church education, drama, education, environment, evangelism, family, feminism, health, and so on. Also needs illustrations and photographs. Requires affiliation with the denomination.

Article length 750 to 2,000 words. Prefers query. Accepts computer disks, simultaneous submissions, and photocopies by negotiation. Buys first and reprint rights. Guidelines and sample copy for SASE. Lead time 6 months. Pays $50 to $350 (on acceptance or publication not stated).

THE CANADIAN CATHOLIC REVIEW, 1437 College Drive, Saskatoon, SK, S7N 0W6 Canada. (306) 966-8959. Fax: (306) 966-8904. Rev. Daniel Callam, CSB, editor. A 40-page magazine published 11 times yearly by the Canadian Catholic Review Corporation. Circulation 1,200.

☐ *The Canadian Catholic Review* serves an adult, Roman Catholic audience. The magazine's purpose is to "be faithful to Magisterium; to maintain a solid spiritual aspect by professing the Gospel of Jesus Christ through saints, writers, founders." Needs are for devotions, meditations, news, opinion, commentary, personal experience, and profiles on theology, doctrine, the arts, Christian living, church education, education, evangelism, family, feminism, history, and leadership. Also needs book, film, video, and television reviews, illustrations, and photographs. Prefers Roman Catholic writers. "Writing must be lucid, articulate, and faithful. The CCR is aimed at intelligent, though not scholarly, Catholics. It aims to enliven the faith of the laity and clergy."

Article length 1,000 to 6,000 words. Prefers query. Accepts computer disks, but no simultaneous submissions or photocopies. Buys first rights. Guidelines and sample copy for SASE. Lead time 3 months. Pays $50 to $300 on publication.

CANADIAN DISCIPLE, 240 Home Street, Winnipeg, MB, R3G 1X3 Canada. (204) 783-5881. Raymond A. Cuthbert, editor. A 16-page quarterly magazine published by the Christian Church in Canada. Circulation 550.

☐ *Canadian Disciple* addresses adults with a Disciples of Christ background. The magazine's purpose is to "strengthen the bonds of fellowship, communicate information, deepen the spiritual life." Needs are for comics, devotions, meditations, humor, news, opinion, commentary, and personal experience on theology, doctrine, Christian living, environment, evangelism, feminism, history, missions, stewardship, natives, social issues. "Articles of interest to an ecumenically inclined audience are warmly received." Also needs illustrations and photographs.

Article length 3 to 6 double-spaced pages. Prefers a query. Accepts simultaneous submissions and photocopies but no computer disks. Buys first and reprint rights. Guidelines and sample copy for SASE. No payment.

THE CANADIAN GIDEON, 501 Imperial Road, North Guelph, ON, N1H 7A2 Canada. (519) 823-1140. Fax: (519) 767-1913. Neil J. Bramble, editor. A 48-page bimonthly digest published by Gideons International of Canada. Circulation 4,200.

☐ *The Canadian Gideon* addresses members of the Gideon, an interdenominational audience with an Evangelical background. The magazine's purpose is to "educate, encourage and motivate members so they can continue to reach others with the gospel of Christ." Needs are for devotions, meditations, how-to, news, personal experience, and profiles on Christian living, evangelism, leadership, missions, and stewardship. Particular needs are for ministry news, testimonies, and world news. Also needs book reviews, illustrations, and photographs. "It is essentially inhouse, Evangelical, focused on Gideon ministry and issues related to our ministry."

Article length 800 to 1,200 words. Prefers a complete manuscript. No simultaneous submissions, photocopies, or computer disks. Requires first and reprint rights. Guidelines and sample copy for SASE. No payment.

THE CANADIAN LUTHERAN, Box 163 Station A, Winnipeg, MB, R3K 2A1 Canada. (204) 832-0123. Fax: (204) 888-2672. Frances A. Wershier, editor. A 16-page bimonthly magazine published by the Lutheran Church–Canada. Circulation 27,500.

☐ *The Canadian Lutheran* addresses a youth, adult, and senior adult audience with a Lutheran background. The magazine's purpose is to "serve the constituency by disseminating information, sharing the Christian faith, familiarizing the people of the church with the institutions of the church and with each other." Needs include features about Lutherans, comics, devotions, meditations, personal experience, and profiles on theology, doctrine, Christian living, church education, environment, evangelism, family, history, leadership, missions, stewardship, natives, and so on. "We welcome articles about or by Lutheran Church–Canada members." Also needs games, quizzes, and puzzles.

Article length 2 to 4 double-spaced pages. Prefers query. Occasionally accepts simultaneous submissions and computer disks. Buys first rights primarily, reprint rights occasionally. Guidelines and sample copy for SASE. Lead time 2 months. Pays (occasionally) on publication.

CANADIAN MESSENGER OF THE SACRED HEART, 661 Greenwood Avenue, Toronto, ON, M4J 4B3 Canada. Rev. F. J. Power, editor. (416) 466-1195. A 32-page monthly magazine published by the Apostleship of Prayer. Circulation 18,000.

☐ *Canadian Messenger of the Sacred Heart* serves an adult, Roman Catholic audience. Needs devotions, meditations, personal experiences, and theology on Christian living, church education, family, missions, seniors. Needs fiction that guides daily Christian living.

Article and fiction run 1,500 words. Prefers a complete manuscript. No simultaneous submissions, photocopies, or computer disks. Buys first rights. Guidelines and sample copy for $1. Reports in 1 month. Lead time 6 months. Pays 4 cents per word on acceptance.

CARAVAN, 90 Parent Avenue Ottawa, ON, K1N 7B1 Canada. (613) 236-9461. Fax: (613) 236-8117. Joanne Chafe, editor. A 16-page quarterly magazine published by the Canadian Conference of Catholic Bishops. Circulation 850.

☐ *Caravan* primarily serves an adult, Roman Catholic audience. The magazine's purpose is to provide "a resource for adult religious educators which acts as an information service, networking vehicle, model for the what and the how of adult religious education." Needs include how-to, news, opinion, personal experience, and profiles on doctrine, church education, adult education, leadership, and social issues.

Article length 5 double-spaced pages. Accepts query or complete manuscript in photocopies or as computer submissions, but no simultaneous submissions or reprints. Guidelines and sample copy for SASE. Lead time 2 months. Pays (sometimes) on publication.

THE CATECHIST, 2451 East River Road, Dayton, OH 45439. (513) 294-5785. Patricia Fischer, editor. A 52-page magazine published 7 times yearly with a circulation of 45,000.

☐ *The Catechist* serves an audience of religion teachers with a Roman Catholic background. Needs articles on teaching experience and theology, column material on religion and teaching issues. Also uses photographs.

Article and column material run 1,800 words. Photographic needs are for B&W glossies. Prefers a query, but accepts complete manuscript. Accepts photocopies and computer submissions, but no simultaneous submissions. Buys all rights. Guidelines free for SASE, sample copy for $2.50. Reports in 2 to 4 months. Pays $25 to $75 on publication.

CATHEDRAL AGE, Washington National Cathedral, Massachusetts & Wisconsin Avenues, NW, Washington, DC 20016-5098. (202) 537-6247. Fax: (202) 364-6600. Kelly Ferguson, editor. A 32-page quarterly magazine published by Washington National Cathedral. Circulation 33,000.

☐ *Cathedral Age* serves a clergy audience with an Episcopal background. Needs personal experiences and interviews on current issues and theological topics, meditations as fillers, and photographs.

Article length 1,000 words, meditations 500 words. Model release required with B&W glossies. Prefers a query. Accepts computer submissions in Microsoft Word (Macintosh). Buys all rights. Guidelines and sample copy for $3.75. Pays $50 on publication.

CATHOLIC BIBLICAL QUARTERLY, 415 Administration Building, Catholic University, Washington, DC 20064. (202) 319-5519. Fax: (202) 319-4799. Aelred Cody, OSB. A quarterly journal published by Catholic Biblical Association of America.

☐ *Catholic Biblical Quarterly* addresses a scholarly audience. Needs articles on Scripture and the Bible.

Article length 20 pages. Prefers a complete manuscript. Accepts computer submissions in WordPerfect 5.1. Guidelines and sample copy for $3.75. Reports in 3 months. Pays in 50 copies.

CATHOLIC DIGEST, P.O. Box 64090, St. Paul, MN 55164-0090. (612) 647-5288. Fax: (612) 647-4346. Henry Lexau, editor. Submit fillers to Susan Schaefer. A 144-page monthly digest magazine published by the University of St. Thomas. Circulation 575,000.

☐ *Catholic Digest* serves an adult and senior adult audience, mostly women, with a Roman Catholic background. "As a digest, we're particularly interested in articles which have been published once before. Please include a photocopy, tearsheet, or transcript of the article; the name and address of the original publisher, the date of the issue of the original publication, its copyright statement; any pertinent information about 2nd rights—i.e. do they belong to you, the author or remain with the first publisher?" Needs personal experiences, interviews, and devotional articles. Also needs fillers (anecdotes and humor) and photographs that accompany manuscripts. No fiction or poetry.

Article length 1,500+ words. Fillers run 500 words. Prefers a complete manuscript. Buys first or reprint rights. Guidelines and sample copy for SASE. Reports in 4 weeks. Pays $200 for originals, $100 for reprints on acceptance.

CATHOLIC FAMILY MEDIA GUIDE, P.O. Box 369, 109 East Oak Street, Durand, IL 60124. (815) 248-4407. Fax: (815) 248-2330. Owen C. Phelps, Jr., editor. A 32-page monthly (10 times yearly) magazine with a circulation of 3,000.

☐ *Catholic Family Media Guide* serves laity adults with a Roman Catholic background. Needs articles on Catholic sports and entertainment celebrities, accompanied by photographs.

Article length 250 to 1,000 words. No model release required with B&W glossies. Prefers a complete manuscript. Accepts photocopies, simultaneous, computer, and electronic submissions. Buys all rights. Guidelines free for SASE, sample copy $1. Reports in 1 to 2 months. Lead time 2 to 3 months. Pays 5 cents per word within 30 days of publication.

CATHOLIC LIBRARY WORLD, 461 West Lancaster Avenue, Haverford, PA 19041. (215) 649-5250. Fax: (215) 896-1991. Anthony Prete, editor. A 68-page quarterly magazine published by the Catholic Library Association. Circulation 3,000.

☐ *Catholic Library World* addresses an audience of Roman Catholic scholars. Needs current issues of interest to Catholic librarians and photographs.

Query or send complete manuscript. Accepts computer disks. IBM: WordPerfect, WordStar, or ASCII. Guidelines and sample copy for SASE. No payment.

CATHOLIC NEAR EAST MAGAZINE, 1011 First Avenue, New York, NY 10022-4195. (212) 826-1480. Fax: (212) 838-1344. Michael J. L. LaCivita, editor. A 32-page bimonthly magazine published by Catholic Near East Welfare. Circulation 100,000.

☐ *Catholic Near East Magazine* addresses a clergy and laity audience with an Orthodox Roman Catholic background. The magazine "seeks to educate its readers about the faiths, traditions, history, and culture (not exclusively Christian or Catholic) of Ethiopia, India, the Middle East, and the former Soviet Union." Needs current issues, historical and cultural pieces on the peoples and churches of the Near East. Also needs photographs.

Article length 1,500 to 2,000 words. No model release required with color slides. Prefers a complete manuscript. Buys first rights. Guidelines and sample copy for SASE with 2 stamps. Reports in 1 month. Lead time 3 months. Pays 15 cents per word on publication.

THE CATHOLIC REGISTER, #303 67 Bond Street, Toronto, ON, M5B 1X6 Canada. (416) 362-6822. Fax: (416) 362-8652. Father Carl Matthews, editor. A 20-page tabloid published 47 times yearly with a circulation of 30,000.

☐ *The Catholic Register* addresses a youth, adult, and senior adult audience with a Roman Catholic background. The magazine's purpose is to "inform Catholic people of English Canada on matters of faith." Prefers Roman Catholic writers. "We are English Canada's national, weekly Roman Catholic newspaper." Needs "anything Roman Catholic."

Article length 600 to 1,000 words. Prefers phone queries. No simultaneous submissions, photocopies, or computer disks. Buys first rights. Guidelines and sample copy not available. Reports in 3 to 4 weeks. Pays $50 to $100 on publication.

CATHOLIC TWIN CIRCLE, 12700 Ventura Avenue, Suite 200, Studio City, CA 91604. (818) 766-2270. Fax: (818) 766-2905. Loretta G. Seyer, editor. A 20-page weekly newspaper magazine with a circulation of 35,000.

☐ *Catholic Twin Circle* serves an audience of scholars, clergy, and laity with a Roman Catholic background. Needs personal experiences, devotions, articles on current issues, and theology. Also needs column materials on current issues and theology, and photographs.

Article length 1,000 to 2,000 words. Photographic needs are for B&W glossies and color slides. Prefers a complete manuscript. Accepts photocopies, computer disks in WordPerfect, XyWrite. Buys all rights. Guidelines and sample copy for SASE. Reports in 2 weeks. Pays 3 to 5 cents per word 45 days after publication.

CBMC CONTACT, 1800 McCallie Avenue, Chattanooga, TN 37404. (615) 698-4444. Fax: (615) 629-4434. Robert J. Tamasy, editor. A 24-page bimonthly magazine published by Christian Business Men's Committee of USA. Circulation 17,000.

☐ *CBMC Contact* addresses an Evangelical audience of adult laity, business and professional men. "We use very little freelance material. Generally from persons familiar with and involved in the mission and ministry of the Christian Business Men's Committee of USA. Our purpose is to evangelize and disciple business and professional men for Jesus Christ." Needs personal experiences, interviews, and articles on current issues related to business. Also uses column material on current issues and financial topics.

Article length 700 to 1,000 words, column material 700 words. Must query first. Accepts computer submissions in Macintosh Microsoft Word. Buys first rights. Guidelines and sample copy for $2.50. Reports in 8 weeks. Pays $50 to $75 on publication.

CHAPTER ONE, 12018 State Route 45, Lisbon, OH 44432-9615. Belinda J. Puchajda, editor. A 240-page quarterly magazine with a circulation of 600.

☐ *Chapter One* serves an audience of clergy and laity. Needs fiction, poetry (traditional and free verse, haiku), column material, fillers, and photographs.

Fiction length 10,000 words. Limit poems to 5 per envelope. No model release required for B&W glossies. Prefers a complete manuscript. Accepts computer submissions with IBM compatibility, 5.25" disk. Buys one-time rights. Guidelines for SASE. Sample copy for $1 plus 2 postage stamps. Reports in 4 to 6 months. Pays $50 on publication.

CHARISMA AND CHRISTIAN LIFE, 600 Rinehart Road, Lake Mary, FL 32746. (407) 644-8720. Fax: (407) 333-9753. Steven Strang, editor. Submit features to John Archer, news to Nancy Justice. A 100-page monthly magazine published by Strang Communications. Circulation 200,000.

☐ *Charisma and Christian Life* is an interdenominational magazine which serves a laity audience with a Charismatic, Evangelical background. Needs articles on current issues and theology. Sponsors an annual fiction contest. See "Entering Contests," chapter 5.

Article length 1,500 to 2,500 words. Prefers a complete manuscript. Accepts computer disks in XyWrite. Buys first rights. Guidelines and sample copy for SASE. Reports in 1 month. Pays $75 to $400 on publication.

THE CHRISTIAN CENTURY, 407 South Dearborn Street, Chicago, IL 60605. (312) 427-5380. James M. Wall, editor. A 32-page weekly journal with a circulation of 35,000.

☐ *The Christian Century* serves an audience of scholars and clergy with a Liberal, Protestant background. The magazine is "an ecumenical weekly that examines developments in the contemporary church and probes the religious and moral issues of modern culture." Needs personal experiences, interviews, and devotions on current issues and theological topics. Also needs poetry, fillers, and photographs. "If you are not familiar with the *Century*, we encourage you to examine a copy before submitting your manuscript."

Article length 1,500 to 3,000 words. Free verse poems run 20 lines maximum, fillers (anecdotes, humor, and book reviews) 500 words. Photograph needs are for B&W glossies. Prefers a complete manuscript. Guidelines and sample copy for SASE and $1.75. Reports in 3 to 4 weeks. Lead time 3 months. Pays $75 to $125 on publication.

CHRISTIAN COMPUTING MAGAZINE, P.O. Box 439, Belton, MO 64012. (816) 331-3881. Fax: (816) 331-5510. Steve Hewitt, editor. A 52-page monthly magazine with a circulation of 25,000.

☐ *Christian Computing Magazine* serves a mainline Protestant audience of all ages with either an Evangelical or Liberal background. Needs personal experiences, interviews, articles on current issues in relation to computers or computers in ministry. Also needs advice on computer technology for columns.

Article and column length not stated. Prefers a complete manuscript. Accepts computer and electronic submissions in Microsoft Word. Buys first rights. Guidelines and sample copy for SASE. Pays with trade of software.

CHRISTIAN COURIER, #4, 261 Martindale Road, St. Catherines, ON, L2W 1A1 Canada. (416) 682-8311. Fax: (416) 682-8313. Bert Witvoet, editor. A 20-page newspaper published by Calvinst Contact Publishing, Ltd. Circulation 5,800.

☐ *Christian Courier* serves an interdenominational, adult audience with an Evangelical background. The newspaper's purpose is "to report on happenings in the Reformed and broader Christian community and on world events important to Christianity." Needs comics, humor, news, opinion, commentary, personal experiences on Christian living, drama, education, environment, family, feminism, health, media, stewardship, music, natives, politics, seniors, and social issues. Editor wants "popular style, but clear thinking and in harmony with Scripture. Not interested in proof-texting and propositional approach to the Bible."

Article length 750 to 1,000 words. Prefers a complete manuscript. Accepts simultaneous submissions, photocopies, or computer disks. Buys first and reprint rights. Guidelines and sample copy for SASE. Reports in 1 month. Pays $30 to $70 on publication.

THE CHRISTIAN COURIER, 1933 West Wisconsin Avenue, Milwaukee, WI 53233. (414) 344-7300. Fax: (414) 344-7375. Gayle Ryberg, editor. A monthly newspaper published by ProBusColls Association.

☐ *The Christian Courier* serves an Evangelical audience. Its purpose is to "propagate the Gospel of Jesus Christ in the Midwest." Needs general interest articles and fillers (anecdotes, facts, and newsbreaks).

Articles are 300 to 1,500 words. Filler length is 10 to 100 words. Prefers complete manuscript. Buys first and reprint rights. Reports in 2 months. Guidelines and sample copy for SASE. Pays in copies.

CHRISTIAN DRAMA MAGAZINE, 1824 Celestia Boulevard, Walla Walla, WA 99362-3619. (509) 529-0089. Judy Tash, editor. A 28-page quarterly magazine published by Phillips Music and Drama. Circulation 300.

☐ *Christian Drama Magazine* serves an audience of scholars, clergy, and laity with an Orthodox Roman Catholic or Protestant, Evangelical or Liberal, background. Needs personal experiences related to drama, fiction (sketches and plays), poetry (dramatic readings), columns (drama related how-to's), and photographs.

Article length 250 to 1,000 words and fiction 250 to 5,000 words. Photographic needs are for B&W glossy or matt finish, clear color prints to be used as B&W. Prefers a complete manuscript. Accepts computer submissions in WordStar 5.0. Buys first, reprint, all rights. Guidelines and sample copy for SASE. Reports in 4 months. Pays $25 for articles, $10 for photographs on publication.

CHRISTIAN EDUCATORS JOURNAL, Dordt College, 498 4th Street, NE, Sioux Center, IA 51250-1697. (712) 722-6252. Fax: (712) 722-1198. Lorna Van Gilst, editor. A 36-page quarterly magazine published by Christian Educators Journal Association. Circulation 4,200.

☐ *Christian Educators Journal* serves an Evangelical audience of teachers and scholars with a mainline Protestant background. A thematic magazine which needs articles on current issues in Christian day school education, theory and practice in Christian day schools, sometimes poems related to education. Column material is written in-house.

Article length 600 to 1,200 words. Limit poetry submissions to 5 per envelope. Prefers a query. Buys first and reprint rights. Guidelines, theme list, and sample copy available with 9 × 12 SASE with 98 cents postage. Pays $10 to $25 on publication.

CHRISTIAN HISTORY, 465 Gundersen Drive, Carol Stream, IL 60188. (708) 260-6200. Fax: (708) 260-0114. Kevin Miller, editor. A 52-page quarterly magazine published by Christianity Today, Incorporated. Circulation 50,000.

☐ *Christian History* serves an audience of laity and church leadership with a Protestant, Evangelical background. A thematic magazine which needs articles on church history.

Article length is 1,000 to 2,000 words. Must query first. Buys first rights. Guidelines, theme list, and sample copy for $4. Pays 10 cents per word on acceptance.

CHRISTIAN HOME AND SCHOOL, 3350 East Paris Avenue, SE, Grand Rapids, MI 49512. (616) 951-1070. Fax: (616) 957-5022. Dr. Gordon L. Bordewyk, editor. Submit to Roger Schmurr. A 36-page bimonthly magazine published by Christian Schools International. Circulation 52,500.

☐ *Christian Home and School* serves an adult audience of laity with a Protestant, Evangelical background. Needs personal experiences on parenting topics and current issues in education. Also buys photographs.

Article length 500 to 2,000 words. No model release required for B&W glossies or color slides. Prefers a complete manuscript. Accepts photocopies. Usually buys all rights, but negotiable. Guidelines free for SASE, sample copy for 9 × 12 SASE with $1 postage. Reports in 3 weeks. Pays $50 to $110 on publication.

CHRISTIAN INFO, 5375 Alderley Road, Victoria, BC, V8Y 1X9 Canada. (604) 658-2644. Fax: (604) 658-8481. Madge Bowes, editor. A 20-page monthly newspaper published by the Vancouver Island Christian Communication Society. Circulation 14,000.

☐ *Christian Info* serves an interdenominational audience of all ages with an Evangelical background. Needs devotions, meditations, how-to's, news, opinion, personal experience on theology, Christian living, evangelism, family, missions, stewardship, music, natives, and social issues. Also needs poetry and book, music, film, and video reviews.

Article length 400 to 500 words. Prefers a complete manuscript. Accepts simultaneous submissions, but no photocopies or computer disks. Buys first and reprint rights. Guidelines and sample copy for SASE. Reports in 1 month. No payment.

NOTE TO USERS OF THIS BOOK

As you search in chapters 2, 3, and 4 for appropriate publishers for your material, be sure to use the indexes in the back of the book to help you find the periodicals and publishers you are looking for.

Chapter 5, *Branching Out,* has additional lists of publishers and information you will want if you are writing poetry, greeting cards, curriculum, or devotionals; preparing material for newspapers and syndicates, regional publications and nonprofit organizations; or marketing cartoons or drama and scripts for radio, television, videos, or film.

In chapter 7, you will also find a list of literary agents who have expressed interest in helping writers market religious material.

CHRISTIANITY TODAY, 465 Gundersen Drive, Carol Stream, IL 60188-2498. Fax: (708) 260-0114. David Neff, managing editor. A 90-page biweekly magazine published by Christianity Today, Incorporated. Circulation 180,000.

☐ *Christianity Today* addresses an audience of scholars, clergy, and laity with an Orthodox, Evangelical background. Uses scholarly articles on theology, ethics, and current issues. Also uses column material (profiles on ordinary Christians doing extraordinary service for the Lord).

Article length 1,000 to 4,000 words, columns 900 to 1,000 words. Must query first. Buys few free-lance articles. Buys first and reprint (please notify when, where, and how first used) rights. Guidelines and sample copy for 9 × 12 SASE with 3 first-class stamps. Reports in 2 months. Lead time 8 months. Pays negotiable rates on acceptance.

THE CHRISTIAN LIBRARIAN, Box 4020, Three Hills, AB, T0M 2A0 Canada. (403) 443-5511. Fax: (403) 443-5540. Ron Jordahl, editor. A 32-page quarterly journal published by the Association of Christian Librarians. Circulation 450.

☐ *The Christian Librarian* serves an interdenominational audience of "Christian librarians, Bible college faculty, and students with an Evangelical background." The magazine's purpose is the "Communication of Christian interpretation of librarianship and publication of articles on the theory and practice of library science, bibliographic articles, and reviews of Christian literature." Needs how-to's, opinion, personal experience, and profiles on librarianship, "most topics if approached from a bibliographic slant." Also needs book reviews.

Article length 1,000 to 5,000 words. Prefers query. Accepts simultaneous submissions, photocopies, and computer disks in WordPerfect. Requires first, reprint, simultaneous, and one-time rights. Guidelines and sample copy for SASE and $5. Reports in 2 weeks. No payment.

CHRISTIAN LIVING, 616 Walnut Avenue, Scottdale, PA 15683. (412) 887-8500. Fax: (412) 887-3111. David Graybill, editor. A 28-page magazine published 10 times yearly by the Mennonite Publishing House. Circulation 6,500.

☐ *Christian Living* serves an adult audience of laity (65 percent women) with an Anabaptist, Mennonite background. Needs personal experiences and articles on current issues. Also needs nonformula fiction, poetry (free verse and haiku), and photographs.

Article length 700 to 1,200 words. Limit poems to 4 to 24 lines, 6 poems per envelope. Model release for B&W glossies preferred, but not required. Prefers a complete manuscript. Accepts photocopies. Buys one-time rights. Guidelines and sample copy for SASE. Reports in 1 month. Pays 5 cents per word for prose, $1 per line for poems, $35 for photos on acceptance.

CHRISTIAN MEDICAL & DENTAL SOCIETY JOURNAL, Box 830689, Richardson, TX 75083. (214) 783-8384. Fax: (214) 783-0921. Hal Habecker, editor. A 32-page quarterly journal published by the Christian Medical and Dental Society. Circulation 8,000.

☐ *Christian Medical & Dental Society Journal* serves an Evangelical adult and senior adult audience of laity and professionals from an Independent Protestant background. Needs personal experiences, interviews, and devotionals on current issues and missions experiences. Also needs humorous fillers.

Article length 2,500 to 3,000 words. Prefers a query. Accepts computer submissions in WordPerfect 5.0 or 5.1. Pays on publication. Rate not stated.

CHRISTIAN MINISTRY, 407 South Dearborn Street, Chicago, IL 60605. (312) 427-5380. James M. Wall, editor. A 40-page bimonthly journal published by Christian Century Foundation. Circulation 12,000.

☐ *Christian Ministry* serves a nondenominational audience of ministers, chaplains, denominational workers, and church counselors with a Liberal background. It's a "practical magazine for thinking clergy." A thematic magazine that needs "articles that deal thoughtfully with issues confronting local parish ministers in their day-to-day work. Deals with anything from theological treatment of a particular issue, to preparing and presenting better sermons, to putting together a church budget. We seek to be inclusive or nonsexist in language and presentation. Therefore, inclusive language should be used when referring to people (including clergy). We respect an author's view in references to God."

Article length to 3,000 words. Photograph needs are for B&W glossies. Prefers a complete manuscript. Accepts photocopies, but no simultaneous submissions. Buys all rights. Guidelines, theme list, and sample copy for SASE and $2.25. Guidelines for submitting photographs and artwork available for SASE. Reports in 3 to 4 weeks. Pays $10 to $75 on publication.

CHRISTIAN PARENTING TODAY, P.O. Box 3850, Sisters, OR 97759-0850. (503) 549-8261. David Kopp, editor. A 60-page bimonthly magazine published by Good Family Magazines, a division of David C. Cook Publishing. Circulation 225,000.

☐ *Christian Parenting Today* "is a positive, practical magazine that targets real needs of the contemporary family with authoritative articles based on fresh research and timeless truths of the Bible." It serves an Evangelical adult and senior adult audience of clergy and laity with an Orthodox Roman Catholic or Protestant background. A thematic magazine that needs personal experiences, interviews, and anecdotes of a personal nature for fillers.

Article length 850 to 1,000 words. "Parent Exchange" and "Life in Our House" run 25 to 100 words. "My Story," a first-person story, high on human interest and inspiration of how one family or parent faced and overcame a parenting challenge, 850 to 1,000 words. Prefers a query for SASE. Buys first rights. Guidelines, theme list, and sample copy for 9 × 12 SASE and $1.50 postage. For guidelines only, #10 envelope with one first-class stamp. Reports in 2 months. Lead time 6 months. Pays 15 to 25 cents a word for articles, $40 for "Parent Exchange," and $25 for "Life in Our House" on acceptance.

THE CHRISTIAN READER, 465 Gundersen Drive, Carol Stream, IL 60188. (708) 260-6200. Fax: (708) 260-0114. Bonne Steffen, editor. A 110-page bimonthly magazine with a circulation of 200,000.

☐ *The Christian Reader* serves an Evangelical audience, primarily women. Uses personal experiences, devotionals, articles on current issues. Also uses humorous fillers.

Article length 1,000 words, fillers 200 words. Prefers a complete manuscript. Accepts photocopies. Buys first and reprint rights. Guidelines and sample copy for SASE. Lead time 6 months. Pays variable amounts on publication.

CHRISTIAN RENEWAL, Box 777, Jordan Station, ON, L0R 1S0 Canada. (416) 562-5719. Fax: (416) 562-7828. John Van Dyk, editor. A 20-page news magazine published 20 times yearly by the Abraham Kuyper Foundation. Circulation 4,500.

☐ *Christian Renewal* serves an adult audience with a Reformed Church background. The magazine's purpose is to "inform, educate, and inspire members of the Reformed community of churches in North America. Content includes church-related as well as world news and analysis of events and trends." Needs devotions, meditations, news, opinion, personal experience, and profiles on the arts, Christian living, education, family, history, missions, music, politics, social issues, and theology. Also uses poetry, book reviews, and illustrations. Prefers Reformed Church writers.

Article length to 7 double-spaced typed pages. Prefers full manuscript. Accepts simultaneous submissions, photocopies, no computer disks. Buys first and reprint rights. Lead time 4 months. Pays on publication. Rate not released.

CHRISTIAN RETAILING, 600 Rinehart Road, Lake Mary, FL 32746. (407) 333-0600. Fax: (407) 333-9753. Brian Peterson, editor. Submit book reviews to Tom Winfield, music reviews to Ana Gascon. A 72-page monthly magazine published by Strang Communications Company. Circulation 10,000.

☐ *Christian Retailing* addresses an audience of Christian bookstore personnel and managers. Needs articles of interest to the Christian retailing industry and photographs.

Article length 1,000 to 2,000 words. Must query first. Buys all rights. Guidelines free for SASE, sample copy for $3. Reports in 6 weeks. Pays $50 on publication with a $35 kill fee.

CHRISTIAN SCHOOL, 1308 Santa Rosa, Wheaton, IL 60187. (708) 653-4588. Phil Landrum, Publisher. A 48-page quarterly magazine published by Landrum Specialty Publishers. Circulation 3,000 schools.

☐ *Christian School* serves an audience of Christian school educators. Needs articles on educational tools and how-to's. Also uses fiction, column materials (educational topics), and fillers (anecdotes and humor).

Article length 5 double-spaced pages, fiction 1,000 to 1,500 words, columns and fillers 500 words. Prefers a query. Guidelines and sample copy for SASE. No payment at this time.

CHRISTIAN SINGLE, 127 Ninth Avenue N, Nashville, TN 37234. (615) 251-2277. Leigh Neely, interim editor. A 50-page monthly magazine published by the Baptist Sunday School Board. Circulation 90,000.

☐ *Christian Single* serves an adult and young adult audience with a Southern Baptist background. Needs personal experience and devotions, inspirational fiction related to singleness, column material, traditional poetry, humorous fillers, and photographs.

Article and fiction length 600 to 1,200 words. Column materials are on health and fitness and financial advice for single persons. Prefers a complete manuscript. Accepts computer and electronic submissions. Buys first, reprint, one-time, and all rights. Guidelines and sample copy for 9 × 12 SASE with 98 cents postage. Reports in 4 to 6 weeks. Lead time 12 months. Pays 5 cents per word 30 days after acceptance.

CHRISTIAN SOCIAL ACTION (formerly *Engage/Social Action*), 100 Maryland Avenue, NE, Washington, DC 20002. (202) 488-5632. Lee Ranck, editor. Published by the General Board of Church and Society of the United Methodist Church. A monthly magazine of 32 pages, with an international circulation of 3,000.

☐ *Christian Social Action* is looking for articles that "discuss current social issues and reflect a thorough knowledge of the subject. Examples: peace issues, race relations, economic and labor issues, environmental concerns, international relations." Audience is mainline Protestant clergy and general lay readers.

Articles should be 1,500 to 2,000 words. Guidelines and sample copies available. Reports in four weeks. Pays $50 to $100 per article, on publication.

CHRISTIAN STANDARD, 8121 Hamilton Avenue, Cincinnati, OH 45231. (513) 931-4050. Fax: (513) 931-0904. Sam E. Stone, editor. A 23-page weekly magazine published by Standard Publishing Company. Circulation 65,000.

☐ *Christian Standard* serves a nondenominational audience of scholars and clergy with an Evangelical background. Needs devotions, articles on current issues and theology, and photographs.

Article length 400 to 1,600 words. Photographic needs are for B&W glossies and color slides. Prefers a complete manuscript. Buys first and reprint rights. Guidelines and sample copy for SASE and $1. Reports in 3 to 4 weeks. Pays $10 to $80 on publication.

CHRISTIANWEEK, Box 725, Winnipeg, MB, R2K 2E9 Canada. (204) 943-1147. Fax: (204) 947-5632. Harold D. Jantz, editor. A 16-page biweekly newspaper with a circulation of 12,000.

☐ *Christianweek* serves an interdenominational audience of Evangelical adults. The magazine's purpose is to "provide a window on the Christian faith and life in Canada which is shaped by a commitment to historic, Evangelical Christianity." Needs news, opinion, and profiles on any topic. Also needs book, music, film, and video reviews. "We're a Canadian newspaper, Evangelical in orientation, that is concerned to communicate to a Canadian audience. Focus is Canadian stories and opinion that will genuinely broaden the understanding for the church in this country. That's something that anyone writing for us must understand."

Article length 600 to 800 words. Prefers phone query. Accepts simultaneous submissions occasionally. No photocopies or computer disks. Buys first rights. Guidelines and sample copies not available. Pays $25 to $100 on publication.

CHRISTMAS: THE ANNUAL OF CHRISTMAS LITERATURE AND ART, 4265 South 5th Street, Box 1209, Minneapolis, MN 55440-1209. (612) 330-3441. Fax: (612) 330-3455. Kristine Oberg, editor. A 64-page anthology digest published annually that celebrates Christmas. Published by Augsburg Fortress Publishers, its circulation is 40,000.

☐ *Christmas* addresses an audience of Mainline Protestant children ages 8 to 12 and adults, mostly women. A thematic magazine that uses family-oriented personal experiences, inspiration, history, and nostalgia on Christmas themes. Needs articles, short stories, and poetry (traditional, free verse, and haiku).

Article and short story length 1,500 to 4,000 words, poems 25 to 100 lines (limit 5 per envelope). Prefers a complete manuscript. Accepts computer submissions in Microsoft Word, WordPerfect, or as an ASCII file. Buys first, one-time, reprint, and all rights. Guidelines and theme list free for SASE. Sample copy for $12.95 plus postage. Call (800) 328-4648 for sample copy. Reports in 12 weeks. Lead time 18 months. Pays $75 to $500 on acceptance.

CHURCH & STATE, 8120 Fenton Street, Silver Spring, MD 20910. (301) 589-3707. Fax: (301) 495-9173. Joseph L. Conn, editor. A 24-page monthly magazine published by the Americans United for Separation of Church and State. Circulation 25,000.

☐ *Church & State* serves a Liberal audience of scholars, clergy, laity, and lawyers with Baptist, Seventh Day Adventist, Christian Science, or Unitarian backgrounds. Uses articles on current issues or church-state matters. No fiction or poetry.

Article length 1,500 to 2,000 words. Prefers a query. Accepts computer submissions in WordPerfect 5.1. Buys one-time rights. Guidelines and sample copy for SASE. Reports in 2 to 4 weeks. Pays $200 to $250 on acceptance.

CHURCH AND SYNAGOGUE LIBRARIES, P.O. Box 19357, Portland, OR 97280-0357. (503) 244-6919. Lorraine E. Burson, editor. A 20-page bimonthly newsletter published by Church and Synagogue Library Association. Circulation 3,300.

☐ *Church and Synagogue Libraries* serves an interfaith audience of congregational librarians with either an Evangelical or Liberal background. Needs articles on librarianship, how-to's, practical methods, and techniques. Also needs column materials on librarianship and photographs.

Article length 750 to 900 words. Model release required for B&W glossies and color prints. Prefers a complete manuscript. Buys one-time rights. Guidelines and sample copy for SASE. Reports in 2 to 4 weeks. No payment.

CHURCH BUSINESS, 4040 Creditview Road, Unit 11, Box 6900, Mississauga, ON, L5C 3Y8 Canada. (416) 569-6900. Fax: (416) 569-6915. Terry Hrynsyshyn, editor. A 40-page bimonthly magazine published by Momentum Magazines. Circulation 14,000.

☐ *Church Business* serves an interdenominational audience of clergy with either a Protestant or Roman Catholic background. "Covers all aspects of church building and administration activity, showcasing church-related products, supplies, case history stories, and features." Needs how-to's, news, and personal experiences on church education, education, environment, leadership, stewardship, and music. "Of interest to all denominations regarding the successful implementation of church administration programs and facility management."

Article length 1,000 to 1,500 words. Prefers query. Accepts photocopies, computer disks, but no simultaneous submissions. Buys first and reprint rights. Guidelines and sample copy for SASE. Reports in 3 months. Pays on publication. Rate not stated.

CHURCH EDUCATOR, 165 Plaza Drive, Prescott, AZ 86303. (602) 771-8601. Fax: (602) 771-8621. Robert Davidson, editor. Submit to Linda Davidson. A 32-page monthly journal published by Educational Ministries. Circulation 3,500.

☐ *Church Educator* serves a lay leadership and clergy audience with a Protestant background. Needs articles and column material on any phase of Christian education programming for the church.

Articles and columns 500 to 1,000 words. Prefers a complete manuscript. Buys first rights. Guidelines and sample copy for SASE with 75 cents postage. Reports in 2 months. Pays 2 to 4 cents per word on publication.

THE CHURCH HERALD, 6157 28th Street, SE, Grand Rapids, MI 49506-6999. Jeffrey Japinga, editor. A monthly magazine published by the Reformed Church in America. Circulation 40,000.

☐ *The Church Herald* addresses an adult audience with a Reformed Church in America background. Uses personal experiences, humor, general articles. Also uses fiction with a Christian theme.

Articles and short stories length 500 to 1,500 words. Prefers a query, but accepts complete manuscripts. Buys first, reprint, one-time, and simultaneous rights. Guidelines and sample copy for 9 × 12 SASE with $2. Reports in 1 to 2 months. Lead time 6 months. Pays $50 to $200 on acceptance. Offers 50 percent kill fee.

CHURCH HERALD AND HOLINESS BANNER, P.O. Box 4060, 7415 Metcalf, Overland Park, KS 66204. Ray Crooks, editor. A 20-page biweekly magazine published by Church of God (Holiness). Circulation 2,500.

☐ *Church Herald and Holiness Banner* addresses an Evangelical audience of clergy and laity with a Church of God (Holiness) background. Needs devotions and meditations.

Length is 200 to 400 words. Prefers a complete manuscript. Accepts computer submissions in Professional Write. Requires all rights. Guidelines and sample copy for SASE. Reports in 2 months. No payment.

CHURCH HISTORY, 1025 East 58th Street, Chicago, IL 60637. (312) 702-8215. Martin E. Marty, editor. A 160-page quarterly journal published by the American Society of Church History. Circulation 3,400.

☐ *Church History* serves an interdenominational and interfaith audience of clergy and laity. Needs historical studies. "Limited number."

Article length to 6,250 words. Prefers a complete manuscript. Accepts computer disks. WordPerfect 5.1 preferred, but can use others. Requires all rights. Guidelines and sample copy for SASE. Reports in 8 months. No payment.

THE CHURCHMAN'S HUMAN QUEST, JUST THE HUMAN QUEST, 1074 23 Avenue, N, St. Petersburg, FL 33704. (813) 894-0097. Edna Ruth Johnson, editor. A 24-page bimonthly newspaper published by The Church Associates Incorporated. Circulation 10,000.

☐ *Churchman's Human Quest* serves an adult and senior adult audience of scholars, clergy, and laity with a Liberal, Humanist background. Needs personal experiences, traditional poetry, and fillers (meditations, anecdotes, and humor).

Articles to 1,000 words. Short poems, 2 per envelope. Guidelines and sample copy for SASE. No payment.

CHURCH MEDIA LIBRARY MAGAZINE, 127 Ninth Avenue N, Nashville, TN 37234. (615) 251-2752. Floyd B. Simpson, editor. A 50-page quarterly magazine published by the Baptist Sunday School Board. Circulation more than 30,000.

☐ *Church Media Library Magazine* addresses church librarians in the Southern Baptist Convention. Needs personal experiences and how-to's on all phases of running church libraries: promotion and displays on books, videotapes, audio resources, filmstrips, and so on.

Article length 90 to 195 lines at 55 characters per line. Prefers query, but accepts complete manuscript. Accepts photocopies and computer disks. Buys first, reprint, and all rights. Guidelines and sample copy for SASE. Reports in 1 to 2 months. Pays 5 cents per word on acceptance.

CHURCH OF GOD EVANGEL, P.O. Box 2250, 922 Montgomery Avenue, Cleveland, TN 37311-2250. (615) 476-4512. Fax: (615) 478-7521. Homer G. Rhea, editor. A 36-page monthly magazine published by Church of God. Circulation 50,000.

☐ *Church of God Evangel* serves an audience of laity and clergy with an Evangelical, Church of God background. Needs personal experiences, devotional articles, articles on current issues. Also needs photographs.

Article length 1,200 words maximum. Model release required for B&W glossies and color slides. Prefers a complete manuscript. Accepts photocopies and simultaneous submissions. Buys first rights. Guidelines and sample copy for 9 × 12 SASE with postage for 4 ounces. Reports in 1 month. Lead time 4 months. Pays $10 to $50 on acceptance.

CHURCH TEACHERS MAGAZINE, 1119 Woodburn Road, Durham, NC 27705. (919) 490-5552. Shirley Strobel, editor. A 40-page bimonthly magazine published 5 times yearly by Harper-Collins Publishers. Circulation 8,000.

☐ *Church Teachers Magazine* serves an interdenominational audience of church educators: teachers and directors of Christian education with a Liberal background. A thematic magazine that needs articles on curriculum ideas and teaching strategies. All column material (video and book reviews, religious art) assigned. Also needs fillers (cartoons) and photographs.

Article length 1,000 to 1,500 words. No model release required for photographs. All photographs B&W glossies except for the cover. Prefers a complete manuscript. Accepts computer submissions in Microsoft Word. No simultaneous submissions. Buys all rights. Guidelines, theme list for SASE, sample copy for $1 postage. Reports in 2 months. Lead time 2 1/2 months before September and October. Pays $50 to $150 on publication.

CHURCHWOMAN, Church Women United, 475 Riverside Drive, Room 812, New York, NY 10115. (212) 870-2347. Fax: (212) 870-2338. Margaret Schiffert, editor. A 24-page bimonthly magazine published by Church Women United. Circulation 10,000.

☐ *Churchwoman* serves an interdenominational audience of women, both Evangelical and Liberal, with a Roman Catholic or mainline Protestant background. Needs interviews and devotional articles, articles on current issues, theology, environment, health care, justice, poverty of women, economic alternatives.

Article length to 3 double-spaced pages. Must query. Guidelines for SASE, sample copy for $1. No payment.

CHURCH WORSHIP, 165 Plaza Drive, Prescott, AZ 86303-5549. (602) 771-8602. Fax: (602) 771-8621. Robert G. Davidson, editor. A 24-page monthly newspaper published by Educational Ministries, Incorporated. Circulation 1,200.

☐ *Church Worship* serves a Protestant clergy audience with a Liberal or Evangelical background. Needs religious poetry, column material on special seasons and worship services.

Column material length 750 words. Prefers a complete manuscript. Buys first rights. Guidelines and sample copy for SASE. Lead time 3 months. Pays 3 cents per word on publication.

CIRCUIT RIDER, 201 Eighth Avenue S, Nashville, TN 37202. (615) 749-6137. Fax: (615) 749-6079. J. Richard Peck, editor. A 28-page monthly magazine published by The United Methodist Publishing House. Circulation 40,000.

☐ *Circuit Rider* serves an audience of United Methodist clergy. Needs articles on theology and church administration.

Article length 1,600 words or less. Prefers a complete manuscript. Accepts computer submissions in ASCII. Buys all rights. Guidelines and sample copy for SASE and $1. Reports in 3 months. Pays $25 to $200 on publication.

CLARION, 41 Amberly Boulevard, Ancaster, ON, L9G 3R9 Canada. (416) 575-3688. Fax: (416) 575-0799. Rev. J. Geertsema, editor. A 24-page bimonthly magazine published by Premier Printing. Circulation 2,600.

☐ *Clarion* serves an audience of all ages with a Canadian Reformed Church background. The magazine's purpose is to "serve the members of the Canadian Reformed churches and to build them up in the faith." Needs Bible studies, devotions, and meditations on doctrine, Christian living, church education, education, environment, evangelism, family, history, missions, and social issues. "Biblically and confessionally bound." Also needs book reviews, illustrations, and photographs. Prefers Canadian Reformed Church writers.

Article length 3 to 8 double-spaced pages. Prefers a complete manuscript. Accepts simultaneous submissions and computer disks, but no photocopies. Requires first and reprint rights. No seasonal material. Guidelines and sample copies not available. No payment.

CLCL (CHANGING LIVES, CALLING LEADERS), Box 50434, Indianapolis, IN 46250. (317) 576-8140. Larry Mitchell, editor. A 32-page bimonthly magazine published by the Youth Department, The Wesleyan Church. Circulation 3,000.

☐ *CLCL* addresses an audience of laity and clergy from an Evangelical, Wesleyan background. Needs interviews and column material on current issues. Prefers a query, but accepts a complete manuscript. Buys first rights. Reports in 2 months. Pays on acceptance. Rate not stated.

THE CLERGY JOURNAL, 6160 Carman Avenue, E., Inver Grove Heights, MN 55076. Submit to "The Editor." A 48-page monthly (10 yearly) magazine with a circulation of 15,000. Published by Logos Productions, Inc., Seymour, IN.

☐ *The Clergy Journal* addresses a clergy audience with a mainline Protestant background. Needs articles on church administration. Prefers query but accepts complete manuscript. Accepts photocopies. Buys all rights. No guidelines, but sample copy for $3.50. Reports in 2 weeks. Lead time 4 months. Pays $25 to $50 on publication.

CLUBHOUSE, Box 15, Berrien Springs, MI 49103. (616) 471-9009. Elaine Trumbo, editor. A 32-page bimonthly magazine published by Your Story Hour. Circulation 8,000.

☐ *Clubhouse* addresses an audience of children and youth, both Christian and non-

Christian. Needs articles and fiction (adventure), traditional and free verse poetry, fillers (humor and cartoons).

Article and story length 1,200 words maximum. Limit poems to 24 lines, 5 poems per envelope. Prefers a complete manuscript. Accepts photocopies and simultaneous and computer submissions. Buys first, reprint, one-time, and simultaneous rights. Guidelines and sample copy for 6 × 9 SASE with enough postage for 3 ounces. Reports in 4 to 6 weeks. Pays $10 to $25 after acceptance.

CLUBHOUSE/CLUBHOUSE JR., 420 North Cascade Avenue, Colorado Springs, CO 80903. (719) 531-3400. Lisa Brock, assistant editor. A 16-page monthly magazine published by Focus on the Family. Circulation 100,000.

☐ *Clubhouse Jr.* and *Clubhouse* serve nondenominational children's audiences ages 4 to 7 and 8 to 12 respectively with an Evangelical background. Primarily needs quality fiction that will relate to the age groups of each magazine.

Stories 500 to 1,400 words. Prefers a complete manuscript. Buys first rights. Guidelines and sample copy for SASE. Reports in 4 to 6 weeks. Lead time 5 months. Pays $30 to $400 on acceptance.

CO-LABORER, P.O. Box 5002, Antioch, TN 37011-5002. (615) 731-6812. Fax: (615) 731-0049. Melissa Riddle, editor. A 32-page bimonthly magazine published by the National Association of Free Will Baptists. Circulation 15,000.

☐ *Co-Laborer* serves an Evangelical women's audience with a Free Will Baptist background. Needs articles, plays, anecdotes, and programs on missions.

Article length 1,000 words; poetry, any style, any length. Guidelines and sample copy for $2. Pays in copies.

COLUMBIA, THE MAGAZINE FOR THE KNIGHTS OF COLUMBUS, One Columbia Plaza, New Haven, CT 06510. (203) 772-2130. Fax: (203) 777-0114. Richard McMunn, editor. A 32-page monthly magazine with a circulation of 1.5 million.

☐ *Columbia* addresses an audience of Roman Catholic adults. Needs articles dealing with Catholic family life, the Catholic church, and Knights of Columbus stories. Also needs photographs.

Article length 1,500 words maximum. Model release required for color slides and prints. Prefers a query. Buys first rights. Guidelines and sample copy for SASE. Lead time 6 months. Pays $500 on acceptance.

COMMONWEAL, 15 Dutch Street, New York, NY 10038. (212) 732-0800. Patrick Jordan, managing editor. Margaret Steinfels, editor. A 32-page biweekly newspaper published by Commonweal Foundation. Circulation 18,000.

☐ *Commonweal* addresses a lay leadership audience, predominantly Roman Catholic. Needs personal experiences, articles on current issues, theological topics, and public affairs. Uses quality poetry.

Article length is 1,000 to 3,000 words. Prefers query but accepts complete manuscript. Buys all rights. Guidelines and sample copy for SASE. Reports in 3 to 4 weeks. Pays 3 cents per word on acceptance.

COMPASS: A JESUIT JOURNAL, C #300, 10 St. Mary Street, Toronto, ON, M4Y 1P9 Canada. (416) 921-0653. Fax: (416) 921-1864. Robert Chodos, editor. A 52-page bimonthly magazine published by the Jesuits of the Upper Canada Province. Circulation is 3,700.

☐ *Compass: A Jesuit Journal* addresses an adult, Roman Catholic audience. "Ecumenical in spirit, it provides a form for lively debate and an ethical perspective on social and religious questions." Needs opinion, personal experience, doctrine on arts, education, environment, feminism, health, history, media, natives, politics, and social issues. "Articles should be accessible and intellectually engaging; very few unsolicited articles used." Also uses book, film, and video reviews.

Article length 1,000 to 2,000 words. Prefers a complete manuscript. Buys first rights only. Accepts simultaneous submissions, photocopies, and computer disks. Guidelines and sample copy for SASE. Pays $250 to $600 on publication.

CONGREGATIONAL JOURNAL, Box 298 Fairfax Avenue, Ventura, CA 93003. (805) 644-3397. Dr. Henry David Gray, editor. Submit to Rev. Raymond A. Waser. A 72-page semiannual journal published by the American Congregational Center. Circulation 1,500.

☐ *Congregational Journal* addresses an audience of scholars and clergy with a Congregational background. Needs articles on theology and history. "Each issue of Congregational Journal carries at least fifteen book reviews. Submissions of book reviews welcome. Preference is given books by or about Congregationalists, theology, New Testament, Old Testament, Church history. But every issue has also several books on varied aspects of the common life, viz. art, music, architecture, exceptional literature. We encourage breadth as well as depth. Book reviews are edited to fit space available." Also uses prayers.

Article length 4 to 20 pages. Limit prayers to 3 per envelope. Prefers a complete manuscript. Buys first rights. Guidelines and sample copy for SASE. Reports in 2 weeks. Pays in copies.

CONNECTING POINT, Box 685, Cocoa Beach, FL 32923. Linda G. Howard, editor. A monthly publication.

☐ *Connecting Point* is "for mentally challenged (retarded) persons. Articles should be written for adults who read on the primary level." Needs articles and devotionals with "the issues of interest to the community of mentally challenged persons." Also uses poetry.

Article length 200 to 350 words. Guidelines and sample copy for SASE. Reports in 6 weeks. Pays in copies.

THE CONQUEROR, 8855 Dunn Road, Hazelwood, MO 63042. (314) 837-7300. Darrell Johns, editor. A 16-page bimonthly magazine published by United Pentecostal Church International. Circulation 6,300.

☐ *The Conqueror* addresses a teenage audience with a United Pentecostal Church background. Needs personal experiences and devotionals on current issues, fiction, traditional and free verse poetry, fillers (devotions, meditations, anecdotes, and humor), and photographs.

Articles and fiction 1,000 to 2,000 words, fillers 300 words or less. No model release required for B&W glossies, color slides, or color prints. Prefers a complete manuscript. Accepts photocopies and computer submissions. Buys first, reprint, simultaneous, and one-time rights. Guidelines and sample copy for SASE. Reports in 6 months. Pays $30 for text, $20 for poetry on publication.

CONSCIENCE, 1436 U Street, NW, Suite 301, Washington, DC 20009-3916. (202) 986-6093. Maggie Hume, editor. A 48-page quarterly magazine published by Catholics for a Free Choice. Circulation 12,000.

☐ *Conscience* serves an audience of laity and clergy with a Liberal, Roman Catholic background. Needs personal experiences and interviews on current issues and theology. Also needs traditional, free verse, and haiku poetry.

Article length 1,000 to 3,500 words. Prefers a query, but accepts complete manuscript. Buys first and second rights. Guidelines and sample copy for 9 × 12 envelope with 98 cents postage. Reports in 8 weeks. Pays $25 to $100 on publication.

CORNERSTONE, 939 West Wilson Avenue, Chicago, IL 60640. (312) 989-2080. Fax: (312) 989-2076. Dawn Herrin, editor-in-chief. Submit to Jennifer Ingerson, Submissions editor. A 40-page bimonthly magazine published by Cornerstone Communications, Incorporated. Circulation 60,000.

☐ *Cornerstone* serves an audience of mainline Protestant young adults ages 18 to 25 with a Conservative, Evangelical background. "A display of creativity which expresses a biblical world view without cliches or cheap shots at non-Christians is the ideal. We are known as one of the most avant-garde magazines in the Christian market yet attempt to express Orthodox beliefs in language of the nineties. Any writer who does this may well be published by Cornerstone. Creative fiction is begging for more Christian participation. We anticipate such contributions gladly. Interviews where well-known personalities respond to the gospel are also among strong publication possibilities." Needs personal experiences, interviews, devotions on current issues and theological topics. Needs good quality general fiction and traditional, free, haiku poetry (no epics). Also needs column materials on current issues, theological topics, film and book reviews. Other needs include filler material such as devotions, meditations, and anecdotes and photographs.

Articles run 2,700 words maximum. Fiction length ranges from 250 to 2,500 words. Limit poem submissions to 5 per envelope. Column material ranges from 200 to 2,000 words. Photographic needs are for B&W glossies, color prints, and 35mm color slides. Identify subjects in photographs. No model release required. Prefers a complete manuscript. "Submit copies only, not the original. No SASE needed as we'll contact them only if we're interested in publishing their work. Name, address, and phone and fax numbers should appear on each submitted item." Accepts simultaneous, computer, and electronic submissions in WordStar, BDE, or Microsoft Word. Buys first and second serial reprint rights. Guidelines and sample copy available with 11 × 15 SASE with 6 first-class stamps. Pays around 8 cents per word (negotiable) for prose, $10 to $25 for poems after publication.

COUNSELOR, Box 632, Glen Ellyn, IL 60138. (708) 668-6000. Fax: (708) 668-3806. Janice Burton, editor. A 4-page weekly take-home paper published by Scripture Press Publications, Incorporated.

☐ *Counselor* serves an interdenominational audience of children ages 8 to 11 with an Evangelical background. A thematic magazine needing children's personal experiences, interviews slanted for children. Fiction with emphasis on how God enters into a child's daily experiences. "Our take-home papers correlate with the 'Bible for Today Curriculum' published by Scripture Press. We try to show God at work in the lives of children, emphasizing how to practically apply the truths of God's Word in everyday living. Accompanying photographs appreciated." Needs fillers (cartoons), "no religious cartoons, please." Also needs photographs.

Articles and fiction 900 to 1,000 words. Photographic needs are for B&W glossies, color slides, and color prints. Prefers a complete manuscript. Accepts photocopies and computer printouts. Buys first, one-time, all rights. Guidelines, theme list, and sample copy for SASE. Reports in 6 to 8 weeks. Lead time 9 to 12 months. Pays 5 to 10 cents per word (depending on rights), $5 to $35 for photos on acceptance.

COVENANT COMPANION, 5101 North Francisco Avenue, Chicago, IL 60625. (312) 784-3000. Fax: (312) 784-4366. James R. Hawkinson, editor. A 48-page monthly magazine published by The Evangelical Covenant Church. Circulation 23,000.

☐ *Covenant Companion* addresses an audience of all ages. Adult readers are scholars, clergy, laity with an Evangelical Covenant background. Needs personal experiences, devotions, current issues, theology. Also uses poetry (traditional and free verse), fillers (devotions, meditations, and anecdotes), and photographs.

Article length 1,000 words. Limit poems to 8 per envelope. Model release required for B&W glossies. Prefers a complete manuscript. Accepts photocopies, simultaneous, and computer submissions. Acceptable software WordPerfect or Microsoft Word. Buys first, one-time, and simultaneous rights. Guidelines and sample copy for SASE. Reports in 2 months. Lead time 2 to 4 months. Pays $10 to $15 before publication.

CREATION SOCIAL SCIENCE AND HUMANITIES QUARTERLY, 1429 North Holyoke, Wichita, KS 67208. (316) 683-3610. Dr. Paul D. Ackerman, editor. A 32-page quarterly journal published by Creation Social Science. Circulation 600.

☐ *Creation Social Science and Humanities Quarterly* serves an Evangelical audience of scholars, clergy, laity with an Orthodox, Roman Catholic background. Needs articles on social sciences, literature, art. Also uses poetry (traditional, free verse, and haiku), and fillers (devotions and meditations).

Article length 2,000 to 3,000 words preferred. Limit poems to 1 page maximum. Prefers a complete manuscript. Accepts photocopies and computer disks in IBM compatible software. Requires all rights. Guidelines and sample copy not available.

CREATOR MAGAZINE, Box 100, Dublin, OH 43017. (614) 889-0012. Fax: (614) 792-3585. Marshall Sanders, editor. A 48-page bimonthly magazine with a circulation of 6,000.

☐ *Creator Magazine* serves an adult and senior adult audience who work in music ministry with all age groups. They come primarily from a Protestant, Evangelical background. Needs articles on any phase of music ministry as it relates to all age groups. Also needs photographs.

Article length 2 to 10 double-spaced pages. No model release is required for B&W glossies or color slides. Prefers a complete manuscript. Accepts computer submissions in Microsoft Word, PageMaker, WordPerfect, or ASCII. Buys simultaneous rights. Guidelines and sample copy for SASE. Reports in 3 months. Lead time 2 to 3 months. Pays $25 to $150 on publication.

CRISIS MAGAZINE, 1511 K Street, NW, Suite 525, Washington, DC 20005. (202) 347-7411. Dinesh D'Souza, editor. Scott Walter, managing editor. A 56-page monthly magazine with a circulation of 8,000.

☐ *Crisis Magazine* serves an audience of scholars, clergy, laity from a Roman Catholic background. Needs personal experiences, current issues, theology. Also needs column material on current issues and theology.

Article and column length 2,500 to 3,500 words. Prefers a query. Buys first rights. Guidelines and sample copy for SASE and $3. Reports in 6 weeks. Pays on publication. Rate not stated. Offers a kill fee.

THE CRITIC, 205 West Monroe Street, 6th Floor, Chicago, IL 60606-5097. (312) 609-8880. Fax: (312) 609-8891. John L. Sprague, editor. A 130-page quarterly journal with a circulation of 3,000.

☐ *The Critic* serves a Roman Catholic audience of scholars, clergy, and laity. Needs nonfiction articles, fiction, traditional and free verse poetry.

Articles and fiction 3,500 words. Prefers a complete manuscript. Buys first rights. Guidelines and sample copy for $5. Reports in 1 month. Payment rate varies on acceptance.

CROSS CURRENTS, College of New Rochelle, New Rochelle, NY 10805-2308. (914) 654-5425. Fax: (914) 654-5554. William Birmingham, Joseph Cunneen, and Nancy Malone, OSU, co-editors. Ronnie DelliCarpini, managing editor. A 144-page quarterly journal, published by The Association for Religion and Intellectual Life (ARIL). Circulation 4,200.

☐ *Cross Currents* addresses an Ecumenical audience of intellectual individuals. Needs essays, poetry, and correspondence by academicians, religious leaders, and laypeople of all faiths involved in the intellectual life. Occasionally uses B&W photographs.

Essays can be up to 7,000 words. Accepts complete manuscripts. Buys first rights. Reports in one month. Guidelines and sample copy available for free. No payment.

CRUSADER, Box 7259, Grand Rapids, MI 59510-5616. (616) 241-5616. Fax: (616) 241-5558. G. Richard Broene, editor. Submit games and puzzles to Robert DeVonge. A 24-page magazine published 7 times yearly by the Calvinist Cadet Corps. Circulation 13,500.

☐ *Crusader* addresses a boys' audience ages 9 to 14 with an Evangelical, Reformed Calvinist background. A thematic magazine that needs nature articles and fiction (adventure and mystery), and fillers (cartoons, games, and word puzzles).

Article length 400 to 1,200 words, fiction 800 to 1,500 words, fillers 20 to 200 words. Prefers a complete manuscript. Accepts photocopies and simultaneous submissions. Buys first, reprint, and one-time rights. Guidelines, theme list, and sample copy for 9 × 12 SASE with 3 first-class stamps. Reports in 3 to 6 weeks. Pays 2 to 5 cents per word on acceptance.

CRYSTAL RAINBOW, 340 Granada Drive, Winter Park, FL 32789-3425. Louise M. Turmenne, editor. A 20- to 22-page quarterly newsletter published by The Mirrored Image. Circulation 140.

☐ *Crystal Rainbow* serves an Evangelical audience of youth, but mostly scholars, clergy, laity. Needs personal experiences, articles on current issues, biblical theology. Also needs fiction (mystery, adventure, and romance), column material (advice, current issues, and theology), poetry (any style), fillers, and photographs.

Article and fiction length 300 to 500 words, columns to 300 words, fillers 100 to 300 words. Limit poems to 4 per envelope. Photographic needs are for B&W glossies and color close-ups. Prefers a query. Accepts photocopies, simultaneous, computer, and electronic submissions. Computer disks 3.5" Mac compatible. Buys first, reprint, and simultaneous rights. Guidelines and sample copy for SASE with 52 cents postage and $3.50. Reporting time indefinite. "Please be patient with response time. Crystal Rainbow is a side-line, so response may be noticeably slow." Lead time varies. Pays in 2 copies.

CSSR BULLETIN, CSSR Executive Office, Valparaiso University, Valparaiso, IN 46383. (219) 464-5515. Fax: (219) 464-6714. Richard Busse, editor. A 32-page quarterly journal with a circulation of 6,000.

☐ *CSSR Bulletin* addresses an audience of scholars from all theological positions in the mainline Protestant and Roman Catholic churches. Needs articles on current issues and theology.

Article length to 3,500 words. Prefers a query, but accepts complete manuscript. Accepts computer submissions in WordPerfect. Requires varied rights. No payment.

CURRENTS, #203, 9 Clintwood Gate, North York, ON, M3A 1M3 Canada. (416) 445-8623. Fax: Same as phone. Jim Taylor, editor. A 24-page newsletter published 5 times yearly by Wood Lake Books, Incorporated. Circulation 1,400.

☐ *Currents* addresses an interdenominational audience of adults with a mainline Protestant background. Needs devotional and inspirational material linked to the common lectionary and based on real-life personal experience. Also needs Bible studies, devotions, meditations, humor, personal experience, Christian living, drama, environment, evangelism, family health, history, media, missions, music, natives as they relate to a person's living out or discovery of faith. "Read Currents first, then write to suit the publication." Uses photographs.

Prefers a complete manuscript. Accepts simultaneous submissions, photocopies, computer disks. Buys first and reprint rights. Guidelines and sample copy for SASE. No payment. Reports in 6 months.

DECISION, 1300 Harmon Place, Minneapolis, MN 55403-1988. Roger Palms, editor. A 42-page monthly magazine published by the Billy Graham Evangelistic Foundation, with an international circulation of 2 million.

☐ *Decision* is looking especially for "conversion testimonies written in the first person and personal experience articles in which biblical principles are applied so that readers can identify and apply the same principles in [their] own life." Uses some poetry. No reprints. Readers are youth and adults from a Protestant Evangelical background.

Full-length articles number 1,800 to 2,000 words, vignettes and shorter articles 400 to 1,000; "Where Are They Now?" (testimonies of Graham crusade converts) 600-800 words. Complete manuscripts preferred. Guidelines available for SASE, sample copy for $1. Reports in 8 weeks. Pays for article by length, $35 to $200; poetry word count, $10 to $40 on publication.

DISCIPLESHIP JOURNAL, P.O. Box 35004, Colorado Springs, CO 80935. (719) 548-9222. Fax: (719) 598-7128. Susan Maycinik, editor. Submit to Deena Davis. A 72-page bi-monthly magazine published by the Navigators. Circulation 90,000.

☐ *Discipleship Journal* serves an Evangelical audience of scholars, clergy, and laity from a mainline Protestant background. "Our purpose is to help believers develop a deeper relationship with Jesus Christ and to provide practical help in understanding the Scriptures and applying them to everyday life." A thematic magazine needing how-to and teaching articles. "Most of the articles we publish fall into three categories. (1) Teaching on a Scripture passage, such as a study of an Old Testament character or a short section of an epistle, or explaining the meaning and showing how it applies to daily life. (2) Teaching on a topic, such as what Scripture says about forgiveness or materialism. (3) How-to, such as tips on deepening your devotional life or witnessing in the workplace. We do not publish devotionals, purely theological material, book reviews, news articles, or articles about Christian organizations."

Article length 1,500 to 2,500 words. Must query first. Accepts photocopies. Buys first rights. Guidelines, theme list, and sample copy for $1.69. Reports in 8 weeks. Lead time 3 months. Pays 17 cents per word on acceptance.

DISCIPLESHIP TRAINING, 127 Ninth Avenue N, Nashville, TN 37234. (615) 251-2831. Richard Ryan, editor. A 64-page quarterly magazine published by the Baptist Sunday School Board. Circulation 30,000.

☐ *Discipleship Training* addresses a Southern Baptist audience of adults and leaders in Discipleship Training. Needs personal experiences, practical how-to's for leaders of Discipleship Training.

Article length 100 lines, 45 characters per line. Prefers a query. Accepts computer submissions. Buys all or first rights for a lesser pay rate. Guidelines and sample copy for SASE. Lead time 12 months. Pays 5 cents per word 30 days after acceptance.

DISCOVERIES, 6401 The Paseo, Kansas City, MO 64131. (816) 333-7000, ext. 2250. Fax: (816) 333-1683. Latta Jo Knapp, editor. Submit to Darla Hulett, editorial assistant. A 4-page weekly take-home paper published by WordAction Publishing Company. Circulation 30,000.

☐ *Discoveries* addresses a Nazarene/Wesleyan audience of children ages 8 to 12. A thematic magazine that needs "contemporary, true-to-life stories of 8 to 10 year old children." Also uses cartoons and humor for 8- to 10-year-olds.

Story length 500 to 700 words. Prefers a query, but accepts complete manuscript. Accepts photocopies. Buys all rights. Guidelines, theme list, and sample copy for SASE. Reports in 3 to 6 months. Lead time 14 months. Pays 5 cents per word on publication. Offers a $15 kill fee.

THE DOOR, Box 530, Yreka, CA 96097. (916) 842-2701. Mike Yaconelli, editor. Submit queries and complete manuscripts to Bob Darden, 118 North 30 Street, Waco, TX 76710, or Karla Yaconelli, managing editor. A 36-page bimonthly magazine published by Youth Specialties, 1224 Greenfield Drive, El Cajon, CA 92021. Circulation 10,000.

☐ *The Door* serves a mixed audience of Orthodox Roman Catholic and Protestant adults with either an Evangelical or Liberal background. A thematic magazine that needs personal experiences and interviews on current issues and theology, all with a satirical twist. Also needs column materials on current issues and theology which satirize the church and religious issues, humorous fillers (cartoons, mock advertisements, etc.), an occasional poem, all satirical. "Hold a mirror in front of the Evangelical church with the hope that humor and satire will provide an avenue of reform and renewal as the church looks at its antics and learns to laugh at its absurdities." Buys some photographs.

Article and column length 750 to 2,000 words, interviews 1,500 words. No model release required with B&W glossies, color slides, or prints. Prefers a query. Accepts photocopies and computer submissions. Buys first rights. Guidelines and theme list available for SASE, sample copy for $2. Reports in 6 to 10 weeks. Pays $50 to $300 for text, $40 to $100 for poems, $50 to $75 for fillers on publication. Assigned interviews are paid upon delivery.

THE EDGE, 455 North Service Road, East Oakville, ON, L6H 1A5. Canada. (416) 845-9235. Fax: (416) 845-1966. Captain Bruce Power, editor. A 20-page magazine published 11 times yearly by The Salvation Army. Circulation 4,000.

☐ *The Edge* serves a youth audience with a mainline Protestant background. The magazine's purpose is "to discuss issues relevant to youth/young adults, present the Christian perspective, provide tools for Bible study, encourage growth in Christian faith." Needs Bible studies, comics, devotions, meditations, humor, personal experience on Christian living, media, music, social issues, other topics. Also uses poetry, column material (book, video, music reviews), and photographs.

Article length 200 to 1,200 words. Accepts simultaneous submissions, photocopies, computer disks. Buys first and reprint rights. Guidelines and sample copy for SASE. Reports in 6 months.

THE EGG: AN ECO-JUSTICE QUARTERLY, Anabel Taylor Hall, Cornell University, Ithaca, NY 14853. (607) 255-2445. Dieter T. Hessel, editor. William E. Gibson, senior editor. A 20-page quarterly, cosponsored by the Eco-Justice Project and Network of the Center for Religion, Ethics, and Social Policy at Cornell University, and by the Eco-Justice Working Group of the National Council of Churches. Circulation is more than 4,000.

☐ *The Egg* serves a diverse audience of readers in the church and university communities and environmental and social justice organizations. "As a concept, 'eco-justice' regards ecological wholeness and social/economic justice as necessary and inseparable components of a desirable future." Ecumenically oriented.

Article length 1,600 to 2,400 words. Sample copies available to prospective writers upon request. No payment.

EMPHASIS ON FAITH AND LIVING, P.O. Box 9127, Fort Wayne, IN 46899. (219) 456-4502. Fax: (219) 456-4903. Robert Ransom, editor. A 16-page bimonthly magazine published by Missionary Church, Incorporated. Circulation 13,500.

☐ *Emphasis on Faith and Living* addresses an adult and senior adult audience of laity with an Evangelical, Missionary Church background. Needs personal experiences, interviews, and devotions on current issues and theological topics and photographs (B&W glossies).

Article length 300 to 600 words. Prefers query, but accepts complete manuscript. Accepts photocopies, simultaneous and computer submissions in WordPerfect, PageMaker 4, or an ASCII file. Buys all rights. Guidelines and sample copy for SASE. Reports in 30 to 60 days. Pays $5 to $35 on publication.

ENCOUNTER, Box 82867, 1000 West 42nd Street, Indianapolis, IN 46208. (312) 924-1331. Clark M. Williamson, editor. A 100-page quarterly journal with a circulation of 1,000.

☐ *Encounter* addresses an audience of mainline Protestant and Roman Catholic scholars, clergy, and laity. Needs articles on theology.

Article length 25 typed, double-spaced pages. Prefers a complete manuscript. Buys first rights. Guidelines and sample copy not available. Reports in 1 month. No payment.

EPISCOPAL LIFE, 815 2nd Avenue, New York, NY 10017. (212) 922-5398. Fax: (212) 949-0859. Jerrold F. Hames, editor. Submit to Nan Cobbey, features editor, or Edward Stannard, news editor. A 28-page monthly newspaper published by the Episcopal Church, USA. Circulation 189,000.

☐ *Episcopal Life* addresses a mainline Protestant audience of clergy and laity with an Episcopal background. Needs personal experiences, interviews, and articles on current issues and theology. Also needs column material on current issues and theology and photographs (B&W glossies).

Article length 500 words, column material 300 to 500 words. Prefers a query but accepts complete manuscripts. Accepts computer submissions in WordPerfect 5.1. Buys all rights. Sample copy for SASE. Pays $50 on publication.

ESPRIT, 1512 St. James Street, Winnipeg, MB, R3H 0L2 Canada. (204) 786-6707. Fax: (204) 783-7548. Gwen Hawkins, editor. A 52-page bimonthly digest published by the Evangelical Lutheran Women. Circulation 8,000.

☐ *Esprit* serves an audience of Lutheran women. It is "a resource for women; offers inspiration toward growth in faith, supports recognition of God-given abilities and opportunities; heightens awareness of issues challenging Christians' beliefs daily." Needs devotions, meditations, humor, opinion, personal experience, profiles, doctrine on Christian living, environment, evangelism, family, feminism, health, leadership, stewardship, natives, and social issues. Also uses some poetry and reviews. Prefers Evangelical Lutheran writers. "Desire Christ-centered material that is contemporary, offers hope, but does not preach. Inclusive—no gender, racial, ethnic, religious material or physical bias."

Article length to 1,200 words. Prefers a complete manuscript. Accepts simultaneous submissions, computer disks. Buys first and reprint rights. Guidelines and sample copy for SASE. Reports in 3 months. Pays $12.50 per printed published page on publication.

EVANGEL, Box 535002, Indianapolis, IN 46253-5002. (317) 244-3660. Fax: (317) 244-1247. Vera Bethel, editor. An 8-page weekly take-home paper published by the Free Methodist Church. Circulation 26,000.

☐ *Evangel* serves an Evangelical audience of adults. Needs personal experiences, devotional articles, fiction, poetry (traditional, free verse, haiku), column material (devotionals), and photographs.

Article length 1,000 words, short stories 1,200 words, columns 600 words. Limit poems to 6 poems per envelope. No model release required for B&W glossies. Prefers a complete manuscript. Accepts simultaneous submissions, photocopies. Buys first, reprint, one-time, and simultaneous rights. Guidelines and sample copy for 6 × 9 envelope with 2 stamps. Reports in 1 month. Lead time 3 months. Pays $10 to $45 prior to publication.

THE EVANGELICAL BAPTIST, 679 Southgate Drive, Guelph, ON, N1G 4S2 Canada. (519) 821-4830. Fax: (519) 821-9829. Tom Scura, editor. A 32-page magazine published 11 times yearly by The Fellowship of Evangelical Baptist Churches in Canada. Circulation 5,000.

☐ *The Evangelical Baptist* serves an interdenominational audience of adults from an Evangelical background. "We are Christ-centered, evangelism-oriented, and conservatively Christian." It's purpose is "to promote the cause of Christ through the FEBC by informing its people of Fellowship news in local church and national and international ministries." Needs Bible studies, devotions, meditations, opinion, personal experience, doctrine on Christian living, church education, education, environment, evangelism, family, leadership, missions, stewardship, seniors, and social issues. Also uses column material (book, video, film reviews). "Good issue-oriented feature articles with pictures." Prefers Evangelical Baptist writers.

Prefers a query. Buys first rights. Accepts simultaneous submissions, photocopies, and computer disks. Guidelines and sample copy for SASE. Reports in 8 weeks. Payment is negotiable.

THE EVANGELICAL BEACON, 901 East 78th Street, Minneapolis, MN 55420. Carol Madison, editor. A 40-page magazine published 8 times yearly by the Evangelical Free Church of America. Circulation 38,000.

☐ *The Evangelical Beacon* serves a mixed audience of clergy and laity with an Evangelical Free background. A thematic magazine that needs articles and fillers.

Article length 1,200 to 1,800 words, fillers 500 to 800. Prefers a complete manuscript. Accepts photocopies and simultaneous submissions. Buys first, reprint, and simultaneous rights. Guidelines, theme list, and sample copy for SASE and $1. Reports in 6 weeks. Pays 3 to 7 cents per word on publication.

EVANGELISM, 12800 North Lake Shore Drive, Mequon, WI 53092-7699. (414) 243-4207. Fax: (414) 243-4351. Dr. Joel D. Heck, editor. A 48-page quarterly journal published by Concordia University, Wisconsin. Circulation 1,000.

☐ *Evangelism* addresses an audience of clergy and laity with an Evangelical Protestant background. Needs articles and personal experiences on current issues, theology, and practical ideas on evangelism. Needs column material for Evangelism committees. Buys photographs.

Articles run 1,000 to 4,000 words. Columns run 500 to 2,000 words. Runs B&W glossies of authors. Prefers a complete manuscript. Accepts computer submissions in IBM compatible word processing. Guidelines and sample copy for $1. Reports in 3 weeks. No payment.

EVANGELIZING TODAY'S CHILD, Box 348, Warrenton, MO 63383. (314) 456-4321. Fax: (314) 456-2078. Elsie Lippy, editor. A 72-page bimonthly magazine published by Child Evangelism, Fellowship, Incorporated. Circulation 25,000.

☐ *Evangelizing Today's Child* serves an Evangelical audience of clergy and laity from a Protestant background who work with child evangelism. Needs interviews and theology slanted to the teachers of 4- to 12-year-olds. Also needs contemporary fiction for children 4 to 12 dealing with problems they face today. Must have a scriptural solution worked into the text practically and believably. Needs photographs. All columns assigned.

Article length 1,500 to 2,000 words. Prefers a query. Buys first, reprint, and one-time rights. Guidelines and sample copy for SASE and $1. Reports in 6 weeks. Pays 8 to 10 cents per word for nonfiction, 6 cents per word for fiction on acceptance.

EXALTATION, 127 Ninth Avenue N, Nashville, TN 37234. (615) 251-2967. Crystal Waters Mangrum, editor. A 24-page quarterly magazine published by the Baptist Sunday School Board. Circulation 15,000.

☐ *Exaltation* serves a Southern Baptist youth and adult audience. Needs articles on music.

Article length 4 to 8 pages. Prefers a complete manuscript. Buys one-time rights. Guidelines and sample copy for SASE. Pays 5 cents per word on publication.

FAITH 'N STUFF, The Magazine for Kids, 16 East 34th Street, New York, NY 10017. (212) 251-8100. Fax: (212) 684-0679. Mary Lou Carney, editor. Submit articles to Wally Metts, fiction to Lurline McDaniel. A 32-page bimonthly magazine published by Guideposts Association. Circulation 110,000.

☐ *Faith 'n Stuff* serves an interdenominational audience of children ages 7 to 12. Needs "tough, issue-oriented, controversial, thought-provoking articles." Needs fiction (fiction and fantasy)—"fast-paced, well-crafted stories that reflect Christian values." Uses some humorous poetry. Also uses puzzles, mazes, and jokes. "No Bible word searches or unscrambling disciples' names." Also buys color slides. Only top-quality material. This is not a beginner's market. "Study our magazine before submitting!"

Article length 1,500 words including sidebars. Fiction length 1,400 to 1,600 words. Limit poetry to 4 per envelope. Prefers a complete manuscript for fiction, query for all others. Buys all rights. Guidelines for SASE, sample copy for $3.25. Reports in 6 weeks. Lead time 5 months. Pays $200 to $300 for features, $100 to $200 for fiction on acceptance.

FAITH TODAY, Box 8800, Station B, Willowdale, ON, M2K 2R6 Canada. (416) 479-5885. Fax: (416) 479-4742. Brian C. Stiller, editor. An 80-page bimonthly magazine published by Evangelical Fellowship of Canada. Circulation 17,500.

☐ *Faith Today* serves an interdenominational adult audience from an Evangelical background. It's purpose is "to inform on issues of concern to Canadian church and society on events and trends within the church." Needs comics, news, opinion, profiles, the arts, church education, evangelism, family, leadership, politics, social issues. "Solid, journalistic features (not essays) on issues within the Canadian context. 2 emphases—Canadian and journalistic." Also uses illustrations.

Article length 400 to 800 words. Prefers query. Accepts photocopies and computer disks, but no simultaneous submissions. Buys first rights. Guidelines and sample copy for SASE. Pays $50 to $80 on acceptance.

THE FAMILY, 50 St. Paul's Avenue, Boston, MA 02130. (617) 522-8911. Fax: (617) 541-9805. Sister Mary Lea Hill, editor. Submit to Sister Donna William, managing editor, Sister Kathryn James, assistant editor. A 40-page monthly magazine published by Daughters of St. Paul. Circulation under 10,000.

☐ *The Family* addresses Roman Catholic parents and their families. A thematic magazine which needs personal experiences, interviews, other types of articles relating to family life, "slice of life" fiction, traditional and free verse poetry, column material on current issues, and fillers.

Articles and fiction 750 to 2,000 words. Columns run 650 to 1,200 words. Fillers run 50 to 200 words. Prefers a complete manuscript. Buys first and reprint rights. Guidelines, theme list, and sample copy for 8 1/2 × 11 SASE. Reports in 2 to 3 months. Pays $50 to $150 for articles and stories, $10 to $30 for fillers on publication.

THE FELLOWSHIP LINK, 679 Southgate Drive, Guelph, ON, N1G 4S2 Canada. (519) 821-4830. Fax: (519) 821-9829. Dr. A. Timothy Starr, editor. A 24-page quarterly magazine published by Fellowship of Evangelical Baptists. Circulation 4,000.

☐ *The Fellowship Link* serves an Evangelical audience of senior adults with a Baptist background. Its purpose is "to exalt Jesus Christ, to enhance and edify Christian seniors 55 and over." Needs comics, drama, humor, opinion, personal experience, profiles, Christian living, environment, evangelism, health, history, missions, stewardship, seniors, social issues, travel. "Our approach to ministry to seniors is well-balanced and the emphasis is on the practical." Also needs poetry and illustrations.

Article length 250 words. Accepts simultaneous submissions, photocopies, computer disks. Requires first or reprint rights. Guidelines and sample copy for SASE. Reports in 3 months.

FELLOWSHIP MAGAZINE, Box 237, Barrie, ON, L4N 4T3 Canada. (705) 737-0114. Ed McCaig, editor. A 36-page magazine published 5 times yearly by the United Church Renewal Fellowship. Circulation 2,500.

☐ *Fellowship Magazine* serves adults with a United Church background. "We primarily serve United Church members within the Orthodox/Evangelical tradition." Its purpose is "to serve the reform and renewal movement within the United Church of Canada with news coverage and articles focusing on spiritual growth from a biblical perspective." Needs Bible studies, devotions, meditations, news, opinion, personal experience, doctrine, Christian living, church education, evangelism, family, and missions. Also uses photographs. Prefers United Church writers.

Article length 1,200 to 1,800 words. Prefers query. Accepts simultaneous submissions, photocopies, computer disks. Buys first and reprint rights. Guidelines and sample copy for SASE. Reports in 4 months. Pays $25 to $50 on publication.

FOCUS ON THE FAMILY, 420 North Cascade Avenue, Colorado Springs, CO 80995. (719) 531-3400. Fax: (719) 531-3499. Mike Yorkey, editor. Submit to Sandra Aldrich. A 16-page monthly magazine published by Focus on the Family. Circulation 1.5 million.

☐ *Focus on the Family* addresses a nondenominational audience of clergy and laity with an Evangelical background. Uses personal experiences on current issues and fillers (anecdotes and humor).

Article length 800 to 1,200 words. Prefers a query. Buys first rights. Guidelines and sample copy for SASE. Pays $50 to $500 on publication. "Due to completed plans for future issues, we are unable to accept unsolicited manuscripts at this time."

FOURSQUARE WORLD ADVANCE, 1910 West Sunset Boulevard, Suite 200, Los Angeles, CA 90026-3282. (213) 484-2400, ext. 310. Fax: (213) 413-3834. John R. Holland, editor. Submit to Ronald D. Williams, managing editor. A 24-page bimonthly magazine published by International Church of the Foursquare Gospel. Circulation 97,000.

☐ *Foursquare World Advance* serves an Evangelical audience of youth and adults in the clergy and laity with a Foursquare background. Needs articles.

Article length 1,200 words. Prefers a complete manuscript. Buys first and reprint rights. Guidelines and sample copy for SASE. Reports in 3 months. Pays $75 on publication.

FREEWAY, P.O. Box 632, Glen Ellyn, IL 60183. (708) 668-6000. Amy J. Cox, editor. A 4-page weekly take-home paper published by Scripture Press Publications.

☐ *Freeway* serves an audience of Evangelical youth ages 15 to 20. A thematic magazine needing fiction, nonfiction, and poetry from teens only, photographs to accompany the articles when available. All submissions should "encourage a biblical lifestyle, sexual purity, and abstinence from anything that causes harm to the body."

Articles and fiction 600 to 1,200 words. Prefers a complete manuscript. Buys first, reprint, one-time rights. Guidelines, theme list, and sample copy for SASE. Pays 5 to 10 cents per word (depending on rights) on acceptance.

GOD'S WORLD, P.O. Box 2330, Asheville, NC 28802. (704) 253-8063. Fax: (704) 253-1556. Norm Bomer, editor. An 8-page weekly magazine with a circulation of 235,000.

☐ *God's World* addresses a children's audience ages 9 to 13. "All published manuscripts must present a Christian world view without being moralistic. Simple vocabulary and simple sentence structure." Needs articles on nature, science, human interest, history, and so on.

Article length 600 to 800 words. Prefers a complete manuscript. Buys one-time rights. Guidelines and sample copy for SASE. Pays $75 on publication.

GOSPEL TIDINGS, 5800 South 14th Street, Omaha, NE 68107-3584. (402) 731-4780. Fax: (402) 731-1173. Robert L. Frey, editor. A 16-page bimonthly newsletter published by the Fellowship of Evangelical Bible Churches. Circulation 2,200.

☐ *Gospel Tidings* serves an Evangelical audience of all ages from a Baptist background. Needs personal experiences, devotional articles, and articles on current issues. Also needs fillers (anecdotes), and photographs.

Article length 400 to 1,500 words, fillers 100 to 250 words. Model release required with B&W glossies. Accepts simultaneous submissions. Also computer submissions in WordPerfect or ASCII file. Buys all rights. Guidelines and sample copy not available. No payment.

GROUP/CHILDREN'S MINISTRY/JR. HIGH MINISTRY MAGAZINES, Box 481, Loveland, CO 80539. (303) 669-3836. Fax: (303) 669-3269. Rick Lawrence, editor. Submit to Allie Storey, administrative assistant. These monthly magazines are 50, 55, and 38 pages with circulations of 57,000, 25,000, and 20,000 respectively.

☐ *Group, Children's Ministry*, and *Jr. High Ministry* magazines serve audiences of children's and youth leaders. They need articles on current issues related to children and youth. They also need photographs.

Article length 500 to 1,700 words *(Group)*, 500 to 1,400 words *(Children's Ministry)*, 500 to 1,200 words *(Jr. High Ministry)*. Model release required with B&W glossies. Prefers a complete manuscript. Buys all rights. Guidelines and sample copy for SASE. Pays $75 to $150 on acceptance.

GUIDE MAGAZINE, 55 West Oak Ridge Drive, Hagerstown, MD 21740. (301) 791-7000. Fax: (301) 791-7012. Jeannette Johnson, editor. A 32-page weekly magazine published by Review and Herald Publishing Association. Circulation 40,000.

☐ *Guide Magazine* addresses an audience of youth ages 10 to 14 with an Evangelical, Seventh Day Adventist background. Needs personal experiences, humor, devotions on personal spiritual growth, and fiction (adventure and mystery).

Articles and short stories 1,000 to 1,200 words. Prefers a complete manuscript. Accepts simultaneous submissions. Buys first, reprint, simultaneous, and one-time rights. Guidelines and sample copy for SASE. Reports in 2 weeks. Pays 3 to 4 cents per word on acceptance.

GUIDEPOSTS, 16 East 34th Street, New York, NY 10016. (212) 251-8100. Fax: (212) 684-0679. Fulton Ourssler, Jr., editor-in-chief. Submit short features to Rick Hamlin. A 48-page monthly magazine published by Guideposts Associates, Incorporated. Circulation 3,900,000.

☐ *Guideposts* serves a general audience of Christian and non-Christian adults and youth. Needs personal experience stories, an occasional poem, fillers, and photographs.

Feature articles run 750 to 1,500 words, short features 250 to 750, anecdotes and humor 1 to 3 sentences. Prefers a complete manuscript. Buys all rights. Guidelines and sample copy for SASE. Reports in 2 to 4 weeks. Lead time 4 months. Pays $200 to $400 for features, $50 to $200 for short features on final, edited, approved manuscript with a 25 percent kill fee.

HARVARD THEOLOGICAL REVIEW, 45 Francis Avenue, Cambridge, MA 02138. (617) 495-5786. Fax: (617) 495-9489. Helmut Koester, editor. A 125-page quarterly journal published by the Harvard Divinity School. Circulation 1,800.

☐ *Harvard Theological Review* addresses a Liberal audience of scholars, clergy, and laity with a mainline Protestant or Roman Catholic background. Needs articles on theology, New Testament, philosophy of religion, ethics, American religion, all scholarly in tone.

Prefers a complete manuscript. Requires all rights. Guidelines and sample copy for $10. Reports in 8 weeks. No payment.

HEARTBEAT, P.O. Box 5002, Antioch, TN 37011-5002. (615) 731-6812. Fax: (615) 731-0049. Don Robirds, editor. A 16-page bimonthly magazine published by the National Association of Free Will Baptists. Circulation 42,000.

☐ *Heartbeat* serves an Evangelical audience of clergy and laity with a Free Will Baptist background. Needs personal experiences and interviews about missionaries. Also needs photographs.

Article length to 1,000 words. Prefers a complete manuscript. Buys one-time rights. Pays 3 cents per word on publication.

HELPING HAND, Box 12609, Oklahoma City, OK 73157-2609. (405) 787-3957. Fax: (405) 789-3957. Doris Moore, editor. A 20-page bimonthly magazine published by the General Women's Ministries of the Pentecostal Holiness Church. Circulation 4,000.

☐ *Helping Hand* primarily serves a women's audience with an Evangelical, Pentecostal Holiness background. A thematic magazine that needs articles (personal experiences and devotionals on current issues) and fiction with themes that relate to women. Buys traditional poetry, devotions, and meditations as fillers, and photographs (B&W glossies).

Article and fiction length 500 to 1,200 words, fillers to 500 words. Limit poems to 4 per envelope. Prefers a query, but accepts complete manuscript. Accepts simultaneous submissions. Buys first, reprint, simultaneous, one-time, and all rights. Guidelines, theme list, and sample copy for SASE. Lead time 3 to 4 months. Pays $20 for articles and fiction, $10 to $20 for poetry on publication.

HERALD OF HOLINESS, 6401 The Paseo, Kansas City, MO 64131. (816) 333-7000, ext. 230. Fax: (816) 333-1748. Dr. Wesley D. Tracy, editor. A 44-page monthly magazine published by Church of the Nazarene. Circulation 80,000.

☐ *Herald of Holiness* serves an Evangelical audience of adult laity with a Nazarene background. Needs personal experiences, interviews, devotional articles, articles on current issues and theology. Also uses traditional poetry and photographs.

Article length 700 to 2,000 words. Photographic needs are for B&W glossies and color slides. Prefers a complete manuscript. Buys one-time rights. Guidelines and sample copy for SASE. Reports in 8 weeks. Lead time 7 months. Pays 5 cents per word on acceptance.

HICALL, 1445 Boonville Avenue, Springfield, MO 65802-1894. (417) 862-2781, ext. 4349. Deanna Harris, editor. An 8-page weekly take-home paper published by the Assemblies of God. Circulation 73,000.

☐ *HiCall* addresses an audience of Evangelical youth ages 12 to 17 with an Assemblies of God background. Needs personal experiences, devotions on current issues, fiction (adventure, mystery, romance), traditional, free, haiku poetry, fillers (devotions, meditations, humor), photographs.

Article length to 1,000 words, short stories to 1,500 words and up "if the work is exceptional." Limit poems to 5 per envelope. Filler length to 500 words. Model release required with photographs. Prefers a complete manuscript. Accepts photocopies and simultaneous submissions. Buys first, reprint, simultaneous, and one-time rights. Guidelines available for SASE. Reports in 6 to 8 weeks. Lead time 18 months. Pays 2 to 3 cents per word for prose, 25 cents per line ($5 minimum) for poetry, $25 to $35 for photographs.

HIGH ADVENTURE, 1445 Boonville Avenue, Springfield, MO 65802-1984. (417) 862-2781. Fax: (417) 862-8558. Marshall Bruner, editor. A 16-page quarterly magazine published by the General Council of the Assemblies of God. Circulation 86,000.

☐ *High Adventure* serves an audience of children and youth ages 6 to 17 with an Assemblies of God background. A thematic magazine needing personal experiences and devotional articles on current issues and a wide variety of outdoor topics. Also uses fiction (mystery and adventure), column material (fitness and current issues), and fillers (devotionals and humor).

Article length 1,000 words, columns 700 to 800 words, fillers 300 to 400 words. Prefers a complete manuscript. Accepts computer submissions in WordPerfect or Word for Windows software. Buys first and reprint rights. Guidelines, theme list, and sample copy for SASE. Reports in 1 to 2 months. Pays 3 cents per word on acceptance.

HOME LIFE, 127 Ninth Avenue N, Nashville, TN 37234. (615) 251-2271. Charlie Warren, editor. A 68-page monthly magazine published by the Baptist Sunday School Board. Circulation 650,000.

☐ *Home Life* serves an Evangelical audience of Southern Baptist families. Needs personal experiences, interviews, and articles on current issues or any topic pertinent to family life. Needs fiction on family relationships. Buys traditional poetry and cartoons.

Articles and short stories 1,500 words. Limit poems to 5 per envelope. Prefers query, but accepts complete manuscript. Accepts simultaneous and computer submissions. Buys first and all rights. Guidelines free with SASE, sample copy for $1. Reports in 2 months. Lead time 1 year. Pays 4.75 to 5.5 cents per word for all rights, $15 to $25 for poetry, $38 to $50 for cartoons on acceptance.

HOME TIMES, P.O. Box 16096, West Palm Beach, FL 33416-6096. (407) 439-3509. Dennis Lombard, editor and publisher. A 24-page weekly newspaper with a circulation of 10,000.

☐ *Home Times* "goes to the general public. It is not a Christian newspaper, but a paper produced by Christians." Needs personal experiences and interviews. Especially needs articles on current issues in terms the general public can relate to. "The general news section is an alternative to the Liberal press—it's Judeo-Christian and traditional in morals, Conservative in politics, patriotic and positive." Also needs fiction, traditional poetry, columns (advice, health and fitness, especially current issues), fillers (anecdotes and humor), and photographs.

Articles and columns 900 words, fiction to 1,200 words. Model release required with B&W glossies. Submit complete manuscript only. No queries. Accepts photocopies, simultaneous submissions, and computer submissions in WordStar, WordPerfect, Microsoft Word (5.25" IBM disk). Buys one-time rights. Guidelines and sample copy for $1 and SASE with 3 stamps. "We are very open to new writers. Our publication is very different. You need to study our guidelines." Reports in 1 month. Lead time 6 to 8 weeks ahead. Pays $5 to $25 for articles and stories, $5 to $10 for op-eds, poems, cartoons, and photographs or art on publication. No payment for fillers.

HORIZONS, 100 Witherspoon Street, Louisville, KY 40202. (502) 569-5379. Fax: (502) 569-8085. Barbara Roche, editor. A 40-page bimonthly magazine published by Presbyterian Women. Circulation 30,000.

☐ *Horizons* addresses a women's audience with a Presbyterian background. Needs personal experiences, interviews, devotional articles, articles on current issues and theology. Also needs fiction that shares "insight into life's experiences, particularly for women." Uses poetry (traditional and free verse, haiku), fillers (devotions, meditations, anecdotes, and humor), and photographs.

Article and fiction length 1,500 to 2,000 words. Prefers a complete manuscript. Accepts photocopies, computer and electronic submissions in IBM compatible software. No simultaneous submissions. Buys all rights. Guidelines and sample copy for SASE. Reports in 4 weeks. Lead time 6 weeks. Pays $50 per page on publication.

HORIZONS, JOURNAL OF THE COLLEGE THEOLOGY SOCIETY, Villanova University, Villanova, PA 19085. (215) 645-7302. Fax: (215) 645-7599. Walter E. Conn, editor. A 200-page semiannual journal with a circulation of 1,450.

☐ *Horizons* serves an audience of educators, scholars, and clergy of all faiths. Needs articles on theology and book reviews.

Article length 20 to 30 double-spaced pages. Prefers a complete manuscript. Payment rate, if any, is not stated.

HORIZONS IN BIBLICAL THEOLOGY, 616 North Highland Avenue, Pittsburgh, PA 15206. (412) 362-5610. Donald E. Gowan, editor. A 100-page semiannual journal published by Pittsburgh Theological Seminary. Circulation 500.

☐ *Horizons in Biblical Theology* serves an audience of scholars and clergy with either a Protestant or Roman Catholic background. Needs articles on theological topics.

Article length 15 to 35 double-spaced pages. Prefers a complete manuscript. No payment.

HYMN SOCIETY IN THE UNITED STATES AND CANADA, Box 30854, Texas Christian University, Fort Worth, TX 76129. David W. Music, editor. A 48-page quarterly journal with a circulation of 3,500.

☐ *Hymn Society* addresses an audience of clergy ranging from Evangelical to Liberal, mainline Protestant to Roman Catholic. Needs interviews, devotional articles, and hymnology, column material (current issues and hymnology), fillers (devotions and hymn interpretations), original hymns, photographs.

Must query. No model release required for B&W glossies. Requires all rights. Guidelines and sample copy for SASE. Reports in 6 months. No payment.

I.D., 850 North Grove Avenue, Elgin, IL 60120. Douglas C. Schmidt, editor. An 8-page weekly take-home paper published by David C. Cook Publishing. Circulation 120,000.

☐ *I.D.* addresses a nondenominational audience of youth ages 13 to 18 with an Evangelical background. Needs personal experiences, interviews, devotions, current issues, and theology. Also uses fiction (adventure) and photographs.

Article length 900 to 1,000 words. Model release required for B&W glossies and color slides. Prefers a complete manuscript. Accepts simultaneous submissions and computer submissions in Microsoft Word 5.0. Buys all rights. Guidelines and sample copy for SASE. Reports in 6 to 8 weeks. Lead time 18 months. Pays 10 cents per word on acceptance.

INSIGHT, P.O. Box 23152, Charlotte, NC 28212. (704) 545-6161. Fax: (704) 753-0712. Millie H. Griswold, editor. An 8- to 12-page quarterly newsletter published by Advent Christian Conference. Circulation 2,500.

☐ *Insight* serves an Evangelical audience of adult laity with an Advent Christian background. This publication "is changing to become more of a marketing newsletter with 'snippets' of inspiration and ideas for church leaders." Needs personal experiences and fillers (anecdotes) on teaching and leadership development.

Article length 1,500 words, fillers 1,000 words. Information on submissions and payment not stated.

THE INSPIRER, 737 Kimsey Lane, #620, Henderson, KY 42420. (502) 826-5720. "Callers must be aware that I am speech impaired and they may have difficulty understanding me." Billy Edwards, editor. An 8-page quarterly newsletter with a circulation of 2,000.

☐ *The Inspirer* serves a nondenominational audience of adults with physical disabilities and an Evangelical background. "Although we welcome manuscripts from any Christian writer, we are especially interested in articles from writers with physical disabilities." Needs personal experiences and devotions, traditional poetry, devotions, meditations, and anecdotes as fillers.

Article length 500 words. Limit poems to 5 per envelope. Fillers 25 to 100 words. Prefers a complete manuscript. Accepts computer submissions in IBM compatible software. Buys simultaneous rights. Sample copy is available for SASE, but no formal guidelines. Reports in 2 weeks. No payment.

INTERPRETER, P.O. Box 320, Nashville, TN 37202-0320. (615) 742-5400. Ralph E. Baker, editor. A 36-page magazine published 8 times yearly by United Methodist Communications. Circulation 300,000.

☐ *Interpreter* serves an audience of clergy, laity, and congregational officers with a United Methodist background. "We accept VERY LITTLE freelance because of the publication's responsibility to the denomination's general agencies." Does need photographs.

Model release required when submitting color transparencies and color prints showing United Methodist churches in action. Buys one-time rights. Pays on publication.

INTERVARSITY, Box 7895, Madison, WI 53707-7895. (608) 274-9001. Fax: (608) 274-7882. Neal Knude, editor. A 24-page quarterly magazine published by InterVarsity Christian Fellowship of the USA. Circulation 50,000.

☐ *InterVarsity* is a nondenominational magazine that serves an audience of laity and clergy with a Protestant, Evangelical background. It informs contributors and readers of InterVarsity's work on campus. Needs personal experiences and interviews on current issues as they relate to the college campus. Also needs photographs.

Article length 750 words maximum. Photograph needs are for B&W glossies and color slides. Prefers query. Accepts photocopies. Buys first rights. Guidelines available for SASE. Pays $250 on publication.

ISSUES & ANSWERS, Route 4 Box 274, West Frankfort, IL 62896-9661. (618) 937-2348. Fax: (618) 937-2405. Dan I. Rodden, editor. Submit to JoAnne Tegtmeyer, managing editor. An 8-page monthly newspaper with a circulation of 15,000.

☐ *Issues & Answers* serves an audience of youth and adults, in laity and leadership. Some have an Evangelical background, others are non-Christians. A thematic magazine which needs interviews and articles on current issues and theological topics. Buys photographs.

Article length 4 pages double-spaced. No model release required with B&W glossies. Accepts photocopies. Buys all rights. Guidelines, theme list, and sample copy for $1. Lead time 1 month. Pays in complimentary copies.

JOURNAL OF BIBLICAL LITERATURE, Divinity School, University of Chicago, Chicago, IL. (312) 702-6943. John J. Collins, editor. A 190-page quarterly magazine published by the Society of Biblical Literature. Circulation 7,000.

☐ *Journal of Biblical Literature* addresses a Roman Catholic and mainline Protestant scholarly audience with an Evangelical or Liberal background. Needs theological articles.

Article length not specified. No other information given.

JOURNAL OF CHRISTIAN CAMPING, P.O. Box 646, Wheaton, IL 60189. (708) 462-0300. Fax: (708) 462-0499. John Ashman, editor. Submit to Hollis Pippin, assistant editor. A 32-page bimonthly magazine published by Christian Camping International/USA. Circulation 8,000.

☐ *Journal of Christian Camping* addresses an Evangelical audience of clergy and laity with a Nazarene background. "Our publication mainly serves the leaders of Christian camp, conference, and retreat centers. Our purpose is to equip and enable them in their profession through updates on camping trends, information on current issues in camping, and news about members in our organization." Needs personal experiences, interviews, articles on current issues, conference center issues relating to staff, finances, fundraising, and so on. Also uses column material (health and fitness as it relates to mental and emotional health), and fillers (anecdotes, humor).

Article length 1,000 words. Prefers a query. Accepts photocopies. Buys first rights. Guidelines and sample copy for SASE. Pays $25 to $75 on publication.

JOURNAL OF CHRISTIAN NURSING, 5206 Main Street, P.O. Box 1650, Downers Grove, IL 60515. (708) 964-5700. Fax: (708) 964-1251. Judith Allen Shelly, editor. Submit to Melodee Yohe, managing editor. A 40-page quarterly magazine published by Nurses Christian Fellowship. Circulation 10,000.

☐ *Journal of Christian Nursing* serves an Evangelical audience of professional nurses, with a mainline Protestant or Roman Catholic background. Its purpose is "to help Christian nurses view nursing practice through the eyes of faith." Needs personal experience and interviews of nurses. Potential topics include Christian concepts in nursing, spiritual care, ethics, values, healing and wholeness, psychology and religion, personal and professional life, and other pertinent subjects. Needs "clear photographs for our 'Speaking Out,' opinion column."

Article length 4 manuscript pages. Buys first, reprint rights on a case-to-case basis. Guidelines and sample copy for $4. Lead time 9 to 12 months. Pays $25 to $80 on publication.

JOURNAL OF CHURCH AND STATE, Baylor University, J. M. Dawson Institute of Church-State Studies, P.O. Box 97308, Waco, TX 76798-7308. (817) 755-1510. Fax: (817) 755-3740. James E. Wood, Jr., editor. A 200+ page quarterly journal published by the J. M. Dawson Institute for Church-State Studies. Circulation 1,600.

☐ *Journal of Church and State* addresses an adult interfaith audience of scholars. Readers are, however, primarily mainline Protestants. Needs essays that deal with church-state issues.

Article length 30 double-spaced pages with footnotes. Prefers a complete manuscript (3 copies plus a diskette, if available) in Mass-11, Microsoft Word, WordStar, WordPerfect on IBM or compatibles (5.25" disk); Mass-11 on DEC Rainbow (5.25" disk); MacWrite on Macintosh (3.5" disk). Buys all rights. Guidelines and sample copy for SASE. Reports in 3 to 6 months. No payment.

JOURNAL OF ECUMENICAL STUDIES, Temple University, (022-38), Philadelphia, PA 19122. (215) 787-7714. Fax: (215) 787-4569. Dr. Leonard Swidler, editor. Submit to Dr. Paul Mojzes. A 160-page quarterly journal with a circulation of 2,000.

☐ *Journal of Ecumenical Studies* addresses an audience of Roman Catholic and Protestant scholars and laity with an Orthodox, Evangelical, or Liberal background. Needs articles with interreligious dialogue and book reviews, theology, religious news as column material.

Article length about 30 pages double-spaced. Query first for columns. Prefers a complete manuscript (one original and 3 photocopies). Accepts computer disk, but only after manuscript is accepted and revised. Must be in IBM compatible software, preferably WordPerfect. Guidelines and sample copy for SASE. Reports in 3 months. Information on payment and rights not stated.

JOURNAL OF FEMINIST STUDIES IN RELIGION, Harvard Divinity School, 45 Francis Avenue, Cambridge, MA 02138. (617) 495-5751. Fax: (617) 495-9489. Judith Plaskow and Elisabeth Schüssler Fiorenza, co-editors. Submit to Elizabeth Prichard, managing editor. A 135-page semiannual journal. Circulation 1,100.

☐ *Journal of Feminist Studies in Religion* primarily serves a scholarly women's audience with a Liberal background. Needs articles on current issues and theology on scholarly feminist work in religion, traditional, free, and haiku poetry.

Article length 20 to 35 double-spaced pages. Prefers a complete manuscript. Buys one-time rights. Guidelines and sample copy for SASE. Reports in 9 months. No payment.

JOURNAL OF PASTORAL CARE, 1068 Harbor Drive, SW, Calabash, NC 28467. (919) 579-5084. Fax: (919) 579-5084. Orlo Strunk, Jr., Ph.D., editor. A 104-page quarterly journal with a circulation of 14,000.

☐ *Journal of Pastoral Care* addresses a Liberal audience of clergy and laity. Needs personal experiences, devotional articles, and pastoral theology. Also uses poetry (traditional and free verse).

Article length unspecified. Limit poems to 3 per envelope. Prefers a complete manuscript. Buys first rights. Guidelines and sample copy for $5. Lead time 12 months. Payment in copies.

JOURNAL OF PSYCHOLOGY AND CHRISTIANITY, Department of Psychology, Grave City College, Grave City, PA 16127. (412) 458-2004. Peter C. Hill, Ph.D., editor. Submit Applied Clinical articles to Siang-Yang Tan, Ph.D., Fuller Theological Seminary, 180 North Oakland Avenue, Pasadena, CA 91101. A 96-page quarterly journal published by the Christian Association for Psychological Studies. Circulation 2,200.

☐ *Journal of Psychology and Christianity* serves an audience of professional psychologists and clergy with a Protestant, Evangelical background. Needs articles on theoretical, empirical, and applied articles in psychology and theology and book reviews.

Article length 25 double-spaced pages maximum, book reviews 2 double-spaced pages. Prefers a complete manuscript. Guidelines and sample copy for $5 to $8 depending on issue. Reports in 90 days. No payment.

JOURNAL OF PSYCHOLOGY AND THEOLOGY, 13800 Biola Avenue, La Mirada, CA 90639. (310) 903-4867. Fax: (310) 903-4864. Subscriptions: (310) 903-4727. Patricia L. Pike, Ph.D., editor. A 90-page quarterly journal published by Rosemead School of Psychology, Biola University. Circulation 2,000.

☐ *Journal of Psychology and Theology* intends "to communicate recent scholarly thinking on the interrelationships of psychological and theological concepts and to consider the application of these concepts into a variety of professional settings." Needs articles on scholarly thinking and application of the integration of psychology and theology.

Article length is 20 manuscript pages. Prefers a complete manuscript. Requires all rights. Guidelines available for SASE. Reports in 3 months. No payment.

JOURNAL OF RELIGION AND HEALTH, Box 1077, Southwest Harbor, ME 04679, (c/o Meserve). (207) 244-7124. Harry C. Meserve, editor. An 80-page quarterly digest published by Institutes of Religion and Health. Circulation unspecified.

☐ *Journal of Religion and Health* addresses an adult audience of scholars and clergy with a Liberal mainline Protestant or Roman Catholic background. Needs articles on religion and health and how they interrelate.

Article length 40 double-spaced pages maximum. Prefers a complete manuscript. Accepts photocopies. Guidelines and sample copy for SASE. Lead time 9 months. No payment.

JOURNAL OF RELIGIOUS ETHICS, Theology Department, Georgetown University, Washington, DC 20057-0998. (202) 687-1647. Fax: (202) 687-8000. D. M. Yeager, editor. A 200-page semiannual journal with a circulation of 1,145.

☐ *Journal of Religious Ethics* serves an audience of Roman Catholic and mainline Protestant scholars with either an Evangelical or Liberal background. Needs scholarly articles.

Article length 5,000 to 10,000 words. Prefers a complete manuscript. Accepts photocopies and computer submissions in any DOS or Macintosh applications. Requires all rights. Guidelines free for SASE, back copies available at $9 each. Reports in 2 months. No payment.

JOURNAL OF RELIGIOUS STUDIES, Cleveland State University, Euclid Avenue at East 24th Street, Cleveland, OH 44115. (216) 687-2170. Dr. Derwood C. Smith, editor. Submit to co-editor Richard E. Barnes. A 185-page annual digest published by Cleveland State University. Has an international circulation.

☐ *Journal of Religious Studies* serves an audience of scholars. Needs articles on theology. Article length unspecified. Must query. Guidelines and sample copy for SASE. No payment.

JOURNAL OF WOMEN'S MINISTRIES, 815 Second Avenue, New York, NY 10017. (800) 334-7626. Marcy Darin, editor. A 36-page semiannual magazine published by the Council for Women's Ministries. Circulation 10,000.

☐ *Journal of Women's Ministries* serves a Liberal audience of women with an Episcopal background. Needs personal experiences, interviews, devotional articles, and articles on current issues, issues confronting women in the church and society, theology. Also uses poetry (traditional and free verse), and photographs.

Article length 1,200 to 1,500 words. Limit poems to 2 per envelope. No model release required for B&W glossies. Prefers a query. Accepts computer submissions in IBM compatible software. Buys first rights. Guidelines and sample copy for SASE. Reports in 1 month. Lead time 8 weeks. Pays $50 per article on publication.

THE JOYFUL WOMAN, 118 Shannon Lake Circle, Greenville, SC 29615. (803) 234-0289. Elizabeth Handford, editor. A bimonthly magazine with a circulation of 15,000.

☐ *The Joyful Woman* serves a nondenominational audience of women from a mainline conservative, Evangelical background. "Our purpose is to encourage, stimulate, teach, and develop the Christian woman to reach her full potential, joyful and fulfilled, a useful servant of Christ regardless of her situation." Needs articles that relate to women's concerns.

Article length 400 to 2,000 words. Buys little fiction, poetry, or fillers. Accepts either a query or complete manuscript. Accepts simultaneous submissions. Buys first and reprint rights. Guidelines for SASE. Reports in 6 weeks. Lead time 4 months. Pays 2 to 4 cents per word on publication, occasionally on acceptance.

JUNIOR TRAILS, 1445 Boonville Avenue, Springfield, MO 65802. (417) 862-2781. Sinda S. Zinn. An 8-page weekly take-home paper published by Gospel Publishing House. Circulation 55,000.

☐ *Junior Trails* serves an audience of children ages 10 to 12 (slanted toward the older group) with an Evangelical, Assemblies of God background. Primarily needs "fiction that presents realistic characters working out their problems according to Bible principles; presenting Christianity in action without being preachy. Especially needs inner city stories." Also needs historical, scientific, or nature articles or fillers with a spiritual lesson and "reader appeal, emphasizing some phase of Christian living." Occasionally uses traditional and free verse poetry "expressing feelings or reactions."

Fiction length 1,000 to 1,500 words, nonfiction 500 to 800 words, fillers 300 words.

Prefers a complete manuscript. Accepts simultaneous submissions. Buys first, reprint, and simultaneous rights. Guidelines and sample copy for SASE. Reports in 4 to 6 weeks. Lead time 12 to 15 months. Pays 2 to 3 cents per word on acceptance.

JUST BETWEEN US, Magazine for Ministry Wives, 1529 Cesery Boulevard, Jacksonville, FL 32211. (904) 734-5994. Jill Briscoe, editor. Submit to Michael Duduit, managing editor. A 32-page quarterly magazine published by Preaching Resources, Incorporated. Circulation 8,000.

☐ *Just Between Us* serves a clergy audience and their spouses with an Evangelical background. "Written by and for ministry wives. Editorial content emphasizes practical counsel and encouragement for women who serve in this challenging role." Needs personal experiences and devotionals on current issues and items of interest to ministry wives.

Prefers a query, but accepts complete manuscript. Accepts photocopies and computer submissions in WordPerfect. Buys first rights. Guidelines and sample copy for $2. Reports in 2 to 3 months. Lead time 6 to 9 months. "Most manuscripts are not paid; author receives sample copy."

KEYS FOR KIDS, Box 1, Grand Rapids, MI 49501. (616) 451-2009. Hazel Marett, editor. A 95-page bimonthly daily devotional guide published by Children's Bible Hour. Circulation 40,000.

☐ *Keys for Kids* serves a children's audience ages 8 to 14. Needs devotions. "Our daily devotional for kids consists of a fictional story which is used to teach a biblical principle, a Scripture reading, a memory verse, and a key thought."

Devotion length 400 words. Prefers a complete manuscript. Buys first, reprint, and simultaneous rights. Guidelines and sample copy for 6 1/2" × 9 1/2" SASE with $1.05 postage. Reports in 3 weeks. Pays $10 to $14 per devotional on acceptance.

KEY TO CHRISTIAN EDUCATION, 8121 Hamilton Avenue, Cincinnati, OH 45231. (513) 931-4050. Lowellette Lauderdale, editor. Submit to Lowellette Lauderdale. A 16-page quarterly magazine published by Standard Publishing. Circulation 66,000.

☐ *Key to Christian Education* addresses Evangelical Sunday school teachers and youth workers. "Provides practical helps, encouragement, new information, and challenge for Sunday school teachers and youth workers." A thematic magazine which needs personal experiences and devotions on current issues of importance to Sunday school teachers. Also buys photographs.

Article length 700 to 1,200 words. Model release required for B&W glossies. Prefers a complete manuscript. Accepts simultaneous submissions. Buys all rights. Guidelines, theme list, and sample copy for SASE and 75 cents postage. Pays 2 to 3 cents per word on publication.

KIDS' STUFF, 55 West Oak Ridge Drive, Hagerstown, MD 21740. (301) 791-7000. Fax: (301) 791-7012. Mark Ford, editor. A 32-page quarterly magazine published by Review and Herald Publishing Association. Circulation 2,561.

☐ *Kids' Stuff* addresses a Seventh Day Adventist audience, mostly women, involved in children's ministries. This magazine was "created to inspire and provide practical help for teachers and leaders of children from birth through eighth grade." A thematic magazine needing practical how-to's: "helping children of divorce, encouraging family involvement with children, reaching unchurched children, handling kids who are live wires," and so forth. Also needs fillers (lists of information) and photographs (B&W glossies and color prints).

Prefers a query. Accepts computer submissions in WordPerfect 4.2 or higher. Buys first rights. Guidelines, theme list, and sample copy for SASE. Reports in 2 months. Pays $25 to $100 on acceptance.

LEADER, P.O. Box 2458, Anderson, IN 46018. (317) 642-0255. Joseph L. Cookston, editor. Submit to Melanie Cole, managing editor. A 16-page bimonthly magazine published by the Board of Education of the Church of God. Circulation 4,000.

☐ *Leader* serves an audience of scholars, clergy, and laity in the Church of God. Needs personal experiences and articles on current issues, Christian education, family, children's and youth ministry. Uses poetry (any type) and column material related to Christian education topics. Also needs fillers (meditations, anecdotes, and humor).

Article length 800 words or less. Prefers a complete manuscript. Buys reprint and simultaneous rights. Guidelines and sample copy for SASE. Reports in 2 months. Pays $10 to $25 on publication.

LEADER IN THE CHURCH SCHOOL TODAY, P.O. Box 801, Nashville, TN 37202. (615) 749-6475. Submit to Editor, Leader in the Church School Today. A 64-page magazine published quarterly by The United Methodist Publishing House. Circulation 12,000.

☐ *Leader in the Church School Today* is intended to nurture and support persons who answer the call to serve as leaders in Christian education in the local church; to equip these persons with knowledge and skill to enable them to perform their tasks as leaders; and to provide information about resources, training events, and programs. *Leader* is for pastors, directors of Christian education, educational assistants, age-level coordinators, the chairperson and members of the work area on education, counseling teachers, and Sunday school superintendents. Single issues are often devoted to a particular theme.

Article length varies. Description and writer's guidelines available on request. Prefers complete manuscript. Pays 5 cents per word on acceptance.

LEADERSHIP, 465 Gundersen Drive, Carol Stream, IL 60188. (708) 260-6200. Fax: (708) 260-0114. Marshall Shelley, editor. A 140- to 150-page quarterly magazine published by Christianity Today, Incorporated. Circulation 70,000.

☐ *Leadership* serves an adult audience, both laity and clergy, with an Orthodox Catholic or Protestant (Evangelical and Liberal) background. A thematic magazine which needs personal experiences, interviews, and devotions.

Article length 100 to 3,000 words. Prefers a complete manuscript. Buys first rights. Guidelines, theme list, and sample copy for $3. Reports in 6 weeks. Lead time 3 months. Pays $30 to $300 on acceptance with a 50 percent kill fee.

LEVEL C TEACHER, 6401 The Paseo, Kansas City, MO 64131. (816) 333-7000. Fax: (816) 333-1683. Lynda T. Boardman, editor. A 64-page quarterly magazine published by Word-Action Publications. Circulation 30,000.

☐ *Level C Teacher* addresses an audience of adult laity with a Nazarene background. A thematic magazine. Needs curriculum writers, traditional poetry, fillers (activities), and photographs (B&W glossies and color slides).

Curriculum length one unit. (See also the curriculum section in chapter 5.) Poems are 4 lines each, 4 poems to the envelope. Activities are 20 lines. Model release required for photographs. Prefers a complete manuscript. Accepts photocopies. Buys all rights. Guidelines, theme list, and sample copy for SASE. Reports in 2 to 3 months. Lead time 1 year. Pays 3.5 cents per word on publication.

LIBERTY, 12501 Old Columbia Pike, Silver Spring, MD 20904. (310) 680-6691. Fax: (310) 680-6695. Roland R. Hegstad, editor. A 32-page bimonthly magazine published by the Seventh Day Adventist Church with a circulation of 250,000.

☐ *Liberty Magazine* addresses an audience of scholars, clergy, government officials, lawyers, judges, civic leaders, and laypeople. Needs articles on religious liberty issues such as separation of church and state, amendment violations.

Article length 2,000 to 3,000 words. Prefers query. Buys first or reprint rights. Sample copy and guidelines free for SASE. Reports in 4 weeks.

LIBRARIANS WORLD, P.O. Box 353, Glen Ellyn, IL 60138. (708) 668-0519. Nancy Dick, editor. A 48- to 50-page quarterly magazine published by the Evangelical Church Library Association. Circulation more than 450.

☐ *Librarians World* serves an Evangelical audience of church librarians, scholars, clergy, and laity. Needs technical or inspirational articles geared to church librarians.

Article length 1 to 2 double-spaced pages. Prefers a query. Guidelines and sample copy for SASE. Pays $20 to $50 on publication.

LIFEGLOW, 4444 South 52nd Street, Lincoln, NE 68516 or P.O. Box 6097, Lincoln, NE 68506. (402) 488-0981. Richard J. Kaiser, editor. A 65-page quarterly magazine published by Christian Record Services. Circulation 27,000.

☐ *Lifeglow* "is a magazine for visually-impaired adults over age 25." The audience includes laity and clergy from a "Conservative Christian" background. "From a Christian perspective, *Lifeglow* seeks to provide wholesome reading material that brightens, inspires, and entertains." Needs articles on adventure, biography, career opportunities, devotion/inspiration, experiences involving the handicapped, health, history, hobbies, holidays, marriage, nature, nostalgia, relationships, sports, and travel. "While it is true that many blind and visually-impaired adults have the same interest as sighted people, manuscripts focusing on the lives and needs of the sight impaired are given preferential treatment." No fiction except when it's a true story written with fiction techniques. Whenever possible good quality photographs should accompany the manuscript.

Article length 800 to 1,400 words, devotionals 250 to 600 words. Model release required for B&W glossies or color slides that accompany the manuscript. Prefers query, but will accept complete manuscript. "Computer printouts need to be dark enough to be easily read." Buys one-time rights. Guidelines and sample copy for SASE. Reports in 3 to 4 months. Lead time 12 months. Pays 3 to 5 cents per word for text, $5 to $10 for B&W glossies on publication.

LIGHT AND LIFE, P.O. Box 535002, Indianapolis, IN 46253-5002. (317) 244-3660. Fax: (317) 244-1247. Robert B. Haslam, editor. A 32-page monthly magazine published by the Free Methodist Church of North America. Circulation 33,000.

☐ *Light and Life* accepts "only articles that are written from a Christian perspective and are in the top 10% of skill in writing." It serves an Evangelical audience of clergy and laypeople with a Free Methodist background. Needs personal experiences and devotionals on current issues and theology. Also buys fiction, traditional and free poetry, column material, and photographs.

Article and fiction length 500 to 1,200 words, columns 600 words. Limit poems to 6 per envelope. Model release required with B&W glossies. Prefers a complete manuscript. Accepts simultaneous, computer, and electronic submissions in WordPerfect 5.0 or 5.1. Buys first and simultaneous rights. Guidelines free for SASE, sample copy for $1.50 postpaid. Reports in 4 weeks. Lead time 6 months. Pays 4 cents per word on publication.

LIGUORIAN, One Liguori Drive, Liguori, MO 63057. (314) 464-2500. Fax: (314) 464-8449. Allan Weinert, C.S.S.R., editor. Submit to Francine M. O'Connor, managing editor. Published by Redemptionist Fathers. A 72-page monthly magazine of the Redemptionist Fathers with a circulation of 380,000.

☐ *Liguorian* serves a general Roman Catholic audience. Needs include personal experience and interviews, inspirational fiction, and traditional poetry. Columns and art work are assigned.

Articles and fiction 1,500 to 2,000 words. Limit poems to 2 per envelope. Prefers a complete manuscript. Accepts no simultaneous submissions. Computer submissions should be IBM compatible. Buys all rights. Sample copy and guidelines available with 9 × 6 SASE. Reports in 6 weeks. Lead time 6 months. Pays 10 to 12 cents per word on acceptance.

LISTEN, 6401 The Paseo, Kansas City, MO 64131. (816) 333-7000. Fax: (816) 333-1683. Janet R. Reeves, editor. Submissions to Amy Lofton or Rosemary Postel. A 4-page weekly take-home paper published by WordAction Publishing. Circulation 35,500.

☐ *Listen* addresses an Evangelical children's audience, ages 4 to 5, with a Holiness background. A thematic magazine that needs short third-person narratives on current issues. Also uses fiction, traditional, free verse, and haiku poetry, activities for preschool children as fillers, and photographs.

Article and fiction length 300 to 400 words. Limit poetry to 4 to 12 lines. Uses color slides. Prefers a complete manuscript. Buys multi-use rights. Guidelines, theme list, and sample copy for SASE. Reports in 1 month. Lead time 1 to 3 years. Pays 3.5 cents per word on acceptance.

LISTENING: JOURNAL OF RELIGION AND CULTURE, Lewis University, Rt. 53, Romesville, IL 60441-2298. (815) 838-0500, ext. 324. Fax: (815) 838-9456. Victor S. LaMotte, editor. Submit to Marilyn Missim-Sabat. A 90-page quarterly journal published by Lewis University. Circulation 800.

☐ *Listening* serves a Roman Catholic audience of clergy and laity, primarily men. Needs articles on theology.

Article length not specified. Must query. Accepts computer submissions in WordPerfect 5.0 or 5.1. Requires all rights. Guidelines and sample copy for SASE. No payment.

LITURGY, 8750 Georgia Avenue, Suite 123, Silver Spring, MD 20910. (301) 495-0885. Fax: (301) 495-5945. Blair Gilmer Weeks, editor. A 90-page quarterly journal published by The Liturgical Conference with a circulation of 3,000.

☐ *Liturgy* serves an adult, general audience with a Protestant or Roman Catholic background. A thematic magazine which needs expositional and how-to articles on theology, Christian education, rituals, worship renewal, poetry and B&W glossies.

Prefers query. Accepts computer disks and electronic submissions in WordPerfect or ASCII file. Buys all rights. Free guidelines and theme list for SASE, sample copy for $10.95. Reports in 3 months. Lead time 3 months. Pays $50 on publication.

LIVE, 1445 Boonville Avenue, Springfield, MO 65802-1984. (417) 862-2781. Lorraine Mastrorio, editor. A weekly take-home paper published by the General Council of the Assemblies of God. Circulation 165,000.

☐ *Live* addresses an adult audience of laity with an Assemblies of God background. Needs personal experiences, devotional articles, articles on current issues. Also uses fiction, poetry (traditional, free verse, haiku), and fillers (humor, anecdotes).

Article and short story length 500 to 1,500 words, fillers 200 to 500 words, poems

12 to 50 lines. Prefers complete manuscript. Buys first, reprint, one-time, or simultaneous rights. Guidelines and sample copy for #10 SASE with 1 first-class stamp. Reports in 12 weeks. Lead time 6 months. Pays $5 to $50 on acceptance.

THE LIVING CHURCH, 816 East Juneau Avenue, Milwaukee, WI 53202. (414) 276-5420. Fax: (414) 276-7483. David Kalvelage, editor. Submit articles to John Schuessler, managing editor, Travis Du Priest, book review editor. A 16-page weekly magazine with a circulation of 10,000.

☐ *The Living Church* addresses an adult, Protestant, general audience. Needs include personal experiences and devotions on current issues. Uses traditional, free verse, and haiku poetry related to church year themes. Submit 5 per envelope. Columns are personal experiences and inspirational pieces on current issues and theology. Filler needs include devotions, meditations, anecdotes, and humor. Uses B&W glossies.

Article length 1,000 words, columns 300 to 600 words, fillers to 200 words, poems 3 to 15 lines. Prefers a complete manuscript. Buys one-time rights. Sample copy and guidelines free for SASE. No payment.

LIVING FAMILY MAGAZINE, Rt. 2 Box 656, Grottoes, VA 24441. (703) 249-3177. Fax: (703) 249-3177. Eugene K. Souder, editor. A 36-page quarterly tabloid magazine published by Shalom Foundation, Incorporated. Circulation 135,000.

☐ *Living Family Magazine* serves an audience of all ages and "reaches a cross section of America. We approach family values from a Judeo-Christian perspective, but we avoid much of the religious jargon that would offend many of our readers. We go to every household in a community by saturation, direct mail. Keep material positive. Light a candle rather than curse the darkness." Needs personal experiences and interviews "to help strengthen family and community." Needs advice and health and fitness as column material. Good morals without being preachy. Needs anecdotes and humor as fillers about family and community relationships. Also uses photographs.

Article length to 1,000 words, fillers 100 to 300 words. Normally doesn't require a model release with B&W glossies or color slides. Prefers a complete manuscript. Accepts photocopies and simultaneous submissions. Buys first, reprint, simultaneous, one-time, and all rights. Guidelines and sample copy for SASE. Reports in 2 months. Pays on publication. Rate not stated.

LIVING WITH PRESCHOOLERS/LIVING WITH CHILDREN, 127 Ninth Avenue N, Nashville, TN 37234. (615) 251-2229. Ellen Oldacre, editor. Fifty-page quarterly magazines published by the Baptist Sunday School Board. Circulation 42,000 each.

☐ *Living with Preschoolers* and *Living with Children* address an Evangelical audience of parents of preschoolers and children with a Southern Baptist background. Each magazine needs personal experiences, interviews, devotional articles on current issues, theological and family-related topics like "AIDS, blended families, child abuse, divorce, entertainment, sibling rivalry, sex education, etc." They also use fiction (adventure), poetry (traditional, free verse, haiku), column material on family issues, and fillers (devotions, meditations, anecdotes, and humor).

Article length 800 to 1,200 words, fiction 1,000 to 1,200 words, columns 800 to 1,200 words, poems and fillers 1 manuscript page or less. Prefers a complete manuscript or query. Prefers to buy all rights, but will consider others. Guidelines and sample copy for SASE. Reports in 3 months. Lead time 12 months. Pays 5.5 cents per word on acceptance.

LIVING WITH TEENAGERS, 127 Ninth Avenue N, Nashville, TN 37234. (615) 251-2229. Ellen Oldacre, editor. A 50-page quarterly magazine published by the Baptist Sunday School Board. Circulation 40,000.

□ *Living with Teenagers* addresses an Evangelical audience of parents of teenagers with a Southern Baptist background. Needs personal experiences, interviews, devotional articles on current issues and topics like "parent/youth relationships, adolescence, dating, self-concept building, high school issues, driving, teen pregnancy, etc." Also uses fiction on family and theological issues, traditional, free verse, and haiku poetry, column material on family issues, fillers (devotions, meditations, anecdotes, humor).

Article and column length 800 to 1,200 words, fiction 1,000 to 1,200 words, fillers and poetry 1 manuscript page or less. Prefers a complete manuscript or query. Prefers to buy all rights, but will consider others. Guidelines and sample copy for SASE. Reports in 3 months. Lead time currently 12 months, but changing to shorter time. Pays 5.5 cents per word on acceptance.

THE LOOKOUT, 8121 Hamilton Avenue, Cincinnati, OH 45231. (513) 931-4050. Fax: (513) 931-0904. Simon J. Dahlman, editor. A 16-page weekly magazine published by Standard Publishing Company with a circulation of 120,000.

□ *The Lookout* addresses an adult audience of laity with a Protestant, Evangelical background. Needs include personal experiences and devotions on current issues, with biblical application; contemporary fiction. Column needs are reader opinion essays.

Article length 400 to 1,800 words, fiction 1,000 to 1,800, columns 500 to 900. Uses B&W glossies and color slides. Model release required. Accepts complete manuscripts, photocopies, and simultaneous submissions. Buys one-time rights. Sample copy for 50 cents, guidelines for SASE. Reports in 10 to 12 weeks. Lead time 3 to 12 months. Pays 5 to 6 cents per word on acceptance with 33.3 percent kill fee.

THE LUTHERAN, 8765 West Higgins Road, Chicago, IL 60631. (312) 380-2540. (312) 380-1465. Edgar R. Trexler, editor. Submit to Senior Features editor, David L. Miller, and Senior News editor, Sonia C. Groenewold. A 68-page monthly magazine published by the Evangelical Lutheran Church in America. Circulation 950,000.

□ *The Lutheran* addresses an audience of youth, adults, senior adults, clergy, laity, Lutherans. Needs personal experiences, interviews, news in the world of religion and current social issues. Also needs humorous fillers and photographs.

Article length 300 to 2,000 words, fillers 25 to 100 words. Model release required with B&W glossies, color slides, and color prints. Prefers a query. Buys first rights. Lead time 3 months. Pays $400 to $1,000 for assigned articles; $50 to $400 for unsolicited articles, $5 for fillers, $10 to $50 for photographs on acceptance. Offers a kill fee.

LUTHERAN FORUM, P.O. Box 327, Delhi, NY 13753-0327. (607) 746-7511. Fax: (607) 829-2158. Rev. Dr. Paul R. Hinlicky, editor. Submit to Martin A. Christiansen, managing editor. A 64-page quarterly magazine published by the American Lutheran Publicity Bureau. Circulation 4,000.

□ *Lutheran Forum* primarily serves an audience of scholars and clergy with a Lutheran background, some with an Orthodox, Roman Catholic background. Needs articles on current issues, scholarly theological research and commentary.

Article length 500 to 2,000 words. Accepts computer submissions in WordPerfect or any other IBM compatible software, 3.5" or 5.25" disks. Guidelines available on request, sample copy for donations of $5 to $10. Reports in "2 years or so." No payment.

THE LUTHERAN JOURNAL, 7317 Cahill Road, Medina, MN 55439. (612) 941-6830. Fax: Same as telephone. Rev. Armin U. Deye, editor. A 32-page quarterly magazine with a circulation of 130,000.

☐ *The Lutheran Journal* addresses a conservative audience of adults, middle age or older, with a Lutheran background. Needs articles and fiction, poetry (free and traditional verse), fillers (anecdotes, humor, jokes, and cartoons).

Article and short story length 1,500 to 2,000 words. Limit poems to 3 per envelope. Prefers complete manuscript. Accepts simultaneous submissions. Buys first and one-time rights. Sample copy and guidelines for SASE. Reports in 60 days. Pays 1 to 3 cents per word on acceptance.

THE LUTHERAN LAYMAN, 2185 Hampton Avenue, St. Louis, MO 63139. (314) 647-4900. Gerald Perschbacher, editor. A 16-page monthly newspaper published by the International Lutheran Laymen's League. Circulation 85,000.

☐ *The Lutheran Layman* addresses an audience of adults, senior adults, clergy, and laity with a Lutheran background. Needs news, personal experiences, and interviews. "We have a substantial pool of writers already. What we especially want are Lutheran writers and reporters who can work on stories related to the work of 'The Lutheran Hour.'"

Article length 500 to 700 words. Prefers a query. Buys all rights. Guidelines and sample copy for SASE. Reports in 2 weeks. Pays negotiable fees on acceptance.

THE LUTHERAN WITNESS, 1333 South Kirkwood Road, St. Louis, MO 63122. Rev. David L. Mahsman, editor. Submit to David Strand, managing editor. A 24-page monthly magazine published by the Lutheran Church—Missouri Synod. Circulation 340,000.

☐ *The Lutheran Witness* serves an audience of adult laity from a Lutheran—Missouri Synod background. Needs devotional articles, fillers (anecdotes and humor), and photographs (B&W glossies).

Article length 400 to 800 words, fillers 30 to 60 words. Prefers a complete manuscript. Buys first rights. Guidelines and sample copy for SASE. Reports in 6 to 8 weeks. Lead time 6 to 8 months. Pays $100 ($150 with photographs) on acceptance. Offers a kill fee.

THE MAGAZINE FOR CHRISTIAN YOUTH, P.O. Box 801, 201 Eighth Avenue S, Nashville, TN 37202. (615) 749-6319. Fax: (615) 749-6079. Anthony E. Peterson, editor. A 48-page monthly magazine published by The United Methodist Publishing House. Circulation 35,000.

☐ *The Magazine for Christian Youth* addresses a youth audience, ages 11 to 18, with an Evangelical or Liberal background in The United Methodist Church, and the unchurched. Needs personal experiences, interviews, and devotional articles on current issues, theology, helps for the Christian life, health, topics that "deal with their concerns, pleasures, and questions." Also needs youth-oriented fiction (adventure and mystery) from teenage writers only, column material (advice, health and fitness, current issues, theology), humorous fillers, and photographs.

Articles and fiction 500 to 1,500 words, columns 500 words, fillers 500 words maximum. Type manuscripts double-spaced with a 53-character line. Writers are encouraged "to offer photography and illustration suggestions for their articles." No model release required for photographs. Prefers a query, but accepts complete manuscript. Accepts simultaneous submissions. Buys first, reprint, one-time, and all rights. Guidelines and sample copy for SASE. Pays 5 cents per word on acceptance.

MATURE YEARS, 201 Eighth Avenue S, Nashville, TN 37203. (615) 749-6292. Fax: (615) 749-6512. Marvin W. Cropsey, editor. A 112-page quarterly magazine published by Abingdon Press/The United Methodist Publishing House with a circulation of 80,000.
☐ *Mature Years* "is designed to help persons in and nearing the retirement years understand and appropriate the resources of the Christian faith in dealing with specific problems and opportunities related to aging." The audience is primarily lay. Needs nonfiction and fiction for "older adult or intergenerational interests; humorous or serious." Also buys poetry, columns (health and fitness, inspiration), fillers (puzzles, cartoons, and jokes), and photographs which accompany articles.

Articles and short stories 1,200 to 2,000 words. Poems to 16 lines maximum and 10 per envelope. Columns 900 to 1,800 words, fillers to 75 words. Submit color prints or slides only. Requires model release. Prefers a complete manuscript. Buys first or reprint rights. Free guidelines for SASE, sample copy for $3.50. Reports in 6 to 8 weeks. Lead time 12 months. Pays 4 cents per word on acceptance.

MENNONITE BRETHREN HERALD, C 3-169 Riverton Avenue, Winnipeg, MB, R2L 2E5 Canada. (204) 669-6575. Fax: (204) 654-1865. Ron Geddert, editor. A 32-page biweekly magazine published by the Canadian Conference of Mennonite Brethren.
☐ *Mennonite Brethren Herald* addresses an adult audience from a Mennonite background. Needs comics, devotions, meditations, news, personal experience, theology, Christian living, church education, evangelism, family, leadership, missions, stewardship, seniors, social issues. Also needs column material and poetry. Prefers Mennonite writers.

Article length 1,500 words. Prefers a complete manuscript. Accepts simultaneous submissions and computer disks, but not photocopies. Buys first and reprint rights. Guidelines and sample copy for $1. Reports in 4 months. Pays $30 per page on publication.

THE MENNONITE QUARTERLY REVIEW, Goshen College, Goshen, IN 46526. (219) 535-7435. Fax: (219) 535-7438. Theron F. Schlabach, interim editor. Submit to John D. Roth, editor designate. A 120-page quarterly journal published by The Mennonite Historical Society. Circulation of 930.
☐ *The Mennonite Quarterly Review* addresses an international audience of scholars and clergy with a Mennonite background. Needs "all Mennonite studies, especially historical, sociological, theological, and literary." Occasionally needs photographs if necessary for illustration with article.

Article length 25 to 30 manuscript pages. No model release required for B&W glossies or color prints. Prefers a complete manuscript. Accepts computer diskettes in all standard word processors or ASCII. Reports in 1 year. Guidelines available for SASE, sample copy for $6. Requires all rights. No payment.

MESSAGE OF THE OPEN BIBLE, 2020 Bell Avenue, Des Moines, IA 50315. (515) 288-6761. Fax: (515) 288-2510. Ray E. Smith, editor-in-chief. Submit to Delores Winegar, managing editor. A 20-page monthly (10/year) magazine published by Open Bible Standard Churches. Circulation 4,300.
☐ *Message of the Open Bible* is intended "to inspire, inform and unify the Open Bible family, to provide a quality magazine to Open Bible people, by Open Bible people." Its audience is adult, lay, leadership, Evangelical with an Open Bible Church background. Needs testimonies, devotions, inspiration, original sermons or teachings or challenges.

Maximum article length is 1,600 words. Prefers to work with members of Open Bible churches. Submit a query or a complete manuscript. Guidelines and sample copy are available for SASE. Reports in 2 weeks. No payment.

THE MESSENGER, P.O. Box 1568, Dunn, NC 28334. Donna Hammond, editor. A 16-page monthly magazine.

☐ *The Messenger* addresses an adult audience with an Evangelical, Pentecostal Free Will Baptist background. This publication "is designed primarily to provide devotional and inspirational reading for members, to promote denominational events and programs, and to report denominational and local church news." Needs article and devotional materials. "Most themed articles are assigned although freelance." Also uses photographs.

Article length does not exceed 6 double-spaced pages. Uses clear B&W glossies. Color transparencies are used only for seasonal or special issues. Prefers a complete manuscript. Rights must be indicated in the upper right-hand corner. Sample copy available for 65 cents. Pays on publication. Rate not stated.

METHODIST HISTORY, P.O. Box 127, Madison, NJ 07940. (201) 822-2787. Fax: (201) 408-3909. Charles Yrigoyen, Jr., editor. A 64-page quarterly journal with a circulation of 1,200.

☐ *Methodist History* addresses an audience of scholars, clergy, and laity with a United Methodist background. Needs articles on the history of Methodism.

Length of articles 5,000 words maximum. Prefers a complete manuscript. Buys first rights. Free guidelines for SASE. Reports in 3 months. No payment.

MINISTRY TODAY, P.O. Box 9127, Fort Wayne, IN 46899. (219) 456-4502. Fax: (219) 456-4903. Robert Ransom, editor. A 4-page bimonthly newsletter published by the Missionary Church, Incorporated. Circulation 4,100.

☐ *Ministry Today* addresses an adult, lay audience ages 20 to 40 with an Evangelical, Missionary Church background. Needs personal experiences, interviews, devotionals on current issues and family. Also needs photographs (B&W glossies).

Article length 200 to 250 words. Prefers a query, but accepts complete manuscripts. Accepts photocopies, simultaneous and computer submissions in WordPerfect, Pagemaker 4, or ASCII. Buys all rights. Guidelines and sample copy for SASE. Reports in 30 to 60 days. Pays on publication. Rate not stated.

THE MIRACULOUS MEDAL, 475 East Chelten Avenue, Philadelphia, PA 19144. (215) 848-1010. Rev. John W. Gouldrick, CM, editor. A 30-page quarterly magazine.

☐ *The Miraculous Medal* addresses an adult and senior adult audience with a Roman Catholic background. "We do not want unsolicited articles or editorial viewpoints of a political or religious nature." Needs fiction: "Any subject matter is acceptable, provided it does not contradict the teachings of the Roman Catholic Church." Also buys poetry: "Must have a religious theme, preferably about the Blessed Virgin Mary."

Fiction length 1,600 to 2,400 words, poetry length 20 lines maximum. Prefers a complete manuscript. Buys first rights only. Guidelines and sample copy for SASE. Reports in 6 to 8 weeks. Pays 2 cents per word for fiction, 50 cents per line for poetry on acceptance.

MISSIOLOGY, Asbury Theological Seminary, Wilmore, KY 40390. (618) 664-3518, ext. 215. Fax: Same as phone. Darrell L. Whiteman, editor. A 128-page quarterly journal published by the American Society of Missiology, 616 Walnut Avenue, Scottdale, PA 15683.

☐ *Missiology* serves an audience of Roman Catholic and mainline Protestant scholars and clergy with an Evangelical or Liberal background. Needs articles on theology, scholarly articles on missiological subjects.

Article length 20 double-spaced pages. Prefers a complete manuscript (3 photocopies). Accepts computer submissions. Requires all rights. Guidelines free for SASE. No payment.

MISSIONARY TIDINGS, P.O. Box 535002, Indianapolis, IN 48253-5002. (317) 244-3660. Fax: (317) 244-1247. Daniel V. Runyon, editor. A 40-page bimonthly magazine published by Free Methodist World Missions. Circulation 9,000.

☐ *Missionary Tidings* addresses an audience of adult laity with an Evangelical, Free Methodist background. Needs personal experiences as they relate to Free Methodist mission work. Uses fillers (devotions, meditations, anecdotes, and humor) and photographs.

Length on articles and fillers not stated. No model release required by B&W glossies. Prefers a complete manuscript. Accepts photocopies, simultaneous and computer submissions in IBM WordPerfect or an ASCII file. Requires one-time rights. Reports in one month. No payment.

MISSION FRONTIERS, 1605 Elizabeth Street, Pasadena, CA 91104. (818) 398-2121. Fax: (818) 398-2263. Ralph D. Winter, editor; Rick Wood, managing editor. A 40-page bimonthly magazine published by the U.S. Center for World Missions.

☐ *Mission Frontiers* addresses an Evangelical adult audience. Needs interviews, articles on current issues, and reports on news of Frontier Missions. Also needs photographs.

Article length is 1,500 words. Photograph needs are for B&W glossies and color prints. Prefers a query. Accepts computer submissions in Macintosh RSG 4.5. Guidelines and sample copy for SASE. No payment.

MODERN LITURGY, 160 East Vironia Street, #290, San Jose, CA 95112. (408) 286-8505. Fax: (408) 287-8748. Kenneth Guentert, editor. Submit to Charlotte Pace, managing editor. A 48-page monthly (10 times/year) magazine published by Resource Publications, Incorporated. Circulation 10,000.

☐ *Modern Liturgy* addresses an adult, Roman Catholic audience. Needs articles on theological topics.

Article length is 1,000 to 2,000 words. Prefers a query. Buys first and reprint rights. Guidelines available for SASE. Reports in 6 weeks. Pays on publication. Rate not stated.

MOMENTUM, Suite 100, 1077 30th Street, NW, Washington, DC 20007-3852. (202) 337-6232. Fax: (202) 333-6706. Patricia Feistritzer, editor. An 84-page quarterly journal published by the National Catholic Educational Association. Circulation 24,000.

☐ *Momentum* addresses an audience of "Catholic administrators and teachers in diocesan offices, schools, religious education centers and seminaries, board members and parents K through seminary." Needs "theoretical and practical articles for educators," column material on justice and peace, and book reviews.

Article length 1,000 to 2,000 words. Column material such as book reviews 300 words, "From the Field" 400 to 500 words. Prefers a complete manuscript. Accepts computer submissions. Guidelines free for SASE, sample copy with 9 × 12 SASE with $1.05 postage. Reports in 3 months. Pays 3 cents per word for articles and $15 for book reviews and "From the Field" on publication.

MOODY MAGAZINE, 820 North LaSalle Boulevard, Chicago, IL 60610. (312) 329-2163. Fax: (312) 329-2149. Andrew Scheer, managing editor. An 84-page monthly magazine (July and August issues combined) published by Moody Bible Institute with a circulation of 135,000.

☐ *Moody Magazine* "exists to encourage and equip Christians to live biblically in a secular culture." The audience is adult laity with a Protestant, Evangelical background. Needs personal experiences and reporting articles on current issues, fiction that "like our nonfiction, shows people grappling with the need to apply scriptural principles to their daily circumstances." Also needs material for columns: "Just for Parents" and "First Person," salvation testimonies.

Article length 1,800 to 2,200 words, fiction 1,800 to 2,400 words, "Just for Parents" 1,300 words, "First Person" 800 words. Query required. Buys first rights. Guidelines and sample copy for SASE. Reports in 2 to 3 months. Lead time 9 months. Pays 10 to 15 cents per word on acceptance with a kill fee for assigned articles.

MY FRIEND, 50 St. Paul's Avenue, Boston, MA 02130. Sister Anne Joan Flanagan, editor. A 32-page monthly magazine with a circulation of 32,000.

☐ *My Friend* serves an audience of children ages 6 to 12 with a Roman Catholic background. "Through this publication we intend to provide wholesome and entertaining reading for young people while imparting Christian values and basic Catholic doctrine." Needs devotional articles and articles on current issues. Uses fiction about kids, humorous poetry, column material on coping for kids, and fillers (puzzles and jokes).

Article, column, and story length 500 words. Limit poems to 5 per envelope. Prefers a complete manuscript. Buys first rights. Guidelines and sample copy for 9 × 12 SASE and 75 cents postage. Reports in 4 weeks. Pays $20 to $250, $5 for fillers on acceptance.

NATIONAL & INTERNATIONAL RELIGION REPORT, Box 21433, Roanoke, VA 24018. (703) 989-7500. Stephen Wike, publisher.

☐ *National & International Religion Report* addresses a general Christian audience. Wants religious newsstories and clippings on religious stories in your local newspaper. Story length a paragraph or two. Query for more details. Pays $50 per item.

NETWORKS, P.O. Box 685, Cocoa, FL 32923. (407) 632-0130. Fax: (407) 631-8207. Linda G. Howard, editor. An 8-page bimonthly newsletter published by the Christian Council on Persons with Disabilities. Circulation 1,700.

☐ *Networks* is for "pastors, professionals or ministers who are involved in specialized ministries to mentally challenged (retarded) persons." A thematic newsletter "written for people who are associated with or ministering (bringing the Gospel) to mentally challenged persons." Needs articles on current issues, theology on ministering to the disabled population. Also uses poetry (traditional, free verse, and haiku), column material on current issues and theology, fillers (humor). "A specialized publication networking with ministries who are sharing the gospel with disabled persons. All materials should relate to the issues which face people in disabled ministries."

Article length 250 to 450 words. Prefers a query, but accepts complete manuscripts. Accepts simultaneous submissions. Requires first rights. Guidelines and sample copy for SASE. Reports in 6 weeks. Lead time 4 months. Pays in copies.

NEW COVENANT, P.O. Box 7009, Ann Arbor, MI 48107. (313) 668-4896. Fax: (313) 668-6104. Jim Manney, editor. A 36-page monthly magazine published by Our Sunday Visitor, Incorporated. Circulation 49,000.

☐ *New Covenant* serves an adult, Roman Catholic audience. Needs personal experiences, interviews, and devotionals.

Article length 1,200 to 3,500 words. Prefers query. Buys one-time rights. Guidelines and sample copy for SASE. Reports in 3 weeks. Pays 10 cents per word on acceptance.

NEW WORLD OUTLOOK, 475 Riverside Drive, Room 1351, New York, NY 10115. (212) 870-3765. Fax: (212) 870-3940. Alma Graham, editor. A 48-page bimonthly magazine published by the General Board of Global Ministries of The United Methodist Church. Circulation 33,000.

☐ *New World Outlook* serves a United Methodist audience of adult and senior adult clergy and laity. "*New World Outlook* buys very few unsolicited articles. Most of our materials are planned and commissioned. However, we are interested in finding writers—especially United Methodists—in parts of the United States and the world where there are missionaries or mission projects sponsored by the General Board of Global Ministries of The United Methodist Church. We cannot be responsible for returning unsolicited manuscripts and photos. Interested writers or photographers should send letters of query." Needs articles about United Methodist missions sponsored by or affiliated with the GBGM. Also needs photographs.

Article length 1,000 to 2,000 words. Uses B&W glossies when color prints or slides not available. Requires model release. Requires a query. Accepts computer submissions in WordPerfect (IBM compatible) software. Buys all rights on articles, first rights on photographs. Guidelines and sample copy for SASE. Lead time 4 months. Pays $150 to $250 on publication.

OBLATES, 15 South 59th Street, Belleville, IL 62223. (618) 233-2238. Jacqueline Lowery Corn, editor. Submit to Priscilla B. Kurz. A 20-page bimonthly magazine with a circulation of 500,000.

☐ *Oblates* serves a senior adult lay audience of both Protestant and Catholic backgrounds. Needs personal experiences and traditional poetry.

Article length 500 to 600 words, poetry to 16 lines. Limit poems to 2 per envelope. Prefers a complete manuscript. Buys first rights. Guidelines and sample copy for SASE with 52 cents postage. Reports in 2 months. Pays $75 on acceptance.

ON THE LINE, 616 Walnut Avenue, Scottdale, PA 15683. (412) 887-8500. Fax: (412) 887-3111. Mary Clemens Meyer, editor. A 32-page weekly take-home paper published by Mennonite Publishing House. Circulation 9,000.

☐ *On the Line* serves an audience of children ages 10 to 14 with a Mennonite background. Needs articles on current issues, science, nature, and health. Needs fiction (adventure and mystery) on everyday problems and situations kids face. Also uses traditional, free verse, and haiku poetry, humor, jokes and riddles as fillers, and photographs.

Article length 350 to 500 words, fiction 1,000 to 1,500 words, poems 3 to 15 lines, 10 per envelope. Model release required for B&W glossies. Prefers a complete manuscript. Accepts photocopies, simultaneous, and computer submissions. Buys first, reprint, and one-time rights. Guidelines and sample copy for SASE. Reports in 1 month. Pays $10 to $20 on acceptance.

THE OTHER SIDE, 300 West Apsley Street, Philadelphia, PA 19144-4221. (215) 849-2178. Dee Dee Risher, editor. Submit nonfiction to Doug Davidson, fiction to Jennifer Wilkins. A 64-page bimonthly magazine with a circulation of 13,000.

☐ *The Other Side* primarily serves an Orthodox, Roman Catholic (and mainline Protestant) audience of adults, both clergy and laity, with an Evangelical or Liberal background. Needs personal experiences, interviews, and devotionals on current issues and theology. Also uses fiction, poetry, column material, and photographs. "Less than 5 percent of submitted articles are accepted."

Articles and fiction 500 to 3,000 words, column material 1,500 words or less, poetry 50 lines maximum (limit 3 poems per envelope), B&W glossies, and color slides. Prefers a complete manuscript. Buys first rights. Guidelines available for SASE, sample copy for $4.50. Reports in 6 weeks. Pay $20 to $350 for articles, $75 to $250 for fiction, $15 for poetry on acceptance.

OUR FAMILY, Box 249, Battleford, SK, S0M 0E0 Canada. (306) 937-7771. Fax: (306) 937-7644. A 40-page monthly magazine with a circulation of 12,000.

☐ *Our Family* addresses an adult Roman Catholic audience. "Popular for the average Roman Catholic." Needs Bible studies, devotions, meditations, opinion, personal experience, theology, Christian living, church education, education, environment, evangelism, family, feminism, missions, natives, and social issues. Prefers Roman Catholic writers.

Article length 1,000 to 3,000 words. Prefers a complete manuscript. Accepts simultaneous submissions and photocopies, but no computer disks. Buys first and reprint rights. Guidelines and sample copy for $2. Reports in 4 months. Pays 7 cents per word on acceptance.

OUR SUNDAY VISITOR, 200 Noll Plaza, Huntington, IN 46750. (219) 356-8400. Fax: (219) 356-8472. Greg Erlandson, editor-in-chief. Submit manuscript to Tricia Hempel, editor. A 24-page weekly take-home paper with a circulation of 160,000.

☐ *Our Sunday Visitor* addresses a Roman Catholic audience of clergy, scholars, and laity, both men and women. "All material must reflect teaching of magisterium of the Catholic Church. Articles should have a specific angle for Catholic readers." Needs interviews and articles on current issues, theology, and spirituality. Also needs column material (current issues, theology, and opinion) and photographs (B&W glossies and color slides).

Article length 1,200 words, column material 700 words. Model release required for photographs. Prefers a query. Buys one-time rights. Guidelines and sample copy for SASE. Reports in 6 weeks. Lead time 2 to 3 months. Pays $100 to $250 on acceptance. Offers a kill fee.

PARENT CARE NEWSLETTER, Box 216, Bethany, OK 73008. (405) 787-7272. Betty Robertson, editor. A 16-page monthly newsletter with a circulation of 200.

☐ *Parent Care Newsletter* addresses both Evangelical and Liberal adult clergy and laity with a mainline Protestant background. Needs personal experiences, issues relating to parent care. Also needs column material (devotions, meditations) related to parent care, fillers (advice, helpful tips) related to parent care.

Article length 750 to 1,200 words, fillers 450 words. Prefers a complete manuscript, simultaneous submissions. Buys one-time rights. Guidelines and sample copy for $2.50. Reports in 4 to 8 weeks. Pays $5 to $10 on publication.

PARENTS OF TEENAGERS, P.O. Box 850, 548 Sisters Parkway, Sisters, OR 97759. Gloria Chisholm, editor. A 40-page bimonthly magazine published by Good Family Magazines, a division of David C. Cook Publishing. Circulation 50,000.

☐ *Parents of Teenagers* is committed to offering practical, positive help to Christian parents rearing teenagers in today's complex world. The audience is youth, adults, scholars, laity, Evangelicals, Liberals, Protestants, and Roman Catholics. "Easy-to-read articles, personal experiences, practical how-to's, serious thought provokers, and interviews on relationship-building, peer pressure, and spiritual growth." Columns and photographs assigned in-house.

Article length 1,000 to 1,800 words. Prefers query. Accepts computer submissions in IBM WordPerfect 5.0. Buys first rights. Guidelines and sample copy available with 9 ×

12 SASE with 5 first-class stamps. Reports in 2 months. Pays 10 to 15 cents on acceptance.

PARISH FAMILY DIGEST, 200 Noll Plaza, Huntington, IN 46750. Corine B. Erlandson, editor. A 48-page bimonthly digest published by Our Sunday Visitor, Incorporated. Circulation 150,000.

☐ *Parish Family Digest* serves an audience of young Roman Catholic families. Needs articles on "family life, parish life, prayer, profiles, seasonal topics, inspirational topics, subjects of interest to the Roman Catholic reader." Also needs anecdotes and short humor as fillers.

Article length 750 to 1,000 words, fillers 100 words average. Prefers a complete manuscript. Buys first rights. Guidelines and sample copy for a 5 × 7 SASE with 52 cents postage. Reports in 3 to 4 weeks. Lead time 7 months. Pays 5 cents per word on acceptance.

PARISH TEACHER, 426 South Fifth Street, Box 1209, Minneapolis, MN 55440. (612) 330-3423. Fax: (612) 330-3455. Carol A. Burk, editor. A 12-page monthly magazine published by Augsburg Fortress Publishers. Circulation not given.

☐ *Parish Teacher* serves a lay audience of Lutheran church school teachers. Needs articles on Christian education in the church school setting.

Article length 4 to 5 double-spaced pages. Prefers a complete manuscript. Accepts simultaneous submissions. Buys first rights. Guidelines and sample copy for $1. Reports in 1 month. Lead time 6 months. Pays $15 to $50 on publication.

PARTNERS, P.O. Box 1126, Harrisonburg, VA 22801. (703) 434-0768. Crystal Shank, editor. An 8-page weekly take-home paper published by Christian Light Publications, Incorporated.

☐ *Partners* serves an audience of Mennonite children ages 9 to 14. A thematic take-home paper that needs "articles and stories with spiritual significance. Stories to which the child can write an ending." No retold Bible stories. Also uses traditional poetry that tells a story, quizzes, and word puzzles.

Article length 200 to 800 words, true stories or fiction 400 to 1,600 words, poems any length in small batches. Prefers a complete manuscript. Buys first, reprint, or all rights. Guidelines, theme list, and sample copy, available with 9 × 12 SASE with 2 stamps. Reports in 4 to 6 weeks. Lead time 7 months. Pays 1.5 to 3 cents per word, 20 to 30 cents per line for poems on acceptance. Payment varies for quizzes and puzzles.

PASTORAL LIFE, Canfield, OH 44406-0595. (216) 533-5503. Fax: (216) 533-1076. Anthony L. Chenevey, editor. A 64-page monthly digest published by the Society of St. Paul with a circulation of 3,200.

☐ *Pastoral Life* serves an audience of adults, clergy, Protestants, and Roman Catholics. Needs articles on current church issues and theology.

Article length 2,000 to 3,000 words. Prefers a query, but accepts complete manuscripts. Accepts photocopies. Buys one-time rights. Guidelines available for SASE. Reports in 3 weeks. Pays 4 cents per word on publication.

PATHWAY I.D., 1080 Montgomery Avenue, Cleveland, TN 37311. (615) 478-7599. Lance Colkmire, editor. A weekly take-home paper, published quarterly, by the Church of God. Circulation 18,200.

☐ *Pathway I.D.* addresses a youth audience ages 15 to 18 with an Evangelical, Church of God background. Needs personal experiences and articles on current issues, and fillers.

Article length 500 to 800 words, fillers 200 to 300 words. Prefers a complete manuscript. Buys first, reprint, simultaneous, one-time, and all rights. Guidelines and sample copy for SASE. Reports in 1 month. Lead time 1 year. Pays $20 to $45 on acceptance.

PENTECOSTAL EVANGEL, 1445 Boonville Avenue, Springfield, MO 65802. (417) 862-2781. Fax: (417) 862-8558. Richard Champion, editor. A 32-page weekly magazine published by the Assemblies of God with a circulation of 275,000.

☐ *Pentecostal Evangel* serves an audience of adults, clergy, lay, Evangelical, Assemblies of God. A thematic magazine that needs personal experiences and articles on current issues. Uses traditional and free verse poems and photographs.

Article length is 800 to 1,000 words. Poems 10 to 40 lines. Prefers a complete manuscript. Requires model release for B&W glossies and color slides. Buys first and reprint rights. Free guidelines and sample copy for SASE. Reports in 2 months. Lead time 4 months. Pays 6 cents per word for articles, 20 to 40 cents per line for poems on acceptance.

THE PENTECOSTAL MESSENGER, P.O. Box 850, Joplin, MO 64802. (417) 624-7050. James D. Gee, editor. Submit to Don K. Allen or Peggy L. Allen. A 32-page monthly magazine published by the Pentecostal Church of God. Circulation 7,000.

☐ *The Pentecostal Messenger* serves an Evangelical audience, both clergy and laity, with a Pentecostal Church of God background. A thematic magazine that needs devotional articles on current issues, traditional and free verse poetry, devotions, meditations, anecdotes, and humor as fillers, and photographs.

Articles and fillers 500 to 2,000 words. Model release required with color slides and color prints. Prefers a complete manuscript. Accepts photocopies, simultaneous submissions, computer disks, preferably in ASCII or in WordPerfect. Buys first, reprint, simultaneous, and one-time rights. Guidelines, theme list, and sample copy for SASE. Reports in 4 to 6 weeks. Lead time 3 months. Pays 1.5 cents per word on publication.

PERSPECTIVES ON SCIENCE AND THE CHRISTIAN FAITH, P.O. Box 668, Ipswich, MA 01938. (508) 356-5656. Fax: (508) 356-4375. J. W. Haas, Jr., editor. A 72-page quarterly journal published by the American Scientific Affiliation. Circulation 3,500.

☐ *Perspectives on Science and the Christian Faith* serves an Evangelical audience of professional scientists, primarily men. Needs articles on current issues, theology and science, interaction of science and theology.

Articles length 10 to 20 manuscript pages. Prefers a complete manuscript (3 photocopies). Requires all rights. Sample copy for $6. Reports in 3 months. Lead time 1 year. No payment.

P.I.M.E. WORLD, 35750 Moravian Drive, Fraser, MI 48035. (313) 791-2100. Fax: (313) 791-8204. Paul Witte, editor. A 32-page monthly magazine (except July and August) published by PIME Missionaries with a circulation of 28,500.

☐ *PIME World* "has a twofold purpose: (1) to give information about the work of PIME missionaries and its 610 members, (2) to educate Catholics about the mission of the church." The audience is adult, lay, Roman Catholic. Needs personal experiences and interviews on current issues with a missions emphasis. Uses photographs.

Article length 800 to 1,200 words. Takes color prints. Does not require model release. Prefers a complete manuscript. Accepts simultaneous submissions. Guidelines and sample copy for SASE. Reports in 2 weeks. Pays 5 cents a word, $5 per color photo on publication.

PIONEER, Brotherhood Commission, 1548 Poplar Avenue, Memphis, TN 38014. (901) 272-2461. Fax: (901) 726-5540. Jene C. Smith, editor. A 24-page monthly magazine published by the Brotherhood Commission of the Southern Baptist Convention. Circulation 25,500.

☐ *Pioneer* addresses an audience of Southern Baptist boys ages 12 to 14. Needs personal experiences on teen activities and interests. "Special interest stories. No preachy articles." Also buys photographs.

Article length 100 to 800 words. Model release required for B&W glossies. Prefers a complete manuscript. Accepts computer submissions that are IBM compatible. Buys one-time and reprint rights. Guidelines and sample copy for $1.20. Reports in 4 weeks. Pays 4.5 cents per word on acceptance.

PIONEER CLUBS PERSPECTIVE, Box 788, Wheaton, IL 60189. (708) 293-1600, ext. 340. Fax: (708) 293-3053. Rebecca Powell Parat, editor. A 32-page magazine published 3 times yearly by Pioneer Clubs. Circulation 28,000.

☐ *Pioneer Clubs Perspective* addresses an audience of Pioneer Club leaders. Pioneer Clubs operate in a nondenominational, Evangelical setting with children ages 2 through 18. Needs personal experiences as a club leader and interviews, inspiring ideas for club activities and meetings, and leadership development. Needs ideas for club activities, tips for more effective club leadership as fillers. Also needs photographs.

Article length 900 to 1,800 words, fillers 100 to 200 words. Model release required for B&W glossies. Prefers a query. Accepts photocopies and simultaneous submissions. Accepts computer submissions in WordPerfect software. Buys first, reprint, one-time, and all rights. Guidelines and sample copy for $1.75. Reports in 1 month. Pays $20 to $75 on acceptance.

PLUMBLINE, 1700 Park Street, Syracuse, NY 13208. (315) 472-5147. Jacqueline Schmitt, editor. A 28-page quarterly magazine published by The Episcopal Society for Ministry in Higher Education with a circulation of 1,700.

☐ *Plumbline* is a campus ministry and serves an audience of adults, scholars, clergy, laity, Liberals, and Episcopalians. Nonfiction needs include personal experiences on current issues, theology, anti-racism, or campus ministry; poetry any style, any topic that relates to campus ministry; columns on campus ministry and news items; photographs.

Article lengths "are variable. Can be long." Column length 200 words. Cover photos are B&W glossies cropped square. Prefers query. Accepts computer submissions WordPerfect 4.2 or 5.0. Sample copy and guidelines are available for $3. Payment rate not stated.

POCKETS, 1908 Grand Avenue, Box 189, Nashville, TN 37202. (615) 340-7333. Janet R. McNish, editor. A 32-page magazine published 11 times yearly by The Upper Room. Circulation 72,000.

☐ *Pockets* addresses an interdenominational children's audience ages 6 to 12. Needs children's fiction built around their theme list which is published each autumn, traditional, free, light verse, haiku poetry. Sponsors an annual contest. (See also chapter 5, "Entering Contests.")

Story length 900 to 1,000 words. Poetry to 24 lines, limit 5 per envelope. Prefers a complete manuscript. Accepts photocopies. Buys first rights. Guidelines and theme list available for SASE, sample copy for SASE with $1.05 postage. Reports in 1 month. Lead time 11 months. Pays 12 cents per word for fiction, $20 to $50 for poetry on acceptance.

A POSITIVE APPROACH, P.O. Box 910, Millville, NJ 08332. (609) 451-4777. Patricia Johnson, editor. A 64-page quarterly magazine with a circulation of 200,000.

☐ *A Positive Approach* serves an adult and senior adult audience of clergy and laity with a Roman Catholic or Protestant background. Nonfiction needs include devotions, a column on health and fitness, and photographs.

Devotion and column length 500 words. Photographs with articles only. Requires model release. Accepts complete manuscript, photocopies, simultaneous and computer submissions. Buys one-time, reprint, and simultaneous rights. Guidelines and sample copy for $2. Reports in two weeks. Payment rate not stated.

POWER AND LIGHT, 6401 The Paseo, Kansas City, MO 64131. (816) 333-7000. Fax: (816) 333-1683. Beula Postlewait, editor. Submit to Melissa Hammer, editorial assistant. An 8-page weekly magazine published by WordAction Publishing Company. Circulation 30,000.

☐ *Power and Light* serves a "Bible-believing audience of youth ages 11 and 12 with a Nazarene, Evangelical Friends, Free Methodist, or Wesleyan background." A thematic magazine that needs contemporary fiction, fillers (cartoons, puzzles, and humor), and photographs.

Fiction length 600 to 750 words. Portfolios may be sent as photograph submissions. Prefers query, but accepts complete manuscript. Accepts photocopies. Buys all rights, occasionally first, reprint, or one-time rights for lower payment. Guidelines and theme list free for SASE. Reports in 3 to 6 months. Lead time 12 months. Pays 1.75 to 5 cents per word for text, $15 for puzzles on publication. Pays $15 kill fee.

POWER FOR LIVING, P.O. Box 632, Glen Ellyn, IL 60138. (708) 668-6000. Donald W. Crawford, editor. An 8-page weekly take-home paper published by Scripture Press Publications.

☐ *Power for Living* serves an audience of Evangelical men and women. Needs profiles and personal experiences, fillers, an occasional poem. "We like well-rounded portrayals of colorful, living evangelical Christians who serve the Lord in unique and effective ways. We welcome dramatic or humorous true accounts of how believers have applied biblical truths or have been changed or challenged by the Lord. Concentrate on a single significant incident and hold the reader's attention by using action and dialogue rather than straight narrative."

Article length to 1,500 words. Must query. Buys first, one-time, and reprint rights. Guidelines and sample copy for SASE. Pays 5 to 10 cents per word (depending on rights) on acceptance.

THE PRAYER LINE, P.O. Box 55146, Seattle, WA 98155-0146. (206) 363-3586. Rev. Jonathan Edward Nisbet, editor. A 4-page quarterly newsletter published by The Prayer By Mail Society, Incorporated. Circulation, approximately 3,900.

☐ *The Prayer Line* addresses an adult, Evangelical audience. Needs personal experiences, interviews, and devotions. Also uses photographs.

No stated length. Uses B&W glossies. Prefers a query. Buys first, reprint, and one-time rights. Guidelines and sample copy for SASE with 52 cents postage. Reporting time indefinite. Pays on acceptance. Rate not stated.

PRAYING, 115 East Armour Boulevard, P.O. Box 419335, Kansas City, MO 64141. (816) 531-0538. Art Winter, editor. A 38-page bimonthly magazine published by National Catholic Reporter. Circulation 15,000.

☐ *Praying* addresses a Liberal, Roman Catholic audience. Needs personal experiences, devotional articles, and fiction on spirituality for everyday living. Also uses cartoons as fillers and photographs.

Articles and fiction 2,000 words. No model release required for B&W glossies. Prefers a complete manuscript. Buys one-time rights. Guidelines and sample copy for SASE. Reports in 1 week. Pays on acceptance. Rate not stated.

THE PREACHER'S MAGAZINE, 10814 East Broadway, Spokane, WA 99206. (509) 226-3464. Randal E. Denny, editor. An 80-page quarterly magazine with a circulation of 18,000.

☐ *The Preacher's Magazine* serves an Evangelical audience of clergy from Holiness denominations. Needs nonfiction articles related to preaching and church administration.

Article length 700 to 2,500 words. Prefers a complete manuscript. Guidelines available for SASE. Pays 3.5 cents per word on publication.

PREACHING, 1529 Cesery Boulevard, Jacksonville, FL 32211. (904) 743-5994. Dr. Michael Duduit, editor. A 64-page bimonthly magazine published by Preaching Resources, Incorporated. Circulation 10,000.

☐ *Preaching* serves an audience of clergy with a Protestant, Evangelical background. Needs practical articles on preaching. "Virtually all articles and sermons published by Preaching are written by active pastors and seminary professors, not by laypersons. Please submit biographical information along with manuscript."

Prefers a query, but accepts complete manuscript. Accepts photocopies and computer submissions in WordPerfect. Buys first rights. Guidelines free for SASE, sample copy for $2.95. Reports in 3 to 4 months. Lead time 12 months. Pays $50 on publication.

PRESBYTERIAN OUTLOOK, 3711 Saunders Avenue, Richmond, VA 23285-5623. (804) 359-8442. Fax: (804) 353-6369. Robert H. Bullock, Jr., editor. Submit book reviews to Lillian M. Taylor, 66 Probasco Road, E, Windsor, NJ 08520. A 16-page weekly (43 times yearly) magazine published by the Presbyterian Outlook Foundation with a circulation of 11,500.

☐ *The Presbyterian Outlook* serves an audience of Presbyterian laity and clergy. Needs nonfiction articles and columns on theological topics.

Article length 4 double-spaced pages, columns 2 double-spaced pages. Prefers query, but accepts complete manuscripts. Accepts photocopies, but no simultaneous submissions. Buys first rights. No guidelines or sample copy available. Reports in 3 weeks. No payment.

PRESBYTERIAN SURVEY, 100 Witherspoon Street, Louisville, KY 40202. (502) 569-5637. Fax: (502) 569-5018. Ken Little, editor. Submit to Catherine Cottingham, managing editor. A 44-page monthly (10 times yearly) magazine published by the Presbyterian Church USA. Circulation 120,000.

☐ *Presbyterian Survey* serves an adult audience with a Presbyterian Church USA background. A thematic magazine needing personal experiences, devotional articles, and articles on current issues and theology. Also needs photographs.

Article length 1,000 to 2,000 words. Model release required for B&W glossies or color slides accompanying the manuscript. Prefers a complete manuscript. Accepts computer submissions in Microsoft Word. Buys first rights. Guidelines, theme list, and sample copy for SASE. Reports in 1 month. Lead time 4 months. Pays $75 to $200 (average $100) sometimes on acceptance, usually on publication.

THE PRIEST, 200 Noll Plaza, Huntington, IN 46750. (219) 356-8400. Fax: (219) 356-8472. Rev. Owen F. Campion, editor. Submit to Robert A. Willems, associate editor. A 48-page monthly magazine with a circulation of 10,000.

☐ *The Priest* serves an audience of clergy and laity with a Roman Catholic background.

Uses personal experiences and devotions on theological topics, column entitled "Viewpoints." Book reviews and other columns written in-house.

Feature length articles 1,500 to 5,000, mini-features to 2,000 words, "Viewpoints" column to 1,500 words. Prefers a complete manuscript. Accepts computer submissions in WordPerfect 5.0, 5.25" or 3.5" diskettes. Buys first rights. Guidelines available for SASE. Reports in 3 to 4 weeks. Lead time 4 months. Pays $175 to $250, $150 for mini-features, $50 for "Viewpoints" on acceptance.

PRIMARY DAYS, Box 632, Glen Ellyn, IL 60138. (708) 668-6000. Fax: (708) 668-3806. Janice K. Burton, editor. A 4-page weekly take-home paper published by Scripture Press, Incorporated.

□ *Primary Days* serves an audience of Evangelical children ages 6 to 8. "Our take-home papers correlate with the Scripture Press 'Bible for Today' curriculum. Stories (preferably true) must reflect God at work in the everyday lives and experiences of children. No mini-sermons or moralizing tacked on at the end, please." A thematic magazine which needs personal experiences and interviews of children 6 to 8 years. Needs adventure stories with definite Christian emphasis. Also buys photographs.

Length for fiction and nonfiction 600 to 700 words. Model release required for B&W glossies, color slides, or clear color prints. Prefers a complete manuscript. Accepts photocopies and computer submissions. Buys first, one-time, and all rights. Guidelines and theme list for SASE. Reports in 6 to 8 weeks. Lead time 12 months. Pays 7 to 10 cents per word (depending on rights), $5 to $35 for photos on acceptance.

PRO ECCLESIA: A JOURNAL OF CATHOLIC & EVANGELICAL THEOLOGY, 5642 Endwood Trail, Northfield, MN 55057. (507) 663-1842. Fax: (507) 663-1842. Carl E. Braaten and Robert W. Jenson, co-editors. A 128-page quarterly journal published by the Center for Catholic & Evangelical Theology. Circulation 2,500.

□ *Pro Ecclesia* serves an audience of scholars and clergy from either an Orthodox Catholic or Lutheran background. Needs articles on theology.

Article length 20 double-spaced pages. Prefers a complete manuscript. Accepts computer submissions with IBM compatibility. Guidelines and sample copy not available. Reports in 2 months. No payment.

PROGRESS, P.O. Box 96019, Kansas City, MO 64131-0609. (816) 763-7800. Jo Reid, editor. Submit to managing editor, Susan Collard. A 64-page bimonthly magazine published by Christian Business and Professional Women of America. Circulation 30,000.

□ *Progress Magazine* serves an interdenominational audience of Evangelical laity. Needs personal experiences, column material on such topics as "how God helped an individual through crisis or stress, ministry in the marketplace, help for Christians in the marketplace." Needs meditations and anecdotes as fillers.

Article length 1,000 words. Column material 1,000 to 1,500 words. Filler length 300 to 600 words. Prefers query. Accepts complete manuscript in photocopies. Buys first rights. Guidelines and sample copy for a 6 × 9 SASE. Reports in 2 to 3 weeks. Lead time 5 months. Pays in copies.

PSYCHOLOGY FOR LIVING, 1409 North Walnut Avenue, Rosemead, CA 91770-0950. (818) 288-7000. Fax: (818) 288-5333. Ruth E. Narramore, editor. A 20-page bimonthly newspaper with a circulation of 18,000.

□ *Psychology for Living* addresses an Evangelical audience of scholars, laity, and clergy with a mainline Protestant background. Needs articles on Christian mental health.

Article length 1,000 to 1,500 words. Buys reprint rights. Guidelines and sample copy for SASE. Reports in 3 months. No payment.

PULPIT AND BIBLE STUDY HELPS, 6815 Shallowford Road, Chattanooga, TN 37421. (615) 894-6060. Fax: (615) 894-6863. Dr. Spiros Zodhiates, editor. Submit articles to Mr. Anastasio Ioannidis. A 28-page monthly newspaper published by AMG International. Circulation 210,000.

☐ *Pulpit and Bible Study Helps* is an interdenominational tabloid that serves laity and clergy with a Protestant, Evangelical background. Needs personal experiences, interviews, and devotionals on current issues and theology. Needs meditations and anecdotes as fillers.

Article length 1,000 to 5,000 words, fillers (10 to 300 words) serve as sermon illustrations. Prefers a complete manuscript. Buys all rights. Lead time 2 months. "We desire donated material."

PURPOSE, 616 Walnut Avenue, Scottdale, PA 15683. (412) 887-8500. Fax: (412) 887-3111. James E. Horsch, editor. An 8-page weekly take-home paper published by the Mennonite Publishing House. Circulation 17,500.

☐ *Purpose* serves an adult audience of clergy and laity with an Anabaptist, Mennonite background. Needs personal experiences, free verse poetry, fillers (devotions and anecdotes), photographs.

Articles and fillers 800 words, poetry 12 lines, model release required with B&W glossies. Prefers a complete manuscript. Buys one-time rights. Guidelines and sample copy for SASE. Reports in 8 to 12 weeks. Lead time 6 months. Pays 3 to 5 cents per word on acceptance.

PURSUIT, 901 East 78th Street, Minneapolis, MN 55403-1360. (612) 853-8491. Carol Madison, editor. A 24-page quarterly magazine published by the Evangelical Free Church.

☐ *Pursuit* is written for non-Christians and the unchurched, including a spectrum of age groups, economic levels, professions, and heritage. A thematic magazine needing feature articles that focus on practical ideas and answers for daily life which are compatible with the world view. Profiles are about Christians who are prominent in or have a prominent relation to secular society. They should include the testimony of God's role in the person's life.

Article length 500 to 2,000 words. Prefers a complete manuscript. Accepts computer submissions with adequate return postage. Buys first and reprint rights. Guidelines, theme list, and sample copy for SASE. Reports in 6 weeks. Pays 3 to 7 cents per word on publication. Additional payment for photographs or assigned articles.

QUAKER LIFE, 101 Quaker Hill Drive, Richmond, IN 47374-1980. (317) 962-7573. James R. Newby, editor. A 52-page magazine published 10 times yearly by Friends United Meeting. Circulation 9,000.

☐ *Quaker Life* addresses an adult audience, both lay and leadership, with a Religious Society of Friends (Quaker) background. "Ninety-five percent of our material is solicited, so opportunities for non-Friends writers to be published are limited." Needs personal experiences and devotions on current theological issues. Occasionally publishes traditional poetry.

Article length 3 to 6 double-spaced pages. Poem length 8 to 32 lines. Limit poem submissions to 3 per envelope. Prefers a complete manuscript. Buys first rights. Sample copy for $2. Reports in 2 to 3 weeks. Lead time 6 weeks. Pays in copies.

QUARTERLY REVIEW: A JOURNAL OF THEOLOGICAL RESOURCES, Box 871, Nashville, TN 37202-0871. (615) 340-7383. Fax: (615) 340-7048. Sharon J. Hels, editor. A 115-page quarterly journal published by the United Methodist Board of Higher Education and Ministry and The United Methodist Publishing House. Circulation 3,000.

☐ *Quarterly Review* addresses an audience of United Methodist scholars and clergy. Needs articles on current issues and theology.

Article length 5,000 words or less. Prefers a complete manuscript. Accepts computer submissions in any MS-DOS, but WordPerfect preferred. Buys first rights. Guidelines are available for SASE. Lead time 6 months. No payment.

QUEEN OF ALL HEARTS, 26 South Saxon Avenue, Bay Shore, NY 11706. (516) 665-0726. Fax: (516) 665-4349. Rev. J. Patrick Gaffney, SMM, editor. Submit to Rev. Roger M. Charest, SMM, managing editor. A 48-page bimonthly magazine published by Montfort Missionaries. Circulation 5,000.

☐ *Queen of All Hearts* addresses an audience of Roman Catholic adults, clergy and laity. Needs personal experiences and devotions about Mother of God, fiction about Our Lady with a moral, free verse poetry, column material for "Editor's Chat" regarding True Devotion to Mary, devotions and anecdotes as fillers, photographs.

Articles and fiction length is 1,500 to 2,000 words. Limit poems to 2 per envelope. "Editor's Chat" 900 words. Uses B&W glossies. Prefers a complete manuscript. Buys first rights. Guidelines available for $2. Reports in 6 weeks. Pays $40 to $60 on acceptance.

R-A-D-A-R, 8121 Hamilton Avenue, Cincinnati, OH 45231. (513) 931-4050. Margaret K. Williams, editor. A 12-page weekly take-home paper published by Standard Publishing Company with a circulation of 110,000.

☐ *R-A-D-A-R* "reaches children with the truth of God's Word, and helps them make it the guide of their lives." Serves children in grades 3 to 6 with a conservative, Evangelical, interdenominational background. A thematic magazine which needs fiction with "believable plots and should be wholesome, Christian character-building, but not preachy. Make prayer, church attendance, and Christian living a natural part of the story." Articles are on hobbies, animals, nature, life in other lands, sports, science, seasonal topics, and so on. Uses a few poems with biblical, seasonal, or nature theme. Also uses Bible puzzles and cartoons.

Fiction length 900 to 1,000 words, articles 400 to 500 words, poems to 12 lines. Prefers a complete manuscript. Prefers not to receive simultaneous submissions, no computer submissions. Buys first and reprint rights. Guidelines, theme list, and sample copy for SASE. Pays 3 to 7 cents per word for articles and fiction, 50 cents per line for poems, $15 to $20 for cartoons on acceptance. Payment for puzzles varies.

REFORMED WORSHIP, 2850 Kalamazoo SE, Grand Rapids, MI 49560. (616) 246-0752. Fax: (616) 246-0834. Dr. Emily R. Brink, editor. A 48-page quarterly journal published by Christian Reformed Church in North America Publications with a circulation of 3,000.

☐ *Reformed Worship* serves an audience of clergy and laity of church musicians and other worship leaders who are mainline Protestants. Needs articles on all phases of worship. Also uses cartoons on worship themes and photographs.

Article length 500 to 1,000 words. Prefers query, but will accept complete manuscripts. Accepts computer submissions, "DOS based preferred, WordPerfect." Buys first rights. Guidelines free for SASE. Back issues $6 per copy. Reports in 8 weeks. Pays $30 on publication.

RELIGION TEACHER'S JOURNAL, P.O. Box 180, Mystic, CT 06355. (203) 536-2611. Fax: (203) 572-0788. Gwen Costello, editor. A 40-page magazine published 7 times yearly with a circulation of 35,000.

☐ *Religion Teacher's Journal* serves a Liberal, Roman Catholic audience of religion teachers and catechists. Needs articles on teaching experiences, filler how-to's relating to teaching religion, short how-to's, and photographs.

Article length to 6 double-spaced pages. Filler how-to's 250 to 500 words, short how-to's 150 to 250 words. Write for guidelines on submitting B&W glossies and color slides. Prefers a complete manuscript. No simultaneous submissions. Buys first rights. Guidelines and sample copy for 9 × 12 envelope with 98 cents postage. Reports in 1 month. Lead time 2 months. Pays $15 per page for articles and fillers, $5 for short fillers just prior to publication.

RELIGIOUS BROADCASTING, 7839 Ashton Avenue, Manassas, VA 22110. (703) 330-7000. Fax: (703) 330-7100. Ron J. Kopczick, editor. Submit to Elizabeth J. Guetschow, features editor. A 56-page monthly magazine published by National Religious Broadcasters. Circulation 9,400.

☐ *Religious Broadcasting* serves an audience of Evangelical adults in and associated with the Christian broadcasting industry. "We are willing and happy to receive well-written articles relating to the Christian broadcasting and promoting excellence within this field." Needs interviews on current issues, anything informational, and photographs. " Typical monthly themes include: radio, television, publishing, music, youth/education, technology."

Article length 1,500 words. Photographs needed include B&W glossies, color slides, color prints, camera ready artwork. Prefers query, but accepts complete manuscript. Guidelines and sample copy for SASE. Reports in 2 months. Pays in copies.

REVIEW FOR RELIGIOUS, 3601 Lindell Boulevard, St. Louis, MO 63108. (314) 535-3048. Fax: (314) 535-0601. Rev. David L. Fleming, S.J., editor. A 160-page bimonthly newspaper with a circulation of 13,000.

☐ *Review for Religious* addresses an audience of laity and clergy from either a Roman Catholic or Protestant background. Needs devotional and theological articles on spirituality and canon lay ministry.

Article length 2,400 words. Prefers computer disk plus hard copy. Buys first rights. Guidelines and sample copy for SASE. Reports within 1 year. Pays on publication. Rate not stated.

ROCK, 850 North Grove Avenue, Elgin, IL 60120. Ann Dinnan, editor. An 8-page weekly take-home paper published by David C. Cook Publishing. Circulation not stated.

☐ *Rock* serves an audience of junior high youth that are Evangelical and interdenominational. "We are entering a phase at *The Rock* in which we will not be buying new manuscripts. Instead we will be recycling material that we have previously published. Writers may want to contact us a year from now for an update on our publishing status."

ST. ANTHONY MESSENGER, 1615 Republic Street, Cincinnati, OH 45210. Norman Perry, editor. A monthly magazine published by Franciscan Friars, St. John's Province.

☐ *St. Anthony Messenger* addresses a Roman Catholic audience ages 40 to 70, mostly women. It is a "general interest, family-oriented magazine. We want to help our readers better understand the teachings of the gospel and Catholic Church, and how they apply to life and the full range of problems confronting us as members of families, the

Church, and society." Needs articles on the church and religion, marriage and family, parenting, social concerns, inspiration and practical spirituality, psychology, and profiles. Also needs fiction. No fillers.

Articles and stories 3,000 words maximum. Prefers a complete manuscript. Buys first rights. Guidelines and sample copy for SASE. Reports in 6 to 8 weeks. Lead time 6 months. Pays 14 cents per word on acceptance.

ST. JOSEPH'S MESSENGER AND ADVOCATE OF THE BLIND, 541 Pavoina Avenue, Jersey City, NJ 07306 or P.O. Box 288, Jersey City, NJ 07303. (201) 798-4141. Sister Ursula Maphet, CSJP, editor. A 16-page quarterly newspaper published by the Sisters of St. Joseph of Peace. Circulation 20,000.

☐ *St. Joseph's Messenger and Advocate of the Blind* serves Roman Catholic adults and senior adults, both laity and clergy, interested in supporting ministry to the aged, young, blind, and needy. Needs articles and fiction on current issues, traditional and free verse poetry, meditations and humor as fillers.

Articles and fiction 800 to 1,800 words. Poetry length 20 to 40 lines, limit 10 per envelope. Filler length 100 to 150 words. Prefers a complete manuscript. Buys first rights. Guidelines and sample copy for SASE. Reports in 3 weeks. Pays $10 to $28 for text, $5 to $20 for poetry on acceptance.

SALLY ANN, 455 North Service Road, E, Oakville, ON, L6H 1A5 Canada. (416) 845-9235. Fax: (416) 845-1966. Margaret Hammond, editor. A 16-page magazine published 11 times yearly by the Salvation Army. Circulation 14,000.

☐ *Sally Ann* serves a nondenominational audience of women with an Evangelical background. Uses Bible studies, how-to, humor, personal experiences, and profiles. Potential topics include Christian living, environment, evangelism, family, feminism, health, money management, and social issues. Also uses photographs.

Article length 800 to 1,200 words. Prefers a query. Accepts simultaneous submissions, but no photocopies. Buys first and reprint rights. Guidelines and sample copy for SASE. Reports in 3 weeks. Lead time 6 to 8 months. Pays an honorarium, but rate not stated.

SALT, 205 West Monroe Street, Chicago, IL 60606. (312) 236-7782. Fax: (312) 236-7230. Rev. Mark Brummel, editor. Submit to Mary Lynn Hendrickson, assistant managing editor. Published by Claretian Publications. Has a circulation of 10,000. Ten issues yearly.

☐ *Salt* addresses an adult Roman Catholic audience "for Christians who seek social justice. Publishes 3 types of articles: (1) Features on social justice issues such as hunger, poverty, prisons, women's rights, etc. (2) Profiles of men and women who are incorporating action for justice in their daily lives. (3) Opinion or short humor on aspects of Christian faith and justice. These can be personal experiences, reflections, or observation."

Feature length 2,000 to 3,000 words, profiles to 2,000, opinion and humor length not stated. Prefers query first. Guidelines and sample copy for SASE. Pays $400 for features, $250 for profiles, $200 for opinion and short humor.

SALT & LIGHT, P.O. Box 531152, Indianapolis, IN 46253-1152. (317) 293-9738. Mary Reynolds-Williams, editor. A 10- to 12-page bimonthly newsletter published by Christian Career Women, Incorporated. Circulation 500.

☐ *Salt & Light* addresses a Conservative women's audience ages 25 to 60. Needs personal experiences, interviews, devotional articles, and articles on current issues. Also uses traditional and free verse poetry.

Article length is 800 to 1,500 words. No length specified on poems. Prefers a complete manuscript. Guidelines and sample copy for 75 cents. Reports in 8 to 10 weeks. Payment in copies.

SCP JOURNAL/SCP NEWSLETTER, Box 4308, Berkeley, CA 94704. (510) 540-0300. Fax: (510) 540-1107. Tal Brooke, editor and president. The journal is a 45-page quarterly, the newsletter a 20-page quarterly published by SCP Incorporated with a circulation of 18,000.

☐ *SCP Journal/SCP Newsletter* address an adult, general audience with a conservative, Evangelical background. Need nonfiction on current issues such as apologetics/analysis of new religious movements such as Gaia, New Age, and so on.

Writers must query! "We have a very high standard. We want established authorities on spiritual counterfeit movements." Buy first and one-time rights. Sample copy $5. Pay $20 to $35 per typeset page.

SEARCH, 127 Ninth Avenue N, Nashville, TN 37234. (615) 251-2074. Fax: same as telephone. Judith S. Hayes, editor. A 66-page quarterly magazine published by the Baptist Sunday School Board with circulation of 10,000.

☐ *Search* serves an audience of scholars with an Evangelical, Southern Baptist background. Needs expositional articles and interviews on current issues and theological topics.

Article length 2,500 to 5,000 words. Prefers query but accepts complete manuscripts. No simultaneous submissions. Buys all rights. Guidelines available for SASE. Reports in 3 months. Pays 5 cents per word 30 days after acceptance.

SEEK, 8121 Hamilton Avenue, Cincinnati, OH 45231. (513) 825-9391. Eileen Wilmoth, editor. An 8-page weekly take-home paper published by Standard Publishing Company with a circulation of 55,000.

☐ *Seek* serves an audience of laity and clergy with an Evangelical, Protestant background. Needs personal experiences and devotions on current issues. Fiction needs are for adventure stories. Also uses humorous fillers and photographs.

Article length 400 to 1,200 words. Humorous pieces to 400 words. Requires model release with B&W glossies. Prefers query, but will accept complete manuscript. Buys first and reprint rights. Guidelines free for SASE. Reports in 4 to 6 weeks. Pays 3 cents per word on acceptance.

SENIOR MUSICIAN, 127 Ninth Avenue N, Nashville, TN 37234. (615) 251-2944. Jere Adams and Crystal Waters Mangrum, editors. Submit literary manuscripts to Jere Adams, music to Crystal Mangrum. A 32-page quarterly magazine published by the Baptist Sunday School Board. Circulation 30,000.

☐ *The Senior Musician* serves a senior adult, Southern Baptist audience. Needs personal experiences, interviews, and devotions on current issues, theology, and music.

Article length 1 to 2 double-spaced pages. Prefers a complete manuscript. Buys first and reprint rights. Guidelines available for SASE. Reports in (varies). Pays 5 cents per word on publication.

SEWANEE THEOLOGICAL REVIEW, School of Theology, University of the South, Sewanee, TN 37375. (615) 598-1475. Christopher Bryan, editor. A 100-page quarterly journal published by University of the South. Circulation 2,500.

☐ *Sewanee Theological Review* addresses an Orthodox Roman Catholic and Anglican (Episcopal) audience of clergy and laity. Needs articles on theology.

Article length 20 double-spaced pages. Prefers a complete manuscript. Accepts computer submissions. Requires all rights. Guidelines for SASE. Reports in 6 months. No payment.

SHARING, A JOURNAL OF CHRISTIAN HEALING, Box 1974, Snoqualmie, WA 98065. (206) 391-9510, ext. 512. Fax: (206) 391-9512. Rusty Rae, editor. A 32-page monthly digest published by The International Order of St. Luke the Physician. Circulation 10,000.

☐ *Sharing* serves an interdenominational audience of laity and clergy with a Protestant, nonmonastic healing background. Needs personal experience and theological articles, traditional, free verse, and haiku poetry, fillers (meditations with healing emphasis), and photographs.

Article length 500 to 2,000 words. Poems any length. No model release required for B&W glossies. Prefers a complete manuscript. Accepts photocopies and computer submissions, preferably in Word for Windows PC or ASCII format. Buys all rights (but negotiable with writer). Guidelines and sample copy for SASE. Reports in 2 weeks. No payment.

SHARING THE PRACTICE, P.O. Box 930, Summersville, WV 26651. (304) 872-2371. Dr. David W. Nash, editor. A 60-page quarterly journal published by the Academy of Parish Clergy, Incorporated, with a circulation of 400.

☐ *Sharing the Practice* serves an audience of Protestant and Roman Catholic adults, scholars, and clergy from either an Evangelical or liberal background. Needs personal experiences, interviews, and devotions on current issues and theological topics. Uses poetry, anecdotes, humor, and photographs.

Accepts complete manuscripts. Sample copy and guidelines available for SASE. No payment.

SHARING THE VICTORY, 8701 Leeds Road, Kansas City, MO 64129. (816) 921-0909. Fax: (816) 921-8755. John Dodderidge, editor. A 24-page monthly (September through May) magazine published by the Fellowship of Christian Athletes. Circulation 50,000.

☐ *Sharing the Victory* serves an audience of interdenominational youth grade 7 through college, adult laity, and athletes. The magazine's purpose is "combining athletics and faith, encouraging and enabling athletes and coaches to take their faith seriously on and off the 'field.'" Needs personal experiences and interviews of athletes, "both widely recognized athletes and deserving unknowns." Uses an occasional free verse poem with an athlete theme and B&W glossies or color slides to accompany articles.

Article length 600 to 800 words. Poem length 24 lines or less, limit 2 per envelope. Requires model release for color slides. Must query first. Buys first rights. Guidelines and sample copy for 9 × 12 envelope with 3 first-class stamps and $1. Pays $100 to $200, $25 for poems on publication.

SHINING STAR MAGAZINE, Box 299, Carthage, IL 62321. (800) 435-7234. Fax: (217) 357-3987. Rebecca Daniel, editor. An 80-page quarterly magazine with a circulation of 15,000.

☐ *Shining Star Magazine* serves an adult audience of educators, both clergy and laity, with either a Roman Catholic or Evangelical Protestant background. A thematic magazine which produces "teacher written materials for teachers and parents of children ages 3 to 12. Puzzles, games, plays, stories, songs, articles, bulletin boards, crafts, recipes, and reproducible units. Bible based stories and Scripture study hints. Memory verse motivators and crafts to reinforce Bible stories are 2 examples of what you will find in our magazine. Also publish two dozen workbooks per year." Needs advice column on parenting/teaching tips and devotionals as fillers.

Article and story length 1 to 3 single-spaced pages. Prefers a complete manuscript. Buys all rights. Guidelines, theme list, and sample copy for $4 and SASE. Guidelines for workbooks P.O. Box 2532, Orcutt, CA 93457. Reports in 4 to 6 weeks. Lead time 9 months. Pays $15 to $100 for articles, $35 to $100 for fiction on publication.

SIGNS OF THE TIMES, P.O. Box 7000, Boise, ID 83707. (208) 465-2577. Fax: (208) 465-2531. Greg Brothers, editor. A 32-page monthly magazine published by the Seventh Day Adventist Church. Circulation 260,000.

☐ *Signs of the Times* serves a non-Christian audience as well as lay members of the Seventh Day Adventist Church. Needs personal experiences and theological articles written with the unchurched person in mind. Also uses photographs.

Article length 650 to 2,000 words. Model release required with color slides. Prefers a complete manuscript. Accepts simultaneous submissions. Buys first rights. Guidelines and sample copy for 9 × 12 SASE. Lead time 8 months. Pays $100 to $350 on acceptance. Offers a $100 kill fee.

SISTERS TODAY, The Liturgical Press, Collegeville, MN 56321. (612) 363-7065. Fax: (612) 363-3299. Sister Mary Anthony Wagner, OSB, editor. Submit poetry to Sister Mary Virginia Micka, CSJ, 1884 Randolph, St. Paul, MN 55105. An 80-page bimonthly journal published by The Liturgical Press/St. John's Abbey. Circulation 7,000 to 8,000.

☐ *Sisters Today* serves a Roman Catholic women's audience of scholars, clergy, and laity. Needs articles on theology and spirituality. Also uses poetry (traditional, free verse, haiku) and photographs (B&W glossies, color prints, and slides) for covers.

Article length 10 double-spaced pages, poems 16 to 20 lines. Prefers a complete manuscript. Buys first rights. Guidelines for SASE, sample copy for $3. Lead time 1 year. Pays $5 per page, $10 for poems, $25 for photos, $50 for cover photos on publication.

SOCIAL JUSTICE REVIEW, 3835 Westminster Plaza, St. Louis, MO 63108. (314) 371-1653. Rev. John H. Miller, CSC, editor. A 32-page bimonthly journal published by Catholic Central Verein of America with a circulation of 1,275.

☐ *Social Justice Review* serves an audience of scholars, clergy, laity, Roman Catholics. Needs articles on current issues, theology, and social science.

Article length 2,000 to 3,000 words. Accepts complete manuscripts. Buys first rights. Guidelines and sample copy free for SASE. Reports in 2 weeks. Pays 2 cents per word on publication. Rate not stated.

SOUTHWESTERN JOURNAL OF THEOLOGY, SWBTS, Box 22000, Fort Worth, TX 76122-0490. (817) 923-1921, ext. 2820. Dr. Russell Dilday, editor. Submit to Dr. William M. Tillman, Jr. A 72-page journal published 3 times yearly by Southern Baptist Theological Seminary. Circulation 1,500.

☐ *Southwestern Journal of Theology* serves an audience of clergy and laity with a Southern Baptist background. Needs articles on theology. Must query first. Buys one-time rights. Pays on a contract basis.

SPICE, Box 10212, Lansing, MI 48901. (517) 484-0016. Laura Deming, editor. A 12-page monthly magazine published by Clergy Family Publications, Incorporated. Circulation more than 1,000.

☐ *Spice* "is a publication for women and men whose spouses are clergy." Needs personal experiences, interviews, and devotionals on current issues and theology. Also uses poetry and devotions, meditations, anecdotes, and humor as fillers, traditional, free verse, and haiku poetry. Articles and fillers should relate specifically to clergy spouses.

Article and filler lengths not specified. Limit 6 poems per envelope. Prefers a query, but accepts complete manuscript. Buys reprint rights. Guidelines and sample copy for SASE. Lead time 2 months. No payment.

SPIRITUAL LIFE, 2131 Lincoln Road, NE, Washington, DC 20002. (800) 832-8489. Fax: (202) 832-8967. Steven Payne, O.C.D., editor. Submit to Edward O'Donnell, O.C.D. A 64-page quarterly journal published by Washington Province of Discalced Carmelites, Incorporated. Circulation 13,000.

☐ *Spiritual Life* serves an audience of Roman Catholic clergy and laity. Needs articles on prayer and spirituality.

Article length 3,000 to 3,500 words. Prefers a complete manuscript. Buys first and one-time rights. Guidelines and sample copy for $1 and SASE with 4 first-class stamps. Reports in 6 to 8 weeks. Pays $50 on acceptance.

SPORTS SPECTRUM, Box 3566, Grand Rapids, MI 49501. (616) 954-1276. Fax: (616) 957-5741. Dave Branon, editor. A 32-page bimonthly magazine published by Radio Bible Class. Circulation 45,000.

☐ *Sports Spectrum* is a nondenominational magazine that serves an audience of Evangelical youth and adults with an Evangelical background. Needs athlete's stories. "Writers must interview athletes featured. Articles must either tell or reflect the athlete's testimony of faith while telling in a compelling way how the athlete lives out biblical principles in his or her life. No high school or college athletes."

Article length 2,000 words. Prefers query. Accepts computer submissions in Microsoft Word. Buys first rights. Guidelines and sample copy for SASE. Reports in 1 month. Pays 10 to 15 cents per word on acceptance.

STANDARD, 6401 The Paseo, Kansas City, MO 64131. (816) 333-7000. Beth A. Watkins, editor. An 8-page weekly take-home paper published by the Church of the Nazarene. Circulation 165,000.

☐ *Standard* serves an adult audience with a Nazarene background. Needs personal experiences, devotional articles, and articles on current issues. Also uses fiction (adventure, mystery, and romance), traditional and free verse poetry, fillers (devotions, meditations, and anecdotes), and photographs.

Article and fiction length 1,700 words maximum. Limit poems to 5 per envelope. Send model release if available. Prefers a complete manuscript. Accepts photocopies and simultaneous submissions. Buys first and reprint rights. Guidelines and sample copy for #10 SASE. Reports in 10 to 12 weeks. Lead time 14 to 18 months. Pays 2.5 to 3.5 cents on acceptance.

THE STANDARD, 2002 South Arlington Heights Road, Arlington Heights, IL 60005. (708) 228-0200. Fax: (708) 228-5376. Julie-Allyson Ieron, managing editor. A 32-page magazine published 10 times yearly by the Baptist General Conference. Circulation 14,000.

☐ *The Standard* serves an Evangelical audience of clergy and laity with a Baptist background. Needs personal experiences, interviews, and articles on current issues. Also uses column material (current issues), fillers (anecdotes and humor), and photographs.

Article length 800 to 2,000 words. Prefers a query. Accepts computer submissions in IBM or Mac, 3.5" disks. Buys first rights. Guidelines and sample copy for SASE. Reports in 2 to 3 weeks. Lead time 3 to 4 months. Payment varies on publication.

STORY FRIENDS, 616 Walnut Avenue, Scottdale, PA 15683. (412) 887-8500. Fax: (412) 887-3111. Marjorie Waybill, editor. A 4-page weekly take-home paper published by the Mennonite Publishing House. Circulation 9,000.

☐ *Story Friends* serves an audience of Mennonite children ages 4 to 9 years. Needs fiction with a Christian message and traditional poetry.

Story length 300 to 800 words. Poems have 4 to 16 lines. Accepts complete manuscripts as simultaneous submissions, photocopies, or computer submissions. Buys one-time rights. Guidelines available with 9 × 12 envelope with 2 first-class stamps. Reports in 2 weeks. Pays 3 to 5 cents per word on acceptance.

STORY MATES, P.O. Box 1126, Harrisonburg, VA 22801. (703) 434-0768. Miriam R. Shank, editor. A 4-page per issue Sunday school take-home paper published by Christian Light Publications, Incorporated. Circulation 5,000.

☐ *Story Mates* addresses a children's audience, ages 4 to 8, with a Mennonite background. A thematic magazine that needs fiction with Bible teaching as central focus. "No retold Bible stories, fantasy, Valentine's Day, Halloween, or secular Christmas and Easter." Also uses traditional poetry and fillers (activities, "especially ones that follow our theme list").

Story length no more than 800 words, poetry any length. Prefers a complete manuscript. Accepts photocopies, computer, and electronic submissions. Buys first, reprint, and all rights. Guidelines, theme list, and sample copy for 6 × 9 envelope or larger with 52 cents postage. Reports in 6 weeks. Pays 2 to 3 cents per word on acceptance.

STRAIGHT, 8121 Hamilton Avenue, Cincinnati, OH 45231. (513) 931-4050. Fax: (513) 931-0904. Carla J. Crane, editor. Submit to associate editor, Kelley Wingo. A 12-page weekly take-home paper published by Standard Publishing Company. Circulation 55,000.

☐ *Straight* serves an audience of Protestant Evangelical youth ages 13 to 19. A thematic magazine which needs personal experiences, interviews, devotions, realistic fiction, all varieties of poetry, humorous fillers, photographs.

Article length 900 to 1,200 words, fiction 1,000 to 1,500 words. Filler length 900 to 1,100 words. Requires a model release for B&W glossies and color slides. Prefers a complete manuscript. Accepts photocopies and simultaneous submissions. Buys all rights. Guidelines, theme list, and sample copy for SASE. Reports in 1 to 2 months. Lead time 9 to 12 months. Pays 3 to 7 cents per word on acceptance.

THE STUDENT, 127 Ninth Avenue N, Nashville, TN 37234. (615) 251-2777. Currently looking for an editor. Submit material to "The editor." A 52-page monthly magazine published by the Baptist Sunday School Board with a circulation of 40,000.

☐ *The Student* addresses college students who are Evangelical and Southern Baptist. Needs personal experiences and interviews on current issues of significance to college students, fiction about life situations at college.

Articles to 1,200 words, fiction to 1,800 words. Accepts complete manuscripts, computer submissions in any software. Buys all rights. Free guidelines and sample copy for SASE. Reports in 2 months. Lead time 12 months. Pays 5 cents per word 30 days after acceptance.

STUDENT LEADERSHIP JOURNAL, P.O. Box 7895, Madison, WI 53707-7895. (608) 274-9001, ext. 413. Fax: (608) 274-7882. Jeff Yourison, editor. A 28-page quarterly journal published by InterVarsity Christian Fellowship. Circulation is 8,000.

☐ *Student Leadership Journal* addresses an Evangelical audience of college students ages 18 to 24 and their leaders, with either a Roman Catholic or mainline Protestant background. "(1) Writers should know, understand, or be part of the current campus culture. (2) Student leaders face all the symptoms, pains and joys of leadership in general.

(3) While a journal, our style is informal, light yet meaty. We avoid general, fluffy articles in favor of those offering profound insight underscored by real life illustrations and stories from the lives of other influential leaders or fellow students." A thematic magazine needing personal experiences, interviews, articles on current issues, and theology. Also needs how-to articles on leadership issues. Needs free verse poetry, fillers (humor and parables), and photographs.

Article length 500 to 2,000 words. Limit poems to 5 per envelope. Model release required for photographs. Model release forms must be supplied by writer. Prefers a complete manuscript. Accepts computer submissions in IBM format ASCII files. Buys first rights. Guidelines and theme list for SASE, sample copy for $3. Reports in 6 months. Lead time 3 months. Pays varied amount on acceptance.

SUNDAY DIGEST, 850 North Grove Avenue, Elgin, IL 60120. (708) 741-0800. Eric Stanford, senior editor. Submit to Christine Dallman, associate editor. An 8-page weekly take-home paper published by David C. Cook Publishing. Circulation 100,000.

☐ *Sunday Digest* serves a lay, nondenominational audience of adults and senior adults with a Protestant, Evangelical background. Needs personal experiences and interviews, inspirational fiction, fillers, and free verse poetry. Also needs photographs.

Article length 400 to 1,500 words, fiction 1,000 to 1,500 words, fillers to 400 words, limit poetry to 10 per envelope. Model release required for B&W glossies, color slides, and color prints. Prefers a complete manuscript. Buys first and reprint rights. Guidelines and sample copy for SASE. Reports in 3 months. Lead time 1 year. Pays $50 to $250 for articles, $50 to $70 for poetry, $20 to $50 on acceptance.

SUNDAY SCHOOL COUNSELOR, LEADER EDITION, 1445 Boonville Avenue, Springfield, MO 65802-1894. (417) 862-2781. Sylvia Lee, editor. A 28-page monthly magazine published by the General Council of the Assemblies of God. Circulation 31,000.

☐ *Sunday School Counselor* addresses an Evangelical audience of lay leaders with an Assemblies of God background. A thematic magazine that needs personal experience articles and interviews on current issues and theology as they relate to Sunday school leadership. "Need more articles on administration." Also buys photographs.

Article length 800 to 2,000 words. Model release required with B&W glossies, color slides, and color prints. Prefers a complete manuscript. Accepts simultaneous submissions. Buys first, reprint, simultaneous, one-time, and all rights. Guidelines, theme list, and sample copy for $2 or 8 1/2 × 11 SASE. Reports in 4 weeks. Lead time 7 months. Pays $25 to $90 on acceptance.

TAKE FIVE, 1445 Boonville Avenue, Springfield, MO 65802-1894. (417) 862-2781. Fax: (417) 862-8558. Tammy L. Bicket. Submit photographs and poetry to Joseph S. Bednar, editorial assistant. A 112-page quarterly devotional guide published by the General Council of the Assemblies of God. Circulation 30,000.

☐ *Take Five* addresses an audience of Evangelical youth ages 12 to 19 years in the Assemblies of God. "We are especially interested in material (art, poetry, devotionals) by teens. When submitting, teens should include their age, grade, and church." Devotionals written on assignment. Needs traditional and free verse poetry written by teens about faith in everyday life. Photographs "by and of teens, all ethnic groups and races, especially urban."

Poem length 15 to 50 lines. Accepts simultaneous submissions and photocopies. No model release required for photographs. Buys all rights. Guidelines available for SASE. Reports in 6 to 12 weeks. Lead time 9 months. Pays $5 to $13 on acceptance for poetry.

TEACHERS IN FOCUS, 420 North Cascade Avenue, Colorado Springs, CO 80919. (719) 531-3400, ext. 1761. Fax: (719) 531-3499. Charles Johnson, editor. This is a brand new 16-page full-color monthly magazine published by Focus on the Family whose circulation has already reached 10,000 to 20,000.

☐ *Teachers in Focus* "encourages staff in public and private schools to provide a values-based education to students in grades K-12. It offers inspiration and information that will equip teachers to meet the challenges presented in today's rocky educational environment." The magazine serves an audience of lay adult leaders, professional educators, mostly with a Protestant, Evangelical background. Needs personal experiences on topics related to public and private education. Also needs column material, classroom anecdotes and appropriate humor that "maintains a Judeo-Christian worldview and appeals to both public and private schools. Areas of interest include classroom success stories, discipline and control, contemporary students and their families, special needs students, social issues and schools, professional relationships and organizations, child development, holidays, curriculum."

Article length 800 to 1,500 words. Prefers a complete manuscript, but queries are acceptable. Buys first and one-time rights. Guidelines are free for SASE, sample copy will be available soon. Reports in 2 to 4 weeks. Payment is up to $300 on publication.

TEACHERS INTERACTION, 3558 South Jefferson Avenue, St. Louis, MO 63122-7295. (314) 268-1091. Fax: (314) 268-1329. Jane Haas, editor. Submit to Tom Nummela. A 32-page quarterly magazine published by The Lutheran Church—Missouri Synod. Circulation 20,000.

☐ *Teachers Interaction* serves an audience of Lutheran laity and clergy. Needs personal experiences in religious education.

Article length 750 words. Prefers a complete manuscript. Buys first rights. Guidelines and sample copy for $1. Reports in 3 to 6 months. Pays $35 on publication.

TEENAGE CHRISTIAN MAGAZINE, P.O. Box 1438, Murfreesboro, TN 37133-1438. Marty Dodson, editor. A 32-page bimonthly magazine published by Christian Publishing Incorporated. Circulation 15,000.

☐ *Teenage Christian* serves a youth audience ages 13 to 19 with a Free Will Baptist background. A thematic magazine needing personal experiences, interviews, devotional articles, articles on current issues. Also uses fiction (adventure, mystery), poetry (traditional and free verse), column material (health and fitness, current issues, music for teens), fillers (devotions, meditations, anecdotes, humor), and photographs.

Article length 500 to 1,200 words, fiction 1,000 to 2,000 words, fillers 100 to 500 words. Model release required for B&W glossies and color slides. Prefers a complete manuscript. Accepts simultaneous submissions. Buys one-time rights. Guidelines, theme list, and sample copy for SASE. Reports in 30 to 60 days. Lead time 4 to 6 months. Pays $25 flat fee on publication.

TEEN POWER, P.O. Box 632, Glen Ellyn, IL 60138. (708) 668-6000. Amy J. Cox, editor. An 8-page weekly take-home paper published by Scripture Press Publications.

☐ *Teen Power* serves an audience of Evangelical youth ages 11 to 15. A thematic take-home paper needing fiction, nonfiction, and some poetry.

Articles and fiction run 800 to 1,200 words. Traditional poetry from young teens. Prefers a complete manuscript. Buys first, reprint, and one-time rights. Guidelines, theme list, and sample copy for SASE. Pays 5 to 10 cents (depending on rights) per word on acceptance.

TEENS TODAY, 6401 The Paseo, Kansas City, MO 64131. (816) 333-7000. Fax: (816) 333-1683. David W. Caudle, editor; Joy Kaiser, editorial assistant. An 8-page weekly magazine published by the Church of the Nazarene. Circulation 45,000.

☐ *Teens Today* serves an Evangelical audience of youth ages 12 to 18 with a Nazarene background. The magazine's purpose is "to model life in Jesus Christ." A thematic magazine which needs personal experiences that speak to the needs and interests of teens. Also needs fiction (adventure, mystery, and romance) on teen issues and problems. Uses photographs.

Fiction and nonfiction ranges from 1,200 to 1,500 words. Model release required for B&W glossies. Accepts complete manuscripts, simultaneous submissions, and photocopies. Accepts computer submissions in Word 5.0 or 5.1. Buys first, reprint, simultaneous, one-time, and all rights. Guidelines and theme list available for SASE. Reports in 3 months. Lead time 12 months. Pays 3 to 3.5 cents per word on acceptance.

THEOLOGICAL STUDIES, Georgetown University, Washington, DC 20057. (202) 338-0754. Robert J. Daly, editor. A 200-page quarterly journal with a circulation of 5,500.

☐ *Theological Studies* serves a Roman Catholic audience of scholars and clergy. Needs theological articles.

Article length 20 double-spaced pages. Guidelines and sample copy for $6 per issue. No mention of payment.

THEOLOGY AND PUBLIC POLICY, 4500 Massachusetts Ave., N.W., Washington, DC 20016-5690. (202) 885-8648. James A. Nash, editor. A 60-page semiannual journal published by the Churches' Center for Theology and Public Policy. Circulation is approximately 1,200.

☐ *Theology and Public Policy* addresses an ecumenical audience of both scholars and advocates. Needs articles that explore "the vital linkage between theological-ethical reflection and Christian action" on peacemaking and disarmament, urban policy, economic justice, poverty and hunger, racial-ethnic and women's rights, health care, and ecological integrity.

Article length to 6,000 words. Author's guidelines available for SASE. No payment.

THEOLOGY TODAY, P.O. Box 29, Princeton, NJ 08542. (609) 497-7714. Fax: (609) 924-2973. Thomas G. Long and Patrick D. Miller, editors. A 148-page quarterly journal published by Princeton Theological Seminary. Circulation 13,500.

☐ *Theology Today* addresses an audience of adults, senior adults, scholars, clergy, and laity with a Protestant background. Needs scholarly nonfiction on current issues and theology. Also uses poetry.

Articles average 3,500 words. Limit poetry submissions to 5 per envelope. Accepts complete manuscript. Guidelines available for SASE. Pays on publication. No rate stated.

TIME OF SINGING: A MAGAZINE OF CHRISTIAN POETRY, P.O. Box 211, Cambridge Springs, PA 16403. (814) 382-5911. Charles A. Waugaman, editor. A 40-page magazine published by High Street Community Church, Conneaut Lake, PA. Circulation 300.

☐ *Time of Singing* addresses an adult and senior adult audience of scholars, clergy, and laity with either a mainline Protestant or Roman Catholic background. "Our purpose is to provide satisfying reading experiences for those who enjoy inspirational poetry, offer valuable resource materials for those engaged in preparing devotional messages, sermons, etc., to provide a reading public for the growing group of Christian poets." A thematic magazine that needs poetry, "all kinds." Sponsors poetry contest. Entrance fee. (See also "Entering Contests," chapter 5.)

Limit poems to 4 to 5 per envelope. Prefers a complete manuscript. Accepts photo-copies and computer submissions. Buys first rights. "We release rights to poets, but retain rights for later anthologies, etc." Guidelines, theme list, and sample copy: $4 for current issue, $2.50 for back issue. Payment in 1 copy.

TODAY'S BETTER LIFE, 5301 Wisconsin Avenue, NW, Suite 620, Washington, DC 20015. (202) 364-8000. Fax: (202) 364-8910. Dale Hanson Burke, editor. Submit to Laura Schramm. A 110-page quarterly magazine published by Thomas Nelson Publishers.
☐ *Today's Better Life* addresses an Evangelical audience of adult (mostly women) laity from a mainline Protestant background. Needs interviews, column material (advice, health and fitness), fillers (devotions), and photographs.
Article length 1,500 words, column material 1,000 to 1,500 words. Photographic needs are for color slides. Prefers a complete manuscript. Accepts computer submissions in IBM WordPerfect. Buys reprint and one-time rights. Guidelines and sample copy not available. Pays $100 to $200 on publication.

TODAY'S CATHOLIC TEACHER, 330 Progress Road, Dayton, OH 45449. (513) 847-5900. Fax: (513) 847-5970. Ruth A. Matheny, editor. Submit to Steve Brittan. A 64-page monthly magazine with a circulation of 50,000.
☐ *Today's Catholic Teacher* serves an audience of scholars and professional educators with a Roman Catholic background. Needs articles on current issues in education or catechetics, columns on Catholic school related subjects, school news as fillers, and photographs.
Article length 1,500 words, column material 800 words. Model release required for B&W glossies. Prefers a query. Buys all rights. Guidelines and sample copy for $3. Reports in 2 months. Pays $75 to $175 on publication.

TODAY'S CHRISTIAN WOMAN, 465 Gundersen Drive, Carol Stream, IL 60188. (708) 260-6200. Fax: (708) 260-0114. Julie Talerico, editor. An 80-page bimonthly magazine pub-lished by Christianity Today, Incorporated. Circulation 200,000.
☐ *Today's Christian Woman* serves an audience of Evangelical women. Needs personal experiences for "One Woman's Story" and humorous fillers. "We do not accept fiction or poetry."
Article length 1,000 words. Send 200 word fillers to "Heart to Heart" department. Prefers query. Buys first rights. Guidelines and sample copy for SASE. Reports in 4 to 6 weeks. Lead time 6 months. Pays 10 to 15 cents per word on publication.

TODAY'S SINGLE, 1933 West Wisconsin Avenue, Milwaukee, WI 53233 (414) 344-7300. Fax: (414) 344-7375. Gayle Ryberg. A quarterly newspaper published by the National Association of Christian Singles.
☐ *Today's Single* serves an Evangelical audience of single adults. Pays in copies.

TOGETHER, Rt. 2 Box 656, Grottoes, VA 24441. (703) 249-3900. Fax: (703) 249-3177. Eugene K. Souder, managing editor. An 8-page bimonthly tabloid magazine published by Shalom Foundation, Incorporated. Circulation 200,000.
☐ *Together* serves an audience of all ages with "free home delivery by direct mail." Needs personal experiences and interviews on how Jesus makes a difference in my life. Also needs devotional articles, anecdotes as fillers, and photographs.
Article length to 1,000 words. Normally no model release required for B&W glossies and color slides. Prefers a complete manuscript. Accepts photocopies and simultaneous submissions. Buys first, reprint, simultaneous, one-time, and all rights. Guidelines and sample copy for SASE. Reports in 1 month. Pays on publication. Rate not stated.

TOGETHER TIME FOR TWOS AND THREES, 6401 The Paseo, Kansas City, MO 64131. (816) 333-7000. Fax: (816) 333-1683. Lynda T. Boardman, editor. A 4-page weekly take-home paper published by WordAction Publications.

☐ *Together Time* serves an audience of adult laity and nonreading children from a Holiness Nazarene background. A thematic story paper that needs contemporary fiction on Christian themes, traditional poetry, and fillers (activities), and photographs.

Fiction length 300 to 350 words, poems 4 to 8 lines, activities, 20 lines. Requires model release for color slides. Prefers a complete manuscript. Buys all rights. Guidelines and sample copy for SASE. Reports in 2 to 3 months. Lead time 1 year. Pays 5 cents per word on publication.

TOUCH, Box 7259, Grand Rapids, MI 49510. (616) 241-5616. Fax: (616) 241-5558. Joanne Ilbrink, editor. Submit to Carol Smith, managing editor. A 24-page monthly magazine published by the Calvinettes. Circulation 15,000.

☐ *Touch* is a thematic magazine. "We publish a theme update twice a year. Write for this publication. Our readers are girls 7 to 14 primarily from the Christian home and school setting. However, Calvinettes is also an outreach program of the church and we have community girls involved as well. The purpose is to bring girls into a living relationship with Jesus Christ. And to help them see how God is at work in their lives and in the world around them." A thematic magazine that needs personal experiences, interviews, devotions, fiction (adventure, mystery, light romance), traditional poetry, devotions, and anecdotes as fillers, and photographs.

Articles and fiction run 500 to 1,000 words. Poetry length 12 lines, limit 10 per envelope. Fillers run 500 words. Uses B&W glossies. Prefers a complete manuscript. Accepts photocopies, simultaneous, and computer submissions. Buys first, reprint, and simultaneous rights. Guidelines, theme list, and sample copy for 8 × 10 SASE. Reports in 3 months. Lead time 9 months. Pays on publication. Rate not stated.

TRINITY NEWS, 74 Trinity Place, Room 406, New York, NY. (212) 602-0705. Fax: (212) 602-0726. Dr. Katherine Kurs, editor. A 24-page quarterly magazine published by the Parish of Trinity Church, New York City. Circulation 12,000.

☐ *Trinity News* serves an Episcopal audience of clergy and laity. Needs interviews and articles on current issues, column materials on current issues, and photographs.

Articles and column materials run 1,000 to 3,000 words. Photograph needs are for B&W glossies. Must query. Guidelines and sample copy for SASE. Reporting time varies. No specifics on payment.

THE UNITED CHURCH OBSERVER, 84 Pleasant Boulevard, Toronto, ON, M4T 2Z8 Canada. (416) 960-8500. Fax: (416) 960-6477. Muriel Duncan, editor. A 52-page monthly news magazine published by the United Church of Canada. Circulation 185,000.

☐ *The United Church Observer* addresses a United Church of Canada audience of all ages. "The Observer follows basic CP style; avoids sexist language; interested in feature material more than news items; interested in social justice, human rights, Christian faith in action and stories of personal courage and triumph." Its purpose is "to provide news of the church, nation, and world." Its goals are "to inform, educate, challenge, to be a forum for dialogue and help people with their faith." Needs news, opinion, personal experience, profiles, theology, church education, education, environment, family, feminism, health, leadership, natives, seniors, and social issues.

Article length not specified. Prefers a complete manuscript. Accepts photocopies, but no simultaneous or computer submissions. Buys first and reprint rights. Guidelines and sample copy for SASE. Reports in 12 weeks. Pays negotiable rate on publication.

UNITED METHODIST REPORTER, P.O. Box 660275, Dallas, TX 75266. (214) 630-6495. Fax: (214) 630-0079. John A. Lovelace, editor. A 4- to 6-page weekly newspaper with a circulation of 450,000.

☐ *United Methodist Reporter* serves an adult lay audience with a United Methodist background. Needs personal experiences and interviews on current issues and news related to United Methodists. Also needs traditional poetry and photographs.

Article length 700 words maximum. Limit poems to 4 to 16 lines, 3 to 5 per envelope. No model release required for B&W glossies and color prints. Prefers query, but accepts complete manuscript. Buys first and one-time rights. Guidelines and sample copy for SASE. Reports in 2 weeks. Pays 4 cents per word for articles, $2 per poem on acceptance.

US CATHOLIC, 205 West Monroe Street, Chicago, IL 60606. (312) 236-7782. Rev. Mark E. Brummel, editor. Submit to Sue Fox, managing editor. Published by Claretian Publications with a circulation of 52,000.

☐ *US Catholic* addresses an audience of "highly educated and intelligent Roman Catholic readers." Publishes articles in 4 categories: (1) Feature articles cover issues on prayer, sacraments, liturgy, parish life, marriage, divorce, family life, everyday morality, and other aspects of everyday Catholic life. (2) "Sounding Board" is a monthly feature sent in advance to readers asking comments about the article. (3) "Gray Matter" comprises opinion pieces discussing issues that are neither black nor white. "A Modest Proposal" suggests a new way of dealing with an old subject of interest to Catholics. (4) "Actual Grace" comprises humor pieces that reflect life as an American Catholic. Also buys fiction with strong characters that cause readers to stop for a moment and consider their relationships with others, the world, and/or God.

Feature article length 2,500 to 4,000 words. "Sounding Board" length 1,100 to 1,300 words. "Gray Matter" and "A Modest Proposal" 1,100 to 1,800 words. "Actual Grace" 1,300 words. Must query first. Guidelines and sample copy for SASE. Pays $500 for features, $250 for "Sounding Board," "Gray Matter," "A Modest Proposal," or "Actual Grace."

USQR (UNION SEMINARY QUARTERLY REVIEW), 3041 Broadway, New York, NY 10027. (212) 280-1361. Fax: (212) 280-1416. Pam Eisenbaum, editor. Submit to William Love, associate editor, Patrick Minges, assistant editor. A quarterly journal published by Union Theological Seminary.

☐ *USQR* serves a Liberal, interdenominational audience of clergy and laity. Needs articles on theology, biblical criticism, church history, book reviews.

Article length 15 to 25 double-spaced pages. Prefers a complete manuscript. Buys all rights. Guidelines and sample copy for SASE. Pays in 10 copies.

VENTURE, P.O. Box 150 Wheaton, IL 60189. (708) 665-0630. Fax: (708) 665-0372. Submit to Deborah Christensen, managing editor. A 32-page bimonthly magazine published by Christian Service Brigade. Circulation 20,000.

☐ *Venture* addresses an interdenominational audience of Evangelical boys ages 10 to 15. "We strive to glorify Christ, not man. Thus, we want our stories to reflect the simple truths of the gospel and its life-changing power." Needs articles on Christian living, fiction (adventure, mystery, humor), photographs.

Article length 1,000 to 1,500 words, fiction to 1,000 words. No model release required for B&W glossies. Prefers a complete manuscript. Buys first and reprint rights. Guidelines and sample copy for $1.85. Reports in 1 week. Lead time 2 months. Pays 5 to 10 cents per word for prose, $75 to $100 for cover use, $35 for inside use of photos on publication.

VIBRANT LIFE, 55 West Oak Ridge Drive, Hagerstown, MD 21740. (301) 791-7000. Fax: (301) 791-7012. Barbara Jackson-Hall, editor. A 32-page bimonthly magazine published by Review and Herald Publishing Association. Circulation around 50,000.

☐ *Vibrant Life* serves an audience of adults and senior adults, both lay and leadership, with a Seventh Day Adventist background. Needs articles on current issues as they relate to total health (physical, mental, spiritual).

Accepts complete manuscript. Buys first rights. Guidelines and sample copy for $1. Reports in 1 month or less. Lead time 6 months. Pays $80 to $250 on acceptance.

VIRTUE, P.O. Box 850, Sisters, OR 97759-0850. (503) 549-8261. Marlee Alex, editor. A 60-page bimonthly magazine published by Good Family Magazines, a division of David C. Cook Publishing. Circulation 150,000.

☐ *Virtue* "is designed for Christian women who are looking for spiritual perspectives and personal enrichment in every aspect of their lives." Readers are both homemakers and career women (most work part-time) with either a Protestant, Evangelical, or Orthodox Roman Catholic background. Needs personal experiences and interviews, fiction, columns entitled "Working Smarter (Not Harder)," "Equipped for Ministry," "One Woman's Journal," "In My Opinion." Also uses traditional, free verse, haiku poetry and household hints as fillers.

Article length 1,500 words maximum, fiction 1,500 to 2,000 words. Limit poems to 3 per envelope. Household hints run 300 words. Must query first except for fiction and column materials. Buys first rights. Guidelines and sample copy for 9 × 12 envelope with $1.50 postage. Reports in 2 months. Pays 15 to 25 cents per word on acceptance for assigned manuscripts, on publication for unassigned manuscripts.

VISION, P.O. Box 50025, Pasadena, CA 91115. (818) 798-1124. Fax: (818) 798-7895. Forrest L. Turpen, editor. Submit material to Mrs. Ranelda Hunsicker, managing editor. A 20-page bimonthly magazine published by Christian Educators Association, International. Circulation 2,500.

☐ *Vision* serves an audience of Evangelical parents and teachers. Needs personal experiences and interviews on current issues that are education related. Uses poetry on education-related topics; advice, current issues, and theology columns related to parents and teachers; devotions, meditations, anecdotes, statistics, and humor as fillers; photographs.

Article length 900 to 1,500 words. Limit poems to 3 per envelope. Columns run 400 words, fillers 150 to 400 words. Biggest need is for B&W glossies. Accepts complete manuscripts, simultaneous and computer submissions in IBM WordPerfect 5.1. Buys one-time rights. Guidelines available for SASE. Reports in 6 weeks. Pays in copies.

VISTA, P.O. Box 50434, Indianapolis, IN 46250. (317) 576-8144. Brenda Bratton, editor. An 8-page weekly take-home paper with a circulation of 70,000.

☐ *Vista* serves an Evangelical audience of adult and senior adult laity with a Wesleyan background. "Please obtain guidelines before submitting." Needs personal experiences and interviews on current issues and humor, column material on "how-to" and current issues, and photographs.

Article and column material length 500 to 600 words. Needs B&W glossies. Prefers a complete manuscript. Accepts simultaneous submissions. Buys first, reprint, and simultaneous rights. Guidelines and sample copy for 9 × 12 SASE. Reports in 6 to 8 weeks. Lead time 9 to 10 months. Pays 2 to 4 cents per word on acceptance or publication.

VITAL CHRISTIANITY, P.O. Box 2499, Anderson, IN 46018. (317) 644-7721. Arlo F. Newell, editor. Submit to Kathleen Buehler, managing editor. A 64-page monthly magazine published by Warner Press. Circulation 21,000.

☐ *Vital Christianity* serves an Evangelical audience of laity and clergy with a Church of God background. A thematic magazine which needs personal experiences, contemporary fiction, and short poetry.

Article length 1,000 to 1,200 words, fiction 1,500 to 1,800 words. Limit poems to 3 per envelope. Prefers a complete manuscript. Buys primarily first or one-time rights, occasionally reprint and simultaneous rights. Guidelines, theme list, and sample copy for 9 × 11 envelope with enough postage for 7 ounces. Reports in 6 to 8 weeks. Lead time 10 to 12 weeks. Pays $10 to $100 on acceptance.

VOICE, P.O. Box 5050, Costa Mesa, CA 92628-5050. (714) 754-1400. Jerry Jensen, editor. A 40-page monthly magazine with a circulation of 300,000.

☐ *Voice* addresses an audience of laity and clergy affiliated with a Full Gospel Business Men's Fellowship. Needs personal experiences and testimonies.

Article length 1,500 to 2,500 words. Prefers a complete manuscript. Guidelines available for SASE. Pays 10 cents per word within 60 days of acceptance.

THE WAR CRY, 615 Slaters Lane, Alexandria, VA 22313. (703) 684-5500. Fax: (703) 684-5539. Colonel Henry Gariepy, editor. Captain Lesa Salyer, youth editor. A 24-page biweekly magazine published by The Salvation Army. Circulation 500,000.

☐ *The War Cry* serves an adult and senior adult audience, both lay and leadership, with a Protestant Evangelical background. Needs personal experiences and devotions on current issues and special days.

Article length 700 to 1,500 words. Prefers a complete manuscript. Buys first and one-time rights. Guidelines and sample copy for SASE. Reports in 6 weeks. Lead time 6 months. Pays 15 cents per word on acceptance.

WEAVINGS: A JOURNAL OF THE CHRISTIAN SPIRITUAL LIFE, P.O. Box 189, Nashville, TN 37202-0189. (615) 340-7254. Fax: (615) 340-7006. John S. Mogabgab, editor. Submit to JoAnn E. Miller, assistant editor. A 48-page bimonthly journal published by The Upper Room. Circulation 30,000.

☐ *Weavings* addresses a mainline Protestant and Orthodox Roman Catholic audience of scholars, clergy, and laity, both men and women. A thematic magazine needing personal experiences and theology related to themes. Also needs poetry (traditional and free verse).

Article length 1,500 to 3,000 words. Prefers a query, but accepts complete manuscript. Buys one-time and all rights. Guidelines and theme list for SASE. Reports in 6 months. Pays approximately 10 cents per word for articles, $50 up for poetry on publication.

THE WESLEYAN ADVOCATE, P.O. Box 50434, Indianapolis, IN 46250-0434. (317) 576-8256. Fax: (317) 577-4937. Norman G. Wilson, editor. Submit to Jerry Brecheisen, managing editor. A 36-page monthly magazine published by the Wesleyan Church. International circulation of 20,000.

☐ *The Wesleyan Advocate* serves an Evangelical audience of clergy and laity with a Wesleyan background. Needs personal experience and devotional articles on current issues. Also uses fiction (adventure), poetry (traditional and free verse), fillers (devotions, meditations, and anecdotes), and photographs.

Article length 100 to 800 words. Prefers complete manuscript. Accepts simultaneous and computer submissions in Microsoft Word. Buys first and simultaneous rights. Guidelines and sample copy for $1. Reports in 2 to 3 weeks. Pays 1 to 3 cents per word on publication.

WHEREVER MAGAZINE, P.O. Box 969, Wheaton, IL 60189. (708) 653-5300. Fax: (708) 653-1826. Jack Kilgore, editor. A 16-page monthly (during the academic year) magazine. It's published by the Evangelical Alliance Mission, and the circulation varies between 6,000 and 17,000.

☐ *Wherever Magazine* addresses an Evangelical adult audience. "We shoot for college and young professionals with an intent on missions." Needs articles on missions issues and experiences. Uses photographs.

Article length is 1,500 words maximum. B&W glossies require a model release. Must query. "Authors can request to be on our mailing list for freelancers. Mailings in the summer and spring will outline upcoming themes for the academic year. Writers may query from the information we provide. They should have some familiarity with overseas missions and church planning. Please don't query before receiving this mailing!" Accepts electronic transmissions on WordPerfect or WordStar. Buys all rights. Guidelines and sample copy for SASE. Reports in 1 month. Pays on publication. Rate not stated.

WITH MAGAZINE, 722 Main, Box 347, Newton, KS 67114-0347. (316) 283-5100. Carol Duerksen and Eddy Hall, co-editors. A 32-page monthly magazine (8 times/year) published by the Mennonite Church and the General Conference Mennonite Church.

☐ *With* serves an Evangelical audience of socially conscious youth ages 15 to 18 with a Mennonite and Brethren background. A thematic magazine which needs personal experiences, occasionally as-told-to's, interviews, how-to's, and devotions on current issues with humor where appropriate. Needs realistic, contemporary fiction with teen protagonist, parables, and humor. Also uses traditional and free verse poetry on nature, humor and cartoons used as fillers, and photographs.

Article length 300 to 1,800 words, fiction 500 to 2,000, model release required for B&W glossies. Prefers a query on as-told-to articles. Accepts complete manuscripts for everything else. Accepts photocopies, simultaneous, and computer submissions. Buys first, reprint, one-time, and simultaneous rights. Guidelines, theme list, and sample copy available with 9 × 12 SASE and $1.21 postage. Reports in 3 to 6 weeks. Lead time 4 to 6 months. Pays 4 cents per word on acceptance.

THE WITNESS, 1249 Washington Boulevard, #3115, Detroit, MI 48226. (313) 962-2650. Jeanie Wylie-Kellerman, editor. Submit to Marianne Arbogast and Julie Wortman; poetry editor, Gloria House. A 28-page monthly magazine published by Episcopal Church Publishing Company. Circulation 4,500.

☐ *The Witness* serves an audience of adults and senior clergy and laity with a Liberal, Episcopal background. A thematic magazine which needs articles and interviews on current issues and theological topics, poetry, and photographs.

Article length 1,000 words. Uses B&W glossies and color slides. Prefers a query. Accepts photocopies, simultaneous and computer submissions. Buys all rights for prose, simultaneous rights for art and photographs. Guidelines, theme list, and sample copy for $2.50. Pays on publication. Rate not stated.

WOMAN OF POWER, P.O. Box 2785, Orleans, MA 02653. (508) 240-7877. Charlene McKee, editor. An 88-page quarterly publication with a circulation of 20,000.

☐ *Woman of Power* primarily addresses an audience of non-Christian women, scholars, clergy, and laity, between the ages of 25 and 45. "We explore a theme in each issue of special interest to women's spirituality." A thematic magazine needing personal experiences, interviews, and articles on current issues. Also uses photographs.

Article length 5,000 words maximum. Model release required with B&W glossies. Prefers a complete manuscript. Accepts photocopies and simultaneous submissions. Accepts computer submissions in Microsoft Word 5.5. Requires first rights. Guidelines and theme list for SASE, sample copy for $8. Reports in 3 to 6 months. Pays in 2 copies and 1 year's subscription to the magazine.

WOMAN'S TOUCH, 1445 Boonville Avenue, Springfield, MO 65802-1894. (417) 862-2781. Fax: (417) 862-8558. Sandra G. Clopine, editor. Submit to Aleda Swartzendruber, associate editor, or Darla Knoth, assistant editor. A 28-page bimonthly magazine published by the General Council of the Assemblies of God. Circulation 18,000.

☐ *Woman's Touch* serves an Evangelical audience of women in lay and leadership positions of the Assemblies of God. A thematic magazine which needs personal experiences on current issues, a few poems, and meditations, anecdotes, and humor as fillers.

Article length 1,200 words maximum. Limit poems to 3 per envelope. Fillers run 400 to 500 words. Prefers a complete manuscript. Buys first and reprint rights. Guidelines, theme list, and sample copy free for SASE. Reports in 6 to 8 weeks. Lead time 8 to 10 months. Pays $10 to $35 for unsolicited articles on acceptance.

WOMEN ALIVE!, P.O. Box 4683, Overland Park, KS 66204. (913) 649-8583. Aletha Hinthorn, editor. A 20-page bimonthly magazine published by Women Alive, Incorporated. Circulation 5,000.

☐ *Women Alive!* "encourages holiness women to apply Scripture to their daily lives." The audience is adult, senior adult women with a Protestant, Evangelical background. Needs personal experiences and devotions on current issues. Uses devotions and meditations as column material and cartoons, jokes, and humor as fillers.

Article length 600 to 1,500 words. Accepts complete manuscripts, simultaneous submissions. Buys first, reprint, simultaneous, and all rights. Guidelines available for $1.50. Reports in 2 to 4 weeks. Lead time 4 months. Pays $15 to $35 on publication.

WONDER TIME, 6401 The Paseo, Kansas City, MO 64131. (816) 333-7000. Fax: (816) 333-1683. Lois Perrigo, editor. Teresa Gillihan, submissions editor. A 4-page weekly take-home paper published by WordAction Publishing Company. Circulation 45,000.

☐ *Wonder Time* addresses an Evangelical audience of children ages 6 to 8 years with a Nazarene background. A thematic magazine that needs nonfiction, fiction, and poetry that coordinate with Sunday school curriculum. Art is assigned.

Article and story length is 350 to 450 words. Poetry is 4 to 8 lines on seasonal and Christian themes. Buys all rights. Guidelines, sample copy, and theme list is available for SASE. Lead time 6 months. Pays 3.5 cents per word on acceptance.

WORD & WORLD: THEOLOGY FOR CHRISTIAN MINISTRY, 2481 Como Avenue, St. Paul, MN 55108. (612) 641-3482. Fax: (612) 641-3425. When using fax number, item must be marked, "Attn: Word & World." Frederick J. Gaiser, editor. Submit book reviews to Jane Strohl. A 104-page quarterly journal published by Luther Northwestern Theological Seminary. Circulation 3,500.

☐ *Word & World* "seeks deliberately to relate theology to Christian ministry and to relate the Christian tradition to the contemporary world. It is read by students and scholars, but its primary audience is parish pastors—who are interested in the best fruits of study and reflection as these are addressed to them in their work." It's read by Roman Catholics, but predominantly by Lutherans of both Evangelical and Liberal theological positions. Nonfiction needs include articles on current issues, theology, and opinion. Columns needed include current issues and theology.

Articles and columns are about 12 pages double-spaced. Accepts complete manuscripts in photocopies or computer submissions. Buys all rights. Guidelines free for SASE, back issues of the magazine are $5 each. Reports in acknowledgment within 10 days, decision within 60 days. Pays a modest honorarium on publication.

WORLD VISION MAGAZINE, 919 West Huntington Drive, Monrovia, CA 91016. (818) 357-1111. Fax: (818) 357-0915. Terry Madison, editor. Submit to Larry Wilson, managing editor. A 24-page bimonthly magazine published by World Vision Incorporated. Circulation of 160,000.

☐ *World Vision Magazine* serves both Evangelical and Liberal laity and clergy, with a mainline Protestant or Roman Catholic background. The magazine "ministers to children, families and communities, provides emergency aid, fosters self-reliance, furthers evangelism, strengthens Christian leadership, and increases public awareness of poverty and its worldwide causes." Needs personal experiences and interviews on current issues. Also uses color slides and illustrations.

Article length 800 to 2,400 words. Model release required for photographs. Must query. Accepts photocopies and computer submissions in Macintosh WordPerfect. Buys first rights. Guidelines and sample copy for SASE. Reports in 2 to 6 weeks. Pays 20 cents per word on acceptance. Offers a kill fee.

WORLDWIDE CHALLENGE, 100 Sunport Lane, Orlando, FL 32809. (407) 826-2390. Fax: (407) 826-2374. Diane McDougall, editor. A 52-page bimonthly magazine published by Campus Crusade for Christ. Circulation is 95,000.

☐ *Worldwide Challenge* addresses adult supporters of Campus Crusade, both lay and leadership, with an Evangelical Protestant and Roman Catholic background. Needs personal experience articles.

Article length 300 to 1,000 words. Prefers query addressed to "Free-lance Editor." Buys first rights. Guidelines and sample copy for $2, addressed to Terri Oesterreich, editorial assistant. Pays $25 to $50 on acceptance.

YOU!, 29800 Agoura Road, Suite 102, Agoura Hills, CA 91301. (818) 991-1813. Fax: (818) 991-2024. Paul Lauer, editor. Submit to Tom Ehart, managing editor. A 28-page monthly magazine published by Veritas Communications, Incorporated. Circulation 35,000.

☐ *You!* addresses an audience of Roman Catholic youth ages 13 to 18. Needs personal experiences and devotional articles on current issues, theology, and family issues. Needs columns on current issues and theology, fillers (anecdotes), and photographs.

Articles and columns run 800 words, fillers 250 to 300 words. Prefers query, but accepts complete manuscript. Accepts photocopies and computer submissions in Macintosh, Microsoft Word. No model release required for B&W glossies, color slides, and color prints. Buys first and one-time rights. Guidelines and sample copy for SASE. Pays 5 cents per word on publication.

YOUNG & ALIVE, 4444 South 52nd Street, Lincoln, NE 68516 or P.O. Box 6097, Lincoln, NE 68506. (402) 488-0981. Richard J. Kaiser, editor. A 65-page quarterly magazine published by Christian Record Services. Circulation 26,000.

☐ *Young & Alive* addresses an audience of blind or sight-impaired young adults, ages 16 to 20 with a conservative Christian background. This magazine "seeks to stimulate the thinking, feelings, and activities of persons with sight impairment. As they test new ideas, form relationships, and develop values, *Young & Alive* seeks to assist in meeting their needs in a positive way." Needs articles on adventure, biography, camping, careers, personal experiences of the handicapped, health, history, hobbies, holidays, marriage, nature, practical Christianity, sports, and travel.

Article length 800 to 1,400 words. Clear B&W glossies should accompany article when possible. Model release required. Prefers query, but accepts complete manuscript. Accepts computer submissions. Buys one-time rights. Guidelines and sample copy for SASE. Reports in 3 to 4 months. Lead time 12 months. Pays 3 to 5 cents per word for text, $5 to $10 for photos on acceptance.

YOUNG MUSICIANS, 127 Ninth Avenue N, Nashville, TN 37234. (615) 251-2960. Clinton E. Flowers, editor. A 52-page quarterly magazine published by the Baptist Sunday School Board. Circulation 85,000.

☐ *Young Musicians* addresses a Southern Baptist children's audience, ages 9 to 11. Needs theological topics for articles, devotional and/or music topics for fiction, religious poetry about God, family, and friends. "I look for inspirational, real life stories for children, especially as they relate to Christian music in the child's life. I purchase stories about major composers such as Bach, Handel, Watts, and Wesley if they are written for a 4th to 6th grade child. Most hymn writers are acceptable if stories relate to where children are—we do not need academic material. I also welcome music activities, stories about biblical instruments, stories relating to the piano and organ. Activities related to any rhythm instrument." Uses photographs.

Article length 60 lines, 30 characters per double-spaced line. Devotional and music topics run 76 to 180 lines, 30 characters per double-spaced line. Model release is required with B&W glossies. Prefers a query. Accepts computer submissions. Buys first rights. Guidelines available for SASE. Reports in 1 month. Pays 5 cents per word on acceptance.

YOUNG SALVATIONIST, 615 Slaters Lane, P.O. Box 269, Alexandria, VA 22313. (703) 684-5500. Fax: (703) 684-5539. Captain M. Lesa Salyer, editor. A 16-page monthly magazine published by the Salvation Army. Circulation 22,000.

☐ *Young Salvationist* presents a Protestant, Evangelical message to high school teens, both Christian and non-Christian. A thematic magazine which needs personal experiences, interviews, and devotions on current issues, general fiction, and photographs.

Article and fiction length 750 to 1,200 words. Needs B&W glossies and color prints. Prefers a complete manuscript. Accepts photocopies, simultaneous, and computer submissions. Buys first, reprint, one-time, all rights. Guidelines, theme list, and sample copy for 9 × 12 SASE. Reports in 1 month. Lead time 3 months. Pays 10 cents per word on acceptance.

THE YOUNG SOLDIER, 455 North Service Road, E, Oakville, ON, L6H 1A5 Canada. (416) 845-9235. Fax: (416) 845-1966. Mrs. Captain Judy Power, editor. An 8-page weekly newspaper published by the Salvation Army. Circulation 20,000.

☐ *The Young Soldier* addresses a nondenominational children's audience with an Evangelical background. The purpose of the newspaper is "to teach children about the gospel; to inform them about the Salvation Army, and to encourage them to live a life of faith." Needs comics, devotions, meditations, games, puzzles, quizzes, how-to's, humor, personal experience, fiction, and poetry. Potential topics are Christian living, church education, environment, evangelism, family.

Article and story length 700 to 800 words. Prefers complete manuscript. No simultaneous submissions, photocopies, or computer submissions. Guidelines and sample copy for SASE. Reports in 2 weeks. Lead time 3 months. No payment.

YOUR CHURCH, 465 Gundersen Drive, Carol Stream, IL 60188. (708) 260-6200. Fax: (708) 260-0114. James D. Berkley, editor. A 56-page bimonthly magazine published by Christianity Today, Incorporated. Circulation 200,000.

☐ *Your Church* serves an audience of Evangelical clergy (primarily men) with a mainline Protestant background. A thematic magazine that needs articles "about church business administration only. The magazine is focused narrowly so sermons, meditations, devotionals, and stories are of no use to us." Also needs column materials on church business administration, fillers (cartoons), and photographs (B&W glossies and color slides).

Article length 1,000 to 1,500 words. Column material length 1,000 to 1,200 words. Model release required with photographs. Prefers a query. Accepts computer submissions, but must state software name and version number. Buys first rights. Guidelines, theme list, and sample copy for SASE. Reports in 1 month. Lead time 4 months. Pays 10 cents per word on acceptance.

YOUTH AND CHRISTIAN EDUCATION, 1080 Montgomery Avenue, NE, Cleveland, TN 37311. (615) 476-4512. Fax: (615) 478-7521. James E. Humbertson, editor. A 32-page quarterly magazine published by the Church of God. Circulation 14,000.

☐ *Youth and Christian Education Leadership* serves an Evangelical audience of adults, scholars, clergy, and laity with a Church of God background. Needs "articles for Christian education workers at the local level." Uses photographs.

Article length is 500 to 1,200 words. Model release required with B&W glossies. Prefers a complete manuscript. Buys first and reprint rights. Guidelines available for SASE. Reports in 2 weeks. Pays $25 on acceptance.

YOUTHGUIDE, 722 Main, Box 347, Newton, KS 67114. (316) 283-5100. Eddy Hall and Carol Duerksen, coeditors. A quarterly journal published by the Mennonite Church. General Conference Mennonite Church, Church of the Brethren, and Brethren in Christ.

☐ *YouthGuide* serves an Evangelical audience of socially conscious youthworkers in lay and leadership positions with a Mennonite or Brethren in Christ background. Needs how-to articles on ministry to youth and cartoons about youth ministry as fillers.

Article length 600 to 1,900 words. Prefers a complete manuscript. Accepts simultaneous submissions. Buys one-time rights. Guidelines and sample copy for 9 × 12 SASE with $1.21 postage. Reports in 1 to 2 months. Payment is on acceptance. Rate not stated.

THE YOUTH LEADER, 1445 Boonville Avenue, Springfield, MO 65802. (417) 862-2781, ext. 4041. Fax: (417) 862-1693. Tom Young, editor. A 24-page magazine published twice quarterly by the Assemblies of God National Youth Department. Circulation 3,200.

☐ *The Youth Leader* addresses an Evangelical audience of laity and clergy, with an Assemblies of God background. These adults work with teenagers in the local church setting. Needs articles on current issues and youth ministry how-to's and anecdotes as fillers.

Prefers query, but accepts complete manuscript. Accepts photocopies and simultaneous submissions. Buys first, reprint, and simultaneous rights. Guidelines and sample copy for SASE. Reports in 4 weeks. Pays 4 cents per word on publication.

YOUTH UPDATE, 1615 Republic Street, Cincinnati, OH 45210. (513) 241-5615. Fax: (513) 241-0399. Carol Ann Morrow, editor. A 4-page monthly newsletter published by St. Anthony Messenger Press. Circulation 25,000.

☐ *Youth Update* serves an audience of high school teens with a Roman Catholic background. Needs articles on life issues with a spiritual perspective.

Article length 2,300 words. Must query. Accepts computer submissions with IBM compatible language or ASCII. Buys first rights. Guidelines and sample copy for SASE. Reports in 6 to 8 weeks. Lead time 4 months. Pays $350 to $400 on acceptance.

YOUTHWORKER, 1224 Greenfield, Drive, El Cajon, CA 92021. (619) 440-2333. Fax: (619) 440-4939. Wayne Rice, editor. Submit to Tim McLaughlin. A 120-page quarterly journal published by Youth Specialties. Circulation 8,000.

☐ *Youthworker* "serves the personal and professional needs of full-time youth workers in the church and parachurch with thoughtful, in-depth articles." The audience is youth leaders and workers from an Evangelical Protestant or Roman Catholic background. A thematic magazine that needs personal experiences and interviews on current issues, anecdotes and humor as fillers, and photographs.

Article length 1,500 to 3,500 words, fillers to 500 words, model release required for B&W glossies. Prefers query. Accepts computer submissions in IBM and Mac compatible software. "We use WordPerfect 5.1." Buys first and reprint rights. Guidelines and theme list free for SASE, sample copy for $5. Reports in 4 weeks. Lead time 3 months. Pays $100 on acceptance. Kill fee negotiable.

YOUTHWORKER UPDATE, 1224 Greenfield Drive, El Cajon, CA 92021. (619) 440-2333. Fax: (619) 440-4939. Wayne Rice, editor. Submit to Tim McLaughlin. An 8-page monthly newsletter published by Youth Specialties. Circulation 9,000.

☐ *Youthworker Update* "is a clipping service that keeps professional and volunteer youth workers informed of the latest trends, research, resources, and news pertinent to the field." The audience is Evangelical laity and lay leaders in either Protestant or Roman Catholic churches. Needs quotations.

Quotations run 10 to 80 words. Prefers a complete manuscript. Accepts computer submissions in IBM or Mac compatible software. "We use WordPerfect 5.21." Buys first and reprint rights. Guidelines and sample copy for SASE. Reports in 4 weeks. Pays on publication. Rate not stated.

* THREE *

Writing for Religious Book Publishers

This chapter lists publishers of religious books in the United States and Canada. Some of them are owned and operated by denominations or church groups and publish exclusively religious titles. Others are independent or family-owned publishers that do religious books. Some are general trade houses with religious departments that publish many religious books each year. Still others are trade houses that only occasionally publish a religious title. However, all publishers listed here have indicated their interest in publishing some religious books. Although the publishers in this chapter have a Christian orientation, we have used the generic "Religious" in the title. The kinds of inspirational books sought by many publishers have a very broad approach to religion as you will discover while reading their entries.

Writing a book is a process quite different from writing a magazine article or a short piece for some other purpose. A book is a large undertaking, and the writer intending to tackle such a project will do well to consider carefully the information contained in each of the entries listed here. You will want to send for catalogs from the houses that seem likely to be interested in the kind of book you are writing. Many publishers also furnish author's guidelines free for a SASE (usually a number 10 envelope is large enough). But if you are sending for a catalog, make your SASE a 9 × 12 envelope. If you are sending for information from a Canadian publisher, use Canadian postage or include an International Reply Coupon for the proper amount.

Most publishers prefer to begin with a query letter rather than a completed manuscript. This is standard procedure in book publishing, and the religious writer venturing into this field ought to follow it. Write a brief letter to the editor. Tell him or her your idea for a book, give a brief, one-paragraph synopsis, and ask if he or she would be interested in seeing a portion or the whole of the manuscript (if you have already written it).

If the editor says yes to your query, reply with more about your book—outline the contents, submit a sample chapter or two, discuss your idea of the market for the book, and give some indication of the time you will require to complete the task. You may want to indicate your anticipated needs for an advance or royalty.

If the publisher is still interested, the next step may be negotiations on a contract. The entries in this chapter give some clues to the usual royalties or advances offered. In all cases, however, this matter is open to negotiation, as is much of the whole process of getting a book published. For this reason, many writers use an agent to do their negotiating for them. Actually, negotiating a contract is not as complicated as it may sound, and if it is done with patience and cooperation there is little to be feared. The publisher's objective is the same as the writer's—to publish the best book possible and to reach the greatest possible number of readers.

The business of publishing religious books has been expanding for several years. The increase in the number of religious bookstore outlets is due to the helpful counsel of such organizations as the Christian Booksellers Association and the Evangelical Christian Publishers Association. As you read the entries in this chapter, you will discover many different kinds of religious publishers having very different needs and objectives. Be sure to match the subject and potential readership of your book with that of the publisher you choose.

Some of the publishers in this chapter publish books intended for a Jewish audience as well as Christian books, but most of the publishers of Judaica are listed in chapter 4. You will also find cross-references within this chapter when a publisher is known by more than one name. For example, information on Gospel Light Press will be found under Regal Books, and information for Nazarene Publishing House will be found under Beacon Hill Press. In all cases both names are found in the alphabetical listing.

As with the chapter on periodical markets, we suggest you make good use of the indexes in the back of this book to help you find the publisher most likely to be interested in the kind of manuscript you intend to produce.

Since many publishers are now asking that writers submit hard copy and computer disks, we queried them about the procedure, and this information is in the entries. We also urge writers to read the information about computers for writers in chapter 7.

Even though you may not feel you are at this stage in your career, we also suggest that all potential book writers read the material on agents in chapter 7. In some cases, the entries suggest that publishers prefer getting their manuscripts from agents. If that is the practice of the publisher you choose, you will find the information on agents and the listing provided essential.

It hardly seems necessary, yet editors tell us that some words need to be said here, too, about being professional in the way that you submit manuscripts as well as the way you write them. Some of the books suggested in chapter 6, on resources for religious writers, will tell you how and what to do in submitting a book manuscript. We don't try to give guidance on the subject here, but the following list of the ten most common faults of book manuscripts will send up a few warning flags. An editor compiled this list after some twenty years of reading book manuscripts. Take heed of these warnings about what not to do.

Ten Faults of Book Manuscripts

1. The manuscript is directed at no one. There is no focus, no special reader in mind.

2. The idea is out of date (or before its time).

3. There is no logical progression in the writing. Like Don Quixote, the manuscript goes in all directions at once.

4. The writing is sloppy. Unforgivable!

5. The author submits copies of the manuscript to more than one publisher at the same time without advising the publishers. Multiple submissions are sometimes permitted, but be sure the publishers know about them.

6. The manuscript is submitted to the wrong publisher. It would fit someone else's line but does not fit ours. Query letters should help avoid this.

7. Footnotes and other similar material are inaccurate or incomplete, which makes permissions and other necessary tasks difficult or impossible.

8. The author has a faulty or inadequate concept of the market at which the book is aimed.

9. An agent is used incorrectly. Agents can be helpful, but sometimes they get in the way if they are only duplicating the work of the author.

10. There is no table of contents.

A careful reading of these and other suggestions from book editors will go a long way toward helping you get your book published by one of the houses in the following list.

PUBLISHERS

ABINGDON PRESS, 201 8th Avenue S., Nashville, TN 37203. (615) 749-6000. Fax: (615) 749-6512. Neil M. Alexander, editorial director. Submit manuscripts to Mary Catherine Dean, general interest books; Rex Matthews, academic books; Paul Franklyn, professional books; Jack Keller, reference books; J. Richard Peck, United Methodist books and resources. Publishing arm of The United Methodist Church releasing 130 originals and reprints yearly, 90 percent paperback.

☐ Abingdon Press addresses a wide audience of all ages from all Christian perspectives. Needs "a wide variety of resources on religious topics for both the specialist and nonspecialist in ministry." Topics include self-help, marriage and family, parenting, Bible studies, reference books, and children's picture books. See entries under Dimensions for Living and Kingswood Books for special interests and requirements.

Requires a query on all materials. Accepts IBM compatible and ASCII submissions. Reports in 12 weeks. Pays varied royalties based on the retail price. Free author guidelines for SASE.

ACCENT BOOKS, 12100 West 6th Avenue, P.O. Box 15337, Denver, CO 80215. (303) 988-5300. Mary Nelson, editor. Publishes several original paperbacks yearly. A division of David C. Cook Publishing.

☐ Accent Books addresses an Evangelical audience. Needs books that "help local churches and their members teach and minister more effectively." Interested especially in books related to Christian education. Publishes curriculum and other resources for all ages. No fiction or poetry.

Requires a query for all submissions. Prefers outline/synopsis/sample chapters. Accepts computer submissions. Pays royalties but seldom gives advances. Free curriculum catalog for 9 × 12 SASE, author guidelines for #10 SASE.

AGLOW PUBLICATIONS, Box 1548, Lynnwood, WA 98046. (206) 775-7282. Fax: (206) 778-9615. Karen E. Anderson, acquisitions editor. The book publishing arm of Women's Aglow Fellowship International. Publishes 6 to 8 paperback originals yearly.

☐ Aglow Publications addresses an Evangelical audience of women, many of them with a Charismatic background. Needs books that "minister to the hearts of women around the world who desire to grow spiritually, intellectually, emotionally, and psychologically." Readers are "contemporary women of all ages who juggle the demands of children, marriage, work, church, and friendships. An increasing number are single mothers, widowed and divorced." Also does some Bible studies.

Length averages 175 to 200 pages. Requires a query. Accepts photocopies, simultaneous and computer submissions. Reports in 6 to 8 weeks. Pays 10 percent royalty on the retail price. Advances average $1,500 to $2,000. Free catalog and author guidelines for SASE with 2 first-class stamps.

ALBA HOUSE, 2187 Victory Boulevard, Staten Island, NY 10314. (718) 761-0047. Fax: (718) 761-0057. Aloysius Milella, editor; Edmund C. Lane, managing editor. Book publishing arm of the Society of St. Paul. Publishes 30 paperback originals and reprints yearly.

☐ Alba House addresses a children's audience, also adult scholars, clergy, and laity with primarily a Roman Catholic background. Needs books on self-help, marriage and family, recovery, social issues, prayer, devotions and meditations, Bible studies. Also does children's picture books. No fiction or poetry.

Prefers a query. Accepts computer submissions. Reports in 4 weeks. Pays 10 percent royalty. No advances. Free catalog and author guidelines for SASE.

THE ALBAN INSTITUTE, 4125 Nebraska Avenue, NW, Washington, DC 20016. (202) 244-7320. Fax: (202) 364-7266. Celia A. Hahn, editor. Produces 10 original paperbacks yearly in association with the Washington Cathedral and the Episcopal Church.

☐ The Alban Institute publishes resources for congregational life and practical tools to enhance the parish ministry. Many publications report the results of congregational research carried out by the Institute or by its authors. The three editorial series are: Congregational Problems and Opportunities, the Clergy Role and Career, and the Ministry of the Laity in the World and in the Church. Also produces videotapes.

Average length is 100 pages. Write for guidelines before submitting a manuscript. Reports in 3 to 4 months. Pays 7 percent royalty on net receipts. Average advance is $100.

AMERICAN CATHOLIC PRESS, 16160 South Seton Drive, South Holland, IL 60473. (708) 331-5485. Father Michael Gilligan. A Roman Catholic publisher of materials on liturgy and liturgical music only.

☐ American Catholic Press publishes 5 books annually, mostly hardback for a Catholic audience. Also publishes audiocassettes, hymnals, choir music.

AMG PUBLISHERS, P.O. Box 22000, Chattanooga, TN 37422. (615) 894-6060. Fax: (615) 894-6863. Spiros Zodhiates and Dale Anderson, editors. Publishing arm of AMG International. Publishes 10 originals and reprints yearly, mostly paperback.

☐ AMG Publishers addresses an Evangelical audience of adults. Needs books on theology, exegesis, and Bible study, reference books. Also interested in books dealing with marriage and family, cults, world religions, and social issues. Uses photographs and illustrations. Does some audiovisuals.

Prefers outline/synopsis/sample chapters. Reports in 8 to 12 weeks. Royalties are negotiable. Catalog for SASE.

AUGSBURG FORTRESS PUBLISHERS, 426 South 5th Street, Box 1209, Minneapolis, MN 55440. (612) 330-3433. Robert Moluff, editorial director, Augsburg Books; Marshall Johnson, editorial director, Fortress Books. The publishing arm of the Evangelical Lutheran Church in America. Publishes 50 books yearly under two imprints as described below.

☐ Augsburg Fortress Publishers addresses a wide spectrum of readership, subjects, and markets. Augsburg Books are primarily for general Christian readers of all ages and denominations, both laity and church leadership. Under this imprint subjects relate to how-to, self-help, marriage and family, prayer, devotions and meditations, congregational life. Most are paperback. Also does children's picture books. Average adult book length is 128 pages.

Fortress Books address students, scholars and clergy from all denominations and backgrounds. Subjects are Bible study, church history, systematic theology, ethics, women and religion, African-American studies, preaching, practical and pastoral theology. Most are hardcover and larger in size than Augsburg Books.

Prefers a query for either imprint. Accepts simultaneous submissions and photocopies. Reports in 6 weeks. Pays an average of 10 percent on the retail price. Offers modest advances. Guidelines for SASE.

AVE MARIA PRESS, Notre Dame, IN 46556. (219) 287-2831. Fax: (219) 239-2904. Frank J. Cunningham, director of publishing. Publishes 18 to 20 paperback original titles annually.

☐ Ave Maria Press is looking for books aimed at a youth, adult, and senior adult audience with either a Roman Catholic or mainline Protestant background. Wants titles related to spiritual formation and growth, catechetical and sacramental subjects. Also produces audiocassettes.

Prefers outline/synopsis/sample chapter submissions. Accepts PC-based software. Reports in 1 month. Pays royalties based on retail price. Guidelines and catalogs free.

NOTE TO USERS OF THIS BOOK

As you search in chapters 2, 3, and 4 for appropriate publishers for your material, be sure to use the indexes in the back of the book to help you find the periodicals and publishers you are looking for.

Chapter 5, *Branching Out*, has additional lists of publishers and information you will want if you are writing poetry, greeting cards, curriculum, or devotionals; preparing material for newspapers and syndicates, regional publications and nonprofit organizations; or marketing cartoons or drama and scripts for radio, television, videos, or film.

In chapter 7, you will also find a list of literary agents who have expressed interest in helping writers market religious material.

BAKER BOOK HOUSE, P.O. Box 6287, Kentwood, MI 49516. (616) 676-9185. Fax: (616) 676-9573. Allan Fisher, director of publications; Jane Dekker, assistant. Publishes 120 originals (a few reprints) yearly. Eighty percent are paperback.

☐ Baker Book House addresses an audience of all ages, mostly with an Evangelical background. Needs academic, reference, and professional books, general trade books on a variety of subjects, as well as fiction (mystery and women's contemporary). Does some textbooks and reference materials.

Prefers outline/synopsis/sample chapters. Accepts photocopies and simultaneous submissions. Reports in 2 to 3 weeks. Pays 14 percent royalty on the wholesale price. Free catalog and author guidelines for SASE.

BARBOUR AND COMPANY, INCORPORATED, P.O. Box 719, 1810 Barbour Drive, Uhrichsville, OH 44683. (614) 922-6045. Fax: (614) 922-5948. Stephen Reginald, editor. An Evangelical publisher producing materials for a general readership of all ages, in all categories except academic titles and Bible study guides. Produces 25 titles annually, mostly paperback, both originals and reprints.

☐ Barbour and Company is seeking devotions, inspirational, romance, and children's picture books. Interested in historical fiction.

Prefers submissions of outline/synopsis/sample chapters. Reports in 3 weeks. Pays royalties and advances of $500 average or outright purchase. Catalogs and author's guidelines available for $1 postage.

BARCLAY PRESS, 600 East Third Street, Newburg, OR 97132. (503) 538-7345. Fax: (503) 538-7033. Dan McCracken, editor. Publishing arm of the Northwest Yearly Meeting of the Friends Church. Publishes two paperback originals and reprints yearly.
☐ Barclay Press addresses a general adult audience. Needs books dealing with spirituality, contemporary issues, prayer, devotions.

Prefers a query. Accepts outline/synopsis/sample chapters. Pays 10 percent royalty.

BEACON HILL PRESS OF KANSAS CITY, P.O. Box 419527, Kansas City, MO 64141. (816) 931-1900. Fax: (816) 753-4071. Bonnie Perry, editor. Publishing arm of the Church of the Nazarene. Produces 30 paperback originals yearly.
☐ Beacon Hill Press addresses an Evangelical audience of all ages and stations in life. Publishes books on a wide variety of subjects: "theology and doctrine; history and biography, especially of the holiness/Wesleyan heritage; home, family, and marriage; inspiration; pastoral and teaching aids; books for women; group Bible studies; devotional reading; applied Christianity." Also does fiction (romance, adventure, biblical, historical).

Average nonfiction book length 150 to 200 pages, average fiction length 200 pages. Prefers to work with a complete manuscript or outline/synopsis/sample chapters. Accepts photocopies and simultaneous submissions. Accepts WordPerfect computer submissions. Reports in 4 months. Pays 10 percent royalty on the retail price. Advances to $500.

BEACON PRESS, 25 Beacon Street, Boston, MA 02108. (617) 742-2110. Fax: (617) 723-3097. Wendy J. Strothman, director; Lauren Bryant, Christian and general religion books; Deborah Chasman, Jewish and Native American books. The publishing arm of the Unitarian Universalist Association. Publishes 5 originals and reprints yearly, 60 percent paperback.
☐ Beacon Press addresses an audience of scholars, clergy, and general laity from a Liberal religious background. Needs books dealing with social issues, books of scholarly content and approach. No fiction or children's books.

Prefers a query and outline/synopsis/sample chapters. Accepts simultaneous submissions. Reports in 6 to 8 weeks. Pays variable royalties, advances, and outright purchases. Free catalog and author guidelines for 9 × 12 SASE.

BETHANY HOUSE PUBLISHERS, 6820 Auto Club Road, Minneapolis, MN 55438. (612) 829-2500. Fax: (612) 829-2503. Carol A. Johnson, editorial director.
☐ Bethany House Publishers is "no longer reviewing manuscript submissions or query letters."

BETHEL PUBLISHING, 1819 South Main Street, Elkhart, IN 46516 (219) 293-8585. Fax: (219) 522-5670. Rick Oltz, editor. Publishing arm of the Missionary Church headquartered in Fort Wayne, Indiana. Publishes for a general readership of all ages with an Evangelical background.
☐ Bethel Publishing is looking for devotional books and other nonfiction, fiction (mystery and adventure), greeting cards, and calendars. All books paperback.

Prefers to work with complete manuscripts. Reports in 90 days. Pays royalties of 10 percent of wholesale, some advance. Will consider simultaneous submissions. Catalogs and author guidelines available for 9 × 12 SASE.

Don Bosco Multimedia, 475 North Avenue, Box T, New Rochelle, NY 10802. (914) 576-0122. Fax: (914) 654-0443. James T. Morgan, editor. A publisher of the Silesian Society, Inc. Releases 30 religiously oriented titles annually for youth and adults: scholars, clergy, laity.

☐ Don Bosco Multimedia is looking for books dealing with youth and family ministry. No fiction. Also does audiovisuals.

Average length 150 pages. Requires a query. Reports in 1 month. Pays negotiable royalties. Catalogs and author guidelines available for SASE.

Bridge Publishing, Incorporated, 2500 Hamilton Boulevard, South Plainfield, NJ 07080. (908) 754-0745. Fax: (908) 754-0613. Guy J. Morrell and Kenneth M. Percy, editors. Publishes 25 paperback originals and reprints yearly.

☐ Bridge Publishing addresses an audience of Evangelical and Roman Catholic adults and has a Charismatic emphasis. Publishes quality Christian books for the general Christian market as well as manuscripts geared especially to the Charismatic reader. Also accepts manuscripts aimed at the secular book industry, especially if they deal with "family and social concerns." Interested in the following topics: "spiritual warfare, discipleship, evangelism, marriage, education, family, church growth and involvement." Also does biblical reference materials, daily devotionals and Bible studies. Will consider some "fiction and poetry of exceptional merit."

Prefers a complete manuscript or outline/synopsis/sample chapters. Accepts computer submissions. Reports in 8 to 12 weeks. Pays variable royalties and advances.

Broadman Press, 127 Ninth Avenue North, Nashville, TN 37234. (615) 251-2433. Charles Wilson, publisher. Submit manuscripts to "submissions editor." The publishing arm of the Southern Baptist Convention under the supervision of the Sunday School Board. Publishes 50 originals yearly, 80 percent of them in paperback.

☐ Broadman Press addresses an Evangelical audience of Southern Baptists of all ages. Seeks a wide range of readers both inside and outside Southern Baptist churches: children, scholars, clergy, and laity. Interested in biographies, humor, devotional reading, reference works, biblical studies, and curriculum. Also does some children's books.

Average length for adult books 96 to 200 pages depending on subject matter and market. Prefers outline/synopsis/sample chapters. Accepts computer submissions. Reports in 6 weeks. Pays standard royalties. Free catalog and author guidelines for SASE.

Brown-ROA, 2460 Kerper Boulevard, Dubuque, IA 52001. (319) 588-1451. Fax: (319) 589-4705. Ernest T. Nedder, president. A division of William C. Brown Communications, Inc. Publishes a few religiously oriented originals and reprints yearly.

☐ Brown-ROA aims at readers of all ages, primarily with a Roman Catholic background. Publishes how-to's, Bible studies, and textbooks. Also does audiovisuals.

Prefers complete manuscripts. Reports in 2 months. Pays varied royalties. Seldom offers advances. Free catalogs available.

Cambridge University Press, 40 West 20th Street, New York, NY 10011. (212) 924-3900. Fax: (212) 691-3239. Sidney Landau, editor. An American subsidiary of Cambridge University Press in England. Publishes 30 originals and reprints yearly, mostly hardcover.

☐ Cambridge University Press addresses an academic and scholarly audience from all religious backgrounds. Needs academic monographs.

Average length is 250 to 300 pages. Prefers outline/synopsis/sample chapters. Accepts computer submissions, but inquire first. Reports in 3 months. Pays royalties of 10 percent on net sales. Advances and outright purchases are rare. Free catalog and author guidelines for SASE.

CATHOLIC UNIVERSITY OF AMERICA PRESS, 620 Michigan Avenue, NE, Washington, DC 20064. (202) 319-5052. Fax: (202) 319-5802. David J. McGonagle, editor.
☐ Catholic University of America Press publishes 5 titles annually, books for scholars of theology, college, and university students, in theology and other religious subjects.

Prefers query and outline/synopsis/sample chapter submissions. Reports in 2 months. Pays varied royalties on wholesale price. No advance. Free catalogs and guidelines available.

CHALICE PRESS (CBP PRESS), P.O. Box 179, St. Louis, MO 63166. (314) 231-8500. Fax: (314) 231-8524. David P. Polk, editor. The publishing arm of the Christian Board of Publication, a unit of the Christian Church (Disciples of Christ). Publishes 15 paperback originals annually for a mainline Protestant, adult readership.
☐ Chalice Press is interested in "books for the thinking church" on the subjects of theology, preaching, social issues, worship, and Bible study.

Prefers outline/synopsis/sample chapter submissions. Accepts computer submissions on any word processing program. Reports in 3 months. Pays royalties of varied amounts. No advances. Author's guidelines available with SASE.

CHARIOT FAMILY PUBLISHING, 20 Lincoln Avenue, Elgin, IL 60120. (708) 741-0800. Cathy Davis, executive editor. Julie Smith, children's editor. A division of David C. Cook Publishing Company releasing 25 adult "LifeJourney" books and 50 juvenile "Chariot" books annually for general readership of mainline Protestants with an Evangelical background.
☐ Chariot Family Publishing is looking for children's books (babies through teens) that "help the child understand himself, his relationship to God, and the message of the Bible in an interesting and readable way." LifeJourney Books for adults deal with "parenting, personal/spiritual growth, and fiction with a strong Christian content and direct application to life." Fiction of any kind is welcome—mystery, romance, adventure, historical, and contemporary.

Prefers complete manuscripts for children's books, outline/synopsis/sample chapter submissions for adults. Make inquiries about acceptable software. Reports in 3 months. Pays royalties and advances on some books—varied amounts. Guidelines available for SASE. All manuscripts should be sent to "submissions editor."

CHOSEN BOOKS PUBLISHING COMPANY, LTD., 6030 East Fulton Road, Ada, MI 49301. Jane Campbell, editor. A division of Baker Book House, Grand Rapids, Michigan. Publishes 3 originals, 2 of them paperback, yearly.
☐ Chosen Books addresses an Evangelical audience of adults and has a Charismatic emphasis. Interested in books dealing with "the spiritual life" on topics of how-to, self-help, recovery, social issues, prayer, devotions and meditations.

Books average 60,000 to 90,000 words. Prefers a query or proposal consisting of an outline/synopsis/sample chapters. Accepts simultaneous submissions. Reports in 1 to 2 months. Pays royalties on net sales. Offers advances. Author's guidelines for #10 SASE.

CHRISTIAN CLASSICS INCORPORATED, 77 West Main Street, Box 30, Westminster, MD 21158. John J. McHale, editor. Roman Catholic publishers of 6 to 8 paperback titles annually.
☐ Christian Classics addresses a general audience of scholars, clergy, and laity. Needs

spiritual, theological, and reference books on self-help, marriage and family, social issues, biography, prayer, devotions, Bible studies, and humor.

Prefers query and outline/synopsis/sample chapters. Reports in 3 weeks. Pays 10 percent royalties on retail price, advances of $500 to $1,000. Some outright purchases. Free catalogs and author guidelines available.

CHRISTIAN EDUCATIONAL PUBLISHERS, 9230 Trade Plaza, Box 261129, San Diego, CA 92126. (619) 578-4700. Jack Cavanaugh, managing editor. Publishes Bible club curriculum.

☐ Christian Educational Publishers addresses an Evangelical audience of children and youth, ages 2 to 3 through high school. Prefers to work with writers from an Evangelical background. Needs writers for Bible club curriculum workbooks and take-home papers.

Bible club curriculum is 1,500 words per lesson, 13 lessons in a book. Requires a query. All writing done on assignment. "Prospective writers should indicate age level interest and sample assignment will be forwarded." Accepts computer submissions in any software. Reports in 90 days. Pays 3 cents per word.

CHRISTIAN LITERATURE CRUSADE, P.O. Box 1449, Fort Washington, PA 19034. (215) 542-1242. Fax: (215) 542-7580. Ken Brown, editor. Publishes 6 original paperbacks yearly.

☐ Christian Literature Crusade needs books on prayer, devotions and meditation, biographies, autobiographies.

Prefers outline/synopsis/sample chapters. Accepts some computer submissions. Pays royalties of 5 to 10 percent on retail price. Occasionally makes advances. Free catalog and author guidelines for SASE.

CHRISTIAN PUBLICATIONS, 3825 Hartzdale Drive, Camp Hill, PA 17011. (717) 761-7044. Fax: (717) 761-7273. Jonathan Graf, editor. Publishing arm of the Christian and Missionary Alliance Church. Publishes 24 originals yearly, mostly paperback.

☐ Christian Publications addresses an Evangelical audience of all ages. Needs books that deal with "general Christian living" topics and that "stimulate the reader to a deeper walk with Jesus Christ." Does some romance and historical fiction.

Length averages 160 to 200 pages. Prefers a query. Accepts outline/synopsis/sample chapters. Accepts photocopies. Reports in 2 to 3 months. Pays varied royalties. Sometimes gives advances and makes outright purchases. Free catalog and author guidelines for SASE.

CHRISTOPHER PUBLISHING HOUSE, 24 Rockland Street, Hanover, MA 02339. (617) 826-7474. Fax: (617) 826-5556. Nancy Lucas, editor. Publishes 6 to 8 originals of religious interest annually. These books are mostly hardcover.

☐ Christopher Publishing House serves an adult audience from all backgrounds. Needs trade books that "range from A to Z" in topic. Religious topics include how-to, self-help, marriage and family, parenting, social issues, biography and autobiography, prayer, textbooks, humor, and gift books. Also uses books of poetry, photographs, and illustrations.

Book length averages 160 pages. Prefers complete manuscript. Reports in 4 to 6 weeks. Pays varied royalties on net sales. No advances or outright purchases. Free catalog and author guidelines for SASE.

CISTERCIAN PUBLICATIONS, WMU Station, Kalamazoo, MI 49008. (616) 387-8920. Fax: (616) 387-8921. E. Rozanne Elder, editor. Publishing arm of the Order of Cistercians of the Strict Observance, American Region. Publishes 8 to 10 originals and reprints annually, hardcover and paperback.

☐ Cistercian Publications addresses an adult audience of scholars and laity with an Orthodox or Roman Catholic background.

COLLEGE PRESS PUBLISHING COMPANY, 233 West Third Street, Box 1132, Joplin, MO 64802. (800) 289-3300. Fax: (417) 623-8250. John Hunter, editor. A publisher of the Christian Church/Church of Christ. Publishes 25 originals and reprints annually, 50 percent hardback.

☐ College Press addresses an audience of Evangelical adults and senior adults, scholars, clergy, and laity. Interested in Bible studies, Christian fiction, nonfiction on current issues, self-help, recovery, reference books. Fiction should be historical or contemporary.

Average length 300 pages. Prefers a query and outline/synopsis/sample chapter submissions. IBM computer submissions acceptable. Reports in 2 months. Pays 10 percent royalty on wholesale price. No advances. Free catalogs and author guidelines available for SASE.

COMPANION PRESS, 167 Walnut Bottom Road, Shippenburg, PA 17257. (717) 532-3040. Fax: (717) 532-9291. Keith Carroll, Larry Walker, and Tom Gardner, editors. Publishes 38 religiously oriented originals and reprints yearly, mostly paperback. Imprint, Destiny Image Books.

☐ Companion Press addresses an adult audience from all Christian backgrounds. Needs books on a wide variety of topics: how-to, self-help, marriage and family, parenting, recovery, social issues, biography and autobiography, prayer, devotions and meditations, Bible studies, textbooks, references, humor, poetry, and gift books. Fiction needs include mainstream, mystery, romance, adventure, historical, and contemporary. Also does some curriculum, audiovisuals, photographs, and illustrations.

Prefers complete manuscript. Accepts photocopies, simultaneous and computer submissions. Reports in 4 weeks. Pays varied royalties. Free catalog and author guidelines for SASE.

COMPCARE PUBLISHERS, 2415 Annapolis Lane, Minneapolis, MN 55441. (612) 559-4800. Fax: (612) 559-2415. Nathan Unseth, editorial director; Rochelle Gloege, editorial assistant. Publisher of Comprehensive Care Corporation, producers of recovery and emotional health resources in a biblical context. Publishes paperback originals and reprints for an Evangelical, mainline Protestant audience of youth and adults.

☐ Compcare Publishers seeks books on self-help, marriage/family, recovery, devotions and meditations, humor, and gift/coffee table books.

Prefers outline/synopsis/sample chapter submissions. Reports in 8 weeks. Pays advances up to $1,000. Free catalogs and author guidelines available for SASE.

CONCORDIA PUBLISHING HOUSE, 3558 South Jefferson Avenue, St. Louis, MO 63118. (314) 268-1000. Fax: (314) 268-1329. David V. Koch, chief editor of books. Other editors include: Bruce Camelon, theology books; Wil Rosin, contemporary theology; Ruth Geisler, children, youth, family books. The publishing arm of the Lutheran Church—Missouri Synod. Publishes 50 to 60 books annually for a conservative, mainline Protestant audience of all ages. Readers are both laity and scholars.

☐ Concordia Publishing is looking for adult nonfiction on how-to, marriage and family, parenting, social issues, prayer, devotions, Bible study, curriculum, reference works;

children's ethnic books and picture books. Does some children's fiction and audio-visuals.

Prefers query and outline/synopsis/sample chapter submissions. Pays 8 to 10 percent royalty on the retail price. Some advances. Free catalogs and author guidelines available for SASE.

CONTEMPORARY DRAMA SERVICE. See MERIWETHER PUBLISHING, LTD.

DAVID C. COOK PUBLISHING COMPANY. See CHARIOT FAMILY PUBLISHING.

CORIZON HOUSE PUBLISHERS. See CHRISTIAN PUBLICATIONS.

CORNELL UNIVERSITY PRESS, P.O. Box 250, 124 Roberts Place, Ithaca, NY 14851. (607) 257-7000. Fax: (607) 257-3552. Bernhard Kendler and Roger Hayden, editors. A publisher of scholarly materials of broad, nonsectarian, academic interest. Publishes 6 to 8 hardback originals annually.

☐ Cornell University Press is looking for scholarly books in literary, philosophical, historical, and religious studies.

Average length, 100,000 words. Prefers a query and outline/synopsis/sample chapter submissions. Reports in 3 months. Pays some advances and royalties of 5 to 10 percent on the retail price. Free catalogs and author guidelines available for SASE.

COVENANT PUBLISHERS, Box 26361, Philadelphia, PA 19141. (215) 638-4324. Dr. Matthew Sasiku, editor. Publishes 2 religiously oriented paperbacks annually for an adult, mainline Protestant readership.

☐ Covenant Publishers is interested in books on "Christian living" topics. Average length, 250 pages. Prefers complete manuscripts. Accepts WordPerfect submissions. Pays 10 percent royalties on the wholesale price. No advances. Reports in 2 weeks. Free catalogs available for SASE.

COWLEY PUBLICATIONS, 28 Temple Place, Boston, MA 02111. Cynthia Shattuck, editor. An Episcopal Church–related publisher sponsored by the Society of St. John the Evangelist of Cambridge, Massachusetts. Publishes 14 books annually, both originals and reprints, mostly paperback.

☐ Cowley Publications addresses an audience of clergy and scholars with a mainline Protestant background. Seeks books on spirituality (especially Anglican), pastoral concerns, Christian education, liturgy, biblical studies, and books about Christianity and culture.

Prefers outline/synopsis/sample chapters. Accepts computer submissions in Word-Perfect. Average royalty 7.5 percent on the retail price. No advances. Free catalogs available.

CREDO PUBLISHING CORPORATION, Box 3175, Langley, BC, V3A 4R5 Canada. Jocelyn Cameron, acquisitions editor. Publishes 3 to 6 paperbacks yearly.

☐ Credo Publishing addresses an Evangelical audience of all ages, clergy, and laity. Needs biography, autobiography, meditations, reference, theology. Interested in doing more children's books.

Average adult book length is 112 to 350 pages. Prefers proposal with outline/sample chapters. Accepts simultaneous submissions. Reports in 90 days. Pays royalties of 7 to 10 percent. Makes advances. Free guidelines for SASE.

CROSSROAD PUBLISHING COMPANY, 370 Lexington Avenue, New York, NY 10017. (212) 532-3650. Fax: (212) 532-4922. Michael Leach, publisher; Robert T. Heller and Frank

Oveis, editors. Independent publishers with Liberal, Roman Catholic orientation. Produces 50 originals and reprints annually, 50 percent hardback.

□ Crossroad Publishing Company needs books for an adult readership, clergy, scholars, and general laity, on "spirituality, ministry, theology, religious and biblical studies, liturgy, women's studies, world religions." Also interested in self-help, prayer, social issues, and reference books.

Average length 50,000 to 75,000 words. Accepts either a complete manuscript or an outline/synopsis/sample chapters. Computer submissions acceptable in any software. Free catalogs and author guidelines available for large-size SASE.

CROSSWAY BOOKS, 1300 Crescent Street, Wheaton, IL 60187. (708) 682-4300. Jan P. Dennis, editor. Submit manuscripts to "Acquisitions Dept." A division of Good News Publishers. Releases 45 originals yearly, mostly paperback.

□ Crossway Books aims at an Evangelical audience of children, youth, and adults (clergy and laity). Nonfiction topics include marriage and family, social issues, Bible studies, and other contemporary concerns to Christians. Also publishes mainstream, mystery, romance, adventure, and contemporary fiction for adults.

Prefers outline/synopsis/sample chapters. Accepts simultaneous submissions. Reports in 4 to 8 months. Royalties and advances negotiable. Catalogs and guidelines for $1.

CSS PUBLISHING COMPANY, 628 South Main Street, P.O. Box 4503, Lima, OH 45804. (419) 227-1818. Fax: (419) 228-8184. Fred Steiner, editor. Publishes 52 original paperbacks annually with a Protestant orientation.

□ CSS Publishing seeks nonfiction books on marriage, parenting, recovery, prayer, devotions, Bible studies, humor, reference subjects. Especially interested in sermons, chancel dramas, seasonal worship services, and other congregational resources. Call for specific details. No fiction or poetry.

Prefers complete manuscripts. Accepts photocopies, simultaneous and computer submissions. Reports in 3 months. No advances. Some outright purchases. Free catalogs and author guidelines available for SASE.

DESTINY IMAGE BOOKS. See COMPANION PRESS.

DIMENSION BOOKS, Box 811, Denville, NJ 07834-0811. (201) 627-4334. Thomas P. Coffey, editor. Publishes 20 originals and reprints yearly, 75 percent paperback.

□ Dimension Books addresses an adult audience of Liberal Roman Catholics. Needs how-to's, self-help, recovery, social issues, prayer, devotions and meditations, Bible studies, textbooks, references, poetry.

Most manuscripts are 150 pages or more. Prefers a query. Reports in 2 weeks. Pays 10 percent royalty on list price. Advances up to $1,000.

DIMENSIONS FOR LIVING, P.O. Box 801, Nashville, TN 37202. (615) 749-6301. Fax: (615) 749-6512. Mary Catherine Dean, senior editor. Submit to Sally Sharpe, Patricia Augustine, or Marvin Cropsey, editors. A new imprint from The United Methodist Publishing House. Publishes 12 to 15 originals yearly, mostly paperback.

□ Dimensions for Living addresses a youth and adult Christian audience. Nonfiction books "inspire average laypersons in their lives and ministries. They offer a Christian perspective on topics that relate to daily life." No fiction. See also entry for Abingdon Press.

Requires a query before manuscript is submitted. Reports in 6 to 8 weeks. Pays varied royalties on the retail price. Sometimes makes outright purchases. Free author guidelines for SASE.

EDUCATIONAL MINISTRIES, 165 Plaza Drive, Prescott, AZ 86303. (602) 771-8601. Fax: (602) 771-8621. Robert Davidson, editor. Annually publishes 10 paperback originals on Christian education subjects.

☐ Educational Ministries addresses a mainline Protestant audience. Needs books dealing with Christian education topics.

Book length averages 40 to 100 pages. Prefers a complete manuscript. Reports in 3 months. Pays 10 percent royalty on the retail price. Outright purchases of $500. Free catalog and author guidelines for 9 × 12 SASE and $1 postage.

WILLIAM B. EERDMANS PUBLISHING COMPANY, 255 Jefferson Avenue, SE, Grand Rapids, MI 49503. (616) 459-6540. Jon Pott, editor. Submit children's manuscripts to Amy Eerdmans. Publishes 85 titles yearly, mostly originals.

☐ Eerdmans publishes books for an audience of all ages, but primarily for general laity, scholars, and clergy with a Protestant background. Needs "books of a religious nature for the educated non-specialist." Especially interested in "the areas of women's studies, spirituality, family, religious history, and social issues." Also publishes textbooks and some children's picture books.

Prefers to work with authors rather than agents. Accepts outline/synopsis/sample chapters. Photocopies acceptable. Pays royalties of 7 to 10 percent on retail price. Free guidelines and catalogs available.

EVANGELICAL TRAINING ASSOCIATION, Box 327, 110 Bridge Street, Wheaton, IL 60187. (708) 668-6400. Fax: (708) 668-8437. Richard Patterson, president. A publisher of 1 or 2 paperback books annually for an Evangelical readership.

☐ Evangelical Training Association books are Bible and ministry-oriented manuals for use in training adult volunteers for ministry.

All books are 96 pages, 12 chapters. Queries are required. Accepts computer submissions in WordPerfect. No royalties. Outright purchases for $1,000 to $2,000. Reports in 4 to 6 weeks. Free guidelines available for SASE.

EVERGREEN COMMUNICATIONS, INCORPORATED, 301 West Rising Street, P.O. Box 220, Davison, MI 48423. (313) 658-1143. Fax: (313) 653-0226. Robert and Mary Busha, publishers. A nondenominational publisher releasing 8 to 10 originals and reprints yearly, mostly paperback.

☐ Evergreen Communications addresses an Evangelical audience of youth and adults. Needs "inspirational and devotional books, both fiction and nonfiction." Topics include 23 areas on all aspects of family life, life in the workplace, and the single life. Especially interested in books on "coping with grief, joblessness, relationships, illness-injury, and death." Fiction needs include mainstream, romance, and adventure.

Prefers an outline/synopsis/sample chapters. Send SASE for guidelines on submitting individual devotions in a specified pattern. Reports in 6 to 8 weeks. Pays 12 percent royalties on books. For individual submissions payment is in a free copy of the book. Pays advances up to $500.

FOCUS ON THE FAMILY PUBLISHING, 420 North Cascade Avenue, Colorado Springs, CO 80903. (715) 531-3400. Al Janssen and Larry Weeden, editors. Gwen Weising, managing editor. The book publishing arm of the Jim Dobson organization. Publishes 22 originals yearly, mostly hardback.

☐ Focus on the Family Publishing addresses an audience of all ages with a Protestant Evangelical background. Publishes on topics exclusively for families and family members: self-help, how-to, humor, and books that appeal to children and youth.

Average length is 185 pages. Prefers a query before manuscripts or proposals are submitted. Accepts computer submissions. Reports in 8 weeks. Pays royalties and advances of varied amounts. Catalogs and author guidelines available for SASE.

FORTRESS PRESS. See AUGSBURG FORTRESS PUBLISHERS.

FORWARD MOVEMENT PUBLICATIONS, 412 Sycamore Street, Cincinnati, OH 45202. (513) 721-6658. Fax: (513) 421-0315. Charles Long, director and editor. Sponsored by the Episcopal Church, this publisher releases 8 to 10 paperback originals and reprints yearly. Also publishes 30 booklets each year and the daily devotional publication, *Forward Day By Day*.

□ Forward Movement Publications addresses a general readership of adults in mainline Protestant churches. Needs books related to "the life and concerns of the church, especially within the Anglican Communion. Recent subjects have included church history, meditations and spiritual readings, information on current issues" such as drugs and AIDS.

Average length for books is 80 to 128 pages. Booklet length is 4 to 32 pages. Prefers queries. Accepts photocopies and computer submissions after manuscript is accepted. Reports in 1 month. No royalties. Outright purchases on the basis of the length of the manuscript. Catalogs and sample pamphlets for 75 cents postage.

FRIENDSHIP PRESS, 475 Riverside Drive, Room 860, New York, NY 10115. (212) 870-2496. Fax: (212) 870-2550. Audrey Miller, executive director; Margaret Larom, theme materials; Don Parker-Burgard, assistant editor. The publishing division of National Council of Churches of Christ in the USA. Publishes 12 to 20 originals and reprints yearly, mostly paperback.

□ Friendship Press addresses an audience of all ages from all Christian backgrounds. Needs books for programs in mission study for the churches of the National Council, but in addition, several books of general interest especially in the areas of social justice, global issues, and other subjects related to worldwide Christian interests. Also does some children's picture books, audiovisuals, and maps.

Average book length is 120 pages. Prefers complete manuscript. Most theme study books are assigned. Reports in 4 to 6 weeks. Pays standard royalties and advances. Makes some outright purchases. Free catalog and author guidelines for SASE.

FRIENDS UNITED PRESS, 101 Quaker Hill Drive, Richmond, IN 47374. (317) 962-7573. Fax: (317) 966-1293. Ardith Talbot, editor. The publishing arm of Friends United Meeting. Releases 6 originals and reprints yearly, mostly paperback.

□ Friends United Press has a special interest in nonfiction books on "Quaker history, doctrine, and spirituality" as well as biography, autobiography, prayer, devotions, meditations, and textbooks, curriculum. Also publishes some fiction.

Average nonfiction book 200 pages, fiction 120 pages. Prefers a query. Accepts IBM compatible submissions. Pays 7 percent royalty on the wholesale price. Seldom offers advances. Guidelines and catalogs available.

MICHAEL GLAZIER BOOKS. See LITURGICAL PRESS.

GOLD 'N' HONEY BOOKS. See QUESTAR PUBLISHERS.

GOOD NEWS PUBLISHERS. See CROSSWAY BOOKS.

GOSPEL LIGHT PRESS. See REGAL BOOKS.

GOSPEL PUBLISHING HOUSE, 1445 Boonville Avenue, Springfield, MO 65802, (417) 862-2781. Glen Ellard, editor. The publishing house of the Assemblies of God, issuing 20 religious books annually, mostly paperbacks.

☐ Gospel Publishing House issues books for children, youth, and adults, primarily general lay readers of the Assemblies of God Church. The viewpoint of all books must be in harmony with that of the denomination, an Evangelical, Charismatic church. Topics of interest include Bible studies, Christian living, evangelism, healing, Holy Spirit, prophecy, and theology. Publishes some fiction in the realms of adventure, history, and mystery for both juvenile and adult readers.

Manuscripts can be of varying lengths as appropriate for the type of book and reader. Prefers queries with outline/synopsis/sample chapter. Accepts simultaneous submissions. Reports in eight weeks. Guidelines and catalogs available on request. Pays standard royalties.

GREENWOOD PRESS, 88 Post Road West, P.O. Box 5007, Westport, CT 06881. (203) 226-3571. James Sabin and Cynthia Harris, editors. A scholarly publisher specializing in reference books for academic libraries, mostly hardcover.

☐ Greenwood Press is looking for religiously related titles appealing to an academic market. Books should be "academic and appeal to a scholarly audience with sound scholarship and objectivity being as important as the subject."

Average book length 250 to 300 pages. Prefers a query with outline/synopsis/sample chapters. Reports in 3 months. Pays in standard royalties. Free catalog for SASE.

GROUP PUBLISHING, Box 481, Loveland, CO 80539. (303) 669-3836. Fax: (303) 669-3269. Steve Parolini, editor. Publishes 75 paperback originals yearly.

☐ Group Publishing publishes for an audience of teachers and workers with children and youth in all Christian denominations. Materials are curriculum and instructional materials for Christian education in a classroom setting. Also publishes calendars.

Manuscript length ranges from 96 to 120 pages. Prefers a query for all products. Reports in 4 to 6 weeks. Pays 10 percent royalty on net sales. Sometimes advances up to $1,000. Also purchases materials outright. Free catalogs and author guidelines available for SASE.

HARPER SAN FRANCISCO, 1160 Battery Street, San Francisco, CA 94111-1213. (415) 477-4400. Fax: (415) 477-4444. Tom Grady, publisher; John Shopp, senior editor, religious reference, religious trade; John Loudon, senior editor, academic religious; Kandace Hawkinson, editor, feminist, Judaica religious. A division of HarperCollins Publishers. Publishes 80 originals and reprints yearly, 60 percent of them hardcover.

☐ Harper San Francisco addresses readers of all levels of readership, from all religious backgrounds. Interested in "books for the seeker" on a variety of subjects: how-to, self-help, marriage and family, parenting, recovery, social issues, biography and autobiography, prayers, devotions and meditations, Bible studies, textbooks, reference materials, humor, poetry, gift and coffee table books. Also does fiction (mainstream, historical, and contemporary).

Prefers an outline/synopsis/sample chapters. Accepts simultaneous submissions and computer submissions in any format. Reports in 6 to 8 weeks. Pays standard royalties and advances. Free catalog and author guidelines for SASE.

HARRISON HOUSE, P.O. Box 35035, Tulsa, OK 74153. (918) 502-2126. Submit manuscripts to "submissions editor." Publishes 36 originals yearly, mostly paperback.

☐ Harrison House addresses an Evangelical audience from a Charismatic perspective.

Interested in books that "teach Christian doctrine with a Charismatic emphasis." Subjects of interest include how-to, self-help, marriage and family, parenting, prayer, devotions and meditations, Bible studies.

Average book length 160 pages. Requires a query. Accepts outline/synopsis/sample chapters. Accepts simultaneous submissions. Reports in 6 weeks. Pays standard royalties on the wholesale price. No advances or outright purchases. Guidelines for SASE.

HARVEST HOUSE PUBLISHERS, 1075 Arrowsmith, Eugene, OR 97402. (503) 343-0123. Address manuscripts to "Manuscript Coordinator." Publishes 50 books yearly.

☐ Harvest House addresses an Evangelical audience of all ages. Needs "study books, Bible-related material, topical and contemporary fiction and nonfiction with a message that promotes the Gospel. Books that help the hurts of people and nurture spiritual growth." Topics range from evangelism and theology to marriage and family, prayer, and family life. Publishes children's books and some adult fiction (no romance). Does not publish poetry, sermons, or biographies.

Prefers a query and outline/synopsis/sample chapters. Reports in 2 to 8 weeks. Pays standard royalties. Free author guidelines for SASE.

HENDRICKSON PUBLISHERS, INCORPORATED, 137 Summit Street, P.O. Box 3473, Peabody, MA 01961-3473. Dr. Philip H. Anderson, managing editor; Patrick H. Alexander, editor. Publishes 12 religiously oriented books annually for scholars, clergy, and general laity in all theological perspectives. Half are hardback.

☐ Hendrickson Publishers publishes textbooks, biblical studies, and reference books. Average length 250 pages. Reports in 3 months. Catalogs available.

VIRGIL W. HENSLEY, INCORPORATED, 6116 East 32nd Street, Tulsa, OK 74135. (918) 664-8520. Fax: (918) 664-8562. Terri Kalfas, editor. Publishes 5 or 6 originals yearly, mostly paperback.

☐ Virgil W. Hensley addresses an audience of all ages, primarily from a mainline Protestant background. Interested in Christian fiction and nonfiction on a variety of subjects: Bible studies, self-help, marriage and family, parenting, biography and autobiography, and prayer. Fiction needs include: mainstream, mystery, adventure, historical, or contemporary. Also does curriculum.

Average book length 250 to 300 pages. Prefers a query, but accepts an outline/synopsis/sample chapters or complete manuscript. Accepts simultaneous submissions. Reports in 4 to 8 weeks. Pays 5 percent royalties. No advances. Free catalog and author guidelines for SASE.

HERALD PRESS, 616 Walnut Avenue, Scottdale, PA 15683. (412) 887-8500. Fax: (412) 887-3111. David Garber, editor. The book division of Mennonite Publishing House. Publishes 30 originals annually, mostly paperback, for an audience of all ages in all Christian perspectives.

☐ Herald Press seeks "a wide variety of books in the areas of current issues, peace and justice, missions and evangelism, family life, personal experience, juvenile and adult fiction, Bible study, inspiration, church history, Christian ethics, and theology." Books should be "consistent with Scripture in the Anabaptist/Mennonite tradition, honest in presentation, clear in thought, and stimulating in content." Interested in children's books dealing with contemporary topics and picture books.

Prefers a query and book proposal. Accepts computer submissions in most software. Reports in 6 weeks. Pays 10 percent royalty on the retail price, higher for larger sales.

No advances. Free catalogs and author guidelines available for SASE with 60 cents postage.

HOLMAN BIBLE PUBLISHERS, 127 Ninth Avenue N, Nashville, TN 37234. (615) 251-2446. Fax: (615) 251-3752. Trent Butler and Marsha Ellis Smith, editors. A Southern Baptist sponsored publisher of Bible-related materials for an Evangelical, mainline Protestant readership of all ages.

☐ Holman Bible Publishers produces Bible and Bible reference books exclusively. Prefers a query. Accepts computer submissions in WordPerfect or other software. Pays varied royalties. Catalogs and guidelines available for SASE.

HONOR BOOKS, P.O. Box 55388, Tulsa, OK 74155. (918) 585-5033. Submit manuscripts to "Submissions Editor." Publishes 12 originals yearly, 50 percent of them hardcover.

☐ Honor Books addresses an Evangelical audience of Christian business professionals and laity. Seeks books that are "highly motivational" and aimed at business professionals interested in expressing Christian principles in daily life. Potential topics include self-help, marriage and family, parenting, devotions and meditations, Bible studies. Also has a special interest in gift books.

Average book length 192 pages. Requires a query. Accepts photocopies and computer submissions in WordPerfect format. Reports in 6 weeks. Pays standard royalties. No advances or outright purchases. Guidelines available.

IGNATIUS PRESS/GUADALUPE ASSOCIATE, INCORPORATED, 2515 McAllister Street, San Francisco, CA 94118. (415) 387-2324. Fax: (415) 387-0896. Joseph D. Fessio, editor; Caroline Avakoff, editor's secretary. Publishes 45 originals and reprints yearly.

☐ Ignatius Press addresses an Orthodox, Roman Catholic audience of clergy and scholars. Publishes books on a variety of subjects: marriage and family, biography and autobiography, devotions and meditations, textbooks. Also does some audiovisuals and videos.

Prefers a query, but accepts an outline/synopsis/sample chapters or complete manuscript. Accepts photocopies. Pays 8 to 10 percent royalty on the retail price. Advances up to $500.

INHERITANCE PUBLICATIONS, Box 154, Neerlandia, AB, T0G 1R0 Canada. (403) 674-3949. Roelof A. Janssen, editor. Annually publishes five paperbacks of religious interests.

☐ Inheritance Publications addresses an audience of all ages primarily from a Reformed Church background. Needs books on church history, theology, Bible studies, biography, and some historical fiction. Pays royalties and advances.

INTERVARSITY PRESS, P.O. Box 1400, 5206 Main Street, Downers Grove, IL 60515. (708) 964-5700. Fax: (708) 964-1251. Andrew T. LePeau, editorial director. The publishing arm of InterVarsity Christian Fellowship, a campus ministry, headquartered in Madison, Wisconsin. An interdenominational publisher of 70 titles annually for all ages. Most are paperback.

☐ InterVarsity Press publishes "books for the Christian market that fill empty niches with quality books that help people grow personally. This includes Bible study materials and reference books." Also publishes children's picture books.

Average length 120 to 220 pages. Prefers outline/synopsis/sample chapters. Pays negotiable royalties on retail price. Advances negotiable. Some outright purchases. Works with both agents and writers. Reports in 10 weeks. Free catalogs and author guidelines available for 9 × 12 SASE with 5 first-class stamps.

BOB JONES UNIVERSITY PRESS, LIGHT LINE BOOKS, 1500 Wade Hampton Boulevard, Greenville, SC 29614. (803) 242-5100, ext. 4311. George Collins, editor. Submit to Gloria Repp. Publishes 6 originals and reprints yearly, mostly paperback.

☐ Bob Jones University Press addresses a Conservative, Evangelical audience of various ages. Needs adult books of history, biography, and humor. Also interested in realistic fiction (mystery, adventure, historical). Children's books and youth books, both fiction and nonfiction, should "have a good moral tone."

Average adult book length is 15,000 to 30,000 words. Prefers queries and outline/synopsis/sample chapters. Accepts IBM compatible submissions. Reports in 2 months. Pays no advances or royalties. Makes outright purchases up to $1,000. Free catalog and author guidelines for SASE.

JUDSON PRESS, Box 851, Valley Forge, PA 19482-0851. (215) 768-2118. Fax: (215) 768-2056. Mary Nicol, editorial manager; Kristy Pullen, editor. The publishing arm of the American Baptist Churches USA. Produces 5 to 15 originals and reprints annually, mostly paperback. Audience is all ages from all Christian perspectives.

☐ Judson Press looks for practical books for local church leaders and members, especially the African-American Church, books on Baptist history, polity, and practice, how-to's, marriage/family, social issues. No fiction.

Prefers a query with outline/synopsis/sample chapters. Reports in 6 months. Pays varied royalties and advances. Free catalogs and author guidelines available for SASE.

KINDRED PRESS, #4, 169 Riverton Avenue, Winnipeg, MB, R2L 2E5 Canada. (204) 669-6575. Fax: (204) 654-1685. Marilyn Hudson, editor. Publishing arm of the Mennonite Brethren Conference, which releases 3 paperback originals and reprints yearly.

☐ Kindred Press addresses an interdenominational, Evangelical audience. Nonfiction needs include Bible studies, curriculum, biography, and autobiography. Also publishes fiction for adults. Especially looking for children's books and devotionals. No history.

Prefers proposal and outline/synopsis/sample chapters. Accepts simultaneous submissions. Payment schedule under consideration. Reports in 6 to 8 weeks. Free author guidelines for SASE.

KINGSWOOD BOOKS, 2495 Lawrenceville Highway, Decatur, GA 30033. (404) 636-6001. Fax: (404) 636-5894. Rex Matthews, editor. Submit manuscripts to Ulrike Guthrie or Robert Ratcliff. A publisher whose specialty is Wesleyan and Methodist books. Publishes 6 original paperbacks yearly. An imprint of The United Methodist Publishing House.

☐ Kingswood Books addresses an audience of scholars. Publishes monographs in Wesleyan and Methodist studies only. Requires a query. Reports in 12 weeks. Pays varied advances and royalties. Some outright purchases.

JOHN KNOX PRESS. See WESTMINSTER PRESS.

KREGEL PUBLICATIONS, Box 2607, Grand Rapids, MI 40501. (616) 451-4775. Fax: (616) 459-6049. Al Bryant, editor. Publishes 45 religiously oriented, mostly paperback, books annually for an audience of clergy, scholars, and general laity.

☐ Kregel Publications looks especially for Bible study related books of prayer/meditation, textbooks, reference materials, biography/autobiography.

Prefers a query and outline/synopsis/sample chapters. Pays 10 percent royalty on the wholesale price.

KRIEGER PUBLISHING COMPANY, Box 9542, Melbourne, FL 32902. (407) 724-9542. Fax: (407) 951-3671. Mary Roberts, editor. Publishes 1 or 2 originals and reprints yearly, mostly hardcover textbooks.

☐ Krieger Publishing addresses an adult audience of scholars. Needs books "that have originated as reprints of adult education titles based in religion." Primarily interested in books that deal with social issues related to religion.

Prefers a complete manuscript or outline/synopsis/sample chapters. Free catalog and author guidelines for SASE.

LIBRA PUBLISHERS, INCORPORATED, 3089C Clairemont Drive, Suite 383, San Diego, CA 92117. (619) 571-1414. William Kroll, editor. Publishes 3 to 5 religiously oriented originals yearly, mostly hardback.

☐ Libra aims at a general adult audience with a mainline Protestant background. Open to fiction and nonfiction in all categories. Prefers complete manuscript. Reports in 2 to 3 weeks. Pays 10 to 15 percent royalties on the retail price. No advances. Catalogs and author guidelines available for $1.50 and SASE.

LIFE CYCLE BOOKS, P.O. Box 420, Lewiston, NY 14092. (416) 690-5860. Fax: (416) 690-5860. Paul Broughton, editor. Publishes 1 to 3 paperback originals and reprints yearly.

☐ Life Cycle Books addresses a youth and adult general audience from all Christian backgrounds. Publishes books, pamphlets, and brochures relating to "pro-life and pro-family topics." All materials are biblically based discussions of marriage and family related issues. No fiction.

Prefers either a query or a complete manuscript. Reports in 6 weeks. Pays varied royalties. Offers advances of $100 to $300. Outright purchases of brochure manuscripts up to $250. Free catalog and author guidelines for SASE.

LIFEJOURNEY BOOKS. See CHARIOT FAMILY PUBLISHING.

LIGUORI PUBLICATIONS, One Liguori Drive, Liguori, MO 63057-9999. (314) 464-2500. Paul J. Coury, editor. Submit manuscripts to Kass Dotterweich, Audrey Vest, or Patrick Kaler. A publisher of Redemptionists, Roman Catholic order. Publishes paperback originals for clergy, general laity, all ages.

☐ Liguori Publications "produces pastoral, doctrinal, biblical, self-help and educational materials in language that speaks to the contemporary Christian—books targeted to both parishes and individuals." Publishes prayer and devotional books, Bible studies, 24-page pamphlets, and children's picture books. No fiction.

Prefers outline/synopsis/sample chapters. Accepts computer submissions in Word-Perfect. Reports in 6 to 8 weeks. Pays 10 percent royalty on retail price. Some advances. Also outright purchases for small manuscripts. Free catalogs and author guidelines available for SASE.

LILLENAS PUBLISHING COMPANY, P.O. Box 41927, Kansas City, MO 64141. (816) 931-1900. Paul M. Miller, editor. Publishes the following religiously oriented materials annually: 5 program builders and 15 drama resource books.

☐ Lillenas Publishing is seeking manuscripts for books and booklets that relate to drama for Evangelical and mainline Protestant, some Roman Catholic markets. Program builders are materials for special days such as Christmas. Worship resources should be aimed at specific age groups. Drama resources can be on any topic that has a Christian stance.

Manuscripts of various lengths are needed: one-act plays, full-length plays, sketches and skits, short recitations, and so on. Prospective writers may request a "need sheet."

Accepts simultaneous submissions if informed. Prefers to see full manuscripts. No reprints. Accepts computer submissions. Reports in 8 to 12 weeks. Pays royalties for drama resources; flat fees for program builder materials. Free catalog and author guidelines for SASE.

LION PUBLISHING, 1705 Hubbard Avenue, Batavia, IL 60510. (708) 879-0707. Robert Klausmeier, editor. Submit manuscripts to Bob Bittner, assistant editor. Publishes 15 hardback originals yearly. A division of David C. Cook Publishing.

☐ Lion "aims to publish a wide range of titles that present a Christian perspective for general readers" on how-to, marriage and family, social issues, biography, and humor. Publishes some children's picture books and fiction (mystery and historical).

Average length for adult books 60,000 to 80,000 words. Prefers complete manuscript, but accepts outline/synopsis/sample chapters. Accepts computer submissions. Reports in 1 to 3 months. Pays varied advances and royalties. Free catalogs and author guidelines available.

LITTLE DEER BOOKS. See STANDARD PUBLISHING.

LITURGICAL PRESS, Collegeville, MN 56321. (612) 363-2213. Fax: (612) 363-3299. Mark Twomey, managing editor. Sponsored by St. John's Abbey, publisher of 120 originals yearly, mostly in paperback.

☐ Liturgical Press addresses an audience of scholars, clergy, and general laity. Needs books on theology, Scripture, monastic studies, liturgy, worship, and spirituality. Also publishes 2 other imprints: Michael Glazier Books and Pueblo Books.

Prefers outline/synopsis/sample chapters. Accepts IBM compatible submissions. Reports in 2 months. Pays 10 percent royalty. Free catalogs and author guidelines available.

LOIZEAUX BROTHERS, INCORPORATED, P.O. Box 277, 1238 Corlies Avenue, Neptune, NJ 07754. (908) 922-6665. Marjorie Carlson, managing editor. Publishes 10 religiously oriented originals and reprints yearly, mostly in paperback.

☐ Loizeaux Brothers addresses an Evangelical audience of adults. Primarily interested in commentaries and Bible study materials. Requires a query. Accepts any major DOS program submissions. No unsolicited material. All acquisitions under contract.

LOYOLA UNIVERSITY PRESS, 3441 North Ashland Avenue, Chicago, IL 60657. (312) 281-1818. Fax: (312) 281-0555. Joseph F. Downey, editor. Values and Ethics imprint, Dr. Rugh McGugan, editor. Publishes 12 to 15 (mostly paperback) originals and reprints annually. The audience is clergy or general laity with a Liberal, Roman Catholic background.

☐ Loyola University Press seeks books of Jesuit studies, spirituality, biography, history, social ministry, theology. Interested especially in interface between theology and literature and the arts. Also publishes on Chicago subjects involving church art, neighborhood, and personalities.

Books average 180 to 230 pages. Prefers a query and outline/synopsis/sample chapters. Accepts computer submissions in Macintosh Word or IBM compatible software. Pays 10 percent royalty on the retail price. Free catalogs and author guidelines available for SASE.

MERIWETHER PUBLISHING, LTD., 885 Elkton Drive, Colorado Springs, CO 80907. (719) 594-4422. Fax: (719) 594-9916. Arthur Zapel, editor. Rhonda Wray, religion editor. Through its imprint subsidiary, Contemporary Drama Service, Meriwether publishes about 5 books and 45 play scripts yearly. They are both originals and reprints, all in paperback.

☐ Meriwether addresses a mainline Protestant audience. Through Contemporary Drama Service, Meriwether seeks drama-related books and materials, children's picture books, and some curriculum.

Accepts complete manuscripts or outline/synopsis/sample chapters. No phone queries. Accepts photocopies, computer and simultaneous submissions. Reports in 1 month. Pays 10 percent royalty on net sales. Sometimes makes outright purchases. Catalogs and author guidelines available for $1.

MOODY PRESS, 820 North LaSalle Boulevard, Chicago, IL 60610. (312) 329-2101. Fax: (312) 329-2144. Submit manuscripts to "Acquisitions Editor." The book publishing arm of Moody Bible Institute. Releases 80 to 90 originals yearly. Sixty-five percent are in paperback.

☐ Moody Press addresses an audience of all ages in all perspectives. Needs nonfiction books on finance, business, counseling, social and contemporary issues, Christian living, marriage and family, parenting, some children's picture books. Fiction needs include mystery, romance, adventure, and historical.

Prefers a query and outline/synopsis/sample chapters. Accepts simultaneous submissions. Reports in 6 to 8 weeks. Pays royalties on the retail price. Guidelines and catalogs available for 9 × 12 SASE.

MOREHOUSE PUBLISHING GROUP, 871 Ethan Allen Highway, Ridgefield, CT 06877. (203) 431-3927. Fax: (203) 431-3964. E. Allen Kelley, director; Deborah Grahame-Smith, senior editor. Publishes 25 originals and reprints yearly, mostly paperback.

☐ Morehouse Publishing addresses an audience of all ages, scholars, clergy, and general laity. Primary market is among members and parishes of the Episcopal church, but also appealing to Roman Catholic and mainline Protestant readers. Needs books that "enhance church life, participation and personal education and enrichment." Nonfiction needs include how-to, self-help, marriage and family, prayer, devotions, Bible studies, curriculum, reference and gift books, children's picture books.

Length (except for juveniles) averages 80 to 200 pages. Prefers query and outline/synopsis/sample chapters. Reports in 6 to 12 weeks. Pays 6 to 10 percent royalty on the retail price. Some advances. Free catalogs and author guidelines available for SASE.

THOMAS MORE PRESS, 205 West Monroe Street (6th Floor), Chicago, IL 60606. (312) 609-8880. Fax: (312) 609-8891. Joel Wells, editor. The book publishing arm of Thomas More Association. Releases 6 to 10 paperback originals yearly.

☐ Thomas More Press addresses an audience of Liberal Roman Catholic and Protestant adults. Needs books on "theology, commentary, reflection, spirituality and reference."

Average length is 40,000 words. Prefers complete manuscript. Accepts outline/synopsis/sample chapters. Reports in 2 weeks. Pays 7.5 percent royalty on retail price. Some advances. Free catalogs and author guidelines available for SASE.

MOTT MEDIA, 1000 East Huron Street, Milford, MI 48181. (313) 685-8773. Address correspondence to Joyce Bohn. Primarily publishes curriculum and curriculum related products.

☐ Mott Media publishes curriculum for "home schools" and other purposes. Also does a series of biographies for children and youth.

Prefers a query. Reports in 12 weeks. Royalties and outright purchases negotiated.

MULTNOMAH PRESS. See QUESTAR PUBLISHERS.

NAVPRESS, P.O. Box 35001, Colorado Springs, CO 80935. (719) 548-9222. Fax: (719) 260-7223. Bruce Nygren, editor; Debby Weaver, submissions editor. Publishing arm of the Navigators. Releases 35 to 40 originals yearly, mostly paperback.

☐ NavPress primarily addresses an Evangelical audience with a mainline Protestant background. Needs books dealing with marriage and family, recovery, social issues, and Bible studies. Does some fiction: mainstream and contemporary. Also does some audio-visuals.

Average book length 200 pages. Must query. No unsolicited manuscripts. Accepts outline/synopsis/sample chapters. Reports in 2 months. Pays royalties based on whole-sale price. Offers varied advances. Free catalog and author guidelines for SASE.

NAZARENE PUBLISHING HOUSE. See BEACON HILL PRESS OF KANSAS CITY.

NEIBAUER PRESS, 20 Industrial Drive, Warminster, PA 18974. (215) 322-6200. Fax: (215) 322-2495. Nathan Neibauer, editor. An independent publisher of 8 religiously oriented paperbacks yearly.

☐ Neibauer Press addresses an Evangelical audience. Primarily publishes how-to books for church leaders and clergy. Also produces calendars, clip art, and church newspapers. Prefers a query. Reports in 2 weeks. Pays royalties on the wholesale price.

THOMAS NELSON PUBLISHERS, Box 141000, Nashville, TN 37214. (615) 889-9000. Darryl Winburne, managing editor; Bruce R. Barbour, editorial director; Ken Stephens, trade editor; Bob Sanford, Bible editor; Phil Stoner, reference books; Jeff Bowden, audiovisuals. Publishes 300 originals, 50 percent of them paperback, yearly.

☐ Thomas Nelson Publishers addresses readers of all ages and Christian backgrounds, but primarily Evangelical and mainline Protestant. Needs nearly every category of religious book and product and range of subjects: how-to, self-help, marriage and family, parenting, recovery, social issues, biography and autobiography, prayer, devotions and meditations, Bible studies, reference books, humor, and gift books. Fiction needs include mainstream, historical, contemporary. Does children's picture books, puzzles, games, and so on. Also does greeting cards, audiovisuals, calendars, and music.

Prefers complete manuscript for fiction, outline/synopsis/sample chapters for nonfiction. Accepts computer submissions on accepted material. Pays standard royalties and advances. Makes some outright purchases. Free catalog and author guidelines for SASE.

NEW HOPE, Box 12065, Birmingham, AL 35202-2065. (205) 991-8120. Cindy McClain, editor. An imprint of the Woman's Missionary Union of the Southern Baptist Convention. Publishes 15 originals and reprints yearly, mostly paperback.

☐ New Hope addresses an audience of all ages on missions. Needs "books with a mission focus (implicit or explicit). Topics include foreign missions, missions and ministry within the US, personal spiritual growth, witnessing, prayer, missiology, global concepts, etc." Does children's story books and mission idea books for young children.

Books average 24 to 100 pages for children, 100 to 300 pages for adults. Also does audiovisuals, curriculum, and textbooks on missiology. Prefers complete manuscript, but accepts outline/synopsis/sample chapters. Accepts computer submissions on manuscripts after acceptance. No phone queries. Pays 10 percent royalty on the retail price. No advances. Some outright purchases. Free author guidelines available for SASE.

NEW LEAF PRESS, P.O. Box 311, Green Forest, AR 72638. Tim Dudley, president. Publishes "conservative testimonial books designed to be edifying to the body of Christ. Also books that will lead people to Jesus."

☐ New Leaf Press addresses a Christian and non-Christian audience from a Pentecostal perspective. Needs books on Pentecostalism, prophecy, prayer, testimonies.

Length is 180 to 300 pages. Does not publish poetry or children's books. Prefers complete manuscript. Pays royalties, but no advances.

NOVALIS, 223 Main Street, Ottawa, ON, K1S 1C4 Canada. (613) 236-1393. Fax: (613) 236-5278. Michael O'Hearn, acquisitions editor. The publishing arm of the University of St. Paul. Produces 18 originals yearly, mostly paperback.

☐ Novalis addresses an audience of mainline Protestants and Roman Catholics of all ages including scholars and general readers. Nonfiction needs include Bible studies, curriculum, devotionals, liturgical aids and books of theology and doctrine. Especially looking for prayer books, materials on revised rites for funerals, and books on marriage and family life.

Average length is 200 pages. Prefers queries or proposals with outline/synopsis/sample chapters. Accepts simultaneous submissions. Reports in 12 weeks. Pays either a flat rate or royalty. No advances.

OLD RUGGED CROSS PRESS, 1160 Alpharetta Street, Suite K, Roswell, GA 30075. (404) 518-1890. Jay Walton and Karen Alford, editors. Publishes 10 originals yearly, mostly paperback.

☐ Old Rugged Cross Press addresses a mainline Protestant, Evangelical audience. Looking for books that "glorify God and help Christians nurture their faith." Nonfiction needs include how-to, self-help, marriage and family, parenting, recovery, social issues, biography, prayer, devotions and meditations, Bible studies, and poetry. Fiction needs include mainstream, adventure, historical, contemporary. Also does audiovisuals.

Average book length is 200 pages. Prefers a query and outline/synopsis/sample chapters. Accepts photocopies and simultaneous submissions. Reports in 2 to 3 weeks. Pays royalty of 10 percent. Advances average $500. Free catalog and author guidelines for SASE.

OPEN COURT PUBLISHING COMPANY, 407 South Dearborn, Suite 1300, Chicago, IL 60605. (312) 939-1500. Fax: (312) 939-8150. David Ramsay Steele, editor. Publishes 4 scholarly, academic books of religious interest yearly, 65 percent of them paperback.

☐ Open Court Publishing addresses a scholarly audience from all religious backgrounds. Nonfiction needs include philosophy, religion, science, psychology, and Asian studies.

Book length averages 350 pages. Prefers a query. Accepts outline/synopsis/sample chapters. Accepts photocopies and computer submissions. Reports in 3 months. Pays varied royalties on the retail price. Advances are $1,000. Free catalog and author guidelines for SASE.

ORBIS BOOKS, Maryknoll, NY 10545. (914) 941-7590. Fax: (914) 945-0670. Robert Ellsberg and Bill Burrows, editors. Publishing arm of the Catholic Foreign Mission Society of America. Publishes 50 originals and reprints yearly, mostly paperback.

☐ Orbis Books primarily addresses a Liberal audience of adults from a Roman Catholic or mainline Protestant background. Seeks "books for scholars and general readers addressing global dimensions of Christianity with a strong Third World emphasis." Interested in a variety of subjects: theology, social issues, devotions and meditations, Bible studies, textbooks, and reference materials.

Prefers outline/synopsis/sample chapters. Reports in 2 months. Pays 10 percent royalty on the wholesale price. Free catalog and author guidelines for SASE.

OUR SUNDAY VISITOR, 200 Noll Plaza, Huntington, IN 46750. (219) 358-8400. Jacquelyn M. Murphy, editor. Publishes 25 books yearly.

☐ Our Sunday Visitor addresses a Roman Catholic audience of clergy and laity. Interested in biography, reference books, devotional reading, biblical studies, and other forms of devotional and instructional material on the Catholic faith.

Average book length 30,000 to 50,000 words. Prefers a query. Accepts simultaneous submissions. No reprints. Reports in 4 weeks. Pays 10 percent royalty on net sales. Negotiates advances.

OXFORD UNIVERSITY PRESS, 200 Madison Avenue, New York, NY 10016. Canadian address: 70 Wynford Drive, Don Mills, ON, M3C 1J9 Canada. (212) 679-7300. Cynthia A. Read, senior editor. Publishes 25 to 30 originals yearly, mostly hardcover.

☐ Oxford University Press primarily addresses an adult audience from a mainline Protestant background. Nonfiction book needs include theology, religious history, Asian religious, Judaica, as well as all areas of American religion.

Average book length 500 pages. Prefers a query with outline/synopsis/sample chapters. Accepts photocopies. Pays 10 percent royalty on net sales.

PACIFIC PRESS, Box 7000, Boise, ID 83707. (208) 465-2500. Fax: (208) 465-2531. Russell Holt, editor. Marvin Moore, acquisitions editor. Publishes 30 original paperbacks yearly.

☐ Pacific Press addresses an Evangelical audience of all ages with a Seventh Day Adventist background. Needs books that deal with "doctrine, inspiration, relationships, health—prefer true stories written in good fictional style." Interested in books on prayer, self-help, recovery, how-to, marriage and family, devotions, Bible study, and curriculum.

Books average 128 to 224 pages. Prefers a query, but accepts complete manuscript or outline/synopsis/sample chapters. Accepts computer and simultaneous submissions. Reports in 2 months. Pays 12 to 16 percent royalties on wholesale price. Advances are $500. Free catalogs and author guidelines available for SASE.

THE PASTORAL PRESS, 225 Sheridan Street, NW, Washington, DC 20011. (202) 723-1254. Fax: (202) 723-2262. Lawrence Johnson, editor. Publishing arm of the Roman Catholic National Association of Pastoral Musicians. Releases 12 paperback originals yearly.

☐ The Pastoral Press addresses a clergy and scholar audience with a Roman Catholic background. Nonfiction book needs include theology and liturgical music, mostly from the Catholic tradition. Also interested in Bible studies, reference materials, and books on prayer.

Average book length 250 pages. Prefers complete manuscript. Pays 10 percent royalty on the wholesale price.

PAULIST PRESS, 997 MacArthur Boulevard, Mahwah, NJ 07446. (201) 825-7300. Fax: (201) 825-8345. Kevin A. Lynch, editor; Donald F. Brophy, managing editor. Other editors: Douglas Fisher, Lawrence Boadt, Maria Maggi, Richard Sparks. Publishes 80 to 100 originals yearly, mostly paperback.

☐ Paulist Press is a Roman Catholic oriented press that addresses an audience of all ages, all Christian backgrounds, and some Jewish. Seeking books in many categories: "adult education, Bible Study, ecumenism, family life, healing, church history, Jewish/Christian dialogue, liturgy/worship, pastoral ministry, personal growth, philosophy, prayer and spirituality, religious education, social issues, theology, and world missions." Also does books for children and youth.

Book length varies according to age level and need. Prefers a query. Accepts outline/synopsis/sample chapters. Reports in 4 to 6 weeks. Pays 10 percent royalty on the retail price. Pays advances of $500. Free catalog and author guidelines for SASE.

PELICAN PUBLISHING COMPANY, INCORPORATED, 1101 Monroe St., P.O. Box 189, Gretna, LA 70053. (504) 368-1175. Nina Kooij, editor. Publishes 2 religiously oriented hardback originals annually.

☐ Pelican is interested in books aimed at an evangelical audience of general laity with a Southern Baptist background. Needs inspirational and life guidance books.

Average length is 100 printed pages. Query required. No simultaneous submissions. Reports in 1 month. Pays 10 percent royalty on the wholesale price. Some advances. Free guidelines available for SASE.

PENN STATE PRESS, Barbara Building, Suite C, University Park, PA 16802. (814) 865-1327. Fax: (814) 963-1408. Philip Winsor, editor. Publisher sponsored by Pennsylvania State University. Releases 10 religiously oriented originals (hardcover) and reprints (paperback) yearly.

☐ Penn State Press addresses a scholarly audience from all religious backgrounds. Needs works of original academic scholarship dealing with issues of relevance to the Christian message in a global setting. Interested in scholarly material only.

Average book length 200 to 300 pages. Reports in 2 to 3 weeks on queries, 2 to 4 months on manuscripts. Pays up to 10 percent royalty on the wholesale price. Rarely offers advances. Free catalog and author guidelines for SASE.

PICKWICK PUBLICATIONS, 4137 Timberlane Drive, Allison Park, PA 15101. (412) 487-2159. Fax: (412) 487-8862. Dikran Y. Hadidian, editor. Publishes 5 paperback originals or reprints yearly.

☐ Pickwick Publications addresses an audience of scholars and clergy from all perspectives. Needs nonfiction books on church history, biblical studies, and theology. Pays 8 to 10 percent royalty on the retail price. Free author guidelines available for SASE.

PILGRIM PRESS/UNITED CHURCH PRESS, 700 Prospect Avenue, E, Cleveland, OH 44115-1100. (216) 736-3725. Fax: (216) 736-3703. Richard E. Brown, editorial director. The publishing arm of the United Church of Christ. Publishes 15 to 20 originals and reprints yearly, mostly paperback.

☐ Pilgrim Press addresses an adult audience from a Liberal mainline Protestant background. Especially looking for books dealing with ethics and social issues. Needs biography, textbooks, and books of children's sermons.

Prefers an outline/synopsis/sample chapters. Accepts computer submissions in WordPerfect software. Pays royalties. Free catalog and author guidelines for SASE.

PILLAR BOOKS AND PUBLISHING COMPANY, 5840 South Memorial Drive, Suite 111, Tulsa, OK 74145. (918) 665-3240. Fax: (918) 663-7690. Nancy Manley and Elizabeth Sherman, editors. Publishes 5 religiously oriented paperbacks yearly.

☐ Pillar Books are "biblically based from a spirit filled perspective and with a scholarly approach." Especially interested in Bible studies and books on marriage and family.

Books average 100 to 200 pages. Prefers a query. Reports in 4 weeks. Pays royalties on the wholesale price. No advances.

PRESCOTT PRESS, P.O. Box 53777, Lafayette, LA 70505. (318) 237-8578. Fax: (318) 237-7060. David England, editor. Publishes 20 paperback originals and reprints yearly.

☐ Prescott Press addresses an Evangelical youth and adult audience. Needs books on conservative, family-oriented subjects: self-help, marriage and family, parenting, recovery, social issues. Also needs fiction: adventure, historical, and contemporary.

Average length is 20,000 to 50,000 words. Prefers outline/synopsis/sample chapters. Accepts IBM compatible submissions. Reports in 8 weeks. Pays 10 percent royalty on the wholesale price. Free catalogs and author guidelines available for SASE.

PRINCETON UNIVERSITY PRESS, 41 William Street, Princeton, NJ 05840. (606) 452-4900. Sanford G. Thatcher, editor. Publishes 12 religiously oriented paperbacks yearly.

☐ Princeton University Press addresses an academic audience. Publishes nonfiction books "that make an original contribution to scholarship." Books should be based on original research. Interested primarily in biography, history, biblical studies, archeology, philosophy of religion, comparative religion, and Kierkegaard studies.

Average length 400 pages. Prefers a query. Interested in reprints. Sometimes accepts simultaneous submissions. Reports in 2 weeks on prospectus; 1 to 4 months on manuscripts. Hardcover royalties vary from 10 percent on first editions to 15 percent for larger sales. Paperback royalties vary from 5 percent to 7 percent. Sometimes pays advances. Free catalog and author guidelines for SASE.

PUEBLO BOOKS. See LITURGICAL PRESS.

QUESTAR PUBLISHERS, Box 1720, Sisters, OR 97759. (503) 549-1144. Fax: (503) 549-2044. Thomas Womack, vice-president, editorial. Publishes two imprints: "Multnomah" books for adults and "Gold 'n' Honey" for children. Publishes 50 or more titles yearly.

☐ Questar Publishers serves an Evangelical audience of all ages and all types of readers. A 1992 combination with former Multnomah Press of Portland, is looking for adult books that are biblically based. Interested in a broad range of topics on Christian living: how-to, self-help, marriage and family, parenting, social issues, prayer, devotions, and so on. Interested in gift books, but no reference books or poetry. Also seeks historical and contemporary fiction for adults. The "Gold 'n' Honey" children's books continues the line begun by Questar.

Average length for adult books 180 to 200 pages. Prefers a query/proposal for all books with an outline/synopsis/sample chapters. Accepts simultaneous submissions. Pays standard royalties and advances. Free catalog and author guidelines for SASE.

RAINBOW BOOKS, INCORPORATED, P.O. Box 430, Highland City, FL 33846. (813) 648-4420. Fax: Same as phone. Betsy A. Lampe, editor; in-home study books, Marilyn Ratzlaff; general topics, Peggy Bryant. Publishes 10 titles annually for an adult audience of Protestant laity.

☐ Rainbow Books is looking for "in-home study titles" and other broad readership books: how-to, self-help, marriage/family, parenting, biography, autobiography. No fiction.

Requires a query. Accepts simultaneous submissions. Reports in 6 to 8 weeks. Pays 6 to 8 percent royalty on the retail price. Some advances. Free catalogs and author guidelines available for SASE.

REALLY READING BOOKS. See STANDARD PUBLISHING.

REGAL BOOKS, 2300 Knoll Drive, Ventura, CA 93003. (800) 235-3415. Fax: (815) 644-4729. Kyle Duncan, editor. A division of Gospel Light Press publishing twelve originals and reprints yearly, 50 percent of them paperback.

☐ Regal Books addresses a conservative adult audience of mainline Protestants. Needs books on prayer, devotions, and meditations, Bible studies.

Average length is 250 to 300 pages. "Since June 1991 Regal Books has accepted no unsolicited manuscripts."

REGINA PRESS, 145 Sherwood Avenue, Farmingdale, NY 11735. (516) 694-8600. Fax: (516) 694-2205. George Malhame, editor. Publishes five originals yearly, 50 percent of them in hardcover.

☐ Regina Press primarily addresses an audience of children ages 3 to 8. Needs biography, prayer, devotions and meditations, and children's picture books.

Requires a query. Accepts an outline/synopsis/sample chapters. Pays varied royalties on the wholesale price. Sometimes offers advances and outright purchases.

REGNERY GATEWAY, 1130 17th Street, NW, Suite 600, Washington, DC 20036. (202) 457-0978. Fax: (202) 457-0774. Jennifer Reist, production editor. Submit manuscripts to Alfred S. Regnery. A general book publisher issuing 2 or 3 religiously oriented titles yearly, 50 percent of them paperback.

☐ Regnery Gateway addresses an audience of scholars and general laity from both Roman Catholic and Protestant backgrounds. Issues 25 secular titles yearly on politics, history, current affairs, biography, and public policy. Religious books should relate to these areas. No fiction.

Average length 200 to 300 pages. Prefers a query with outline/synopsis/sample chapters. Reports in 2 to 3 months. Pays 10 percent royalty on the retail price. Rarely makes advances. Free catalogs and author guidelines available for SASE.

RELIGIOUS EDUCATION PRESS, 5316 Meadow Brook Road, Birmingham, AL 35242. (205) 991-1000. Fax: (205) 991-9669. Dr. James Michael Lee, editor. Submit queries to Nancy J. Vickers, managing editor. Publishes 5 to 6 originals yearly, mostly paperback.

☐ Religious Education Press addresses an audience of scholars and clergy from all theological perspectives. Needs books "related to religious education with solid research and theory underlying practical application on an ecumenical level."

Average length is 250 to 300 pages. Prefers query on all proposals. Pays standard royalties. Free catalog and author guidelines for SASE.

RESOURCE PUBLICATIONS, INCORPORATED, 160 East Virginia Street, #290, San Jose, CA 95112. (408) 286-8505. Kenneth E. Guentert, editor. Publishes 15 originals yearly, mostly paperback.

☐ Resource Publications addresses an audience of Roman Catholic and mainline Protestant scholars and clergy. Needs books on professional resources for ministry. Also does story and drama collections and curriculum.

Average length is 150 pages. Prefers an outline/synopsis/sample chapters. Reports in 3 months. Pays 8 percent royalty on the wholesale price. Free catalogs and author guidelines available for 2 first-class stamps.

RESURRECTION PRESS, LTD., P.O. Box 248, Williston Park, NY 11596. (516) 742-5686. Fax: (516) 746-6872. Emilie Cerar, editor. Publishes 4 paperback originals and reprints yearly.

☐ Resurrection Press addresses a Roman Catholic audience of youth and adults (clergy and laity). Needs books on "spirituality, healing, Christian living, and devotions." Also seeks books on marriage and family, parenting, social issues, prayer, and meditation. Publishes some audiocassettes with teaching and music.

Average length is 100 to 200 pages. Prefers an outline/synopsis/sample chapters.

Accepts computer submissions in WordPerfect software. Reports in 3 to 6 weeks. Pays 10 percent royalty on the wholesale price. Offers advances. Free catalogs and author guidelines available for SASE.

FLEMING H. REVELL PUBLISHING COMPANY, Box 6287, Grand Rapids, MI 49516. (616) 676-9185. Fax: (616) 676-9573. William J. Peterson, editor. A longtime publishing house that's now a division of Baker Book House. Publishes 40 originals, 75 percent of them paperback, yearly.

☐ Fleming H. Revell addresses an adult, Evangelical audience. Publishes books on a variety of subjects: how-to, self-help, marriage and family, parenting, recovery, social issues, prayer, devotions and meditations, Bible studies. Also does fiction: mystery, romance, and historical.

Requires a query. Reports in 30 days. Pays varied royalties and advances.

REVIEW AND HERALD PUBLISHING ASSOCIATION, 55 West Oak Ridge Drive, Hagerstown, MD 21740. (301) 791-7000. Penny Estes Wheeler, editor. Publishes 35 titles yearly, mostly paperback.

☐ Review and Herald Publishing addresses a Protestant audience of all ages, primarily with a Seventh Day Adventist background. Needs books on "practical, inspirational value," books on marriage and family, parenting, recovery, social issues, prayer, devotions and meditations.

Average length is 128 pages. Accepts either a complete manuscript or an outline/synopsis/sample chapters. Accepts computer submissions in WordPerfect software. Pays 15 percent royalty on the net price. Free guidelines available for SASE.

RUSSELL HOUSE PUBLISHING COMPANY, 1545 Pioneer Way, El Cajon, CA 92020. (619) 588-0629. Fax: (619) 588-4384. Paul Russell, editor. Publishes drama, scripts, and musical skits.

☐ Russell House addresses a mainline Protestant, Evangelical audience. Publishes drama with religious orientation.

Prefers 20 pages or more. Reports in 3 months. Pays 10 percent royalty plus royalty from performance rights. Free catalog and author guidelines for SASE.

ST. ANTHONY MESSENGER PRESS, 1615 Republic Street, Cincinnati, OH 45210. (513) 241-5615. Fax: (513) 241-0399. Rev. Norman Perry, editor; Lisa Biedenbach, managing editor. Publishes 12 originals yearly, mostly paperback.

☐ St. Anthony Messenger Press addresses an adult audience of Roman Catholic clergy and laity. Seeks to publish "practical, popular, affordable books that nurture Catholic Christian life in our culture." Categories of books include "aids for liturgy and sacraments; aids to prayer and spirituality; books for understanding theology, Scripture, and the church; parish ministry resources and Franciscan resources; books of poetry." Also produces audiocassettes.

Prefers a query. Accepts IBM compatible computer submissions. Reports in 3 to 5 weeks. Pays 10 percent royalty based on the net price. Offers $600 advance. Free catalog and author guidelines for SASE.

ST. BEDE'S PUBLICATIONS, P.O. Box 545, North Main Street, Petersham, MA 01366. (508) 724-3407. Fax: (508) 724-3574. Sr. Scholastica Crilly, editor. Publishing house of Saint Scholastica Priory releasing 7 to 10 paperback originals and reprints yearly.

☐ St. Bede's Publications addresses a Roman Catholic audience of clergy and scholars. Needs nonfiction books on spirituality, theology, philosophy, biography. The special emphasis of this publisher is on patristics and Benedictine monasticism.

Query required. Prefers an outline/synopsis/sample chapters. Accepts computer submissions with IBM compatibility. Reports in 2 months. Pays 5 to 7 percent royalty on the retail price. Catalogs and author guidelines available for 2 first-class stamps.

ST. MARY'S PRESS, Winona, MN 55987. (507) 452-9090. Stephan M. Nagel, editorial director. Sponsored by the Christian Brothers of Minnesota, 807 Summit, St. Paul, MN. Publishes 6 to 10 paperbacks yearly.

☐ St. Mary's Press has a primary editorial focus on religious education materials for Roman Catholic high school students and their teachers. Terms and contracts are negotiated on an individual basis.

ST. PAUL BOOKS & MEDIA, 50 St. Paul Avenue, Jamaica Plain, Boston, MA 02130. (617) 522-8911. Fax: (617) 541-9805. M. Eileen Heffernan, editor. Publishing arm of the Daughters of St. Paul. Releases 15 paperback originals and reprints yearly.

☐ St. Paul Books & Media addresses an adult Roman Catholic audience and a children's audience preschool through grade 12. Interested in "books with a religious and/or moral orientation, adult religious education, marriage and family life, healing and coping, books on Papal documents." Also does children's Bible story books.

Adult books average 150 to 200 pages. Prefers a query and outline/synopsis/sample chapters. Accepts computer submissions with IBM compatibility. Reports in 8 to 10 weeks. Pays 7 to 13 percent royalties. Offers advances up to $1,000. Free catalog for 9 × 12 SASE with four ounces postage, author guidelines for #10 SASE.

SCARECROW PRESS, 52 Liberty Street, P.O. Box 4167, Metuchen, NJ 08840. (908) 548-8600. Fax: (908) 548-5767. Norman Horrocks, editor. Co-publisher with the American Theological Library Association, Kenneth E. Rowe and Donald W. Dayton, editors; Pietist and Wesleyan studies, David Bundy and J. Steven O'Malley, editors; studies in Liturgical Musicology, Robin Leaver, editor. Scarecrow publishes 10 religiously oriented originals yearly, mostly hardcover.

☐ Scarecrow Press addresses an adult audience of all religious backgrounds. Primarily needs scholarly and reference materials in the specialties just listed.

Prefers queries first, then either complete manuscript or outline/synopsis/sample chapters. Accepts computer submissions on accepted manuscripts. Pays 10 percent royalty on typed copy, 15 percent royalty on camera-ready copy, based on wholesale price. Free catalog and author guidelines for SASE.

SCRIPTURE PRESS, INCORPORATED. See VICTOR BOOKS.

SERVANT PUBLICATIONS, P.O. Box 8617, 840 Airport Boulevard, Ann Arbor, MI 48107. (313) 761-8505. Fax: (313) 761-1577. Ann Spangler, editor. Publishes 40 originals and reprints yearly.

☐ Servant Publications addresses an "ecumenical, charismatic audience of Roman Catholics and Protestants." Needs nonfiction books on how-to, self-help, marriage and family, recovery, parenting, prayer, devotions and meditations. Also interested in mainstream, mystery, and historical fiction.

Average length is 70,000 to 100,000 words. Prefers to work with writers on fiction. Works only with agents on nonfiction. Prefers queries. Pays 10 percent royalty on the retail price. Offers advances. Free catalogs available for SASE.

HAROLD SHAW PUBLISHERS, P.O. Box 567, Wheaton, IL 60187. (708) 665-6700. Fax: (708) 665-6793. Ramona Cramer Tucker, editor. Carol Pleuddemann, Bible study editor. Publishes 30 paperback originals and reprints yearly.

☐ Harold Shaw Publishers addresses an Evangelical audience of youth and adults with a mainline Protestant background. Needs books of "general religious interest and literary value on self-help and biblical study." Subjects include marriage and family, parenting, social issues, prayer, Bible studies, textbooks, and humor. Also looking for mainstream and historical fiction.

Average length is 150 pages. Prefers a query and outline/synopsis/sample chapters. Accepts IBM compatible submissions. Reports in 2 to 4 weeks. Pays standard royalties and advances. Catalogs and author guidelines available for SASE and $1.25.

SHEED & WARD, 115 East Armour Boulevard, Kansas City, MO 64111. (816) 531-0538. Fax: (816) 931-5082. Robert Heyer, editor. A publisher sponsored by National Catholic Reporter releasing 30 paperback originals yearly.

☐ Sheed & Ward addresses a Roman Catholic and Liberal mainline Protestant audience of scholars, clergy, and laity. Needs books and booklets on "theology, ministry, women's studies, prayer, homiletic resources, ethics, bioethics, medical ethics, religious education, AIDS ministry, pastoral counseling, and small group faith-sharing." Also publishes curriculum, religious clip art, and one-page hand-outs.

Average length is 100 to 200 pages. Prefers complete manuscript. For larger projects, outline/synopsis/sample chapters. Accepts most computer software. No simultaneous submissions. Reports in 3 months. Pays 6 percent royalty on the retail price. No advances. Free catalogs and author guidelines available for SASE.

SHEER JOY! PRESS, Rt. 1 Box 110E, Pink Hill, NC 28572. (919) 568-6101. Fax: (919) 568-568-4171. James and Patricia Adams, editors. Publishes one or two religiously oriented paperbacks yearly.

☐ Sheer Joy! Press addresses a mainline Protestant audience. Interested in manuscripts for inspirational books on a variety of subjects and also manuscripts for drama and puppetry.

Average book length 20,000 to 30,000 words. Prefers a complete manuscript. Reports in 3 to 4 weeks. Pays royalties on the retail price.

SHINING STAR PUBLICATIONS, 1204 Buchanan Street, Box 299 Carthage, IL 62321. (217) 357-3981. Fax: (217) 357-3987. Becky Daniel, editor. Publishes 20 paperback originals yearly.

☐ Shining Star Publications addresses an audience of children and adults from all Christian perspectives. Primarily needs "Bible-based activity books for children, supplementary materials for school, Sunday School, clubs, children's church, vacation Bible schools, etc." Also produces posters, puzzles, activity cards.

Prefers a query and outline/synopsis. Accepts computer submissions. No royalties. Makes outright purchases at $10.50 per page. Free catalogs and author guidelines available for SASE.

STANDARD PUBLISHING, 8121 Hamilton Avenue, Cincinnati, OH 45231. (513) 931-4050. Fax: (513) 931-0904. Mark Plunkett, new products director. Diane Stortz, children's editor. Submit manuscripts and correspondence to "Acquisitions Editors" for general books, children's books, or program books. Publishes 100 originals and reprints, mostly paperbacks, annually. Special imprints include Little Deer and Really Reading books.

☐ Standard Publishing addresses an audience of all ages with a Protestant Evangelical background. Needs short stories, activity books centered in the Bible, and puzzle books. Looking for program materials for holidays celebrated in the church. Also publishes resource materials for church leaders and teachers. No poetry or adult fiction.

Prefers queries for all materials. Accepts complete manuscripts for children's fiction. Reports in 2 to 3 months. Pays varied royalties and advances depending on projects. Free catalogs and author guidelines available for SASE.

STARBURST PUBLISHERS, P.O. Box 4123, Lancaster, PA 17604. (717) 293-0939. Fax: (717) 293-1945. Ellen Hake, editorial director. Publishes 10 to 15 paperback originals annually.

☐ Starburst Publishers addresses an Evangelical audience of children and adults. Needs Evangelical, inspirational fiction and nonfiction in "general areas of business, cookbooks, health issues, self-help, parenting, sports, gardening, etc." Also does Bible-oriented juvenile books. Interested in mainstream, romance, and historical fiction.

Average length is 200 pages or 60,000 words. Prefers an outline/synopsis/sample chapters. Reports in 1 month. Pays 6 to 15 percent royalty on the wholesale price. Free author guidelines available for SASE, catalog for 9 × 12 SASE with 4 first-class stamps.

STAR SONG PUBLISHING GROUP, 2325 Crestmoor, Nashville, TN 37215. (615) 269-0196. Fax: (615) 385-2708. Matthew A. Price, editor. Publishes 25 to 30 paperback originals and reprints yearly.

☐ Star Song Publishing addresses an Evangelical audience of youth, scholars, clergy, and general laity with a mainline Protestant background. Needs nonfiction books on marriage and family, parenting, social issues, biography, autobiography, prayer, devotions and meditations, Bible studies, textbooks, references, humor, and gift books. Also wants mainstream, historical, and contemporary fiction. Publishes curriculum and audiovisuals.

Prefers a query with an outline/synopsis/sample chapters. Accepts computer and simultaneous submissions. Reports in 6 to 8 weeks. Pays 15 percent royalty on the wholesale price. Offers advances to $1,500. Free catalogs and author guidelines available for SASE.

STILL WATERS REVIVAL BOOKS, 4710 - 37A Avenue, Edmonton, AB, T6L 3T5 Canada. (403) 450-3730. Reg Barrow, president. A Reformed Church publisher releasing 15 titles yearly, mostly hardcover.

☐ Still Waters Revival Books addresses an audience of all ages from all Protestant backgrounds. Needs biographies, autobiographies, how-to, reference, and children's books. Especially interested in out-of-print titles of Puritan and Reformed thought. Looking for "hard-line Reformed or Reconstructionist works." Accepts simultaneous submissions. Payment variable. No guidelines available.

TABOR PUBLISHING, 25115 Avenue Stanford, Suite 130, Valencia, CA 91355. Cullen W. Schippe, president; Carol Prochaska, managing editor. Publishes 6 to 8 paperbacks annually.

☐ Tabor Publishing addresses an audience of Roman Catholic parishes providing catechetics, resources for personal growth, and parish ministry resources. Wants "books by reputable authors that are directed to a parish audience." Manuscripts vary in length, 75,000 words maximum. Query is required. Reports in 1 month.

TRINITY FOUNDATION, P.O. Box 700, Jefferson, MD 21755. (301) 371-7155. Fax: (301) 371-9201. John W. Robbins, editor. Publishes 6 paperback originals and reprints yearly.

☐ Trinity Foundation addresses an Evangelical audience of clergy and scholars. Needs nonfiction books on doctrine, philosophy, and theology. Also needs biblical studies and textbooks. Produces cassette tapes on the same subjects.

Average length is 200 pages. Requires a query. Reports in 3 months. No royalties or advances. Makes outright purchases. Free catalogs available for SASE.

TRINITY PRESS INTERNATIONAL, P.O. Box 851, Valley Forge, PA 19482. (215) 768-2120. Fax: (215) 768-2056. Harold W. Rast, director. Publishes 20 to 25 originals and reprints yearly, mostly paperback.

☐ Trinity Press International addresses an audience of scholars, clergy, and laity from all backgrounds. Interested in academic and theologically oriented books in all branches of Christian and Judaic studies. Seeks textbooks, biblical studies, books relating to theology, and other disciplines. Does some books on general, popular subjects.

Prefers a complete manuscript or an outline/synopsis/sample chapters. Reports in 8 weeks. Pays 10 percent royalty on hardcovers, 7.5 percent on paperbacks based on the retail price. Advances $500 and up. No outright purchases. Free catalog and author guidelines for SASE.

TRIUMPH BOOKS, 333 Glen Head Road, Old Brookville, NY 11545. (516) 759-7402. Fax: (516) 759-8619. Patricia A. Kossman, executive editor. An imprint of Liguori Publications, formerly part of Gleneida Publications. Publishes 10 originals and reprints yearly, 50 percent hardcover.

☐ Triumph Books addresses an adult audience with a Roman Catholic or mainline Protestant background. Needs books that are "intellectually challenging, dealing with social, cultural, and religious issues that affect the way faith and values are lived out. Also interested in general inspiration, self-help, and recovery books." Works with writers or agents.

Prefers an outline/synopsis/sample chapters. Reports in 3 to 4 weeks. Pays varied royalties and advances based on the retail price. Free catalog and author guidelines for SASE.

TYNDALE HOUSE PUBLISHERS, 351 Executive Drive, Box 80, Wheaton, IL 60189. (708) 668-8300. Fax: (708) 668-6885. Carole Johnson, editorial manager. Publishes 100 originals and reprints, mostly paperback, yearly.

☐ Tyndale House Publishers addresses a conservative, Evangelical audience of all ages. Needs books that "cover a wide range of categories: home and family, Christian growth, spirituality, recovery, devotional, motivational, inspirational, theology, doctrine, general reference and fiction." Also produces Bibles, Bible reference products, calendars, and videos. Does some humor, puzzle books, and various types of adult fiction.

Requires a query for all projects. Accepts computer submissions in IBM compatible software. Works with both writers and agents. Reports in 2 months. Pays 10 to 18 percent royalty on the wholesale price. Pays advances up to $5,000. Makes outright purchases up to $1,000 for some children's stories. Catalogs and author guidelines available for $2.40 postage and a 9 × 12 SASE.

UNITED CHURCH PUBLISHING HOUSE, 85 St. Clair Avenue, E, Toronto, ON, M4T 1M8 Canada. (416) 925-5931. Fax: (416) 925-9692. Peter White, editor. The publishing arm of the United Church of Canada releasing 15 paperback originals yearly.

☐ United Church Publishing House addresses an adult audience with a mainline Protestant background. Needs Bible studies, biographies, autobiographies, devotionals, poetry, reference works, and books on theology, social issues, justice, and women's studies.

Prefers a query. Accepts simultaneous submissions. No reprints. Reports in 4 weeks. Pays 10 percent royalty on the retail price. Some advances. Free author guidelines for SASE.

UNITED METHODIST PUBLISHING HOUSE. See ABINGDON PRESS, KINGSWOOD BOOKS, and DIMENSIONS FOR LIVING.

UNIVERSITY PRESS OF AMERICA, 4720 Boston Way, Lanham, MD 20706. (301) 459-3366. Fax: (301) 459-2118. Jonathan Sisk, editor; Julie Burnham, acquisitions editor; Maureen Muncaster, director of co-publishing. An academic press publishing an unstated number of titles each year, 60 percent of them hardcover.

☐ University Press of America addresses an audience from all religious backgrounds. Interested in scholarly books dealing with Bible studies, social issues, as well as textbooks and reference volumes.

Requires a query. Accepts outline/synopsis/sample chapters. Pays royalty on the retail price.

VALUES AND ETHICS BOOKS. See LOYOLA UNIVERSITY PRESS.

VICTOR BOOKS, 1825 College Avenue, Wheaton, IL 60187. (708) 668-6000. Fax: (708) 668-3806. Linda Holland, senior acquisitions editor. This house publishes 100 originals yearly, mostly paperback.

☐ Victor Books addresses an audience of all ages, all types of readers, primarily from an Evangelical background. Needs nonfiction on how-to, self-help, marriage and family, parenting, recovery, social issues, prayer, devotions and meditations, Bible studies, textbooks, reference materials, and humor. Also does children's picture books and adult fiction: mainstream, mystery, adventure, and contemporary.

Average length for adult books is 230 to 350 pages, children's books 16 to 32 pages. Prefers an outline/synopsis/sample chapters. Accepts simultaneous submissions. Reports in 60 to 90 days. Pays varied royalties and advances. Free catalogs and author guidelines available for SASE.

VICTORY HOUSE, INCORPORATED, P.O. Box 700238, Tulsa, OK 74170. (918) 747-5009. Fax: (918) 747-1970. Lloyd B. Hildebrand, editor. Publishes 5 to 7 originals and reprints yearly, mostly paperback.

☐ Victory House addresses an Evangelical audience of youth and adults. Needs books on a variety of topics: self-help, marriage and family, parenting, recovery, social issues, biography, autobiography, prayer, devotions, Bible studies, reference and gift books. Also interested in mainstream, mystery, and historical fiction.

Prefers to work with complete manuscript. Reports in 8 weeks. Pays flexible royalties on the wholesale price. Offers advances. Sometimes makes outright purchases. Free catalog and author guidelines for SASE.

WALKER AND COMPANY, 720 Fifth Avenue, New York, NY 10019. (212) 265-3632. Fax: (212) 307-1765. Beth Walker, editor of large-print religious books. A general publisher of books in several areas. Religious works are limited to reprints, large-type "inspirational classics" from all faiths and emphases.

☐ Walker and Company aims at a general readership, especially senior adults. Interested primarily in nonfiction, but does some fiction.

WARNER PRESS, P.O. Box 2499, Anderson, IN 46018. (317) 644-7721. Fax: (317) 649-3664. Arlo F. Newell, editor-in-chief. Submit manuscripts to Dan Harmon, book editor. Publishes 15 originals, yearly, mostly paperback.

☐ Warner Press addresses an adult audience of clergy and laity with a Protestant, Evangelical background. Needs books on "Christian education, doctrine, church growth and church history." Topics include self-help, marriage and family, recovery, biography, Bible study, gift books. Also does curriculum, audiovisuals, calendars, and so on.

Prefers a query and outline/synopsis/sample chapters. Reports in 2 weeks. Pays 15 percent royalty on the wholesale price. Few advances. "Warner is not a freelance house, as such, but will look at material submitted."

WELLNESS PUBLICATIONS, Box 2397, Holland, MI 49422. (616) 335-5553. Darrell Franken, editor. Publisher of "health and faith" books. Releases one religiously oriented title annually for the Evangelical audience.

☐ Wellness Publications seeks books on self-help and marriage/family subjects. Prefers to see complete manuscript. Reports in 3 months. Pays 10 percent royalty on the retail price.

WESTMINSTER PRESS/JOHN KNOX PRESS, 100 Witherspoon Street, Louisville, KY 40202-1396. (502) 569-5043. Fax: (502) 569-5018. Davis Perkins, editorial director; Walter Sutton and Alexa Smith, professional and general books; Cynthia Thompson and Jeffries Hamilton, academic books; Harold Twiss, general books. Publishing arm of the Presbyterian Church USA, producing 80 to 100 paperback originals and reprints yearly.

☐ Westminster/John Knox addresses an adult audience of all types of readers from all Christian backgrounds. Needs "academic and professional books that promote dialogue on issues of concern and importance to the religious community." Subjects include self-help, marriage and family, parenting, recovery, social issues, biography, autobiography, prayer, devotions and meditations, Bible studies, textbooks, reference materials, poetry, gift books. Emphasizes ethics and theology.

Average length is 200 pages. Prefers a query and outline/synopsis/sample chapters. Accepts computer submissions. Reports in 2 to 3 months. Pays varied rate royalties and advances. Free catalogs and author guidelines available for SASE.

WINSTON-DEREK, INCORPORATED, 1722 West End Avenue, Nashville, TN 37203. (615) 321-0535. Fax: (615) 329-4824. Brian Reed, editor. Matalyn Rose Peebles, children's books. James W. Winston, nonfiction religious titles. A nondenominational publisher of 55 religiously oriented titles yearly, mostly paperback.

☐ Winston-Derek Publishers primarily addresses an Evangelical audience of all ages. Needs books on social studies, biography, autobiography, Bible studies, textbooks, poetry, children's picture books. "Open to any well constructed work to add to our list." Primary product is "fiction with an emphasis on black studies." Also publishes greeting cards, audiovisuals, black studies, and paintings.

Prefers complete manuscript or outline/synopsis/sample chapters. Accepts photocopies. Reports in 6 to 8 weeks. Pays royalties on wholesale price and advances of $1,000 to $5,000. Some outright purchases. Free catalogs and author guidelines available for $1 postage.

WORD PUBLISHING, 5221 North O'Connor Boulevard, Irving, TX 75039. (214) 556-1900. Joseph Paul, vice-president. Laura Minchew, children's products. Publishes 100 paperback and hardback originals yearly. A division of Thomas Nelson Publishers.

☐ Word Publishing addresses an audience of all ages, scholars, clergy, and laity from a mainline Protestant, Evangelical background. Needs books on how-to, self-help, recovery, marriage and family, parenting, social issues, biography, autobiography, Bible studies, textbooks, reference materials, humor, and children's picture books. Interested in mainstream, adventure, historical, and contemporary fiction. Also produces videos.

Requires a query for all book projects. Pays standard royalties and advances. Free catalogs and author guidelines available for SASE.

YALE UNIVERSITY PRESS, 92 A Yale Station, New Haven, CT 06520. (203) 442-0960. Fax: (203) 432-2394. Charles Grench, editor. The Press also has nine separate editors for subject areas in which it is interested. Address submissions to "Acquisitions Editor" for the departments listed below. Publishes 10 to 15 religiously oriented hardbacks yearly. ☐ Yale University Press addresses an audience of scholars and general laity. Needs books oriented to the scholarly humanities in the areas of economics, law and political science, foreign languages, literature classics, philosophy, poetry, theater, anthropology, archeology, history, women's studies, education, psychiatry, psychology, sociology, science and medicine, music, arts and architecture, geography, landscape studies, and general reference books.

Requires a query. Prefers an outline/synopsis/sample chapters. Reports in 1 to 3 months. Pays varied royalties and advances. Some outright purchases.

ZONDERVAN PUBLISHING HOUSE, 5300 Patterson Avenue, SE, Grand Rapids, MI 49530. Address all manuscripts and correspondence to "Manuscript Review." A division of HarperCollins Publishers releasing 120 originals and reprints yearly, mostly paperback. ☐ Zondervan addresses an Evangelical audience of all ages from a mainline Protestant background. Publishes a wide range of materials. "Trade books include general nonfiction: biography, autobiography, self-help, devotionals (for families), and some adult fiction." Also does books on youth and children's ministry, books for teens (primarily nonfiction), children (primarily mystery and adventure novels), some early reader books. Academic and professional books include college and seminary textbooks, books for clergy and other professionals, Bible study resources and other reference books. Does some audio and video products.

Prefers a query on all projects. Pays negotiable royalties and advances. Free author guidelines for #10 SASE.

FOUR

Writing for the Jewish Market

by Lion Koppman,
author, editor, publicist

In this chapter you will find a comprehensive annotated listing of Jewish periodicals and publishers of Judaica in the United States and Canada. As far as possible, we have described the kind of material each publishes and what each is seeking, especially from free-lance writers.

For obvious reasons, the Christian market is much larger than the Jewish market, but the markets listed here are very diversified. They encompass not only the broad topic of religion, but also history, culture, and the experiences of the Jewish people, and current happenings. The questionnaires and resulting entries reflect this wide diversification. As far as possible, we have also provided space for publishers and editors to describe the particular needs of their houses and periodicals.

Cautions and considerations in writing for a Jewish audience are generally the same as for all writing:

- Have a thorough knowledge of your audience.
- Know how much has already been written on the subject you are working on.
- Do you have a different angle?
- Is your material timely?
- Know the publisher to whom you are sending your manuscript. Take no chances! Query first and send for samples of publications and author's guidelines where available.
- Check your facts.
- Don't overwrite.
- Type your manuscript double-spaced, on one side of the paper only.
- Always include a SASE (self-addressed stamped envelope).

Would-be authors of Jewish-interest books are encouraged to read the excellent introduction to chapter 3 in this volume for procedures to follow in getting their books published. Read " Ten Faults of Book Manuscripts." Then read the list over again. Its points are deceptively simple; writers can save themselves much grief by following these points.

In addition to writing for Jewish periodicals and authoring Jewish-interest books, writers may find that Jewish organizations can use their skills, or they may discover outlets in radio or TV where there are a number of local and network programs devoted to issues of Jewish interest.

In chapter 5 of this book, writers of Jewish material will also find many suggestions for branching out into specialized kinds of writing for the religious market.

Queries relating to and additional information for this chapter are welcome. This information will be incorporated into future editions of *Religious Writers Marketplace*.

PERIODICALS OF JUDAICA

AGADA, 2020 Essex Street, Berkeley, CA 94703. (510) 848-0965. Reuven Goldfarb, editor. A 64-page annual magazine with a circulation of 1,000.

☐ *Agada* addresses adult readers from all Jewish backgrounds. Publishes mostly fiction, poetry, essays, and memoirs relating to the Jewish religious, historical, or cultural experience. Uses graphic art and photographs.

Article length 6,000 words. Prefers complete manuscript. Accepts photocopies. Guidelines for SASE. Reports in 6 weeks to 2 months. Pays in 2 copies of the magazine on publication.

AGENDA, 730 Broadway, New York, NY 10003. (212) 529-2000. Fax: (212) 529-2009. Rabbi Arthur Vernon, editor. A 32-page magazine published 3 times yearly with a circulation of 2,000.

☐ *Agenda* readers are from all branches of Judaism. Publishes material of Jewish interests and concerns with a focus on Jewish education policy.

Articles average 1,500 to 2,000 words. Prefers a query. Accepts computer submissions in WordPerfect. Guidelines and sample copy for SASE. No payment.

AMERICAN JEWISH HISTORY, 2 Thornton Road, Waltham, MA 02154. (617) 891-8110. Fax: (617) 899-9108. Marc Lee Raphael, editor. A 140-page quarterly academic journal. Circulation 3,600.

☐ *American Jewish History* serves an audience of scholars and rabbis in all branches of Judaism. Needs material dealing with all aspects of Jewish Americana. Needs book reviews, photographs, and illustrations.

Prefers complete manuscripts. Accepts photocopies. Sample copy for SASE. No payment.

AMIT WOMAN, 817 Broadway, New York, NY 10003. (212) 477-4720. Fax: (212) 353-2312. Micheline Ratzfers Dorfer, editor. A 32-page magazine published 5 times yearly.

☐ *Amit Woman* primarily serves Orthodox women. Needs material about Israel, Jewish interests and concerns, personalities, Jewish Americana, the Holocaust, and other subjects of general Jewish interest. Uses photographs and illustrations.

Article length 1,000 to 2,000 words. Prefers a query. Accepts computer submissions in Macintosh. Buys first rights. Guidelines for SASE. Pays up to $100 on publication.

BALTIMORE JEWISH TIMES, 2104 North Charles Street, Baltimore, MD 21218. (301) 752-3504. Gary Rosenblatt, editor. A weekly magazine of regional interest.

☐ *Baltimore Jewish Times* looks for high quality material "of interest to a varied intelligent readership, from humor to personality profiles to family issues." Interested in fiction with a Jewish theme, articles on Jewish issues and concerns, personalities, Jewish Americana, Israel, the Holocaust, converts to Judaism, book reviews, art, and photographs.

Article length 750+ words; features may run to 2,000 words. Prefers a query. Sample copies for 60 cents. Reports in 2 weeks. Pays $50 to $100 per article on publication.

B'NAI B'RITH INTERNATIONAL JEWISH MONTHLY, 1640 Rhode Island Avenue, NW, Washington, DC 20036. (202) 857-6645. Jeff Rubin, editor. A 48-page bimonthly magazine with a circulation of 200,000.

☐ *B'nai B'rith* addresses an adult audience from all branches of Judaism. Needs material about Israel, Jewish issues and concerns, personalities, Jewish Americana, the Holocaust, converts, Jewish folklore, and Sephardic Judaism. Uses book reviews, photographs, and illustrations.

Article length 1,500 to 2,000 words. Prefers queries. Accepts photocopies and computer submissions. Buys first rights. Guidelines and sample copy for $2 and SASE. Pays on acceptance.

CCAR JOURNAL, Central Conference of American Rabbis, New York, NY. Submit all manuscript correspondence to Rabbi Lawrence Englander, c/o Solel Congregation, 2399 Folkway Drive, Mississauga, ON, L5L 3N7, Canada. (416) 820-5915. Fax: (416) 820-1956. A 96-page quarterly magazine.

☐ *CCAR Journal* primarily addresses an audience of scholars and rabbis from all branches of Judaism. Needs material on Israel, Jewish concerns and issues, the Holocaust, converts, Hasidism, and Sephardic Judaism. Also uses book reviews and poetry.

Prefers complete manuscript. Accepts photocopies. No payment.

CHURCH AND SYNAGOGUE LIBRARIES, P.O. Box 19357, Portland, OR 97280. (503) 244-6919. Lorraine E. Burson, editor; Charles Snyder, book review editor. A 16- to 24-page bimonthly newsletter published by the Church & Synagogue Library Association. Circulation 3,000.

☐ *Church and Synagogue Libraries* publishes material related to the work of libraries and librarians in Christian and Jewish institutions. Needs news articles, features, and fillers concerning the running of local and regional library associations. Uses photographs and many book reviews.

Article length 250 to 700 words, fillers a paragraph or two, news items of varied length. Prefers complete manuscripts. Uses reprints. Reports in 4 weeks. Sample copy for 9 × 12 SASE and 2 ounces postage.

CLEVELAND JEWISH NEWS, 3645 Warrenville Center Road, Cleveland, OH 44122. Cynthia Dettelbach, editor; Bernice Green and Nina Rothman, assistant editors. A 48- to 63-page weekly newspaper with a circulation primarily in northeastern Ohio and the Cleveland area.

☐ *Cleveland Jewish News* serves a youth and adult audience from all branches of Judaism. Looks for "news items and personal pieces relevant to Jewish causes/observances/problems; analyses of political/economical/social issues in Israel and Jewish communities in Diaspora." Needs book reviews and photographs.

Article length to 4 pages. Prefers a complete manuscript. Guidelines and sample copy for SASE. Reports in 3 weeks. Pays $35 on publication for articles of 3 or more pages.

COMMENTARY, 165 East 56th Street, New York, NY 10022. (212) 751-4000. Fax: (212) 751-1174. Norman Podhoretz, editor-in-chief; Neal Kozodoy, editor. A 64-page monthly magazine published by the American Jewish Committee. Circulation 30,000.

☐ *Commentary* serves an adult audience from all branches of Judaism. Publishes fiction with Jewish themes, material on Israel, and all Jewish issues and concerns. Uses book reviews.

Article length 3,000 to 5,000 words. Prefers a query. Buys all rights. Reports in 2 to 3 weeks. Pays on publication.

CONGRESS MONTHLY, 15 East 84th Street, New York, NY 10028. Maier Deshell, editor. A 24-page magazine published seven times yearly with a circulation of 30,000.

☐ *Congress Monthly* serves an audience of scholars, rabbis, and general adult readers from all branches of Judaism. Publishes a variety of subjects of Jewish interest and concern. Uses book reviews. Must query. Buys first rights only. Pays up to $100 on publication.

CONNECTICUT JEWISH LEDGER, 740 North Main Street, Suite M, West Hartford, CT 06117. (203) 231-2424. Fax: (203) 231-2428. David Abramowitz, editor. A 32-page weekly newspaper with a circulation of 25,000.

☐ *Connecticut Jewish Ledger* addresses a family audience from all Jewish backgrounds. Interested in news and stories related to their region about Israel, personalities, folklore, the Holocaust, and other Jewish issues and concerns. Also prints fiction with Jewish themes. Uses book reviews, photographs, and illustrations. Pays on acceptance.

CONSERVATIVE JUDAISM, 3080 Broadway, New York, NY 10027. (212) 678-8060. Fax: (212) 749-9166. Rabbi Shamai Kanter, editor; Rabbi Jules Harlow, executive editor; Lisa Stein, managing editor. A 96-page quarterly journal published by the Rabbinical Assembly with a circulation of 2,000.

☐ *Conservative Judaism* addresses an audience of Conservative and Reform rabbis and scholars. Needs articles on all issues of Jewish interest and book reviews. Prefers a query. Accepts computer submissions. Payment in copies.

FORWARD, 45 East 33rd Street, New York, NY 10016. (212) 889-8200. Fax: (212) 447-6406. Seth Lipsky, editor; Adam Brodsky, news editor; Philip Gourevitch, arts editor. A 14-page weekly newspaper with a circulation of 15,000.

☐ *Forward* serves a general audience in all branches of Judaism. Needs fiction with Jewish themes, news and features on all Jewish issues and concerns: personalities, Jewish Americana, the Holocaust, converts, Hasidism, Sephardic Jews. Uses book reviews, photographs, and illustrations. Specialties are "political analysis, hard news, reviews of arts, drama, etc."

Article length 800 to 1,000 words. Prefers a query. Accepts photocopies and computer submissions. Buys all rights, only original material. Correspond with the appropriate editor. Payment depends on length of articles and stories.

GREATER PHOENIX JEWISH NEWS, 7220 North 16th Street, Suite G, Phoenix, AZ 85016. (602) 870-9470. Fax: (602) 870-0426. Leni Reiss, editor. A 28-page weekly newspaper with a circulation of 6,000.

☐ *Greater Phoenix Jewish News* serves a general Jewish audience from all branches of Judaism. Interested in news and features on a variety of subjects, especially Jewish Americana and folklore, personalities, and all issues of Jewish concern. The emphasis in all material should be on the contemporary.

Article length 1,000 words. Prefers a query. Accepts photocopies and simultaneous submissions. Guidelines and sample copy for $1. Reports in 1 month. Pays $25 on publication.

HADASSAH MAGAZINE, 50 West 58th Street, New York, NY 10019. (212) 333-5946. Fax: (212) 333-5967. Alan M. Tigay, editor; Joan Michel, associate editor. A 60-page monthly magazine published by Hadassah, the Women's Zionist Organization of America, Inc. Circulation 295,000.

☐ *Hadassah Magazine* addresses an adult audience from all branches of Judaism, mostly women. Publishes a variety of subjects: Israel, Jewish Americana, Sephardic Jews, and other issues and concerns to Jewish women. Uses book reviews and some fiction.

Article length 1,500 words. Prefers a query. Accepts computer submissions in Macintosh and other software. No simultaneous submissions. Buys first rights. Guidelines for #10 SASE, sample copy for 9 × 12 SASE. Pays on publication.

HERITAGE FLORIDA JEWISH NEWS, Box 300742, Fern Park, FL 32730. (407) 834-8787. Jeffrey Gaeser, editor; Jill Hayflich, associate editor. A 12- to 16-page newspaper with a regional circulation in central Florida of 6,000.

☐ *Heritage Florida Jewish News* serves an adult audience from all branches of Judaism. Looks for nonfiction material on all aspects of Jewish life: Israel, Jewish humor, issues and concerns, the Holocaust, personalities, Sephardic Jews, and Hasidism. Uses book reviews, artwork, and photographs.

Article length 500 to 750 words. Sample copies available for 85 cents. Reports in 3 weeks. Pays 50 cents per published inch on publication.

INSIDE MAGAZINE, 226 South 16th Street, Philadelphia, PA 19102. (215) 893-5700. Jane Biberman, editor; Traci Barr, managing editor. a 150-page quarterly magazine with a circulation of 65,000.

☐ *Inside Magazine* addresses an adult audience from all branches of Judaism. Needs material about Israel, personalities, Jewish Americana, Jewish humor, folklore, and issues and concerns of interest to Jews. Uses book reviews.

Must query before submitting a manuscript. Buys first rights. Guidelines and sample copy for SASE. Reports in 1 to 3 weeks. Pays $300 for features, $150 for departments on acceptance.

ISRAEL HORIZONS, 224 West 35th Street, New York, NY 10001. (212) 868-0386. Arien Lebowitz, editor; Becky Rowe, assistant editor. A 32- to 48-page quarterly newspaper published by Americans for a Progressive Israel. International circulation of 5,000.

☐ *Israel Horizons* serves an audience of scholars, laity, and clergy from all branches of Judaism. Interested in articles on Jewish issues and concerns, Israel, the Holocaust, the kibbutz life. Uses poetry and book reviews.

Article length 2,000 to 2,500 words. Guidelines free with SASE; sample copies for $3. Reports in 9 weeks. Pays $50 per article on publication.

JCCA CIRCLE, 15 East 26th Street, New York, NY 10010. (212) 532-4949. Fax: (212) 481-4174. Shirley Frank, editor. A 24-page quarterly magazine published by the Association of Jewish Community Centers, YMHAs and YWHAs camps in the United States and Canada. Circulation 22,000.

☐ *JCCA Circle* addresses an adult audience from all branches of Judaism. Publishes a wide variety of subjects of interest to its constituency in Jewish associations in North America.

Prefers complete manuscript. Accepts computer submissions. No payment.

JEWISH CHRONICLE OF PITTSBURGH, 5600 Baum Boulevard, Pittsburgh, PA 15206. (412) 687-1000. Fax: (412) 687-5119. Joel Roteman, editor. A 40-page weekly newspaper with a circulation of 13,000.

☐ *Jewish Chronicle of Pittsburgh* addresses readers from all Jewish backgrounds. Interested in news and stories about Israel, personalities, converts, the Holocaust, Hasidism, Jewish Americana and humor, and other Jewish issues and concerns. Uses book reviews, photographs, and illustrations.

Article length 500 to 600 words. Prefers a query. Buys one-time rights. Pays on publication.

JEWISH CURRENTS, 22 East 17th Street, Suite 601, New York, NY 10003. (212) 924-5740. Morris U. Schappes, editor. A 48-page monthly magazine published in association with the Promotion of Jewish Secularism, Inc. Circulation 3,000.

☐ *Jewish Currents* addresses a youth and adult audience with a Reform background. The magazine is a "committed and critical voice in the Jewish progressive community." Publishes "articles, reviews, fiction, and poetry pertaining to Jewish subjects or presenting a Jewish point of view on an issue of interest."

Article length 3,000 maximum. Prefers complete manuscript. Reports in 2 months. Pays in 6 copies and a free subscription.

JEWISH EXPONENT, 226 South 16th Street, Philadelphia, PA 19102. (215) 893-5700. Al Erlick, managing editor. A weekly newspaper published by the Federation of Jewish Agencies of Greater Philadelphia, with a national distribution of 70,000.

☐ *Jewish Exponent* is interested in Jewish issues and concerns, personalities, Jewish Americana, Israel, the Holocaust, converts to Judaism, Hasidism, Jewish humor and folklore, Sephardic Jews. Also prints book reviews and photographs.

Article length 500 to 1,000 words. Prefers a query. Sample copies available. Pays on publication: $35 to $100 per article depending on length and subject matter.

JEWISH FRONTIER, 275 Seventh Avenue, (17th Floor), New York, NY 10001. (212) 229-2280. Fax: (212) 675-7685. Nahum Guttman, editor. A 32-page bimonthly newspaper with a circulation of 10,000.

☐ *Jewish Frontier* addresses adults from all Jewish backgrounds. Publishes articles and stories on a number of subjects: fiction with Jewish themes, Israel, the Holocaust, Jewish issues, concerns, and folklore. Uses poetry and book reviews.

Article length 1,000 to 1,500 words. Prefers a complete manuscript. Buys first rights. Sample copy for $5. Reports in 6 weeks. Pays 5 cents per word for articles, $20 for poems, $35 for book reviews on publication.

JEWISH JOURNAL, 601 Fairway Drive, Deerfield Beach, FL 33441. (305) 698-6397. Fax: (305) 429-1207. Andrew Polin, editor. A 40- to 90-page weekly newspaper with a circulation of 145,000.

☐ *Jewish Journal* addresses adults from all Jewish backgrounds. Publishes news and feature articles on issues of Jewish concern and from the region of circulation. Topics range among the following: Israel, Jewish humor, personalities, converts, Hasidism, Sephardic Jews, the Holocaust, Jewish issues and concerns, Americana, folklore. Uses book reviews, photographs, and illustrations.

Article length 500 to 1,000 words. Rights negotiable. Reporting time varies. Pays $10 to $75 on publication.

THE JEWISH NEWS, 27675 Franklin Road, Southfield, MI 48034. (313) 354-6060. Fax: (313) 354-6069. Gary Rosenblatt, editor; Alan Hitsky, associate editor; Phil Jacobs, managing editor. A 132-page weekly newspaper with a circulation of 21,000.

☐ *The Jewish News* addresses a general audience from all Jewish backgrounds. Publishes material on Israel, Jewish humor, personalities, Jewish Americana, the Holocaust, converts, Hasidism, Jewish folklore, Sephardic Judaism, and other Jewish interests and concerns. Uses some fiction, photographs, and illustrations.

Prefers complete manuscript. Accepts simultaneous and computer submissions. Rights negotiable. Sample copy for $1. Reports in 1 month. Pays on publication.

JEWISH POST OF NEW YORK, 57 E. 11th St. (Suite 9, 9th floor), New York, NY 10003. (212) 505-6959. Fax: (212) 505-1224. A 112-page, monthly newspaper with a circulation of 180,000.

☐ *Jewish Post of New York* addresses an adult audience of general readers from all branches of Judaism. Interested in news, especially with a local angle, on Israel, the Holocaust, Jewish humor and Americana, converts, Hasidism and other Jewish issues and concerns. Uses poetry, book reviews, photos and illustrations, also pieces on Jewish humor and folklore.

Articles should be 250 to 500 words and sometimes more. Pays on publication for all rights. Author guidelines and sample copies available on request.

THE JEWISH PRESS, 338 Third Avenue, Brooklyn, NY 11215. (718) 330-1100. Fax: (718) 935-1215. Rabbi Sholom Klass, editor; Steve Walz, editorial director; Shimon Golding, books. A 120-page weekly newspaper.

☐ *The Jewish Press* addresses an adult audience with an Orthodox background, but is also read by members of other branches of Judaism. Publishes a variety of issues and concerns to Jews: Israel, personalities, Jewish humor, book reviews. Uses photographs and illustrations.

Must query before submitting. Guidelines and sample copy for SASE. Payment is variable on publication.

JEWISH QUARTERLY REVIEW, 420 Walnut Street, Philadelphia, PA 19106. (215) 238-1290. Fax: (215) 238-1540. David Goldenberg, editor; Bonnie Blankenship, managing editor. A 196-page quarterly academic journal with a circulation of 1,000.

☐ *Jewish Quarterly Review* primarily addresses an audience of scholars. Publishes scholarly articles about history, culture, and language of Judaism.

Must query before submitting. Accepts computer submissions in WordPerfect. Guidelines and sample copy for SASE. Reports in 6 months. Pays in copies.

JEWISH SPECTATOR, 4391 Park Milano, Calbasas, CA 91302. (818) 591-7482. Fax: (818) 591-7267. Robert Bleiseiss, editor. A 68-page quarterly magazine with a circulation of 7,000.

☐ *Jewish Spectator* primarily addresses scholars from all Jewish backgrounds. Publishes material on Israel and subjects of interest and concern to American Jewish readers. Uses some fiction, book reviews, and poetry.

Prefers a query. Guidelines and sample copy for $10. Payment in 4 copies.

THE JEWISH STAR, P.O. Box 130603, Birmingham, AL 35213. (205) 956-3929. Fax: (205) 967-1417. Margie Rudolph, editor. A 32- to 40-page monthly tabloid with a circulation of 8,000.

☐ *The Jewish Star* serves a Jewish audience from all backgrounds plus some readers with a Christian background. Interested in news and features about a variety of subjects related to readers in their region: Israel, personalities, the Holocaust, and other Jewish issues, concerns, and humor. Uses book reviews, photographs, and illustrations.

Article length 300 to 400 words. Pays on publication.

THE JEWISH WEEK, 1501 Broadway, Suite 505, New York, NY 10036. (212) 921-7822. Fax: (212) 921-8420. Charles Baumohl and Maxine Apsel, editors. A 40-page weekly newspaper with a circulation of 111,000.

☐ *The Jewish Week* addresses an audience of youth and adults from all branches of Judaism. Publishes news and articles on Jewish issues and concerns: Israel, personalities, Jewish Americana, the Holocaust, converts, Sephardic Jews. Uses photographs and illustrations.

Prefers a query. Accepts photocopies and computer submissions. Buys first rights. Payment varies with length on publication.

THE JEWISH WEEKLY NEWS, P.O. Box 1569, Springfield, MA 01101. (413) 739-4771. Charles Bennett, editor. A 120-page weekly newspaper with a circulation of 2,500.

☐ *The Jewish Weekly News* addresses a general readership from all Jewish backgrounds. Needs news and features about Israel, personalities, Jewish folklore, the Holocaust, and other Jewish issues and concerns.

Article length 1,200 words. Prefers a query. Guidelines and sample copy for SASE. Reports in 2 months. Pays 50 cents per inch on publication.

JOURNAL OF ECUMENICAL STUDIES, Temple University, PA 19122. (215) 787-7714. Fax: (215) 787-4569. Leonard Swidler, editor. Submit manuscripts to Paul Mojzes, coeditor. A quarterly journal published by Temple University with a circulation of 2,000.

☐ *Journal of Ecumenical Studies* addresses an audience of scholars and clergy from all branches of Christendom and Judaism as well as other faiths. Publishes scholarly manuscripts on any aspect of the interreligious/interideological dialogue from the grass-roots to the international level.

Article length 30 pages. Prefers a query. Ask for information on manuscript needs and computer submissions. Reports in 3 months. Pays in one copy of the publication and 30 tearsheets.

JUDAISM, 15 East 84th Street, New York, NY 10028. (212) 879-4500. Fax: (212) 249-3672. Ruth R. Waxman, editor. A 128-page quarterly magazine with a circulation of 6,000.

☐ *Judaism* addresses an audience of scholars, rabbis, and general readership from all branches of Judaism. Needs articles on a variety of subjects of interest and concern to Jews: Israel, personalities, Jewish Americana, the Holocaust, converts, Hasidism, Sephardic Jews. Uses book reviews.

Article length 7,500 to 10,000 words. Prefers complete manuscript. Guidelines and sample copy for SASE. Reports in 1 month. No payment.

KENTUCKY JEWISH POST AND OPINION, 1551 Bardstown Road, Louisville, KY 40205. (502) 459-1914. Julie D. Segal, editor. Submit all manuscripts to Gabriel Cohen, National Jewish Post and Opinion, 2120 North Heridian, Indianapolis, IN 46202. A 15- to 17-page newspaper.

☐ *Kentucky Jewish Post and Opinion* addresses a youth and adult audience of rabbis and general readers from all branches of Judaism. Publishes material on Israel, the Holocaust, personalities, Jewish Americana, converts, Hasidism, Sephardic Judaism, and other Jewish issues and concerns. Interested in Jewish sports. Uses book reviews, photographs, and illustrations.

Guidelines and sample copy for SASE.

LILITH MAGAZINE, 250 West 57th Street, #2432, New York, NY 10107. (212) 757-0818. Fax: (212) 757-5705. Susan Weidman Schneider, editor; Susan Schnur, features editor. A 40-page quarterly magazine with a circulation of 10,000.

☐ *Lilith* addresses an audience of women from all Jewish backgrounds. Publishes articles dealing with a variety of subjects and issues. Write material from a Jewish feminist viewpoint.

Article length 1,500 to 2,000 words. Prefers a query. Guidelines for SASE, sample copy for $5 (includes postage). Pays on or during the first quarter of publication.

METROWEST JEWISH NEWS, 901 Route 10, Whippany, NJ 07981. (201) 887-3900. Fax: (201) 887-4152. David Frank, editor. A 72-page weekly newspaper with a circulation of 25,000.

☐ *MetroWest Jewish News* addresses a general audience of adults from all Jewish backgrounds in the New York and New Jersey area. Publishes news and articles about community affairs of Jewish interest and topics of general interest such as Israel, Jewish Americana, converts, the Holocaust, and other Jewish issues. Uses book reviews.

Article length 800 to 1,000 words. Prefers complete manuscript. Accepts simultaneous and computer submissions. Pays $25 to $100 on publication.

MIDSTREAM, 110 East 59th Street, New York, NY 10022. (212) 759-6208. Fax: (212) 318-6176. Joel Carmichael, editor. A 48-page magazine published 9 times yearly.

☐ *Midstream* addresses scholars, rabbis, and general readers from all Jewish backgrounds. Uses a topical approach, especially in issues of political importance on a wide variety of topics of Jewish concern: Israel, the Holocaust, Jewish Americana, personalities, Sephardic Jews, and other issues. Uses fiction, book reviews, and poetry.

Article length varies with topic. Prefers complete manuscript or query. Accepts computer submissions. Buys all rights. Guidelines for SASE. Pays on publication.

MODERN JUDAISM, c/o Steven Katz, Department of Near Eastern Studies, 360 Rockefeller Hall, Cornell University, Ithaca, NY 14853. (607) 255-7119. Fax: (607) 255-1345. Steven T. Katz, editor. A 120-page journal published 3 times yearly with a circulation of 900.

☐ *Modern Judaism* addresses an audience of scholars and rabbis from all Jewish backgrounds. Publishes scholarly articles and reviews on topics of concern to Judaism.

Article length 20 to 30 double-spaced pages. Prefers a query. Reports in 3 to 6 months. No payment.

MOMENT MAGAZINE, 3000 Connecticut Avenue, NW, Suite 300 Washington, DC 20008. (202) 387-8888. Fax: (202) 483-3423. Hershel Shanks, editor; Suzanne Singer, managing editor. A 75-page bimonthly magazine with a circulation of 30,000.

☐ *Moment* addresses an audience of adults from all Jewish backgrounds. Publishes material on subjects of Jewish interest: Israel, Jewish Americana, personalities, Jewish folklore, and other Jewish issues and concerns. Uses book reviews.

Article length 1,500 to 2,500 words. Prefers a query. Accepts computer submissions in most software. Buys first rights. Guidelines and sample copy for SASE. Payment is variable.

NA'AMAT WOMAN, 200 Madison Avenue, New York, NY 10016. (212) 725-8010. Judith A. Sokoloff, editor; Gloria Gross, fiction editor. A 32-page magazine published 5 times yearly with a circulation of 25,000.

☐ *Na'Amat Woman* primarily addresses women from all Jewish backgrounds. Needs material related to women's issues, social issues, and other Jewish concerns written from a woman's viewpoint. Uses material on Israel, Jewish humor, personalities, folklore, the Holocaust, Jewish Americana. Uses fiction, reviews of Jewish arts, music, and literature, book reviews, photographs, and illustrations.

Article length 2,500 to 3,000 words. Prefers a query, but accepts complete manuscripts. Accepts photocopies. Buys first and second serial rights on book excerpts. Guidelines and sample copy for SASE. Reports in 6 weeks. Pays 10 cents per word on publication.

NOAH'S ARK, A MAGAZINE FOR JEWISH CHILDREN, c/o 6330 Gulfton, #460, Houston, TX 77081. (713) 771-4143. Debbie Dubin and Linda Block, editors. A monthly newsmagazine.
□ *Noah's Ark* is used as a supplement to English-language Jewish newspapers and is also mailed directly to individual subscribers and in group orders to religious schools and synagogues. Uses puzzles, games, stories, current events, and other feature material that appeals to Jewish children and their teachers and parents. "Items should convey information in a fun, easy to digest way. No didactic teaching." Looking for short holiday stories. Also for, if written for elementary school age children, fiction with a Jewish theme, articles on Jewish issues and concerns, personalities, Jewish Americana, Israel, the Holocaust, Jewish humor and folklore, Jews worldwide, and book reviews.
    Article length 400 to 600 words. Query or complete manuscript. Reports within 1 month. Pays 5 cents per word.

REFORM JUDAISM, 838 Fifth Avenue, New York, NY 10021. (212) 249-0100. Aron Hirt-Manheimer, editor. A 64-page quarterly magazine published by the Union of American Hebrew Congregations. Circulation 290,000.
□ *Reform Judaism* addresses adult readers, primarily from the Reform branch of Judaism. Needs articles about Reform Judaism or topics of interest to members of the movement. Wants articles on Israel, American Judaism, and other issues of interest. Uses photographs and illustrations.
    Article length 2,000 words, department opinion pieces, 600 words. Prefers complete manuscript. Accepts simultaneous submissions and photocopies. Buys first rights. Guidelines for SASE, sample copy for $2.50. Pays 10 cents per word on publication.

RESPONSE: A CONTEMPORARY JEWISH REVIEW, 27 West 20th Street, (9th floor), New York, NY 10011. (212) 675-1168. Fax: (212) 929-3459. Bennett Lovett Groff and Adam Margolis, editors. A 64-page quarterly journal with a circulation of 2,000.
□ *Response* addresses an adult audience from all Jewish backgrounds. Publishes on a variety of issues of Jewish concern with the emphasis on contemporary approaches to these issues: Israel, Jewish humor, personalities, Jewish Americana, the Holocaust, converts, Jewish folklore. Uses fiction and poetry with Jewish themes, book reviews on contemporary literature.
    Article length is less than 30 pages. Prefers a query, but accepts a complete manuscript. Accepts computer submissions. Guidelines and sample copy for SASE. Payment in 5 copies of magazine.

RHODE ISLAND JEWISH HISTORICAL NOTES, 130 Sessions Street, Providence, RI 02906. (401) 723-6315. Fax: (401) 728-5067. Judith W. Cohen, editor. A 120-page annual journal with a circulation of 800.
□ *Rhode Island Jewish Historical Notes* addresses an adult audience from all branches of Judaism. Publishes articles and information about Jewish history in Rhode Island.
    Article length 2,500 to 5,000 words. Prefers a query, but accepts complete manuscript. No payment.

SAN DIEGO JEWISH TIMES, 2592 Fletcher Parkway, El Cajon, CA 92020. (619) 463-5515. Carol Rosenberg, editor. A 40-page biweekly newspaper with a circulation of 17,500.
□ *San Diego Jewish Times* serves an audience from all Jewish backgrounds. Interested in news and feature stories related to readers in their region on Israel, Jewish Ameri-

cana, personalities, and other Jewish interests and concerns. Prints fiction with Jewish themes, photographs, and illustrations.

Article length 1,500 words. Pays $50 on publication.

SHOFAR, 43 Northcote Drive, Melville, NY 11747. (516) 643-4598. Gerald Graydon, editor. A 32-page monthly (two bimonthly issues yearly) magazine with a circulation of 16,000.

☐ *Shofar* addresses an audience of children and youth ages 8 to 13 from all Jewish backgrounds. Publishes material on a variety of subjects on Jewish themes. Uses fiction, nonfiction, poetry, games, puzzles, cartoons, photographs, and illustrations. Especially interested in holiday material.

Article length 500 to 700 words. Prefers complete manuscript, but queries welcome. Accepts photocopies and simultaneous submissions. Guidelines and sample copy for 9 × 12 SASE with 98 cents postage. Pays 5 cents per word plus 5 copies on publication. Additional payment for B&W glossies with articles.

THE SOUTHERN JEWISH WEEKLY, 1832 Evergreen Avenue, Jacksonville, FL 32206. (904) 634-1469. Isadore Moscovitz, editor and publisher. A 24-page weekly tabloid published for a regional audience of 28,500.

☐ *The Southern Jewish Weekly* serves an audience of rabbis and scholars from all branches of Judaism. Prints news of Jewish interest in the southeastern United States. Interested in material on Israel, Jewish folklore, personalities, the Holocaust, and Jewish humor. Also uses fiction, poetry, and photographs.

Article length 500 words. Prefers complete manuscripts. Sample copies for SASE. Reports in 2 weeks. Pays approximately $100 for articles.

STUDIES IN BIBLIOGRAPHY AND BOOKLORE, 3101 Clifton Avenue, Cincinnati, OH 45220. (513) 221-1875. Fax: (513) 221-0321. Herbert C. Zafren, editor. A 50-page journal published irregularly by the library of Hebrew Union College-Jewish Institute of Religion in Cincinnati. Circulation 238.

☐ *Studies in Bibliography and Booklore* addresses an audience of scholars from all branches of Judaism. Needs scholarly material dealing with subjects related to Jewish bibliography and booklore.

Prefers to work with complete manuscript. Accepts computer submissions. No payment.

TIKKUN, 5100 Leona Street, Oakland, CA 94619. (510) 482-0805. Fax: (510) 482-3379. Michael Lerner, editor; Marge Piercy, poetry editor; Anne Roiphe, fiction editor. An 80-page bimonthly magazine with a circulation of 40,000.

☐ *Tikkun* addresses an adult audience from all branches of Judaism. This magazine is "a Jewish critique of politics, culture, and society." Publishes an "analytic" treatment of all subjects of present-day concerns and issues to Jewish readers that have import for the United States and the world.

"Tikkun is unlikely to print articles from non-subscribers or people not closely familiar with what has already been printed." Prefers a query. Accepts computer submissions in WordPerfect or Macintosh. Sample copy for $7. Reports in 5 months. Pays $150 for essays or fiction, $35 for poetry on publication.

TRADITION, 1855 LaVista Terrace, Atlanta, GA 30329. (404) 633-0551. Emanuel Feldman, editor. A 120-page quarterly journal published by the Rabbinical Council headquartered in New York City.

☐ *Tradition* addresses an Orthodox audience of scholars and rabbis. Needs articles on

Israel, the Holocaust, converts, Hasidism, Sephardic Jews, and other Jewish issues and concerns. Uses book reviews.

Article length varies from 2,000 to 5,000 words. Prefers to work with complete manuscript. Reports in 6 weeks. No payment.

UNITED SYNAGOGUE REVIEW, 155 Fifth Avenue, New York, NY 10010. (212) 533-7800. Fax: (212) 353-9439. Lois Goldrich, editor. A 38-page semiannual magazine with a circulation of 255,000.

☐ *United Synagogue Review* primarily addresses a Conservative audience of rabbis and general readers. Needs material on all Jewish issues and concerns, personalities, Israel, the Holocaust. Uses photographs and illustrations.

Prefers a query. Reports in 2 to 3 weeks. No payment.

WELLSPRINGS, 770 Eastern Parkway, Brooklyn, NY 11213. (718) 953-1000. Fax: (718) 771-6553. Baila Olidort, editor. A 40-page quarterly magazine with a circulation of 40,000.

☐ *Wellsprings* addresses a Jewish audience from all backgrounds. Welcomes articles on Jewish issues and concerns, personalities, and Hasidism. Prints some poetry, book reviews, photographs, and illustrations.

Article length 2,500 words. Query required. Pays $250 to $350 on publication depending on the length and nature of the assignment.

WESTERN STATES JEWISH HISTORY, 3111 Kelton Avenue, Los Angeles, CA 90034. (310) 475-1415. Fax: (310) 475-2996. William Krame, editor. A 100-page quarterly magazine.

☐ *Western States Jewish History* addresses an adult audience from all Jewish backgrounds. Needs articles related to Jewish history west of the Mississippi, including Alaska and Hawaii, plus Western Canada and Western Mexico.

Article length up to 50 pages. Prefers a query. Sample copy for $6. Reports in 2 weeks. No payment.

THE WISCONSIN JEWISH CHRONICLE, 1360 North Prospect Avenue, Milwaukee, WI 53202. (414) 271-2992. Fax: (414) 271-0487. Andrew Muchin, editor. A 20-page weekly newspaper with a circulation of 5,000.

☐ *The Wisconsin Jewish Chronicle* addresses an adult audience from all Jewish backgrounds. Needs news and articles of local and regional interest on Israel, Jewish humor, Jewish folklore, and other Jewish issues and concerns. Uses book reviews.

Article length 500 to 750 words. Prefers a query. Accepts photocopies and simultaneous submissions. Accepts computer submissions in Microsoft Word. Guidelines and sample copy for SASE. Pays $25 to $50 for articles.

YOUNG JUDEAN, 130 West 57th Street, New York, NY 10019. (212) 355-7900. Direct all editorial correspondence to Shaffzin & Shaffzin, P.O. Box 173, Merion Station, PA 19066. A 16-page quarterly magazine published by the Young Judean Zionist movement and Hadassah Zionist Youth Commission. Circulation 4,000.

☐ *Young Judean* is interested in "lively stories and articles on Israel and Jewish life that will appeal to readers 10 to 12 years old." Uses fiction, nonfiction, poetry, fillers, and book reviews.

Story length 750 to 1,000 words; articles 500 to 1,000 words; fillers of appropriate length. Prefers complete manuscript. Guidelines available; sample copy for 75 cents. Reports in 8 weeks. Pays 5 cents per word, up to $50 per piece on publication.

PUBLISHERS OF JUDAICA

A.R.E. PUBLISHING, 3945 South Oneida, Denver, CO 80237. (303) 363-7779. Fax: (303) 758-0954. Audrey Friedman Marcus and Raymond A. Swerin, editors. Publishes 4 to 6 books of Jewish interest annually.

□ A.R.E. Publishing addresses readers from all branches of Judaism. Needs educational materials for Jewish schools: curriculum, textbooks, mini-courses, workbooks, tapes, and songs, teachers manuals, drama, craft books. Subjects of interest are the Bible, Israel, biographies, Jewish thought, history, and Americana.

Book length averages 200 pages for textbooks and teachers' manuals. Workbooks less. Uses some reprints. Queries are recommended. Prefers outline/synopsis/sample chapters. No simultaneous submissions. Reports in 8 to 10 weeks. Pays 10 percent royalty on retail price. Variable advances. Free catalog and author guidelines for SASE.

JASON ARONSON, INC., 230 Livingston Street, Northvale, NJ 07647. (201) 767-4093. Fax: (201) 767-4330. Arthur Kurzweil, editor. Publishes 45 originals and reprints yearly, mostly hardcover.

□ Jason Aronson addresses an audience of all ages from all Jewish backgrounds. Needs a wide variety of topics: the Bible, Jewish humor, liturgy and prayer, Hasidism, Jewish history and thought. Accepts photographs and illustrations.

Prefers a query, but accepts outline/synopsis/sample chapters. Reports in 4 weeks. Pays royalties based on the retail price. Advances up to $1,000. Free catalog and author guidelines for SASE.

AUGSBURG FORTRESS PUBLISHERS. See FORTRESS PRESS.

LEO BAECK INSTITUTE, INCORPORATED, 129 East 73rd Street, New York, NY 10021. (212) 744-6400. Fax: (212) 988-1305. Robert Jacobs, executive director. Publishes 5 originals yearly, mostly hardcover, in cooperation with university presses.

□ Leo Baeck Institute addresses an audience of scholars from all Jewish backgrounds. Publishes books on the history and culture of German-speaking Jews. Especially interested in the Holocaust and Jewish thought and history in that context.

Average book length 300 pages. Prefers a query. Accepts outline/synopsis/sample chapters in photocopy. No simultaneous submissions. Reports in 4 weeks.

BEACON PRESS. See entry in chapter 3.

BEHRMAN HOUSE, INCORPORATED, 235 Watchung Avenue, West Orange, NJ 07052. (201) 669-0447. Fax: (201) 669-9769. Adam Siegel, Ruby G. Strauss, and Adam Bengal, editors. Publishes 15 to 20 originals yearly, mostly hardcover.

□ Behrman House addresses children and adults, mostly from Conservative and Reform traditions. Publishes textbooks and curriculum for Jewish religious schools. Its Library of Jewish Studies publishes instructional tools for use in adult education in synagogues and Jewish community centers. Books on a variety of subjects are sought: the Bible, Israel, the Holocaust, Jewish history and thought, liturgy and prayer. Also interested in Hebrew language books. Welcomes photographs and illustrations for textbooks.

Average book length 128 to 160 pages. Prefers a complete manuscript. Accepts simultaneous and computer submissions. Royalties and advances or outright purchases are negotiated. Reports in 8 weeks. Free catalog for SASE.

BENMIR BOOKS, 1529 Cypress Street, Walnut Creek, CA 94596. (510) 933-5356. Fax: (510) 933-4166. Boris Bresler, editor. Publishes 1 or 2 originals and reprints of Jewish interest annually, 60 percent of them paperback.

☐ Benmir Books addresses an audience of adults and scholars from all Jewish backgrounds and traditions. This publisher is a "Judaica publisher specializing in translations, reprints and original nonfiction works of high literary quality on Jewish themes." Especially interested in Israel, biographies, and Jewish history. Uses photographs and illustrations.

Accepts outline/synopsis/sample chapters. Accepts simultaneous submissions. Reports in 3 weeks. Pays 10 to 15 percent royalties. No advances. Free catalog and author guidelines for SASE.

BIBLIO PRESS, 1140 Broadway (1507), New York, NY 10001. (212) 684-1257. Doris B. Gold, editor. Publishes 1 or 2 titles yearly.

☐ Biblio Press primarily addresses a women's audience from all Jewish backgrounds. Interested in reaching feminist academic scholars and rabbis, both men and women. Needs books in the area of women's studies related to Judaism. Wants women's aspects of Jewish history and thought, biographies of Jewish women, Jewish women's Americana, and new women's rituals.

Manuscripts average 200 pages. Must query first. Pays royalties. Also makes "for hire" editorial assignments on topics as needed. Free catalog and author guidelines for SASE.

BLOCH PUBLISHING COMPANY, 37 West 26th Street, New York, NY 10010. (212) 532-3977. Charles Bloch, president. Publishes 8 originals and reprints of Jewish interest annually, 50 percent of them paperback.

☐ Bloch Publishing Company addresses a Jewish audience of scholars, rabbis, and laity from all Jewish backgrounds. Interested in books on the Bible, biographies of Jewish personalities, the Holocaust, Israel, and Jewish Americana. No poetry.

Requires a query. Reports in 3 months. Pays 10 percent royalty. Free catalog and author guidelines for SASE.

BOARD OF JEWISH EDUCATION OF GREATER NEW YORK, 426 West 58th Street, New York, NY 10019. (212) 245-8200. Rabbi Harry Cohenson, editor. An agency of the UJA Federation, the Board publishes books of Jewish interest annually.

☐ Board of Jewish Education of Greater New York serves an audience of children and youth from all branches of Judaism. Publishes Jewish educational materials, usable in classrooms. Their materials are designed to impart Jewish values, concepts, and history. Interested in Bible studies, the Holocaust, liturgy and prayer, Jewish history and holidays.

Manuscripts for juvenile books 20 to 30 pages, Bible study or holiday books 40 to 50 pages. Prefers outline/synopsis. Accepts computer submissions. No reprints. Reports within eight weeks.

BUBER PRESS. See REVISIONIST PRESS.

CCAR PRESS, 192 Lexington Avenue, New York, NY 10016. (212) 684-4890. Fax: (212) 689-1649. Rabbi Elliot L. Stevens, editor. Publishing operation of the Central Conference of American Rabbis. Publishes 3 to 5 originals yearly, 50 percent paperback.

☐ CCAR Press addresses a children's audience, also adult scholars and rabbis from the Reform tradition. Publishes guides to Jewish practices, especially for Reform Judaism. Interested in books of liturgy, prayers, and Jewish celebrations.

Prefers a query. Accepts computer submissions in WordPerfect format. Reports in 4 weeks. Pays advances and flat fees. Free catalog and author guidelines for SASE.

CORNELL UNIVERSITY PRESS, 124 Roberts Place, P.O. Box 250, Ithaca, NY 14851. (607) 257-7000. Fax: (607) 257-3552. Bernhard Kendler, editor. A university press publishing 2 or 3 paperback originals yearly. Rarely does reprints.

☐ Cornell University Press addresses a scholarly audience from all Jewish backgrounds. Seeks scholarly materials of broad academic interest on a wide range of subjects from varied approaches. "Readership of books is made up almost entirely of faculty members at English-language universities throughout the world." Has a special interest in anthropological studies of Jewish communities.

Average book length 100,000 words. Prefers a query. Accepts outline/synopsis/sample chapters. Initial consideration of subject takes 2 weeks, final report in 4 months. Pays royalties of 5 to 10 percent on the retail price. Some advances. Free catalog and author guidelines for SASE.

DECALOGUE BOOKS, INC., 7 North McQuesten Parkway, Mount Vernon, NY 10550. (914) 664-5930. William Brandon, editor. Publishes 3 hardcover originals and reprints of Jewish interest yearly.

☐ Decalogue Books addresses a general audience from all branches of Judaism. Interested in Judaica books on various topics: Jewish Americana, the Holocaust, Jewish thought and history. Especially looking for Jewish cookbooks.

Prefers a query. Accepts outline/synopsis/sample chapters. Pays 10 percent royalty on the retail price. Advances negotiable. Free catalog and author guidelines for SASE.

PHILIPP FELDHEIM, INCORPORATED, 200 Airport Executive Park, Spring Valley, NY 10977. (914) 356-2282. Marsi Tabak, editor. Publishes 10 to 12 books of Jewish interest annually.

☐ Philipp Feldheim seeks "quality Judaica from an Orthodox perspective for readers of all ages." Interested in Bible studies, fiction, Jewish history, Jewish thought, the Holocaust, and biographies of Jewish personalities.

Prefers complete manuscript. No reprints. Accepts computer submissions. Reports in 12 weeks. Pays 10 percent royalty. No advances.

FORTRESS PRESS, Box 1209, 426 South Fifth Street, Minneapolis, MN 55440. (612) 330-3436. Fax: (612) 330-3455. Marshall D. Johnson, editor, Fortress Books. A division of Augsburg Fortress Publishers producing 10 paperbacks of Jewish interest yearly.

☐ Fortress addresses an audience of scholars and rabbis from all Jewish backgrounds. Seeks scholarly books in the areas of "formative and modern Judaism." Interested especially in books on Jewish history and thought, the Holocaust.

Average book length 300 pages. Accepts outline/synopsis/sample chapters. Pays 10 percent royalty on the retail price. Advances average $700. Free catalog and author guidelines for SASE.

THE FREE PRESS, 866 Third Avenue, New York, NY 10022. (212) 702-2000. Erwin Glikes, president and publisher; Adam Bellow, senior editor. Publishes 4 books of Jewish interest annually.

☐ The Free Press "seeks books that make a significant original contribution to knowledge in their field and address issues of concern to a broad intellectual and general readership." The audience is adults, scholars, and general lay readers from all branches of Judaism. Interested in books on the Holocaust, Jewish history and thought, and biographies of Jewish personalities.

Average book length 250 to 500 pages. Accepts outline/synopsis/sample chapters or complete manuscripts. Accepts simultaneous submissions. Reports in 4 to 6 weeks. Pays royalties beginning at 10 percent. Offers advances. Catalogs available.

GREENWOOD PRESS, 88 Post Road West, P.O. Box 5007, Westport, CT 06881. (203) 226-3571. James Sabin and Cynthia Harris, editors. A scholarly publisher specializing in reference books for academic libraries.

☐ Greenwood Press serves an "academic and scholarly audience with sound scholarship and objectivity being as important as the subject." Interested in religious related titles, including Judaism, that will appeal to an academic market.

Average book length 250 to 300 pages. Prefers a query with outline/synopsis. Free catalog and author guidelines for SASE. Pays standard royalty. Reports in 2 or 3 months.

HARPER SAN FRANCISCO, 1160 Battery Street, San Francisco, CA 94111-1213. (415) 477-4400. Fax: (415) 477-5555. Thomas Grady, John Loudon, and JoAnn Moschelle, editors. General publisher producing 10 Jewish originals and reprints yearly, mostly hardcover.

☐ Harper San Francisco addresses general and scholarly audiences. Interested in books on Israel, Jewish Americana, history, and thought. Does some poetry.

Prefers a query. Accepts simultaneous and computer submissions. Reports in 4 months. Pays royalties and advances. Free catalog and author guidelines for SASE.

HEBREW PUBLISHING COMPANY, P.O. Box 157, Rockaway Beach, NY 11693. (718) 945-3000. Charles D. Lieber, editor. Publishes 10 originals and reprints of Jewish interest annually.

☐ Hebrew Publishing Company addresses an audience of all ages from mixed Jewish backgrounds. Interested in biblical studies, liturgy and prayer, Jewish thought, children's books. "Publishes a very heterogeneous list of varying criteria."

Prefers outline/synopsis/sample chapters. Reports in 4 weeks. Pays royalties. Sample catalogs available.

HEBREW UNION COLLEGE PRESS, 3101 Clifton Avenue, Cincinnati, OH 45220-2488. (513) 221-1875. Fax: (513) 221-0321. Michael A. Meyer, editor. Publishing arm of Hebrew Union College—Jewish Institute of Religion. Publishes 2 to 4 titles of Jewish interest yearly.

☐ Hebrew Union College Press addresses an audience of rabbis, scholars, and general readership. "Considers only manuscripts on well-defined topics in Judaica and gives each product a rigorous critical reading by specialists in the field before recommending for publication." Welcomes submissions of high-quality dissertations. Interested especially in "in-depth studies" of subjects of Jewish interest and concern: the Talmud, rabbinic literature, interreligious dialogue, ancient religions, and women's studies in Judaism.

Prefers a query. Accepts outline/synopsis/sample chapters. Accepts photocopies and computer submissions. Pays royalties after publication costs have been met. Free catalog and author guidelines for SASE.

HOLIDAY HOUSE, INCORPORATED, 425 Madison Avenue, New York, NY 10017. (212) 688-0085. Mary S. Cuyler, editor. Publishes two originals of Jewish interest yearly. No reprints.

☐ Holiday House publishes books for children and youth ranging from picture books to young adult fiction and nonfiction. Interested in Bible studies, Israel, Jewish history, humor and thought, the Holocaust, and Jewish Americana. Uses fiction and poetry as well as photographs and illustrations.

Average book lengths are as follows: picture books, 32 pages; middle grades, 49 to 110 pages; young adult, 220 to 250 pages. Prefers complete manuscript for picture books, outline/synopsis/sample chapters for novels. Prefers photocopies, not originals, of artwork. Accepts simultaneous submissions. Reports in 6 to 8 weeks. Pays royalties and advances. Guidelines available.

INDIANA UNIVERSITY PRESS, 601 North Morton Street, Bloomington, IN 47404. (812) 855-4203. Fax: (812) 855-7931. John Gallman, director; Janet Rabinowitch, editor. A university press producing 6 to 8 originals of Jewish interest yearly, 50 percent paperback.

☐ Indiana University Press addresses an audience of scholars from all Jewish backgrounds. Publishes scholarly books of original research on a variety of topics of Jewish interest and concern: Bible studies, Israel, the Holocaust, Jewish history and thought, and fiction.

Prefers a query. Accepts outline/synopsis/sample chapters. Reports in 8 weeks. Pays royalties. Free catalog and author guidelines for SASE.

JEWISH LIGHTS PUBLISHING, P.O. Box 237, Woodstock, VT 05091. (802) 457-4000. Fax: (802) 457-4004. Stuart M. Matlins, editor. Publishes 12 originals and reprints yearly, 50 percent paperback.

☐ Jewish Lights Publishing addresses an audience of all ages from all Jewish backgrounds. "We design books to be of interest to people of all faiths." Seeks books that "stimulate thought and help people learn about who the Jewish People are, where they come from, and what the future can be made to hold." Although the audience is primarily Jewish, "books speak as well to the Christian world and will broaden their understanding of Judaism and the roots of their own faith." Seeking books in the areas of theology, philosophy, spirituality, and recovery.

Average book length 200 pages. Must query first. Accepts outline/synopsis/sample chapters. Accepts photocopies. Pays 10 to 15 percent on net price. Advances up to $3,000. Free catalog and author guidelines for SASE.

JEWISH PUBLICATION SOCIETY, 1930 Chestnut Street, Philadelphia, PA 19103. (215) 564-5925. Fax: (215) 564-6640. Ellen Frankel, editor; Bruce Black, editor of children's books. Publishes 18 to 20 originals and reprints yearly, mostly hardcover.

☐ Jewish Publication Society addresses an audience of all ages from all Jewish backgrounds. Needs Bible and commentary books, scholarly and popular reading, and children's books. No novels, poetry, memoirs, or biography. Interested especially in translations of classic texts and young adult fiction and nonfiction. Also seeking books of Jewish humor, Americana, thought and history.

Prefers a query. Accepts outline/synopsis/sample chapters. Accepts simultaneous and computer submissions. Prefers WordPerfect. Reports in 6 to 8 weeks. Pays 10 percent royalty on the retail price. Variable advances. Free catalog and author guidelines for SASE.

JONATHAN DAVID PUBLISHERS, 68-22 Eliot Avenue, Middle Village, NY 11379. (718) 456-8611. Fax: (718) 894-2818. Alfred J. Kolatch, editor. Publishes 15 originals and reprints yearly, mostly hardcover.

☐ Jonathan David Publishers addresses an audience of all ages from all Jewish backgrounds. Seeks books of "popular Judaica" on a variety of subjects in the general nonfiction category: the Bible, Jewish humor, Israel, Jewish Americana, liturgy and prayer. Requires a query. Accepts outline/synopsis/sample chapters. Pays standard royalties and advances.

JUDAICA PRESS, INCORPORATED, 123 Ditmas Avenue, Brooklyn, NY 11218. (718) 972-6200. Fax: (718) 972-6204. Jack Goldman, publisher; Rachel J. Witty, managing editor. Publishes 5 originals and reprints of Jewish interest annually.

☐ Judaica Press addresses an audience of all ages from all Jewish backgrounds. Especially interested in classic Jewish literature: Bible, Prophets, Writings, Talmud, and so forth. Subjects of books can be of wide range: Israel, Jewish humor, liturgy and prayer, the Holocaust, history and thought, and Jewish fiction. Also does children's books.

Adult books range from 230 to 250 pages. Prefers a query or a complete manuscript. Accepts Macintosh or IBM submissions. Pays 7.5 percent royalty on the wholesale price. No advances. Guidelines are provided for author's under contract.

KAR-BEN COPIES, INCORPORATED, 6800 Tildenwood Lane, Rockville, MD 20852. (800) 4KARBEN. Fax: (310) 881-9195. Madeline Wikler and Judye Groner, editors. Publishes 10 to 12 paperback and hardcover originals yearly.

☐ Kar-Ben Copies addresses a children's audience from all Jewish backgrounds. Seeks juvenile storybooks and nonfiction, especially material about "holidays, the Bible, and life cycles."

Average book length is 1,000 words (32 to 48 pages). Prefers a complete manuscript. Reports in 6 to 8 weeks. Pays 6 to 8 percent royalties on net sales. Advances $500 to $2,000. Free catalog and author guidelines for SASE.

KTAV PUBLISHING HOUSE, 900 Jefferson Street, Hoboken, NJ 07030. (201) 963-9524. Bernard Scharfstein, editor. Publishes 20 originals yearly, mostly hardcover.

☐ KTAV Publishing House addresses an audience of scholars, rabbis, and general readers from all branches of Judaism. Seeks books on a variety of subjects: the Bible, Hasidism, Jewish thought and history.

Prefers a complete manuscript. All software acceptable. Reports in 2 weeks. Pays royalties based on the wholesale price. Offers some advances and outright purchases.

NIGHTINGALE RESOURCES, Box 322, Cold Spring, NY 10516. Lila Teich Gold, editor. Judaica publisher of "books for anyone who is thoughtful and curious." Publishes hardcover and paperback originals and reprints on an "irregular" schedule.

☐ Nightingale Resources addresses readers of all ages from all branches of Judaism. Emphasis of the publishing program is on quality writing, scholarship, and production. Prefers a query. Pays negotiable royalties.

PAULIST PRESS, 997 MacArthur Boulevard, Mahwah, NJ 07430. (201) 825-7300. Fax: (201) 825-8345. Kevin A. Lynch, editor; Donald Brophy, managing editor; Lawrence Boaot, Judaica-related books. A Roman Catholic oriented publisher of 3 or 4 paperbacks of Judaica yearly.

☐ Paulist Press addresses an audience of all ages from all Jewish backgrounds. Seeks books of introduction to Judaism for Christian readers, Jewish/Christian dialogue books, or discussing Judaic/Christian roots. Topics include the Bible, the Holocaust, Jewish history and thought, and liturgy and prayer.

Average book length 160 to 200 pages. Prefers a complete manuscript, but accepts outline/synopsis/sample chapters. Accepts some computer submissions. Reports in 6 weeks. Pays 8 to 10 percent royalties on the retail price. Minimal advances.

PELICAN PUBLISHING COMPANY, INCORPORATED, 1101 Monroe Street, Gretna, LA 70053. (504) 368-1175. Nina Kooj, editor. Publishes Jewish oriented books for children.

☐ Pelican Publishing is looking for stories for picture books that educate children about Jewish traditions.

Average book length 23 pages. Requires a query. Reports in 1 month. Pays 10 percent royalty on the wholesale price.

PERSCA BOOKS, 60 Madison Avenue, New York, NY 10010. (212) 779-7768. Fax: (212) 689-5405. Michael and Karen Braziller, editors. Publishes 4 originals and reprints yearly, 50 percent of them paperback.

☐ Persca Books addresses an adult audience from all Jewish backgrounds. Looking for books of literary merit on subjects of the Holocaust, Jewish history and thought. Uses poetry and fiction.

Prefers a query. Reports in 4 to 6 weeks. Pays standard royalties on the retail price.

PILGRIM PRESS/UNITED CHURCH PRESS, 700 Prospect Avenue, E, Cleveland, OH 44115-1100. (216) 736-3725. Fax: (216) 736-3703. Richard E. Brown, editor. Publisher of the United Church of Christ with a broad-based religious program. Mostly paperback.

☐ Pilgrim Press addresses an adult audience from all branches of Judaism. Especially interested in books on ethics and social issues of interest to Jewish readers, from a Jewish viewpoint.

Prefers an outline/synopsis/sample chapters. Accepts computer submissions in WordPerfect. Pays negotiable royalties. Free catalog and author guidelines for SASE.

REVISIONIST PRESS (also includes BUBER PRESS), G.P.O. Box 2009, Brooklyn, NY 11202. Bezalel Chaim, editor. Publishes 2 to 6 hardcover originals and reprints of Jewish interest annually.

☐ Revisionist Press addresses a scholarly audience from all branches of Judaism. Seeks books on a variety of subjects: the Bible, Israel, the Holocaust, Hasidism, Jewish Americana, history and thought. Also seeks poetry and biographies.

Prefers a complete manuscript. Pays 10 percent royalty on net sales. No advances or outright purchases. Catalog and author guidelines for $7.50.

SCHOCKEN BOOKS, INCORPORATED, 201 East 50th Street, New York, NY 10022. (212) 572-6049. Fax: (212) 572-6030. Bonny Fetterman, editor. Publishes 10 originals of Jewish interest annually, mostly hardcover.

☐ Schocken Books addresses a general adult audience from all branches of Judaism. Needs "quality nonfiction Judaica suitable for both the academic and general trade markets." Topics include all subjects of Jewish interest and concern.

Average book length 70,000 to 100,000 words. Prefers a query. Accepts outline/synopsis/sample chapters. Accepts photocopies. Reports in 6 weeks. Pays royalties.

SCHOLARS PRESS, P.O. Box 15399, Atlanta, GA 30333. (404) 636-4757. Fax: (404) 636-8301. Ernest Frerichs, editor for Brown Judaica Studies; Jacob Neusner for South Florida studies. Publisher for Brown University, Providence, Rhode Island, and South Florida University. Produces 50 hardcover originals annually.

☐ Scholars Press addresses a scholarly audience from all branches of Judaism. Especially looking for books related to the Bible, the Talmud, as well as other areas of Jewish thought and concern.

Prefers an outline/synopsis/sample chapters. Reports in 8 to 12 weeks. Payment is negotiable. No royalties or advances. Free catalog and author guidelines for SASE.

SEPHER-HERMON PRESS, INC., 1265 46th Street, Brooklyn, NY 11219 (718) 972-9010. Fax: (718) 972-9010. Samuel Gross, editor. Publishes six books per year of Jewish interest, both originals and reprints, 50 percent paperback.

☐ Sepher-Hermon Press is seeking material for an adult readership from all branches of Judaism; scholars, rabbis, and general readers. Especially interested in scholarly and semi-scholarly nonfiction on Jewish thought and history, biographies of Jewish personalities, the Holocaust and rabbinic literature.

Average book length is 320 manuscript pages. Prefers query with outline/synopsis and sample chapter. Pays standard advances and royalties. Catalog and guidelines available on request.

SONCINO PRESS, LTD., 123 Ditmas Avenue, Brooklyn, NY 11218. (718) 972-6200. Fax: (718) 972-6204. Jack Goldman, publisher; Rachel J. Witty, managing editor. Publishes 6 originals and reprints of Jewish interest yearly, 50 percent of them paperback.

☐ Soncino Press addresses an adult audience from all Jewish backgrounds. Interested in classic Jewish literature: the Bible, Prophets, Writings, Talmud, and so on. Subjects can be Israel, biographies of Jewish personalities, Hasidism, the Holocaust, Jewish thought, liturgy, and prayer.

Prefers a query, but accepts a complete manuscript. Accepts Macintosh or IBM computer submissions. Pays 7.5 percent royalty on the wholesale price. No advances. Guidelines are furnished for authors under contract.

S.P.I. BOOKS, Shapolsky Publishers, 136 West 22nd Street, New York, NY 10011. (212) 633-2022. Fax: (212) 633-2123. I.E. Mozeson, editor. Publishes 25 originals and reprints of Jewish interest yearly, 80 percent of them in paperback.

☐ S.P.I. Books addresses children and adult readers from all Jewish backgrounds. Interested in books on Israel, Jewish humor, biographies of Jewish personalities, Jewish Americana, history and thought.

Average book length 225 pages. Prefers a query. Accepts WordPerfect computer submissions. Pays royalties on the retail price. Offers advances.

TEMPLE UNIVERSITY PRESS, Philadelphia, PA 19122. (215) 787-8787. Fax: (215) 787-4719. Michael Ames, editor. Publishes 2 or 3 hardcover (some simultaneously in paperback) originals of Jewish interest yearly.

☐ Temple University Press addresses a scholarly audience from all branches of Judaism. Needs books in all areas of Jewish interest, especially "ethnicity, sociology, social justice, and human rights."

Prefers an outline/synopsis/sample chapters. Reports in 12 weeks. Pays varied royalties and advances. Free catalog on request.

TRANSACTION PUBLISHERS, Rutgers University, New Brunswick, NJ 08903. (908) 932-2280. Fax: (908) 932-3138. Esther Luckett, editor. Publishes 15 hardcover originals annually.

☐ Transaction Publishers addresses a scholarly audience from all branches of Judaism. Looking for scholarly works on all subjects of interest: Israel, the Holocaust, Jewish Americana, history, and thought.

Prefers a complete manuscript. Accepts any leading computer software. Reports in 12 weeks. Payment is negotiated.

TRINITY PRESS INTERNATIONAL, P.O. Box 851, Valley Forge, PA 19482. (215) 768-2120. Fax: (215) 768-2056. Harold W. Rast, director. Publishes 4 originals and reprints yearly, mostly paperback.

☐ Trinity Press International serves an audience of scholars, rabbis, and general readers from all branches of Judaism. Interested in academic books on Israel, the Bible, Jewish history and thought. Emphasis is on scholarly titles, but some on popular subjects are also welcome.

Average book length 180+ pages. Prefers a complete manuscript or an outline/synopsis/sample chapters. Accepts photocopies. Pays 7.5 percent royalty on paperbacks, 10 percent on hardcovers on the retail price. Advances of $500 up. Free catalog and author guidelines for SASE.

UAHC PRESS, 838 Fifth Avenue, New York, NY 10021. (212) 249-0100. Fax: (212) 734-2857. Aron Hirt-Manheimer, trade book editor; Don Kasakove, textbook editor. Publishes 12 or more originals of Jewish interest annually, mostly paperback. Also publishes general trade books.

☐ UAHC Press addresses an audience of all age groups, primarily from Reform and Conservative branches of Judaism. Publishes "Jewish textbooks and curriculum for all age groups and Jewish trade books for a wide audience of all ages." Interested in books on the Bible, Israel, the Holocaust, Jewish Americana, history, and thought. Juvenile trade books average 32 pages. Adult books are much longer. Prefers a query.

Accepts an outline/synopsis/sample chapters. Reports in 3 weeks. Pays 6 to 10 percent royalty on the wholesale price. Advances up to $750. Free catalog and author guidelines for SASE.

UNITED SYNAGOGUE OF AMERICA BOOK SERVICE, Department of Education, 155 Fifth Avenue, New York, NY 10010. (212) 533-7800. Rabbi Robert Abramson, editor. Publishes 5 originals and reprints yearly, mostly paperback.

☐ United Synagogue addresses an audience of all ages from the conservative branch of Judaism. Interested in educational materials for conservative Jewish use. Accepts little free-lance material. Manuscripts may be addressed to Youth Program or P.R. departments. Payment varies with project.

THE UNIVERSITY OF ALABAMA PRESS, P.O. Box 870380, Tuscaloosa, AL 35487. (205) 348-5180. Fax: (205) 348-9201. Nicole F. Mitchell, editor; Leon Weinberger, editor of Judaica studies. Publisher of the University of Alabama. Publishes 3 to 5 originals yearly, mostly hardcover.

☐ The University of Alabama Press addresses a scholarly audience from all branches of Judaism. Seeks scholarly books of interest "within the traditional disciplines." Interested in Hasidism, the Holocaust, Jewish Americana, and Jewish history and thought.

Average book length is 200 to 400 pages. Prefers a complete manuscript, but queries acceptable. Accepts computer submissions. Pays royalties on the wholesale price. Free catalog and author guidelines for SASE.

UNIVERSITY OF CHICAGO PRESS, 5801 South Ellis, Chicago, IL 60637. (312) 202-7700. Morris Philipson, director; Alan Thomas, religion editor; T. David Brent, philosophy editor. Publishes 8 to 10 originals and reprints of Jewish interest annually.

☐ University of Chicago Press publishes "original scholarship that contributes to the advancement of knowledge in the humanities and social sciences. Books are reviewed prior to publication by at least two specialists in the field and must be approved by the faculty advisory board." Publishes Chicago Studies in the History of Judaism, edited by Jacob Neusner, in addition to a number of books for Jewish studies in general.

Average book length 60,000 to 120,000 words. Prefers outline/synopsis. Accepts simultaneous submissions "reluctantly." Free catalog and author guidelines for SASE. Reports in 10 weeks. Pays 10 percent royalty on net sales on first printings of cloth books. Also pays advances on signing.

UNIVERSITY PRESS OF AMERICA, INCORPORATED, 4720-A Boston Way, Lanham, MD 20706. (301) 459-3366. Fax: (301) 459-2118. Jonathan Sisk, editor-in-chief; Julie Kirsch, acquisitions editor. Publishes 25 originals and reprints yearly, 50 percent of them in paper-back. Some books are copublished with "Studies in Judaism."

☐ University Press of America primarily addresses an audience of scholars. Publishes scholarly monographs. Books of Jewish interest on subjects of the Bible, Israel, the Holocaust, Jewish history and thought.

Prefers a query. Reports in 4 weeks. Pays varied royalties. Free catalog and author guidelines for SASE.

WAYNE STATE UNIVERSITY PRESS, 5959 Woodward Avenue, Detroit, MI 48202. (313) 577-4600. Fax: (313) 577-6131. Arthur B. Evans, editor. Publishes 6 to 8 originals and reprints of Jewish interest yearly.

☐ Wayne State University Press addresses a scholarly audience from all Jewish back-grounds. Publishes scholarly books in all areas of literature and criticism as well as regional books for the Great Lakes area. Judaica interests are in biographies of Jewish personalities, the Holocaust, Jewish humor, Americana, and history. Especially seeking books of Jewish folklore and anthropology.

Prefers a query. Accepts outline/synopsis/sample chapters. Accepts most computer submissions. Reports in 3 months. Pays varied royalties based on the wholesale price. Rarely offers advances. Guidelines and semiannual catalog available.

MARKUS WIENER PUBLISHING, INCORPORATED, 114 Jefferson Road, Princeton, NJ 08540. (609) 921-1141. Shelly L. Frisch and Jonathan Sarna, editors. Publishes original and reprint books of Jewish interest in cooperation with the Center of the Study of American Jewish Experience at Hebrew Union College in Cincinnati.

☐ Markus Wiener Publishing seeks "high quality nonfiction literature and scholarship" on world culture and women's issues. Publishes "Masterworks of Modern Jewish Writing" which includes fiction, Jewish history, and Jewish Americana.

Average book length 300 pages. Prefers outline/synopsis/sample chapters. No simul-taneous submissions. Reports in 4 weeks. Pays 10 percent royalty.

WOMEN'S LEAGUE FOR CONSERVATIVE JUDAISM, 48 East 74th Street, New York, NY 10021. (212) 628-1600. Fax: (212) 772-3507. Janis Popp and Rhonda Kahn, editors. Publishes 1 to 3 paperback originals annually.

☐ Women's League for Conservative Judaism addresses an adult audience from a Con-servative Jewish background. Interested in a variety of topics, especially contemporary life-styles, health and medicine, Jewish travel.

Prefers a complete manuscript. No reprints or simultaneous submissions. Reports in 10 weeks. Pays royalties.

YALE UNIVERSITY PRESS, 92A Yale Station, New Haven, CT 06520. (203) 432-0900. Fax: (203) 432-2394. Charles Grench, editor. Publishes 10 hardcover originals of Jewish in-terest yearly.

☐ Yale University Press primarily addresses an audience of scholars. Interested in schol-arly books on a variety of subjects: the Bible, Israel, the Holocaust, Jewish thought and history.

Average book length 400 pages. Prefers a query. Reports in 4 weeks. Pays royalties on the wholesale price. Offers advances. Free catalog and author guidelines for SASE.

NOTE TO USERS OF THIS BOOK

As you search in chapters 2, 3, and 4 for appropriate publishers for your material, be sure to use the indexes in the back of the book to help you find the periodicals and publishers you are looking for.

Chapter 5, *Branching Out*, has additional lists of publishers and information you will want if you are writing poetry, greeting cards, curriculum, or devotionals; preparing material for newspapers and syndicates, regional publications and nonprofit organizations; or marketing cartoons or drama and scripts for radio, television, videos, or film.

In chapter 7, you will also find a list of literary agents who have expressed interest in helping writers market religious material.

FIVE

Branching Out: Other Opportunities in Religious Publishing

Chapters 2, 3, and 4 have examined the largest, most obvious markets for writing. This chapter profiles the lesser known (or at least lesser tried) opportunities. Some are right at your doorstep, in your own community, or in your region of the country; others are in your denomination or faith group. This chapter lists the names and addresses of places that need religious writers. Some are bound to fill your needs—or more accurately, you can fill theirs.

More than that, reading this chapter will bring many other places to mind as you plan for honing your writing skills and expanding your experience. Only your time and energy limits the field. We urge you to take advantage of your opportunities as a religious writer.

In each edition of *Religious Writers Marketplace* we have asked successful writers to share their expertise in the various fields available. Some of these writers are new to this edition. We're pleased that our writers have supplied you with helpful guidance and many new resources. Read and discover them!

WRITING FOR THE LOCAL CONGREGATION

by Don M. Aycock

You want to be a writer but don't know where to begin? Go to your church or synagogue! Writing opportunities are hidden all over your congregation. If you take the time to discover them, you will find plenty of chances to write and see your work in print, even if it is only in the weekly bulletin. Writing for your congregation is a good way to get experience in putting words on paper. With a little imagination and some hard work, you can become a published writer. Here are some suggestions.

Most writers are readers. Why not write a short book review of something you have read that really helped you? If the book has broad appeal, publish the review in your bulletin or church newsletter. This is especially helpful if the book is in your congregation's library. You can keep fellow members informed about new additions to the library.

Another helpful service writers can perform for their congregations is to catalog ministry opportunities in the church family and community. These needs might be in the church itself or in the community. But be careful not to embarrass anyone in need by printing his or her name. Simply write about general needs in your church and community.

A pastor has the natural opportunity to write to people's needs in a "Pastor's Paragraph" in the bulletin or church newsletter. When one of our older members died, I wrote a column about him. I gave the printed material to his family, who say they will cherish it. One friend used his pastor's column for several months to write specifically to couples. He then collected them into one volume with a publisher to produce his first book.

A doctor friend serves his church by writing and directing plays and dinner theaters sponsored by the church. He does two to four each year. They are done with such skill that each is a sell-out. Many people in the community are introduced to the church through a play.

Write a meditation or sermon. This material could be copied and distributed to the congregation. Or it might be delivered orally during a worship service or devotion.

Special days are good times for writers to reach out to the local congregation. For Father's Day, one woman wrote about her love for her dad. We printed the piece and distributed it to the church. Not only was her father "famous" for a day, the rest of us benefited from it, too.

Writers can keep the local media informed about events in their congregations by approaching newspapers and radio and television stations. Writing news releases is a valuable skill and a needed ministry.

I have written a great deal of Sunday school curriculum for my denomination. Although that material is used in thousands of other churches, I also use it in my Bible class. Curriculum is not easy to write, but prospective writers can get a foot in the door if they are persistent. (See the section "Writing Curriculum" later in this chapter.)

These suggestions are obvious ways to write for your congregation. Use your imagination, and you will find other opportunities. Writers can't not write. Let your inner drive lead you to find publishing opportunities right in your own congregation.

Don Aycock, pastor of a Baptist church in Lake Charles, Louisiana, is a prolific writer: 11 books, dozens of articles, and other materials in print. His most recent book is Inside Religious Publishing *published by Zondervan.*

WRITING FOR REGIONAL PUBLICATIONS

by William Gentz

Regional publications, especially among the larger denominations, are another market for serious religious writers to investigate. Usually they appear frequently—most are monthly, some are weekly. All look for news and features, and they represent a vast opportunity for the religious writer—right at your doorstep.

Most regional publications do not pay for material, but some do, and once you're known as a writer in your area, other opportunities will present themselves. Investigate first your denomination's papers, since each publication prefers to use people who understand its church and the church's special needs. These publications serve a certain geographic region and are interested almost exclusively in stories about people and events in that area. Keep this in mind when writing for them.

If you do not know the name and address of the regional paper that serves your area, get it from your pastor. Or send for a complete list of denominational papers in your region. This information is available at the headquarters of the jurisdictional division where your church is located.

WRITING FOR NONPROFIT ORGANIZATIONS

by William Gentz

Sometimes the best writing opportunities are closer at hand than we realize. For writers of religious material, such opportunities can be found in writing for nonprofit, charitable organizations, many of which have religious sponsorship or orientation. Most of them need help in preparing material for their members, writing promotional letters and brochures, and finding the means of getting the word out to the media about their organizations.

You may want to donate your time to such endeavors, thus building a reputation and getting experience in such forms of writing. But in many cases, especially after you become known, payment for your services is legitimate. After all, such organizations are accustomed to paying the printer and others who help prepare the final product, and many of them are also eager to pay for the services of a good writer. In recent years I have accepted such assignments from several groups, among them the John Milton Society for the Blind, the Laymen's National Bible Association, Catholic Relief Services, the American Bible Society, and Lutheran Immigration and Refugee Service.

Where do you find out about such writing assignments? Look in the yellow pages of your local telephone directory. Ask your local public library. Look for information in your newspapers and local shopping papers. Read the community bulletin boards in your supermarket or wherever they exist. Watch your mail for the many different kinds of brochures and mailings we all receive. Try the organizations to which you belong.

There are also many sources of information about national, nonprofit organizations. One good source is the *Encyclopedia of Associations,* which you will find in your public library. You may find that many national groups have local chapters or branches in your community. Approach them. Get to know their programs and materials and suggest ways that you might be able to help them. When you first call on a nonprofit organization, it is good to have samples of your writing and a bio (short biography) of yourself explaining who you are, what your background is, and what experience you have.

One good place to start and to acquire experience that can be used elsewhere is your church or synagogue. See "Writing for the Local Congregation" earlier in this chapter for suggestions about what can be done there. The clergy from your congregation can also give you information about agencies sponsored by your denomination or faith group that might need your writing help. You may be amazed at the unexpected doors this will open to you. Here's what I mean.

Sometime ago a friend recommended me to the John Milton Society for the Blind to help construct a pamphlet on the Bible and blindness. After I did this one task for them, they also asked me to prepare a brochure on Helen Keller's religious faith, in anticipation of the 100th anniversary of her birth. (She was one of the founders of the Society and served as its president for thirty years—two facts the Society wanted to emphasize during the celebration.)

In the process, the Society also conceived the idea of a magazine article on Miss Keller's Christian faith. They sent this story to several publications; many used it in part or whole. Many of the publications that used the story do not pay for submissions and were happy to get the article from the John Milton Society.

After I finished writing the story, the Society asked me to search their files and old minutes for vignettes on Miss Keller and her faith that would be suitable as filler in other publications. These reached an even wider audience. In addition, my association with the Society stimulated my interest in religious work with the blind, and I wrote and sold two other stories on blindness.

To prepare yourself for working with nonprofit organizations, you may want to look into the following books: *Jobs for Writers* by Kirk Polking, Writer's Digest Books; and *Let the People Know* by Charles Austin, Augsburg.

MARKETING RELIGIOUS POETRY

by Fannie Houck

Marketing poetry differs from marketing prose. Prose articles are the main dish at most periodicals. Often queried in the idea stage, articles are submitted one at a time.

Like dessert, poems appear on the table less often and on small plates. Poems are fillers. They are not queried, and they are submitted in small batches. However well written, poems differ widely in content and scope. Poetry editors differ widely, too, in their tastes.

Yet another difference—article writers may write for only a few magazines. Poetry pays poorly, thus poets need many sales to many markets to survive economically.

After creating and polishing a worthy product, the poet's principal challenge is to find receptive markets. There are many. One needs much patience to discover them. Local, general markets such as newspapers, newsletters, and bulletins can be a good starting place. They help poets test their poetic wings. Acceptance by these publications both affirms and encourages the poet.

To learn about other publications, study writers' market guides, magazines, and newsletters. This book and others such as *Poet's Market* (Writer's Digest Books) can help you find potential markets.

Choose likely markets, then send for and study writer's guidelines and sample copies. This is tedious and time-consuming but essential. Carefully choose and proofread poems before submitting them. If you persist and send what editors want, you will sell your poetry!

I find it helpful to compile my own market lists for different types of poems. And for each market-ready poem, I also prepare a written market plan that names six or more markets. If my poems return, as they often do, I already know where to submit them next.

Before mailing a batch of poems, I review my information about the editor and the market. Do these poems seem appropriate in tone, content, and style for this market?

Each poem has a submission history, which traces its travels from editor to editor. This helps prevent resubmissions to the same editor who has already published or returned it.

When matching poems to editors and markets, it helps to know the poetry editor's name. When editors move on, there's a new one to please and a new set of preferences. Acquaint yourself with poetry editors at writer's conferences and other meetings of this kind. Even a brief chat can reveal personality and preference clues. Such chats often lead to sales on the spot, or sales at a later time.

I subscribe to the magazines that buy my poems. This keeps me abreast of their editorial slant and choices.

Manuscripts go to the post office with a prayer that they find a receptive home and bring someone pleasure, inspiration, and blessing.

One easy market for me has been a denominational paper I've read for years. With varying degrees of success, I've sent poems to an array of consumer, literary, and Christian markets, usually ones listed in a market book. I've tried general interest magazines and others for women, children, teens, or writers.

Marketing poetry has no end. For alas! Good markets dry up or get overstocked. So it's necessary to be alert always for new markets.

What about contests? Are they worthwhile? I think so. I have entered (and lost) many poetry contests. The process of entering—having to select, evaluate, prepare, and polish something appropriate—is a learning experience in itself. If feedback or critique is offered for a small entry fee, I go for it. Opportunities to review or judge others' work have taught me many things about my writing.

Honing our poetic skills helps us create and market delectable poems that editors crave. We can increase our skills through poetry critique groups and round robins. State poetry associations also help us learn and grow.

Markets come and go and change. But if we continue to learn and grow and persistently and thoughtfully market our work, many readers will relish and remember our work.

Fannie Houck of Port Townsend, Washington, has seen her poetry and other writings appear in 47 publications. *Pebbles on the Path,* her first published collection of poems, is her sixth book.

CREATING CARTOONS
AND
CARTOON ARTICLES

by Larry Neagle

Mark Twain in "How I Edited an Agricultural Newspaper" gave this bit of wisdom: "Turnips should never be pulled, it injures them. It is much better to send a boy up and let him shake the tree."

Now obviously Mark Twain never wrote a Serious Article of Fact. If he had, he would have written more accurately that turnips ought to be plucked with great care so as to avoid the thorns on the vines.

This, then, is a Serious Article of Fact. Peruse the following six steps for creating cartoons and cartoon articles for the religious market.

1. Keep art and text simple and uncluttered. Long or complicated text loses reader interest. Complicated cartoons reduce poorly, and look fussy to the eye.

2. Focus on the elements that shape humor:

    a. Reversals. This is what happens when you have a duck in a hunting blind blowing a human call. Reverse roles; reverse sayings; reverse expected outcomes. Most of my cartoon articles were reversals. It was never "How to" but always "How not to."

b. Exaggeration. Did the preacher at your wedding really look like Bela Lugosi?

c. Incongruity. This refers to things out of place: anachronisms, habits, customs. This could be inmates at a prison banquet placing number cards in front of plates as name tags, or a Roman soldier checking his wrist watch to see if it's time for his replacement to arrive.

So which one is chocolate?

d. Understatement. Two men are marooned on a desert island. One taps the other on the shoulder and says, "Do you have a minute?"

e. Hidden elements. We all love to see someone's bubble burst. And nothing bursts a bubble quicker than situations where we see something hidden from the character that spells disaster to his pompous and otherwise inappropriate actions.

3. Avoid extremes. You need not be preachy or use heavy theological content. A light touch in good taste is always appreciated.

How is it that you know so much about sin?

4. Never use cliches. Or old jokes. Or the one you just heard today.

5. Market energetically. Use guides like *Religious Writers Marketplace.* Markets interested in cartoons usually say so in their listing. However, not everyone interested in a cartoon article will say so. Look through the listings for markets that are interested in both cartoons and your subject matter. Then query, including a sample of your art. I've sold to a number of markets in this way.

6. Make it easy for your editor. Send camera ready copy. Meet any deadlines given. Send a SASE. The easier you make it for the publisher, the easier that publisher is to sell to again.

I sold my first cartoon article to *Church Management: the Clergy Journal.* Since then I've sold almost 150 more to such magazines as *The Alliance Teacher, The Deacon, Lighted Pathway,* and *Pentecostal Conquerors.* I've been paid as little as $15, and as much as $250. You won't get rich. But the market is there. Check the entries in chapter 2 to find them.

_____

Larry Neagle is a free-lance writer and cartoonist living in Fort Worth, Texas. More than 1,000 of his cartoons and more than 300 of his articles, short stories, and video scripts have been published or produced. He has published three books.

WRITING GREETING CARDS

by William Gentz

Many religious writers—especially poets—find greeting cards a good market for their talents. Cards express not only the sender's love, but also God's love to the recipient. Several companies specialize in religious cards, and many general publishers use religious messages and verse for special occasions.

Stores indicate that customers are looking for cards that communicate concern for others, contain a meaningful message, and have a fresh appearance. Religious and inspirational cards are definitely a part of this market.

If you plan to write for the greeting card market, study publishers' needs carefully and request their guidelines on submitting material. These differ greatly. Greeting card publishers, however, give the following general guidelines: Type each verse and message double-spaced on a 3 × 5 or 4 × 6 index card. Use only one side of the card. Put your name and address in the upper left-hand corner. Keep a copy of verses or ideas you submit. It's also advisable to keep a record of what you've submitted to each publisher. Enclose a SASE and limit verses or ideas to ten per submission.

An association of greeting card writers and publishers has recently been formed. Write for information about this group and the services they offer: Greeting Creative Network, 1350 New York Avenue, Suite 615, Washington, DC 20005. Another resource comes from Writer's Digest Books, Cincinnati, Ohio, publisher of *A Guide to Greeting Card Writing* by Larry Sandman, $9.95.

David Taylor of *DaySpring Greetings* at Outreach Publications describes this market thus: "There are two broad based categories: everyday cards and seasonal cards. The everyday cards include cards for birthdays, friendship, sympathy, weddings, anniversaries, encouragement, congratulations, etc. The seasonal cards are generally broken down by counter line or box line (this applies to Christmas in particular). This varies with companies, but for *DaySpring,* Christmas, Valentines, and Mother's Day are the largest sending seasons. A good way to know the needs of the market of any particular company is to review the line mix in a local card or gift store."

Establishing yourself in this market requires talent, determination, and lots of work— because the competition is keen. Professional writers are on the staffs of many companies, but free-lance material is definitely sought. Query publishers to find out what themes are open at each of them. Send for the "tip sheets" or "market letters" that some of them issue.

The following publishers do religious material—some of them mostly for Christmas or other special holidays. Areas of special emphasis are indicated in the parentheses. Note that some are specifically Christian, others general religious, and some specifically Jewish.

Greeting Card Publishers

Abbey Press, Box 128, St. Meinrad, IN 47577 (Christian and religious).

American Greetings, 10500 American Road, Cleveland, OH 44144.

Argus Communications, 200 East Bethany, Allen, TX 75002.

Artforms Card Corporation, 725 County Line Road, Deerfield, IL 60015 (Jewish).

Russ Berrie & Company, 111 Bauer Drive, Oakland, NJ 07436.

Bethel Publishing, 1819 South Main Street, Elkhart, IN 46516.

Black and White Cards, Box 6250, Grand Central Station, New York, NY 10163-6020.

Blue Mountain Arts, Box 1077, Boulder, CO 80306 (Inspirational and religious).

Caring Card Company, Box 90278, Long Beach, CA 90809-0278 (Inspirational and religious).

Celebration, Box 9500, Boulder, CO 80301.

Concordia Publishing House, 3558 South Jefferson Avenue, St. Louis, MO 63125.

Creative Directions Incorporated, 323 South Franklin Building, Chicago, IL 60606.

Current, Incorporated, Box 2559, Colorado Springs, CO 80901 (Holidays and seasonal inspirational).

Dayspring Greeting Cards, Box 1010, Siloam Springs, AR 72761 (Christian/religious).

Freedom Greetings, Box 715, Bristol, PA 19007 (Inspirational and religious).

Gallant Greetings, 2654 West Medill, Chicago, IL 60647 (Inspirational and religious).

The C. R. Gibson Company, 32 Knight Street, Norwalk, CT 06856 (Inspirational and religious).

It Takes Two, 100 Minnesota Avenue, LeSueur, MN 56068.

Life Greetings, Box 468, Little Compton, RI 02837 (Religious and inspirational).

Manhattan Greeting Card Company, 150 East 52nd Street, New York, NY 10022 (General religious and inspirational).

Manuscriptures, 9120 260 2nd Avenue, Salem, WI 53168.

Mister B Greeting Card Company, 3305 Northwest 37th Street, Miami, FL 33142 (Christmas and Jewish).

Morning Star Cards, 810 First Street, South Hopkins, MN 55343 (Christian).

Oatmeal Studios, Box 138, Rochester, VT 05767 (Christmas).

Pacific Paper Greetings, Incorporated, Box 2249, Sidney, BC, V8L 3S8 Canada (Inspirational).

Printery House of Conception Abbey, Conception, MO 64433 (Religious/Catholic).

Red Farm Studio, Box 347, Pawtucket, RI 02862 (Christmas).

Roserich Designs Ltd., 627 Broadway #7, New York, NY 10012-2612 (Inspirational).

MARCEL SCHURMAN COMPANY, 2500 North Whatney Way, Fairfield, CA 94533 (General and religious).

SEEDS EVANGELICAL GREETING CARDS, 9906 Colt Drive, Bahama, NC 27503 (Christian).

SUNRISE PUBLICATIONS, 1145 Sunrise Greeting Court, Bloomington, IN 47402 (Religious and inspirational).

VAGABOND CREATIONS, 2560 Lance Drive, Dayton, OH 45409 (Christmas).

WARNER PRESS, INCORPORATED, P.O. Box 2499, Anderson, IN 46018 (Christian).

WINSTON-DEREK, 1722 West End Avenue, Nashville, TN 37203.

WRITING FOR NEWSPAPERS AND SYNDICATES

by Maynard Head

Newspapers always need material, and if it is well written and timely, editors often seek it out. Christian writers often overlook newspapers as a market, and since newspapers are published weekly, or daily, the demand for quality material remains high. Breaking into a large daily newspaper may be difficult for most writers, but if you wish to expand your market and explore the newspaper field, let me make a few suggestions.

Consider writing a few feature stories for a local weekly newspaper. Provide photographs, if possible. They often help sell a story. Stories abound in most communities and small newspapers frequently neither have the staff nor the time to produce them. Schedule an appointment with the editor and discuss your ideas. The editor may make suggestions and ask for material. If not, try again or approach another newspaper.

Once your features have appeared, and if your interest in newspaper writing continues, consider writing a weekly column. A column occupies a definite spot in the paper each week, and editors depend on this material on a consistent basis. If you're interested in writing a column, produce sample columns before discussing the matter with the editor. Consider a name, subject material, and length carefully. Study columns for ideas about material and structure. You will discover that most columns are short, so you will want to write tightly.

When you can consistently produce weekly material and have developed a good collection of clips of your best columns, approach a syndicate. Most syndicate editors prefer a query letter and a half-dozen sample columns. If the column involves technical material, mention why you are qualified to handle the topic. Include a SASE for the return of your material. A partial list of syndicates is as follows:

AMERICAN NEWS FEATURES SYNDICATE, P.O. Box 46004, Bedford, OH 44146. Syndicate features material to a number of newspapers.

CONTEMPORARY FEATURES SYNDICATE, P.O. Box 1258, Jackson, TN 38301. Seeks material on self-help.

FNA NEWS, P.O. Box 11999, Salt Lake City, UT 84147. FNA uses newspaper columns and features.

HYDE PARK MEDIA, 1314 Howard Street, Chicago, IL 60626. Uses newspaper features with a regional slant.

INTERMEDIA NEWS AND FEATURE SERVICE, 434 Avenue of the Americas, Box 691, New York, NY 10017.

UNIVERSAL PRESS SYNDICATE, 4900 Main Street, Kansas City, MO 64112. Universal is a market for newspaper columns and other material for use in a daily newspaper.

The advantage of syndication is that they make the contacts and do the recordkeeping, for a price of course. Usually 40 to 60 percent.

You may prefer to self-syndicate your column by approaching editors personally with samples of your material. You may self-syndicate by personally approaching other newspapers with your column. Send clips of your column for their consideration. Small newspapers negotiate payment on a case-to-case basis and payment ranges from $10 or less to $50 per column. But if your column appears in ten newspapers, that means $100 to $500 for each column.

The advantages to self-syndication is that you have complete control over your column and you keep all the money. The disadvantage is that you have to make all the contacts and do all the recordkeeping.

A number of publications are available to persons interested in writing a column. The following books may prove helpful in getting you established as a columnist.

The Editor and Publisher Syndicate Directory, 11 West 19th Street, New York, NY 10011.

How to Write and Sell a Column, Julie Raskin and Carolyn Males, Writer's Digest Books, 1507 Dana Avenue, Cincinnati, OH 45207.

Editor and Publishers Yearbook, 11 West 19th Street, New York, NY 10011.

Writing Columns and Departments, Mary Sayler, The Word Center, P.O. Box 730, DeLand, FL 32721-0730. A home study course, PSP Unit N-5.

Maynard Head, from Middlesboro, Kentucky, is an author and columnist and a faculty member of Clear Creek Baptist Bible College in Pineville, Kentucky.

News Services

If you like journalistic writing, here's an area you may want to investigate. News services have "stringers" all over the country who keep them supplied with important religious stories, smaller stories the leading news media miss, and local and regional news and analysis. Many denominational magazines and newspapers subscribe to their services. Query the agencies below for details on their particular needs and requirements.

DICKSON FEATURE SERVICE, 17700 Western #69, Gardena, CA 90248.

EVANGELICAL PRESS NEWS SERVICE, Evangelical Press Association, 485 Earlysville, VA 22936. Ronald E. Wilson, executive director.

NATIONAL CATHOLIC NEWS SERVICE, 1312 Massachusetts Avenue, NW, Washington, DC 20005.

RELIGIOUS NEWS SERVICE, P.O. Box 1015, Radio City Station, New York, NY 10101. (Both Christian and Jewish)

JEWISH TELEGRAPHIC AGENCY and SEVEN ARTS FEATURE SYNDICATE, 165 West 46th Street, New York, NY 10036.

ZONDERVAN PRESS SYNDICATE, Media Relations, B-22, 5300 Patterson, SE, Grand Rapids, MI 49530.

Religious Press Associations

For information on press associations, see the "Christian Writers Clubs, Fellowship Groups, and Critique Groups" section of chapter 6, subsection "Religious Press Associations."

WRITING FOR YOUNG READERS

by Sandra Brooks

One leading cause for rejection of juvenile manuscripts is that writers don't know their readers well enough to address their specific needs and concerns. Even seasoned writers admit they're often uncertain about how to make vocabulary and story complexity fit the needs of specific age groups. As with other forms of writing, there are few hard and fast rules in addressing young readers. Here are some general guidelines.

Toddlers, one- to three-year-olds, need the simplest language possible. Pictures of Jesus, Bible characters, familiar family objects, or family activities accompanied by a word, or two, lay the foundation for a toddler's faith.

Preschoolers, three- to five-year-olds, can handle more sophisticated language, but still not much. They love pictures, repetition, alliteration, and sing-song rhyme. They love stories about animals and other children, and they love to laugh. Two main characters are usually enough for preschool stories. Flashbacks are taboo! Children can't understand them.

Lists of acceptable vocabulary words can often be obtained from publishing houses or from public and Christian school teachers. In addition to these sources, *Writer's Digest* recently published a book by Alijandra Mogilner entitled, *Children's Writer's Word Book.* It contains word lists for kindergarten through sixth grade with grade-level notations for each word.

Early Readers, five- to seven-year-olds, can handle basic doctrinal concepts like salvation, forgiveness, and heaven. Early readers like stories about animals, science, history, and fantasy. Opportunities for nonfiction articles increase with early readers. The secret is keeping the topic fun and interesting, not just rehashing the encyclopedia.

Early readers prefer fiction about contemporary children, usually older than they. They like fast-paced action, suspense, and humor. The basic fiction formula of crisis, conflict, and change works well. Problems or obstacles that would overwhelm a child of this age should be avoided. Flashbacks still don't work for this age group.

Although vocabulary is simple, tossing in an occasional fun word intrigues and stretches the early reading mind.

Older Readers, eight- to eleven-year-olds, can handle deeper doctrine and life-style topics: salvation and personal growth, starting a daily quiet time, Bible study and prayer, handling personal relationships with parents, siblings, extended family, friends, classmates, and so forth.

These readers like a variety of nonfiction: biography, science, environmental issues, computers, electronic technology, and so on. Nonfiction articles can also cover how-to's on topics like handling the bully at school, parental criticism, and other issues they deal with every day. Three main characters are plenty, although others may be in the background, either named or unnamed.

Fiction and nonfiction can involve more sophisticated vocabulary and sentence structure: gerunds, infinitives, participles, and other devices that add color and variety to writing.

Teens, twelve- to eighteen-year-olds, is the group that challenges writers most. It's also the group whose attention is most difficult to capture. Many other things compete with reading for teens' time and attention. Quality word craftspersons can play a significant role in reclaiming teens for the printed page.

Teens want to see the relevance of biblical values to everyday life. They like deep spiritual truth explained in sensitive, honest, down-to-earth ways, incorporating as much humor as possible. Teens are more sensitive to preaching than any other group.

Taking an overall look at the marketplace, your best opportunities to sell are biblical and contemporary fiction (prose and rebuses), and nonfiction articles and columns. Other sections in this chapter help with more specialized kinds of writing for juveniles: poetry, drama, music, games, quizzes, and cartoons. Potential periodical markets include denominational and nondenominational magazines and take-home papers. Graded curriculum offers juvenile writers the advantage of assured income. The section of this chapter entitled "Writing Curriculum" gives help with curriculum markets. Potential book products include board books, picture books, game and activity books, coloring books, chapter books, how-to books, devotionals, Bible studies, and junior novels.

The markets are found in the entries in chapters 2 and 3 for Christian writers, and chapter 4 for Jewish writers.

No matter which age group a juvenile writer chooses, God can direct the words into language young readers can understand and respond to. God helps writers see their readers as living, breathing human beings with distinct needs and concerns. The images planted in young minds, the emotions evoked in their hearts, may have an eternal impact on what they think, do, and become. Juvenile writers can help young readers form ideals and values, make decisions, and establish lifetime goals.

Knowing the juvenile audience and writing to meet their specific needs is the secret of succeeding in the marketplace with young readers.

WRITING CURRICULUM

by Nan Duerling

Opportunities abound for writers who can communicate their love of God to students of a particular age group. Curriculum publishing houses of all types constantly need student books and materials, lesson plans for teachers, and related resources such as story books and puzzles. Much of this material is produced on a quarterly basis for Sunday schools, youth fellowship programs, children's activity groups, or junior worship services. Vacation Bible school resources are issued annually. In addition, many publishers print undated, elective resources that sell for several years. Some companies provide material for weekday schools, preschools, or home instruction.

Curriculum is often written by free-lancers who work under contract to produce a specific number of lessons or articles for a particular publication. Writers interested in fulfilling one or more of these assignments should study curriculum samples. Next the writer approaches the publishers that seem interesting to find out how to receive an assignment. Some publishers ask potential writers to complete a questionnaire asking for background experience and training as well as samples of materials written to determine ability to write for specific age groups.

Successful curriculum writers need not be professional theologians, but they know their personal theological positions. The writer's basic understandings about God and how one reads and interprets the Bible must fit well with the publishing house and its readers. Writers need to be familiar with reference books, such as commentaries, Bible dictionaries, concordances, and other resources.

Effective curriculum writers are educators at heart. They are familiar with the needs and interests of children (birth through elementary school), youth (middle high, junior high, senior high), or adults (young adults, middle adults, older adults). These writers use appropriate vocabulary and real-life examples to reach their age group. They provide a variety of activities to help students learn and grow in their faith. Good curriculum writers know how to focus their work on the content they are expected to cover. They must meet the learning objectives set forth by the publisher. These skills are critical because most houses produce materials according to a master curriculum plan, such as the Uniform Series or one of their own design. The lessons or stories that one writer submits must fit together with the work of other writers to create a coherent whole. Since lessons are often based on familiar Bible passages, writers must also become adept at telling "the old, old story" in fresh ways that excite readers and motivate them to respond to the teaching.

Often the person who writes the student book and lesson plans also prepares guides for the teacher. The writer must provide clear, concise directions that help even an inexperienced teacher to work effectively with students. Publication formats vary, but teacher's books generally include: Bible background, materials that are needed to do the lesson, steps in preparation, a purpose for each activity, suggested times for each activity, and options for adding or substituting activities. Some publishers may want authors to field test their material by having several teachers try it out with their classes and evaluate it.

To make curriculum "user-friendly" for students and teachers, publishers usually have a consistent format for each lesson in a series. To achieve this uniformity, editors provide writers with detailed instructions regarding word and line counts, possibly designating the number of characters that are to appear on each line. Even within a single lesson, there may be detailed guidelines on how to structure the lesson. The editor specifies the number of units or lessons to be completed.

Writers must clarify with the editor deadlines for preliminary drafts, the final manuscript, and check on accepted methods of submission, which may include printed copies, faxes, transmission by modem, or computer disks. A written contract should state the amount of payment and whether payment is made on acceptance or on publication. Ownership rights also should be specified in the contract.

Curriculum writing is challenging, exacting work, but it offers tremendous possibilities for authors who want to share their knowledge and faith with others through educational resources.

Nan Duerling, Ph.D., of Crownsville, Maryland, is a free-lance curriculum writer, teacher, and educational consultant.

Curriculum Markets

Producers of Jewish Curriculum

ALTERNATIVES IN RELIGIOUS EDUCATION, 3845 Oneida Street, Denver, CO 80237.
A.R.E. PUBLISHING, 3945 Oneida Street, Denver, CO 80237.
BEHRMAN HOUSE, INCORPORATED, 235 Watchung Avenue, West Orange, NJ 07052.
BOARD OF JEWISH EDUCATION OF NEW YORK, 426 West 58th Street, New York, NY 10010.
UNITED SYNAGOGUE OF AMERICA BOOK SERVICE, 155 Fifth Avenue, New York, NY 10010.

Producers of Christian Curriculum

ACCENT PUBLISHERS (Accent Bible Curriculum), P.O. Box 15337, Denver, CO 80215. (303) 988-5300. Nondenominational, Evangelical, Fundamental. Mary Nelson, editor.

AUGSBURG FORTRESS, 426 South Fifth Street, Box 1209, Minneapolis, MN 55440. Evangelical Lutheran Church in America. Rebecca Grothe; John Kober, children's; Susan Niemi, youth; Scott Tunseth, adult; Carol Burk, teacher publications.

BAPTIST SUNDAY SCHOOL BOARD, 127 Ninth Avenue N, Nashville, TN 37234. (615) 251-2000. Southern Baptist Church, Evangelical. Currently reorganizing. Address all inquiries to Editorial and Curriculum Specialist, Office of Church Growth and Programs. Requires writers to be members of the Southern Baptist Church.

BRETHREN PRESS, 1451 Dundee Avenue, Elgin, IL 60120. (708) 742-5100. Church of the Brethren. Julie Garber, editor. Requires writers to be members of the Brethren Church.

WILLIAM C. BROWN COMMUNICATIONS, INCORPORATED (Brown-ROA), 2460 Kerper Boulevard, Dubuque, IA 52001. (319) 588-1451. Roman Catholic. Mary Jo Graham, elementary (preschool through eighth grade); Marilyn Bowers Gorun, high school and adult publications; Ernest T. Nedder, teacher publications and special areas and topics.

CHRISTIAN BOARD OF PUBLICATION, Box 179, St. Louis, MO 63166. (314) 231-8500. Christian Church (Disciples of Christ). Joseph H. Bragg, Jr.

CHRISTIAN EDUCATIONAL PUBLISHERS, Box 261129, San Diego, CA 92196. (619) 578-4700. Dr. Lon Ackelson, editor. (See also entry in chapter 3.)

COKESBURY, P.O. Box 801, Nashville, TN 37202. (615) 749-6234. The United Methodist Church. Duane A. Ewers, chief curriculum editor; Sharilyn Adair, children's publications; M. Steven Games, youth publications; Dal Joon Won, adult publications and special areas (Special Language Publications); Keith Kendall, teacher publications.

CONCORDIA PUBLISHING HOUSE, 3558 South Jefferson Avenue, St. Louis, MO 63118. (314) 268-1000. Lutheran Church—Missouri Synod. Earl Gaulke, chief curriculum editor; Arnold Schmidt, Sunday school; Rodney Rathman, day/weekday; Jane Fryar, vacation Bible school; Tom Nummela, youth and adult materials.

DAVID C. COOK PUBLISHING COMPANY, 850 North Grove Avenue, Elgin, IL 60120. (708) 741-2400. Interdenominational, Evangelical. John Conaway, children's publications; Rick Thompson, youth publications; Sue Geiman, adult publications and teacher publications.

EASTON PUBLISHING COMPANY, P.O. Box 5192, Rockford, IL 61125. (815) 398-0177. Roman Catholic. Publishes high school curriculum. Laurine Easton, managing editor.

EDUCATIONAL MINISTRIES, INCORPORATED, 165 Plaza Drive, Prescott, AZ 86303. (602) 771-8601. Nondenominational, Liberal. Robert Davidson, chief curriculum editor, youth and adult publications; Linda Davidson, children's and teacher publications; Henry Rust, adult publications, special areas and topics.

FRANCISCAN COMMUNICATIONS (Winston Press), 1229 South Santee Street, Los Angeles, CA 90015-2566. (213) 746-2916. Roman Catholic. Corrine Hart, chief curriculum editor; Liz Montes, children's publications; Karl Holtsnider, adult publications.

FRIENDS UNITED PRESS, 101 Quaker Hill Drive, Richmond, IN 47374. (317) 962-7573. Friends United Meeting (Quakers), Mary Glenn Hadley, chief curriculum editor. Philip Baisley, children's publications, youth publications. Brian Daniels, adult and teacher publications.

GENERAL CONFERENCE OF SEVENTH DAY ADVENTISTS, CHURCH MINISTRIES DEPARTMENT. 12501 Old Columbia Pike, Silver Spring, MD 20904-6600. (301) 680-6165. Seventh Day Adventist. Aileen Sox, primary (ages 1 to 4) and preschool (ages 6 to 9) materials; Andrea Kristenson, junior (ages 10 to 12) and early teen (ages 13 to 14) materials; Gary Swanson, teenage (ages 15 to 17) and young adult (ages 18 to 35) materials;

Erwin Gane, adult (ages 35 up) materials. Requires writers to be members of the Seventh Day Adventist Church.

GOSPEL LIGHT PUBLICATIONS (Living Word Curriculum), 2300 Knoll Drive, Ventura, CA 93003. (805) 644-9721. Interdenominational. Gary S. Greig, Ph.D., chief curriculum editor; Lynnette Pennings, Sunday school curriculum; Christy Weir, Vacation Bible School curriculum; Kyle Duncan, youth and adult publications; Sheryl Haystead, teacher publications and special areas or topics.

GOSPEL PUBLISHING HOUSE (Radiant Life), 1445 Boonville Avenue, Springfield, MO 65802. (417) 862-2781. General Council of the Assemblies of God. Gary L. Leggett, editor in chief; Dawn Hartman, early childhood; Sinda Zinn, elementary children; Tammy Bickey, youth publications; Paul W. Smith, adult publications; Lorraine Mastrorio, special projects.

GROUP PUBLISHING, INCORPORATED (Group's Active Bible Curriculum, Group's Hand-On Bible Curriculum), P.O. Box 481, Loveland, CO 80539. (303) 669-3836. Nondenominational, Evangelical. Stephen Parolini, chief curriculum editor.

KINDRED PRESS, 4-169 Riverton Avenue, Winnipeg, MB, R2L2E5 Canada. U.S. office: 315 South Lincoln, Hillsboro, KS 67063. (204) 669-6575. Marilyn Hudson, interim editor. Mennonite Brethren.

LIGHT AND LIFE PRESS, P.O. Box 535002, Indianapolis, IN 46253-5002. (317) 244-3660. Free Methodist Church of North America. Jean Ballew, director of curriculum ministries.

LIVING THE GOOD NEWS INCORPORATED, 777 Grant Street, Suite 302, Denver, CO 80203. (303) 832-4427. Roman Catholic/Episcopal. Dina Gluckstensn, children's publications; Dirk deVries, youth publications; Jo Youngquist, adult publications; Sue Macstravic, teacher publications; Liz Riggleman, for special projects.

MENNONITE PUBLISHING HOUSE (Herald Press), 616 Walnut Avenue, Scottdale, PA 15683. (412) 887-8500. Mennonite Church. J. Laurence Martin, chief curriculum editor; Marjorie Waybill, children's and children's teachers publications; David Hiebert, youth, adult, and teacher (youth and adult) publications; James E. Horsch, adult electives and miscellaneous curriculum.

MOREHOUSE PUBLISHING (Episcopal Children's Curriculum), P.O. Box 1321, Harrisburg, PA 17105. (717) 541-8130. The Episcopal Church. Locke Bowman, editor in chief, Episcopal Children's Curriculum.

NATIONAL BAPTIST PUBLISHING BOARD, 6717 Centennial Boulevard, Nashville, TN 37209. (615) 350-8000. National Baptist. Pamela Yates, interim editor.

NAZARENE PUBLISHING HOUSE (WordAction Publishing Company), P.O. Box 419527, 2923 Troost, Kansas City, MO 64141. Church of the Nazarene. Dr. Phil Riley, chief curriculum editor and teacher publications; Mark York, children's publications; David Caudle, youth publications; Gene Van Note, adult publications.

NEW HOPE, Box 12065, Birmingham, AL 35202-2065. (205) 991-8120. Women's Missionary Union of the Southern Baptist Convention. Requires Southern Baptist Writers. (See also entry in chapter 3.)

OUR SUNDAY VISITOR, 200 Noll Plaza, Huntington, IN 46750. (219) 356-8400. Roman Catholic. Greg Erlandson, editor in chief; Jacquelyn Murphy, acquisitions editor.

PACIFIC PRESS, Box 7000, Boise, ID 83707. (208) 465-2500. Russell Holt, editor. Seventh Day Adventist. (See also entry in chapter 3.)

PRESBYTERIAN PUBLISHING HOUSE (PREM; Celebrate; Bible Discovery), 100 Witherspoon Street, Louisville, KY 40202. (502) 569-5000. Presbyterian Church, USA. Donna Blackstock, associate editor for resource development; Martha Pillow and Kent Chrisman, early childhood; Tom Malone, children ages 3 to 4 and family ministries; Faye

Berdick, elementary children and youth; Beth Basham and Jim Clinefelter, youth; Janice Weaver, Bible Discovery (adult); Frank Hainer, adult foundational curriculum; Marvin Simmers, leader development.

RANDALL HOUSE, 114 Bush Road, Box 17306, Nashville, TN 37217. (615) 361-1221. Harold D. Harrison, editor. Free Will Baptist. Requires writers from their denomination.

RESOURCE PUBLICATIONS, Suite 290, 160 East Virginia Street, San Jose, CA 95112. (408) 286-8505. (See also entry in chapter 3.)

SAINT ANTHONY MESSENGER PRESS, 1615 Republic Street, Cincinnati, OH 45210. (513) 241-5615. Roman Catholic. Lisa Biedenbach, adult publications.

SAINT MARY'S PRESS, Winona, MN 55987. (507) 457-7900, (800) 533-8095. Owned by Christian Brothers (Roman Catholic), but publish for all denominations, Liberal to Moderate. Steve Nagel, chief curriculum editor.

SCRIPTURE PRESS, P.O. Box 632, Glen Ellyn, IL 60138. Nondenominational, Evangelical.

SHEED & WARD, Box 419492, Kansas City, MO 64141-6492. (816) 531-0538. Robert Heyer, editor. Roman Catholic. (See also entry in chapter 3.)

STANDARD PUBLISHING, 8121 Hamilton Avenue, Cincinnati, OH 45231. Nondenominational, Evangelical. (513) 931-4050. Fax: (513) 931-0904. Richard C. McKinley, chief curriculum editor; Ruth Frederick, children's publications; David Henning, youth publications; James I. Fehl, adult publications; Barbara Bolton, teacher publications; Mark Plunkett, special areas and topics.

STAR SONG, 2325 Crestmoor, Nashville, TN 37215. (615) 269-0196. Matthew A. Price, vice-president.

SUNDAY SCHOOL PUBLISHING BOARD, 330 Charlotte Avenue, Nashville, TN 37201-1188. (615) 256-2480, (800) 359-9396. National Baptist Convention, USA, Inc. Dr. Cecelia N. Adkins, executive director; Dr. H. Clark Nabrit, Sunday school, vacation Bible school; Rev. Ottie West, adults and youth; Mrs. Rae Hudson Watkins, resources for children.

TEL PUBLISHERS, LTD., 1892 Daimler Road, P.O. Box 5471, Rockford, IL 61125-0471. (800) 835-5835, (815) 398-6730. Roman Catholic. Publishes curriculum for kindergarten through high school. Rev. Michael Librandi, general editor; Laurine Easton, editor.

TWENTY-THIRD PUBLICATIONS, P.O. Box 180, Mystic, CT 06355. (800) 321-0411, (203) 536-2611. Roman Catholic but much material is interdenominational. Neil Kluepfel, publisher in charge of acquisitions.

UNION GOSPEL PRESS, P.O. Box 6059, Cleveland, OH 44101. Fundamental.

UNITED CHURCH PRESS, 700 Prospect Avenue, E, Cleveland, OH 44115-1100. (216) 736-3706. United Church of Christ. Sidney D. Fowler, chief curriculum editor.

WARNER PRESS (Journey with the Word), 1200 East Fifth Street, P.O. Box 2499, Anderson, IN 46011. (317) 644-7721. Church of God. Arlo Newell, chief curriculum editor; Deanna Patrick, children's publications; Bill White, youth publications; John Little, adult and teacher publications.

There are also many curriculum writing opportunities with publishers who produce materials for public and private education.

FOCUS ON THE FAMILY, 420 North Cascade, Colorado Springs, CO 80903, is currently developing a line of curriculum for public and private schools.

SHINING STAR PUBLICATIONS, Box 299, Carthage, IL 62321. Becky Daniel, editor.

The following organizations can provide a complete list of potential publishers. Study the entries in chapter 3 for textbook publishers.

ASSOCIATION OF CHRISTIAN SCHOOLS INTERNATIONAL, P.O. Box 4097, Whittier, CA 90607.

CHRISTIAN SCHOOLS INTERNATIONAL, 3350 East Paris Avenue, SE, Grand Rapids, MI 49508.

EVANGELICAL TEACHER TRAINING ASSOCIATION, Box 327, Wheaton, IL 60187.

For one-on-one help with curriculum writing, request Personalized Study Program (PSP) Unit N-7, "Curriculum Writing," from Mary Harwell Sayler, The Word Center, P.O. Box 790, DeLand, FL 32721-0730.

CREATING PUZZLES, GAMES, AND QUIZZES

by Geri Hess Mitsch

Do you want to earn more money but spend less time doing it? Consider games, puzzles, quizzes, and other short pieces. Beginning writers find these shorter pieces less intimidating and easier to finish. There is the additional advantage of writing for a broad market—from children to adults. Children like to work puzzles, find hidden words, follow mazes, solve coded messages, and figure out rebus puzzles (where pictures stand for words). They're entertained with crafts and experiments. Adults enjoy the challenge of brain teasers, crossword puzzles, anagrams, and various kinds of quizzes.

Furthermore, hundreds of magazines carry many kinds of pencil puzzles, brain teasers, and games.

But there's more, much more than making money. In the inspirational market, you have the opportunity for teaching moral values and biblical concepts. Both children and adults are fascinated with crossword puzzles, anagrams, and mix-and-match. When clues use religious characters or Scripture references, they can teach religious facts and concepts. Even little hands can trace dot-to-dots and learn a religious symbol.

Quizzes can be just for fun, test the reader's knowledge, or help individuals do an evaluation (e.g., "Does Your Youth Program Measure Up?"). Thoughtfully answered quizzes can contribute to the reader's spiritual life (e.g., "Do You Have An Effective Prayer Life?").

But don't be fooled because these items are short. The markets are just as exacting and as individualized as any others. Each publication's distinct personality, style, and types of readers determine the success of selling to that particular editor.

To decide which markets you want to write for, consider your interests. If you enjoy playing Scrabble, you'll probably like making up word searches, anagrams, or crossword puzzles. You can even use Scrabble titles to construct your puzzles. Do you grab a pencil when you spot a crossword puzzle? Then try your hand at creating them. They may not be as difficult as you think. Connie Emerson's *How to Make Money Writing Fillers* (Writer's Digest Books, 1985) has several helpful chapters on composing various puzzles, quizzes, and brain teasers. She also includes several marketing tips.

Start by setting up a market file for the types of items you hope to write. Collect a wide variety of sample copies of magazines that use puzzles, quizzes, and games. Pick up "freebies" at writer's conferences and drugstores, back copies from your friends, doctor's offices, or senior centers, and Sunday school take-home papers (one of your best markets) from your children or your religious education department. Write publishers of other magazines for sample copies and guidelines. Some sample copies are free; others must be purchased. Check your market guide for specific details.

Now separate the magazines according to age groups: Children, juniors, adults. Next, go through and cut out the puzzles, quizzes, or games. *Be certain to add the publication title and date to each.* Then tape (paste, staple) all the adult crossword puzzles together on a sheet of three-hole notebook paper, making sure the magazine title and date are on each. Tape all the children's crossword puzzles on another sheet, and so on for each type of quiz, game, or brain teaser. Leave enough space for marketing tips and comments from editors later on.

Next, file these sheets in a three-ring binder (or in file folders) under the three age groups. Filed this way, items can be submitted at the same time to nonoverlapping markets that accept simultaneous submissions. Or they can easily be rerouted as reprints after you've sold them to publications buying first rights.

In another section of your notebook, set up a sheet for each magazine. Enter the title of the magazine, editor's name, address, telephone number, and even the types and themes of items they purchase. Alphabetize by publication titles, either in one alphabet or three alphabets, according to the three age groups: children, juniors, and adults.

When you mail submissions, list them by date under the proper magazine title, one submission to a line. Include the type of submission and title (e.g., dot-to-dots, Noah's Ark; crossword puzzle, Easter). Leave room to add results later (sold, returned), as well as amount and date of payment. You may also wish to add the date of publication.

As your submissions increase, you will need to set up another file to keep you from resubmitting an item to a publisher who's already purchased it. Enter the title of each submission on a sheet of paper, one per sheet, and list by date the various publications to which you've sent that item. For any items not titled, work out an identifying system, such as numbers, placing them on your file carbon copy.

So, ask yourself: Is this market for me? If you are challenged by brain teasers and pencil puzzles, you may find that writing for this potpourri market is just the answer for you. Check the entries in chapters 2, 3, and 4 for the best periodical and book markets for puzzles, games, and quizzes.

Until her death after a long bout with cancer, Geri Mitsch of Canby, Oregon, was an active writer and friend of writers whose memory is cherished by many. It is with thanks to God and in her memory that we reprint this article, which originally appeared in the third edition of *Religious Writers Marketplace.*

WRITING FOR MUSIC PUBLISHERS

by Cynthia Ann Wachner

To open doors to sales in the songwriter's market, writers and composers need five golden keys.

The first key, *Marketplace Knowledge,* requires research to understand each music medium's marketing requirements. By seeking out professionals who share industry information through six areas of contact, songwriters learn how to gain access to the market. These areas include magazines, newsletters, marketing books, seminars, organizations, and musical showcases at churches, conferences, and concerts. One place to start is with the lists at the end of this article. Note that both Christian and Jewish sources are listed.

The second key, *Reading Industry Magazines* and newsletters, plugs a songwriter into the business. Publisher John Styll (CCM and CCM Update) explains, "Magazines give musicians current business news, publisher updates, and knowledge of trends. They help songwriters learn industry players, know peer interests, and keep in tune with songs, artists, and labels on the charts."

Key number three, *Seminar Attendance,* advances a musician's career. Debbie Atkins, Executive Director at Word, Inc., says, "These events give artists chances to network, showcase their songs, and attract publishers' interest in promoting them to producers and directors." Other happenings include Christian Artist Music Seminars, ASCAP Seminars, Gospel Music Week, Dimensions in Christian Music, and Cantor Conventions.

The fourth key, *Membership in Organizations,* gives musicians publishing opportunities when they join GMA, The Songwriter's Guild of America, ASCAP, The Hymn Society in the United States and Canada, The Conference of American Cantors, The Cantor's Assembly, or The American Society for Jewish Music. Each keeps members abreast of industry news, seminars, networking opportunities, and membership perks. (See addresses below.)

The fifth key, *Marketing Presentation Techniques,* opens the last door to publication for artists' choral music, hymns, liturgical music, and all other media. To approach a gospel music publisher, Debbie Atkins explains, "For artists, we need two or three demo tape songs, a typed lyric sheet, a SASE, and an easy to open package with my name on it. I make appointments by phone to review works."

To market Christian choral music, follow the advice of Executive Director of Print Music for *Word Music,* David Gutherie: "We need four part arrangements of choir music that include soprano, alto, tenor, and bass. We do translate songs into full arrangements. Most of our pieces represent all choral styles based on Scripture and bigger theological points."

With these varied musical medium marketing tips in mind, take the final steps through the last door to sales and approach a publisher with your songs.

Music Periodicals

ASCAP IN ACTION—PLAYBACK, One Lincoln Plaza, New York, NY 10023. Murdoch McBride, editor.

CHURCH MUSIC REPORT, P.O. Box 1179, Grapevine, TX 76051. Bill Rayborn, editor.

CHURCH MUSIC WORKSHOP, 201 Eighth Avenue South, Nashville, TN 37203. Gary Alan Smith, managing editor.

CONTEMPORARY CHRISTIAN MAGAZINE UPDATE, 1913 21st Avenue S, Nashville, TN 37212. Stephen Speer, managing editor.

CONTEMPORARY CHRISTIAN MUSIC (CCM), 1913 21st Avenue S, Nashville, TN 37212. Thom Granger, senior editor.

CREATOR, P.O. Box 100, Dublin, OH 43017. Marshall Sanders, publisher.

GMA TODAY, 7 Music Circle, N, Nashville, TN 37203. Bruce Koblish, editor.

THE HYMN, A JOURNAL OF CONGREGATIONAL SINGING, The Hymn Society, P.O. Box 30854, Fort Worth, TX 76129. **THE STANZA**, same address. David W. Music, editor.

JOURNAL OF SYNAGOGUE MUSIC, The Cantor's Assembly, Jewish Theological Seminary, 3080 Broadway, New York, NY 10027.

MUSIC OF JUDAICA, The American Society for Jewish Music, 129 East 67th Street, New York, NY 10023.

MUSIC REVELATION, 7 Elmwood Court, Rockville, MD 20850. Harry Causey, editor and publisher.

SACRED MUSIC NEWS AND REVIEW, 302 3rd Avenue, S, Franklin, TN 37064. Dr. Timothy Sharpe, editor.

SONG WRITERS & ARTISTS, Box 3, Ashland, OR 97520. James Lloyd, editor.

WORSHIP LEADER, 1913 21st Avenue S, Nashville, TN 37212. Stephen Speer, managing editor.

Seminars and Conferences

ASCAP GOSPEL WRITING SEMINARS, Two Music Square West, Nashville, TN 37203.

CHRISTIAN ARTISTS MUSIC SEMINARS, Christian Artists Corporation, P.O. Box 338950, Denver, CO 80233.

DIMENSIONS IN CHURCH MUSIC, Mount Hermon Christian Conference Center, Mount Hermon, CA 95041.

GOSPEL MUSIC WEEK, Gospel Music Association, 7 Music Circle North, Nashville, TN 37203.

HYMN CONFERENCES, The Hymn Society in the United States and Canada, P.O. Box 30854, Fort Worth, TX 76129.

INTEGRITY MUSIC CONFERENCES, Worship International, P.O. Box 16813, Mobile, AL 36616. Holds four regional conferences yearly: North, South, East, and West.

JEWISH MUSIC CONVENTIONS, The American Conference of Cantors, The Cantor's Assembly, and The American Society for Jewish Music. (See below.)

WORD POWER TEAMS, Word Inc., 3319 West End Avenue, Suite 200, Nashville, TN 37203.

Organizations

THE AMERICAN CONFERENCE OF CANTORS, 170 West 74th Street, New York, NY 10023.

THE AMERICAN SOCIETY FOR JEWISH MUSIC, 129 East 67th Street, New York, NY 10023.

ASCAP (AMERICAN SOCIETY OF COMPOSERS, AUTHORS, AND PUBLISHERS), 350 West Hubbard, Chicago, IL 60610. Also has offices in Los Angeles, Nashville, and New York.

THE CANTOR'S ASSEMBLY, Jewish Theological Seminary, 3080 Broadway, New York, NY 10027.

GOSPEL ARTISTS AND MUSICIANS ASSOCIATION, c/o Russ Houck, 604 McKinney, Corsicana, TX 75010. (214) 964-2132 or (903) 874-7490.

GOSPEL MUSIC ASSOCIATION, 7 Music Circle, N, Nashville, TN 37203.

THE HYMN SOCIETY in the United States and Canada, P.O. Box 30854, Fort Worth, TX 76129.

SONG WRITER'S GUILD OF AMERICA (and FOUNDATION), 276 Fifth Avenue, Suite 306, New York, NY 10001.

Books

THE CHRISTIAN MEDIA DIRECTORY, The James Lloyd Group, Box 3, Ashland, OR. 4,000 listings of record labels, Christian music publishers, etc. $29.95.

THE CHRISTIAN MUSIC INDUSTRY DIRECTORY, Sunshine Publishing Company, P.O. Box 45678, Baton Rouge, LA 70895. (800) 673-5510. Professional phone book for musicians: record companies, booking agents, negotiation, and other vital information.

THE CRAFT AND THE BUSINESS OF SONG WRITING by John Braheny. Writer's Digest Books.

HOW TO GET STARTED IN CHRISTIAN MUSIC by Chris Christian. Home Sweet Home Publications.

THE HYMN SOCIETY BOOK SERVICE, The Hymn Society, P.O. Box 30854, Fort Worth, TX 76129. (800) THE-HYMN.

MUSIC PUBLISHING by Randy Poe. Writer's Digest Books.

RESOURCE GUIDE, Gospel Music Association, 7 Music Circle, N, Nashville, TN 37203. (615) 242-0303. Fax: (615) 254-9755.

THE SONGWRITERS IDEA BOOK by Sheila Davis. Writer's Digest Books.

SONGWRITER'S MARKET 1992, 1507 Dana Avenue, Cincinnati, OH 45207. Writer's Digest Books. Mark Garvey, editor.

THIS BUSINESS OF MUSIC, 6th Edition, Sydney Shemel and M. William Krasilovsky. Billboard Publications.

Cynthia Wachner, through her Good News Literary Service in Visalia, California, assists music writers develop new ideas and market their products.

WRITING FOR THE DEVOTIONAL MARKET

by Cynthia Ann Wachner

Devotional writing differs from other styles in three ways. First, it's vital to center in God's Spirit through biblical meditation and consistent prayer. Next, it requires applying Scripture to life situations, social or religious affiliations, and spiritual concerns. The third hallmark of good devotional writing is motivating readers to love God, self, and others within relationships with family and social or religious communities.

Two practical aspects of devotional writing set it apart from other styles. First, sharing the message without preaching is essential. The second is the demand for tight, concise editing to maintain a brief word limit.

Writers who are serious about breaking into the devotional market need a marketing plan. You're welcome to try what I did to succeed.

First, I queried devotional editors for sample copies and writer's guidelines. (See the list at the end of this article.) I analyzed the information and mapped a strategy for approaching each publication.

Upon completing the market analysis, I prioritized markets according to criteria important to me. Next, I divided my list into two categories: free-lance publications and assignment-only publications. I listed them in order, placing the feasible markets first. Then I listed those with less chance of a sale or without monetary payment. I wrote devotionals tailored to each company's guidelines and audience, responding first to those with editorial requests for writing samples, second to those who specified deadlines.

Targeting the market like this eliminates time wasted on unsalable manuscripts. Although it took time to develop the marketing plan, it increased consistent sales and prepared me to handle rejection returns. Upon receiving rejects, I recycled them to another compatible market on my list.

When devotionals that are sold for first rights appear in print, I send tearsheets and a cover letter to markets open to reprints. For devotionals for which I have sold all rights, I rewrite them with a new slant and submit them as first rights or all rights again.

My marketing plan, hard writing work, and God, who established the work of my hands (Psalm 90:17) have enabled me to step into the reality of publication and propelled me to new horizons of article and book sales.

Devotional Markets

CHRIST IN OUR HOME, Augsburg Fortress Publishing House, 426 South Fifth Street, P.O. Box 1209, Minneapolis, MN 55440. Beth Ann Gaede, editor.

COME YE APART, Nazarene Publishing House, P.O. Box 41527, Kansas City, MO 64141. Paul Martin, editor.

DAILY DEVOTIONS FOR THE DEAF, RR 2 Box 26, Council Bluffs, IA 51503. Duane King, editor in chief.

DAILY MIRACLE, P.O. Box 2187, Tulsa, OK 74102.

DEVOTION (daily), 365 **DEVOTIONS** (yearly/weekly assignments), 8121 Hamilton Avenue, Cincinnati, OH 45231. Eileen Wilmoth, editor.

DISCIPLINES, 1908 Grand Avenue, P.O. Box 189, Nashville, TN 37202-0189. Glenda Webb, coordinating editor.

DISCOVERY HOUSE (Books), P.O. Box 3566, Grand Rapids, MI 49501. Robert DeVries, publisher; Carol Holquist, Associate publisher; Timothy J. Beals, editor.

ENCOUNTER (Southern Baptist for youth), 127 Ninth Avenue N, Nashville, TN 37234. J. William Thompson, editor.

EVERGREEN COMMUNICATIONS (annuals and theme collections), P.O. Box 220, Davison, MI 48423. Robert and Mary Busha, publishers.

FORWARD DAY BY DAY (Episcopal), 412 Sycamore Street, Cincinnati, OH 45202. Charles H. Long, editor.

GOD'S WORD FOR TODAY (Assemblies of God), 1445 Boonville Avenue, Springfield, MO 65802.

GUIDEPOSTS DAILY DEVOTIONAL BOOK (annual), 16 East 34th Street, New York, NY 10016. Stephany C. Samoy, editorial assistant.

THE HOME ALTAR, Augsburg Fortress, P.O. Box 590179, San Francisco, CA 94159-0179. Elaine Dunham, editor; Louise Lystig, assistant editor.

KEYS FOR KIDS, Children's Bible Hour, Box 1, Grand Rapids, MI 49501. Hazel Marrett, editor.

LIGHT FROM THE WORD, Wesleyan Church International Center, 6060 Castleway Drive, P.O. Box 50434, Indianapolis, IN 46250-0434. Brenda K. Bratton, editor.

LIVING FAITH, Creative Communications for the Parish (Roman Catholic), 10300 Watson Road, St. Louis, MO 63127. James E. Adams, editor.

MOMENTS WITH GOD, One South 210 Summit Avenue, Oakbrook Terrace, IL 60181-3994. Dorothy Ganoung, editor. No payment.

MOUNTAIN MOVERS, 1445 Boonville Avenue, Springfield, MO 65802-1894. Joyce Booze, editor.

MY DAILY VISITOR, 200 Noll Plaza, Huntington, IN 46750. William and Catherine O'Dell, coeditors. Focus on Roman Catholic saints, traditions, daily mass readings. Limited publication opportunities.

PATHWAYS TO GOD, Warner Press, Inc. (Church of God), P.O. Box 2499, Anderson, IN 46018. Dan Harman, editor.

PORTALS OF PRAYER, 3558 South Jefferson Avenue, St. Louis, MO 63118-3968.

THE QUIET HOUR, David C. Cook Publishing Company, 850 North Grove Avenue, Elgin, IL 60120. Gary Wilde, editor.

REJOICE! Inter-Mennonite Faith Community, 836 Amidon, Wichita, KS 67203. Katie Funk Wiebe, editor.

THE SECRET PLACE, P.O. Box 851, Valley Forge, PA 19481-0851. Phyllis Frantz, editor.

THESE DAYS (Presbyterian Church USA), 100 Witherspoon Street, Room 5622-A, Louisville, KY 40202-1396.

THE UPPER ROOM, 1908 Grand Avenue, P.O. Box 189, Nashville, TN 37202. Mary Lou Redding, editor.

THE WORD IN SEASON, Augsburg Fortress Publishing House, 426 South 5th Street, Minneapolis, MN 55440. Beth Ann Gaede, editor.

Cynthia Wachner has published a number of devotions as well as other writing. She assists other writers in this field through her Good News Literary Service.

For one-on-one help with "Devotional Writing," request Personalized Study Program (PSP) Unit N-5, Mary Harwell Sayler, The Word Center, P.O. Box 730, DeLand, FL 32721-0730.

ENTERING CONTESTS

by Mary Ann Diorio

If you're looking for a catalyst to launch your writing career, you may find it in writers contests. These competitions not only provide a means for establishing a professional track record through the publication of your winning pieces, but they also serve as a vehicle for widespread exposure and additional income. Moreover, contests offer an opportunity for you to measure your development as a writer against other writers in your area of expertise. Most important of all, perhaps, winning a contest offers a unique avenue of ministry unavailable to you through traditional means of publication.

There are as many different kinds of contests as there are writers. For example, some contests deal with only one topic, such as nostalgia or humor. Other contests are limited to certain types of writing, such as poetry, fiction, or drama. Still other contests limit themselves to specific age groups, to particular geographical locations, or to certain ethnic experiences.

Before entering a contest, request guidelines from the contact person well in advance of the deadline. Always include a SASE (self-addressed, stamped envelope) with your request. Read the guidelines carefully in order to determine that you qualify for the contest and that it is still in progress. Note also whether the contest charges entry fees. Some contests, especially those sponsored by "little" literary magazines, require entry fees.

A few contests require nomination by a publisher. If this is the case, simply ask your publisher to nominate your work. Be sure to allow your publisher ample time to make the nomination before the contest deadline.

Follow closely the contest rules for submission. Failure to do so will disqualify you immediately. Many entries never stand a chance of winning because they do not meet the criteria of the particular contest to which they have been submitted. If you have questions, write to the contact person before entering the contest.

When entering a contest, present yourself and your work with the same degree of professionalism that you would use when submitting to an editor. Your work should be polished to the best of your ability.

Opportunities for entering contests abound in the religious field. Many Christian writers' conferences sponsor contests covering various categories of writing, such as poetry, fiction, nonfiction, and drama. Usually you must attend the conference to qualify for the contest. Some religious writers organizations also sponsor contests. Write to the directors of these conferences and organizations for information. A few Christian magazines sponsor contests as well. Subscribing to the magazine is usually a prerequisite for entering.

There are also many contest opportunities in the secular marketplace. Check the back of *Writer's Market* (Writer's Digest Books) for a complete listing of them.

Listed below are some of the best opportunities in the field of religious writing:

1. *The AMY Writing Awards Program,* The Amy Foundation, P.O. Box 16091, Lansing, MI 48901. President, James Russell. For articles communicating biblical truth published in the secular media between January 1 and December 31 of the year prior to your entry. Deadline for entering, January 31. Cash prizes totaling $34,000. No entry fee.

2. *Catholic Press Association Journalism Awards,* Catholic Press Association, 119 North Park Avenue, Rockville Centre, NY 11570. Contact Owen McGovern. To recognize quality work of journalists who work for a Catholic magazine. Work must be published between January and December of the year prior to the entry. Deadline: mid February. Charges $30 fee.

3. *The Christopher Award,* The Christophers, 12 East 48th Street, New York, NY 10017. Award Director, Peggy Flanagan. Outstanding books published during the calendar year that "affirm the highest values of the human spirit."

4. *New Christian Plays Competition,* Colorado Christian University, 180 South Garrison Street, Lakewood, CO 80226. Theater Coordinator, Patrick Rainville Dorn. Offered annually for unpublished work. "To encourage the development of Christian plays and playwrights and to help make scripts available to producers of Christian plays." Deadline: January 31. SASE for guidelines. Prize $200 cash prize for overall first place. Staged reading/workshop production for top four finalists.

5. *Time of Singing Poetry Contest. Time of Singing: A Magazine of Christian Poetry,* Box 211, Cambridge, PA 16403. Charles A. Waugaman, editor. Annual poetry contest. Send a SASE for rules. Small entry fee.

6. *Pockets Fiction Contest,* Box 189, Nashville, TN 37234. Janet McNish, editor. Annual contest. Children's fiction 1,000 to 1,700 words. Deadline: October 1. No entry fee.

7. *Charisma and Christian Life Fiction Contest.* 600 Rinehart Road, Lake Mary, FL 32746. Steven Strang, editor. Annual contest. Query for contest guidelines.

8. *National Writers Club.* Sponsors annual contests on articles and essays, short stories, nonfiction books, novels, and poetry. Contact Sandy Whelchel, Director, c/o National Writers Club, Suite 424, 1450 South Havana, Aurora, CO 80012. (303) 751-7844. Fax: (303) 751-8539. Entry Fee. Query for contest guidelines.

In addition to those just listed, there are many writers' conferences and magazines that offer prizes and sponsor contests. The rules vary for each one. If you plan to attend a conference, or if you'd like to know more about contests offered by magazines, see a complete list of writers' conferences in chapter 6 and check the periodical entries in chapter 2 for magazines sponsoring contests. You may also want to consider subscribing to a new publication entitled *Bottom Line Publications.* It lists the latest contests for writers (as well as artists and photographers) of poetry, fiction, nonfiction, essays, articles, drama, plays, and so on. The address is Star Route Box 21AA, Artemas, PA 17211.

Mary Ann Diorio of Millville, New Jersey, was the third-place winner ($4,000) in the 1990 AMY Foundation contest and her writing has won placement in contests of the National Writers Club, *Writer's Digest,* and St. David's Christian Writers Conference. She is the author of three published books and more than 200 articles.

WRITING FOR THE CROSSOVER MARKET

by Dennis E. Hensley

For the active free-lance writer, there are two distinct target markets for manuscripts: secular publications and religious publications. Although each market is specific in its needs, the two are not mutually exclusive.

The secret to finding a topic that will cross over from the secular marketplace to the religious marketplace is in finding a way to make the subject fit into a religious context. For example, an article on aerobic exercising can be sold to a variety of secular magazines. However, to make that same article appropriate for religious periodicals, one must show how aerobics can be done to the beat of contemporary Christian music; or how aerobics can be synchronized with the recitation of Bible verses; or how aerobics can be incorporated into a vacation Bible school activity time.

Conversely, the secret to making a religious-oriented article cross over to the secular marketplace is in showing how biblical tenets can be applied in daily life. For example, I once wrote an article entitled, "A Businessman Takes Counsel from the Wise Men." I explained the Christmas story of the Magi, then drew examples of leadership from it, such as the fact that the wise men focused on one goal at a time (a single star), that they prepared for the task at hand (the journey), and that they refused to stop until they had completed their mission (seeing the Christ child).

This article appeared in several religious magazines such as *The War Cry* (December 7, 1991) and *Confident Living* (December 1991), but I also sold it to several secular publications, such as *Business Digest* (December 16, 1991) and *Midwest Weekly* (December 22, 1991). The business aspects did not lessen its appeal to Christian readers, nor did the religious message lessen its appeal to business readers.

When doing background research for a secular article, I constantly ask myself, What aspects of this topic would appeal to readers of religious periodicals? How could I focus this material to meet a religious need or answer a religious question? Usually, getting to the answer is a stepping stone process.

I was once writing a feature for *Essence,* one of the nation's leading periodicals for black women. The topic was "How to Overcome Shyness," and it covered everything from mingling with strangers at parties to meeting new people in your apartment building. To get material, I interviewed psychologists, psychiatrists, job counselors, and drama coaches. Their helpful suggestions on confidence building, body language, and conversation techniques gave me plenty of material for my *Essence* article (August 1983).

In writing about meeting new people in an apartment building, one of the suggestions I shared was to invite someone to a civic theater play or a concert. It occurred to me that an invitation to a church would also be appropriate, as would an invitation to a home Bible study. That led to the sale of "Is Shyness Your Bag?" to *Young Ambassador* (June 1985), "Help! I'm Shy!" to *Contact* (October 1986) and *The Baptist Bulletin* (May

1987), and "Overcoming Shyness in Witnessing" in *Light and Life* (August 1987). In the religious versions of the article, I not only gave the recommendations of the secular experts, I also provided Bible verses for additional encouragement.

To initiate crossover sales, I offer these suggestions: First, use your *Religious Writers Marketplace* and *Writer's Market* to provide you with the names and addresses of magazines that focus on your areas of interest.

Second, approach both religious and secular magazines and request copies of their "Guidelines for Writers." Put these guidelines in a three-ring notebook separated by categories of interest ("Cooking," "Crafts," "Sports," "Travel").

Third, list topics you could write about and challenge yourself to come up with article ideas that would work for both markets. For example, a secular article "Keeping Grandkids Occupied" could become "Tips on Helping in a Church Nursery" (same material, new slant). Or, "Planning the Family Picnic" (secular marketplace) could become "Outdoor Fun for Church Groups."

Fourth, research and write your articles and get them in the mail. Remember this: A religious writer is *not* someone who only writes for religious publications. A religious writer is a writer who writes for a wide variety of publications while still maintaining his or her religious values.

Dennis Hensley is the author of 26 books, including *Writing for the Religious and Other Specialty Markets* (Broadman Press), as well as 2,400 articles.

DRAMA AND SCRIPTS
FOR TELEVISION, RADIO, VIDEO, AND FILM

by William Gentz and Sandra Brooks

Religious drama offers specialized, somewhat limited, yet exciting possibilities for religious writers. Drama is flourishing in churches across the nation. Drama on Jewish themes also is growing. Colleges and universities with a religious background are becoming aware of the educational, spiritual, and outreach possibilities of drama. Further indication of the opportunities available to religious playwrights are: the development of full-time Christian performing groups, the recent appearance of more playwriting contests, the growing interest in Jewish theme drama, and the emergence of clearing houses that serve as a link between the amateur, educational, and professional components of the movements.

Listed below and in chapters 2 to 4 are several publishers of different types of drama for production in the local congregation. Short seasonal programs for children as well as other dramatic presentations to meet special needs are needed. See such entries as Lillenas Publishing Company, Russell House, or Sheer Joy! Press. Several new and unusual publishers of "stories" ready for dramatic presentation are *Children's Story Scripts* (2219 West Olive Ave., Suite 130, Burbank, CA 91506), Deedra Bebout, editor, and *Creatively Yours* (2906 West 64th Plaza, Tulsa, OK 74132), Jill Morris, editor. In addition, many of the producers of children's books or periodicals listed in this book are candidates for dramatic readings, puppet shows, and other forms of drama. Try them!

Religious drama writers should watch the announcements offering prizes in writers' publications. Dramatic associations of interest to playwrights include the Dramatists Guild, 234 West 44th Street, New York, NY 10036, and the Theatre Communications

Group, 355 Lexington Avenue, New York, NY 10017. The latter publishes the annual *Dramatist's Sourcebook.*

Drama writers, of course, will also want to study some of the many "how-to" books prepared for them. One of the classics is *The Thirty-six Drama Situations* by George Polti, published by the Writer Incorporated, Boston, $8.95.

The following is a list of publishers of drama that the playwright can query for their needs and submission requirements.

Of Jewish Interest

JEWISH REPERTORY THEATRE, 344 East 14th Street, New York, NY 10003. (212) 674-7200. Ran Avni, artistic director. Produces 5 plays and 15 readings yearly. Needs all types of play musicals. No biblical plays.

Of Christian and General Interest

AGAPE DRAMA PRESS, INCORPORATED, P.O. Box 1313, Englewood, CO 80110.

AUGSBURG FORTRESS PUBLISHERS, 426 South Fifth Street, Minneapolis, MN 55415.

BAKERS PLAYS, 100 Chauncy Street, Boston, MA 02111.

CONTEMPORARY DRAMA SERVICE, Arthur Meriwether, Inc., Box 7710, Colorado Springs, CO 80933.

CSS PUBLISHING COMPANY, 628 South Main Street, Lima, OH 45804.

FRIENDSHIP PRESS, 475 Riverside Drive, New York, NY 10115.

GROUP, Box 481, Loveland, CO 80539.

HIGLEY PUBLISHING CORPORATION, P.O. Box 2470, Jacksonville, FL 32203.

LAMB'S PLAYERS THEATRE, P.O. Box 26, National City, CA 92050.

LILLENAS PUBLISHING CORPORATION, Box 527, Kansas City, MO 64141.

MERIWETHER PUBLISHING, LTD., Box 7710, Colorado Springs, CO 80903.

PAULIST PRESS, 545 Island Avenue, Ramsey, NJ 07446.

RESOURCE PUBLICATIONS, INCORPORATED, 160 East Virginia Street, San Jose, CA 95112.

SCRIPTURE PRESS PUBLICATIONS, INCORPORATED, 1825 College Avenue, Wheaton, IL 60187.

STANDARD PUBLISHING, 8121 Hamilton Avenue, Cincinnati, OH 45231.

Check for other listings in chapters 2 and 3.

Radio and Television

There are also growing numbers of opportunities for writers in religious radio and television. Many religious stations have been organized. In addition, public-service stations often deal with religious topics or are sponsored by community religious organizations. All of these programs need writers.

Because opportunities in this field are usually local, we will not attempt to list stations or programs here. The best source of information is the *Directory of Religious Broadcasting,* an annual publication that lists radio stations in all localities. This directory can be ordered from the National Religious Broadcasters, Box 2544, Morristown, NJ 07960, (201) 428-5400. Another good resource book is *The Christian Media Directory,* The James Lloyd Group, Box 3, Ashland, OR. It contains more than 4,000 listings of assorted Christian media opportunities. Many of those listings are Christian radio and television stations ($29.95). *Interviews and Reviews*, 2218 Bamboo Street, Mesquite, TX 75150, is a magazine with information and how-tos on preparing interviews for the airways.

Two other sources of information about religious radio and TV are:

The Director of Audio-Visual Communications National Council of Churches, 475 Riverside Drive, New York, NY 10115.

Protestant Radio and TV Center, Incorporated, 1727 Clinton Road, NE, Atlanta, GA 30329.

Video and Film

The religious film and video market continues to present several opportunities to the talented, determined writer. New ideas and materials are needed constantly. Although breaking into this area of the business is not easy, it is possible. Before submitting any material, prepare a complete resume, listing your credentials, experience, availability, fields of interest, background, and credits. Sample scripts you've written should accompany the query, and possibly a one-page story-synopsis of the material you propose. Most companies listed below produce 16mm films, videocassettes, and sound filmstrips for all age groups in an interdenominational setting. Query them first for particular needs and submission guidelines.

Study books and other guides to the preparation of material for film and video use, such as *Writing for Film and Television* by Seward Bronfeld, published by Prentice-Hall. *Christian Film and Video* is a newsletter that reviews the latest in Christian productions as well as the classics in the field. For a sample copy, writer editor Mark Fackler at 501 East Seminary, Wheaton, IL 60187. Writers of these materials will also want to look into the possibility of membership in the Christian Artists International, P.O. Box 2134, Lynnwood, WA 98036; or a subscription to *The American Screenwriter*, Grasshopper Productions, Incorporated, Box 67, Manchaca, TX 78652. Another magazine helpful to film and video writers is *Song Writers and Artists*, Box 3, Ashland, OR 97520. The editor is James Lloyd.

In addition, the following companies offer potential opportunities for scripts since they've indicated through our questionnaires that they produce Christian films, videos, or filmstrips.

Ken Anderson Films, Box 618, Winona Lake, IN 46590. (219) 267-5774. Ken Anderson, president. Religious material with an Evangelical bias.

Don Bosco Multimedia, 475 North Avenue, Box T, New Rochelle, NY 10802.

Cathedral Films, Incorporated, P.O. Box 4029, Westlake Village, CA 91359.

Companion Press, 167 Walnut Bottom Road, Shippenburg, PA 17257.

Concordia Publishing House, Product Development Division, 3558 South Jefferson Avenue, St. Louis, MO 83118.

David C. Cook Publishing Company, 850 North Grove Avenue, Elgin, IL 60120.

Cornerstone Pictures, 2800 Washington Street, Avondale Estates, GA 30002.

Credence Cassettes, NCR Publishers, P.O. Box 419491, Kansas City, MO 64141. Clarence Thomson, editor.

Family Films, 14622 Lanark Street, Panorama City, CA 91402. Paul R. Kidd, director of product development.

Friendship Press, 475 Riverside Drive, Room 860, New York, NY 10115.

Gospel Films, Incorporated, Muskegon, MI 49443. (616) 773-3361.

Ignatius Press, 2515 McAllister Street, San Francisco, CA 94118.

MARK IV PICTURES INCORPORATED OF IOWA, 5907 Meredith Drive, Des Moines, IA 50322. (515) 278-4737.

MERIWETHER PUBLISHING, LTD., P.O. Box 7710, Colorado Springs, CO 80933.

NAVPRESS, P.O. Box 35001, Colorado Springs, CO 80935.

OLD RUGGED CROSS, 1160 Alpharetta Street, Suite K, Rosell, GA 30075.

OUR SUNDAY VISITOR, INCORPORATED, Audiovisual Department, 200 Noll Plaza, Huntington, IN 46750.

ST. ANTHONY MESSENGER PRESS, 1615 Republic Street, Cincinnati, OH 45210.

STAR SONG, 2325 Crestmoor, Nashville, TN 37215.

WARNER PRESS, Box 2499, Anderson, IN 46018.

ZONDERVAN, 5300 Patterson Avenue, SE, Grand Rapids, MI 49530.

Canada

FAITH FILMS LTD., 224 Cayer Street, Box 1096, Coquitlam, BC, V3J 6Z2.

SIX

Getting Help: Additional Resources for the Religious Writer

INTRODUCTION

by Norman B. Rohrer

Why should a fledgling writer invest time and money in a writer's conference, seminar, workshop, or correspondence course to stay writing? Why buy and read books about writing? Why not spend the time practicing instead?

It is true that no amount of listening or reading will put your words on paper or provide the trial and error necessary to make you a published author. It's a little like a carpenter sitting in a lecture hall listening to a woodworker discuss the craft while the carpenter's own tools lie idle at home. But anyone who has attended a conference, bought books on writing, taken a correspondence course, or enrolled for training at a local school knows that time spent on learning the basics puts the beginning writer far ahead. There are at least ten advantages to the writer who seeks help from such sources:

1. *The writer gets a good introduction to the business end of publishing.* Unless you understand the pressures of the editorial process, you are unable to appreciate fully why material is needed on time, why royalties are established at the present scale, and why editors ask for clean, neat manuscripts with proper spacing.

2. *The writer learns how to slant the material for different audiences.* A writer researching a project can use the same research for a variety of markets and audiences. This multiplies dividends paid for the time and money invested in the research.

3. *The writer learns to master the techniques.* Public school and college courses in English composition usually do not offer the kind of concentrated study of writing techniques that a producing, selling author should learn to handle with ease. Such techniques include the use of metaphor, simile, onomatopoeia, alliteration, flashback, and many more.

4. *The writer shares the experiences of veteran writers.* Writing is hard work. The commiseration of fellow wordsmiths is of inestimable value to the suffering writer. It might seem a small matter, but just knowing that someone else has had similar experiences can encourage a writer who might think he or she is the only one enduring the agony.

5. *The writer learns to spot trends.* A writer's success often depends on market trends. A good book or article ahead of its time is rejected just as easily as one written behind the times, after the market has been glutted by literature on a given subject.

189

6. *The writer gets help in keeping records.* Everything from cost-cutting techniques to tips on tax deductions can be learned from writing teachers.

7. *The writer can get to know other writers* in the same locality and take advantage of opportunities for fellowship through writers' clubs.

8. *The writer's awareness of market potentials* can be greatly increased as he or she learns of new book or magazine publishing houses.

9. *A writer can learn* which reference books, magazines, and pamphlets are important.

10. *Finally, the writer's natural talent* can be sharpened through the discipline of study.

Working through a well-organized program can be a shortcut to success. "Iron sharpeneth iron; so a man sharpeneth the countenance of his friend" (Proverbs 27:17). As a student, the writer has the counsel of a trusted mentor to offer sympathy when rejections prevail and to help celebrate when victory is won.

Get help! Light is the task when many share the toil. This chapter can show you how.

————

Norman Rohrer, founder and director of Christian Writers Guild, knows whereof he speaks. In addition to writing myriad books and articles, he's "Fired Writers" from coast to coast for almost thirty years!

CONFERENCES AND WORKSHOPS: THE WRITER'S ENERGIZER

by Gayle Roper

I almost didn't make it to my first writers conference. I was a young mother embarking on a new adventure when I drove fifty miles to St. Davids (Pennsylvania) Christian Writers Conference on a warm Monday morning in June. Between rush hour traffic and winding roads, I was half an hour late arriving at the address in the brochure, a dorm at Eastern College. And when I got there no one was around.

I wandered the halls until I found a maintenance staff person.

"Oh yeah," she said. "I think there are some writers here this week, but they're all across campus at class." She pointed vaguely out the window.

"How do I get from here to there?" I asked.

"Well, you can't drive across campus. No roads. You have to go left at the driveway, then left again and again and again. Then go right and then left under the college sign."

An hour later, I finally arrived at my first class—and the session was only seventy-five minutes long. But that week was more than I ever imagined it could be. It literally changed my life.

I've thought often of how close I came to just driving home. Had I done so, I would have missed what has become one of the most exciting and rewarding experiences of my life—attending writers conferences. At writers conferences I've met people I never would have met in my little office in Coatesville, Pennsylvania:

- professional free-lancers who could tell me how to become a professional, too;
- editors who could tell me what they were looking for and if my work measured up;

- aspiring beginners who could share their enthusiasm and dreams with me; and
- committed Christians who challenged me to settle for nothing less than sharing Christ through excellence in writing.

I've been involved at St. David's for nineteen years now, and I direct Sandy Cove (Maryland) Christian Writers Conference. I've also been privileged to teach at several other conferences. Whether I'm in Florida or California, New York or Colorado, I always find the same thing when I'm with people "in the business"—excellence, commitment, encouragement, instruction, contacts, and acceptance. I find people whose eyes don't glaze over when I talk about writing. In fact, their eyes sparkle and their spirits connect with mine over our shared passion and vision. What could be more wonderful?

Gayle Roper has two decades of experience at writers conferences as a teacher, speaker, director, and always a learner. She's the author of *Controlling Your Emotions* and *Who Cares?* (Shaw), and a junior novel series, *East Edge Mysteries* (Cook).

Writers Conferences and Workshops

Arizona

ARIZONA CHRISTIAN WRITERS SEMINAR. Contact Reg Forder, Box 5168, Phoenix, AZ 85010. (601) 838-4919.

CENTRAL ARIZONA CHRISTIAN WRITERS' WORKSHOP. Contact Mona Hodgson, P.O. Box 999, Cottonwood, AZ 86326-0999. (602) 634-0384.

MINI WRITING WORKSHOPS. Contact Donna Goodrich, 648 South Pima Street, Mesa, AZ 85210. (602) 962-6694.

PRESCOTT CHRISTIAN WRITERS SEMINAR. Contact Barbara Spangler, Box 26449, Prescott Valley, AZ 86312. (602) 772-6263.

SWEETWATER CHRISTIAN WRITERS' WORKSHOP. Contact Clara Bruce, Box 5640, Glendale, AZ 85312.

California

ART OF THE WILD/WRITING WITH THE NATURAL WORLD. Contact Art of the Wild, Department of English, UC-Davis, Davis, CA 95616. (916) 752-1658.

CHRISTIAN WRITERS FELLOWSHIP OF ORANGE COUNTY. Contact Marian Bray, 2420 North Bristol Street, Santa Ana, CA 92706.

FRONTLINE COMMUNICATIONS. Contact Writer's Seminars, 1621 Baldwin Avenue, Orange, CA 92665. (714) 637-1733.

HOPE CHAPEL WRITERS DAY. Contact Dianne Shober, 14100 South Mariposa Avenue, Gardena, CA 90247. (310) 323-6847.

INLAND EMPIRE CHRISTIAN WRITERS SEMINAR. Contact Bill Page, Box 8154, Moreno Valley, CA 92552. (714) 924-0610.

LODI ALL-DAY WRITERS SEMINAR. Contact Dee Porter, Box 1863, Lodi, CA 95241.

MT. HERMON CHRISTIAN WRITERS CONFERENCE. Contact David Talbot, P.O. Box 413, Mt. Hermon, CA 95041. (408) 335-4466.

NARRAMORE CHRISTIAN WRITERS CONFERENCE. Contact Dr. Clyde Narramore, Box 5000, Rosemead, CA 91770. (818) 288-7000.

SAN DIEGO SCHOOL OF CHRISTIAN WRITING. Contact Dr. Shirwood E. Wirt, 14140 Mazatlan Court, Poway, CA 92064.

SAN DIEGO STATE UNIVERSITY WRITERS CONFERENCE. Contact Jan Wahl, SDSU, 5630 Hardy Street, San Diego, CA 92182. (619) 594-2514.

SANTA CLARA VALLEY CHRISTIAN WRITERS SEMINAR. Contact Pamela Erickson, 71 Park Village Avenue, San Jose, CA 95136. (408) 226-2064.

WEST CONTRA COSTA COUNTY CHRISTIAN WRITERS CONFERENCE. Contact Tammy Nichols, 4839 State Court, Richmond, CA 94804.

"WRITE-TO-BE READ" WORKSHOP. Contact Norm Rohrer, 260 Fern Lane, Hume Lake, CA 93628. (209) 335-2333.

YWAM CHRISTIAN WRITER'S SEMINARS. Contact Registrar, YWAM Writer's Seminars, Box 3464, Orange, CA 92665. (714) 637-1733.

Colorado

CHRISTIAN WRITERS CONFERENCE—PIKES PEAK AREA. Contact Lynn Dyatt, 3506 Brady Boulevard, Colorado Springs, CO 80909. (719) 574-2164.

COLORADO CHRISTIAN COMMUNICATORS WRITERS CONFERENCE. Contact Shannon R. Sperte, 1294 Amsterdam Drive, Colorado Springs, CO 80907. (719) 589-1939.

COLORADO CHRISTIAN WRITERS CONFERENCE. Contact Debbie Barker, Box 3303, Lyon, CO 80540. (303) 823-5718.

GLEN EYRIE WRITERS WORKSHOPS. Contact Joab Owinyo, Box 6000, Colorado Springs, CO 80934. (719) 598-1212, ext. 466.

PUBLISHING INSTITUTE. Contact The Publishing Institute, 2075 South University #D-114, Denver, CO 80210. (303) 871-2570.

WRITERS WORKSHOP. Contact CDLL, Workshop Registrar, Box 6000, Colorado Springs, CO 80934.

WRITING FOR THE LOCAL CHURCH . . . AND SOMETIMES BEYOND. Contact Verla Lambert, NBC Box 15749, Colorado Springs, CO 80935. (719) 634-0808 or (800) 944-GLEN.

Connecticut

WESLEYAN WRITERS CONFERENCE. Contact Anne Green, c/o Wesleyan University, Middletown, CT 06457. (203) 347-9411, ext. 2448.

Florida

CHRISTIAN WRITERS & MEDIA CONFERENCE. Contact Dottie McBroom, Box 952248, Lake Mary, FL 32795-2248. (407) 322-0938.

FLORIDA CHRISTIAN WRITERS CONFERENCE. Contact Billie Wilson, 2600 Park Avenue, Titusville, FL 32780. (407) 269-9802.

Georgia

NORTHEAST GEORGIA WRITERS CONFERENCE. Contact Elouise Whitten, 660 Crestview Terrace, Gainesville, GA 30501.

Idaho

NORTHWEST CHRISTIAN WRITERS CONFERENCE. Contact Sheri Stone, P.O. Box 1754, Post Falls, ID 83854. (208) 386-8101.

Illinois

MISSISSIPPI VALLEY WRITERS CONFERENCE. Contact David R. Collins, 3403 45th Street, Moline, IL 61265.

MOODY WRITE-TO-PUBLISH CONFERENCE. Contact Lin Johnson, 820 North LaSalle Blvd., Chicago, IL 60610. (309) 762-8985.

SALVATION ARMY CHRISTIAN WRITERS' CONFERENCE. Contact Editorial Director, 10 West Algonquin Road, Des Plaines, IL 60016. (708) 294-2000. Meets every third year.

Indiana

MIDWEST WRITERS WORKSHOP. Contact Dr. Earl Conn, Department of Journalism, Ball University, Muncie, IN 47306. (317) 285-8200.

THE WRITING ACADEMY SEMINAR. Contact Mary K. Kasting, 5129 Marble Court, Indianapolis, IN 46257. (515) 274-5026.

Iowa

WRITING THAT MAKES A DIFFERENCE. Contact Marvin Ceynar, 104 Meadow Lane, Tipton, IA 52772.

Kansas

BCCC CREATIVE WRITING WORKSHOP. Contact Lois Frieson, 901 South Haverhill Road, El Dorado, KS 67042. (316) 321-5083, ext. 233.

NATIONAL LAMPLIGHTERS INSPIRATIONAL WRITERS CONFERENCE. Contact Sharon Stanhope, Box 415, Benton, KS 67017. (316) 778-1043.

Maryland

REVIEW AND HERALD WRITERS' WORKSHOP. Contact Penny E. Wheeler, 55 West Oak Ridge Drive, Hagerstown, MD 21740. (301) 791-7000, ext. 2595.

SANDY COVE CHRISTIAN WRITERS CONFERENCE. Contact Gayle Roper, R.D. 6, Box 112, Coatesville, PA 19320. (215) 384-8125.

Massachusetts

CAPE COD WRITERS' CONFERENCE. Contact Marion Vuilleumier, c/o Cape Cod Conservatory, Rt. 132, West Barnstable, MA 02668. (508) 775-4811.

Michigan

MARANATHA BIBLE AND MISSIONARY CONFERENCE. Contact Leona Hertel, 4759 Lake Harbor Road, Muskegon, MI 49441. (616) 798-2161.

MICHIGAN NORTHWOODS WRITERS CONFERENCE. Contact Robert Karner, 1 Old Homestead Road, Glen Arbor, MI 49636. (616) 334-3072.

Missouri

GREATER ST. LOUIS INSPIRATIONAL WRITERS WORKSHOP. Contact Lila W. Shelburne, 23 Blackberry, St. Charles, MO 63301. (319) 946-8533.

MARK TWAIN WRITERS CONFERENCE. Contact Dr. James C. Hefley, 921 Center Street, Hannibal, MO 63401. (314) 221-2462.

RIGHT WRITING CHRISTIAN WRITERS WORKSHOP. Contact Teresa Parker, 237 East Clearview Drive, Columbia, MO 65202. (314) 875-1141 or (314) 449-2465.

New Mexico

SOUTHWEST WRITERS SEMINAR. Contact Patricia Burke, Box 2635, Farmington, NM 87499-2365. (505) 327-1962.

New York

ARTSFEST WRITERS' WORKSHOP. Contact Lisa Ledlow, 123 West 57th Street, New York, NY 10019. (212) 975-0170, ext. 53.

THE COMMUNICATION WORKSHOP. Contact Gary Blake, 44A Murray Avenue, Port Washington, NY. (516) 767-9590.

GREATER SYRACUSE CHRISTIAN WRITER'S CONFERENCE. Contact Jeri Doner, RR Box 471, Whiting Road, Jordan, NY 13080. (315) 689-6389.

HEPHZIBAH CHRISTIAN WRITERS CONFERENCE. Contact Lois Ewald, Hephzibah House, 51 West 75th Street, New York, NY 10023. (413) 528-0814.

North Carolina

MONTREAT WRITERS CONFERENCE. Contact Director of Montreat Conference Center, P.O. Box 969, Montreat, NC 28757. (800) 572-2257.

Ohio

CINCINNATI BIBLE COLLEGE CHRISTIAN WRITERS WORKSHOP. Contact Diana Eynon, 2700 Gateway Avenue, Cincinnati, OH 45204. (513) 244-8181.

COLUMBUS CHRISTIAN WRITERS WORKSHOP. Contact Brenda Custodio, 3732 Shoreline Drive, Columbus, OH 43232.

MARIAN AREA CHRISTIAN WRITERS SEMINAR. Contact Marge Taylor, 16944 Th127, Harpster, OH 43323. (614) 496-4565.

NORTHWEST OHIO CHRISTIAN WRITERS SEMINAR. Contact Anne Williman, Box 52, Old Fort, OH 44861. (419) 992-4756.

WRITER'S WORLD CONFERENCE. Contact Tom Raber, Box 966, Cuyahoga Falls, OH 44223.

Oklahoma

PROFESSIONALISM IN WRITING. Contact Norma Jean Lutz, 4308 South Peoria, Suite 701, Tulsa, OK 74105. (918) PIW-5588.

WRITING WORKSHOPS. Contact Kathryn Fanning, 1016 NW 39th, Oklahoma City, OK 73118.

Oregon

CASCADE EAST CHRISTIAN WRITERS SEMINAR. Contact Lois Brenchley, 4773 NE Vaughn, Terrebonne, OR 97760. (503) 548-5773.

OREGON ASSOCIATION OF CHRISTIAN WRITERS COACHING CONFERENCE. Contact Patricia

Harbaugh, 1262 NE Myrtle, Myrtle Creek, OR 97457. Or call Elsie Larson (503) 643-6321.

Pennsylvania

CHRISTIAN WRITERS WORKSHOP. Contact Eva Walker Myer, 1860 Montgomery Avenue, Villanova, PA 19085. (215) 525-6780.

CREATIVE AND FREELANCE WRITING WORKSHOP. Contact Joanne Markel, 1160 Thorn Run Road Extension, Corapolis, PA 15108. (412) 266-7110.

GREATER PHILADELPHIA CHRISTIAN WRITERS CONFERENCE. Contact Marlene Bagnull, 316 Blanchard Road, Drexel Hill, PA 19026. (215) 626-6833.

HIGHLIGHTS AT CHATAUQUA. Contact Jan Keen, 711 Court Street, Honesdale, PA 18431. (717) 253-1192.

MONTROSE CHRISTIAN WRITER'S CONFERENCE. Contact Jim Fahringer, P.O. Box 159, Montrose, PA 18801. (717) 279-1001; Jill Renich-Meyers, 204 Asbury Drive, Mechanicsburg, PA 17055. (717) 766-1100.

PITTSBURGH THEOLOGICAL SEMINARY WRITERS' WORKSHOP. Contact Rev. Mary Lee Talbot, Director of Continuing Education, 616 North Highland Avenue, Pittsburgh, PA 15206. (412) 362-5610, ext. 296.

ST. DAVID'S CHRISTIAN WRITERS CONFERENCE. Contact Shirley Eaby, 1775 Eden Road, Lancaster, PA 15206. (717) 394-6758.

WRITERS' WORKSHOPS. Contact Rita Atwell Holler, 100 Greenwood Road, York, PA 16301. (717) 792-0228.

South Carolina

PRESBYTERIAN COLLEGE WRITER'S WORKSHOP. Contact WRITER'S WORKSHOP, Presbyterian College, Clinton, SC 29325. (803) 833-8563.

Tennessee

SOUTHERN BAPTIST WRITERS WORKSHOP. Contact Bob Dean, 127 Ninth Avenue N, Nashville, TN 37234. (615) 251-2939.

Texas

THE ART OF WRITING, THE ACT OF WRITING. Contact Ernestine Finigan, Box 8513, Marshall, TX 75670. (214) 935-3047.

FRONTIERS IN WRITING. Contact Doris R. Meredith, Box 19303, Amarillo, TX 79114. (806) 352-3889.

PRESTONWOOD CHRISTIAN WRITERS GUILD CONFERENCE. Contact Debra Frazier, 1809 Waterford Lane, Richardson, TX 75082.

Virginia

JOHN TYLER COMMUNITY COLLEGE WRITERS CONFERENCE. Contact Martha O. Donnell, Director of Community Education, JTCC, Chester, VA 23831.

Washington

NORTHWEST CHRISTIAN WRITERS ASSOCIATION SEMINARS. Contact Margaret Sampson, 8227 NE 115th Way, Kirkland, WA 98034.

SDA CAMP MEETING WRITING CLASS. Contact Marion Forschler, 18115-116th Avenue, SE, Renton, WA 98058.

SEATTLE PACIFIC CHRISTIAN WRITERS CONFERENCE. Contact Linda Wagner, Humanities Department, Seattle Pacific University, Seattle, WA 98119. (206) 281-2036.

WORD ARTISTS SEMINARS. Contact Gloria Chisholm, 4915-168th Street, SW, #C-201, Lynnwood, WA 98037.

WRITERS WEEKEND AT THE BEACH. Contact Birdie Etchison, Box 877, Ocean Park, WA 98640. (206) 665-6576.

Wisconsin

GREEN LAKE CHRISTIAN WRITERS CONFERENCE. Contact Arlo Reichter, American Baptist Assembly, Green Lake, WI 54941. (800) 558-8898.

TIMBER-LEE CHRISTIAN WRITER'S CONFERENCE. Contact Gene Schroeppel, 2381 Scout Road, East Troy, WI 53120. (414) 642-7345.

THE WRITER'S TOUGHEST JOB—MARKETING. Contact Eugene Gibas, Director of Continuing Education, 1478 Midway Road, Menasha, WI 54952-8002. (414) 832-2636.

Canada

ANNUAL ALBERTA CHRISTIAN WRITER'S FELLOWSHIP CONFERENCE. Contact Lela Ball, RR #3, Wetaskiwin AB, T9A 1X1 Canada.

CHRISTIAN WRITERS OF BRITISH COLUMBIA. Contact Beryl Henne, 541-56th Street, Delta, BC, V4L 1Z5 Canada. (604) 943-9676.

GOD USES INK WRITERS CONFERENCE. Contact Audrey Dorsch, Box 8800, Station B, Willowdale, ON, M2K 2R6 Canada. (416) 479-5885.

LOCAL AND REGIONAL WRITERS CLUBS

by Norma Jean Lutz

I've been writing professionally since 1979, and I cannot fathom the writing life without the support of a local writer's club. Coincidentally, I located my home club through the first (1980) edition of *Religious Writers Marketplace*. At the time, I lived in a small town near Tulsa, Oklahoma, and had no writer friends. I was overjoyed to learn about a group nearby. I visited the club, which met in a small library in a suburb of Tulsa. Soon after that initial visit, I became club president. We moved the club to Tulsa and renamed it Tulsa Christian Writers Club.

The club eventually became the sponsor of the Professionalism in Writing School held annually in Tulsa. This writer's conference, along with the club itself, has enjoyed steady, healthy growth through the years. The TCW Club supplies a strong support group for area writers.

The advantages of a consistent support group are many. Writing is a lonely occupation. The club meeting is a place where like-minded people can gather. Writers understand writers. Family members may not understand how rejection slips can hurt and discourage, but other writers do.

The meeting provides a place where enthusiasm can be renewed and revitalized. Here successes and failures are discussed openly; here beginners find a safe place to learn the nuts and bolts of the business. Markets are discussed, as are marketing techniques.

If the encouragement and learning were the only gain, I would be greatly in favor of writers groups, but there is more. Friendships! Through the years, my dearest and closest friends have been ones gained through my involvement with our club. What a wonderful bonus—writer friends!

When I first learned about this club through that early edition of *Religious Writers Marketplace*, I thought I had really found a nugget. But I was wrong. I had tapped the whole mother lode!

If you are now a writer, or want to be, don't try to go it alone. Groups are springing up all over the nation. Groups may differ in goals, methods, and costs, but the common denominator of fellowship and encouragement will be present.

Scan the following list and find a group near you and attach yourself to it. If there is none, consider taking the steps to start one. The rewards will be worth your efforts!

Norma Jean Lutz of Tulsa, Oklahoma, is a writer, instructor, and coordinator of writing conferences and also owns a writing service company.

Christian Writers Clubs, Fellowship Groups, and Critique Groups

Arizona

BETHANY CHRISTIAN WRITERS' CLUB, meets at Bethany Bible Church, 6060 North 7th Avenue, Phoenix, Arizona. Membership 25. Open to new members. No annual dues. Monthly meetings: the second Tuesday of each month. Contact Mary Lou Kingler, 16820 North 2nd Avenue, Phoenix, AZ 85023. (602) 863-2231. Millie Barger, co-leader.

FOUNTAIN HILLS CHRISTIAN WRITERS CLUB. Meets at Acumen Resource Office, 16810 East Avenue of the Fountains, Suite 200, Fountain Hills, AZ. Open to new members. No annual dues. Contact Rosemarie D. Malroy, 10413 North Demaret Drive, Fountain Hills, AZ 85268. (602) 990-0266 or Catherine Iobst (602) 837-1638.

GRACE CHAPEL WRITERS CLUB. Meets at Grace Chapel Foursquare Church, Scottsdale, Arizona. Membership 11. Open to new members. Monthly meetings. Contact Frances Klinkert, 4523 North 34th Street, Phoenix, AZ 85018. (602) 946-3464.

MESA CHRISTIAN WRITERS CLUB. Meets at First Church of the Nazarene, 955 East University, Mesa, AZ. Membership 15 to 20. Open to new members. No annual dues. Contact Donna Goodrich, 648 Pima Street, Mesa, AZ 85210. (602) 962-6694.

SWEETWATER CHRISTIAN WRITERS GROUP. Meets at 6608 West Montago Lane, Glendale, AZ, 85306. Membership 16. Open to new members. No annual dues. Monthly meetings. Contact Carla Bruce, 4326 North 50th Avenue, Phoenix, AZ 85031. (602) 247-0174.

California

CHRISTIAN WRITERS FELLOWSHIP OF ORANGE COUNTY. Meeting place at Huntington Beach. Membership 100+. Open to new members. Annual dues $15. Monthly meetings October through March. Newsletter. Writer's Days in April and October. Contact Marian Bray, 2420 North Bristol Street, Santa Ana, CA 92706. (714) 543-2430.

DIABLO VALLEY CHRISTIAN WRITERS GROUP. Meets at Community Presbyterian Church, Danville, California. Membership 8 to 10. Open to new members. No annual dues. Contact Peggy Parker, 2275 Trotter Way, Walnut Creek, CA 94596. (510) 934-3221.

INLAND EMPIRE CHRISTIAN WRITERS GUILD. Varies. Membership 50+. Open to new members. Annual dues $25 initially, $15 per renewal. Two one-day seminars annually in February and September. Contact Bill and Carol Gift Page, Box 8154, Moreno Valley, CA 92552-8154. (909) 924-0610.

LONG BEACH CHRISTIAN WRITERS. Membership 5 to 10. Open to new members. No annual dues. Contact Jessica Shaver, 186 East Cameron Place, Long Beach, CA 90807. (213) 595-4162.

SACRAMENTO CHRISTIAN WRITER'S CLUB. Meets at Fair Oaks Presbyterian Church, Fair Oaks, California. Membership 37. Open to new members. Annual dues $10. Monthly meetings and critique groups. Contact Jeri Honberger, president, 405 Dawnridge Road, Roseville, CA 95678. (916) 783-5888 or (916) 631-0513.

SAN DIEGO COUNTY CHRISTIAN WRITERS' GUILD. Nationwide critique groups. Membership 250. Open to new members. Annual dues $15. Semiannual meetings for entire guild. Annual One Day Writer's Seminar, usually in September. Contact Sherwood E. Wirt, 14140 Mazatlan Court, Poway, CA 92064. (619) 748-0565.

SANTA CLARA VALLEY CHRISTIAN WRITERS, San Jose, California. Critique group. Meets twice monthly. Open to new members. No annual dues. Contact Pamela Erickson, 71 Park Village Place, San Jose, CA 95136. (408) 226-2064.

WEST CONTRA COSTA COUNTY CHRISTIAN WRITERS. Meeting place varies. Membership 6. Open to new members. No annual dues. Monthly meetings. Sponsors Greater Bay Area Christian Writers Conference. Contact Bill Edmunds, 535—38th Street, Richmond, CA 94805. (510) 232-1493. Tammy Nichols, co-leader, (510) 237-9890.

THE WRITE BUNCH. Membership 6. Open to 2 new members. No annual dues. Monthly meetings on first Mondays. Contact Shirley Cook, 3123 Sheridan, Stockton, CA 95219. (209) 477-8375, or secretary, Audrey M. Seitelman, 6303 Herdon Place, Stockton, CA 95219. (209) 477-7300.

Colorado

COLORADO CHRISTIAN WRITERS. Meets in the Denver/Boulder area. Membership 250. Open to new members. Monthly critique groups. Two-day conference in March. Contact Debbie Barker, Box 3303, Lyons, CO 80540. (303) 823-5718.

NATIONAL WRITERS CLUB. Membership open. Annual membership dues. Sponsors annual contests on articles and essays, short stories, nonfiction books, novels, and poetry. Contact Sandy Whelchel, Director, c/o National Writers Club, Suite 620, 1450 South Havana, Aurora, CO 80012. (303) 751-7844. Fax: (303) 751-8539.

Florida

ADVENTURES IN CHRISTIAN WRITING. Meets at First Presbyterian Church, Orlando, Florida. Newly organized. Open to new members. No annual dues. Monthly meetings. Contact Mary Shaw, 350 East Jackson Street, 097709, Orlando, FL 32801. (407) 841-4866.

CHRISTIAN WRITERS FELLOWSHIP INTERNATIONAL. Bimonthly newsletter, prayer fellowship, consultation, critique, referral for professional opportunities. No meetings. Contact Sandra Brooks, Rt. 3 Box 1635, Clinton, SC 29325.

SUNCOAST CHRISTIAN WRITERS GROUP. Meets at Suncoast Bible Church, Largo, Florida. Membership 30. Open to new members. No annual dues. Biweekly meetings on Thursdays. Elaine Creasman, 13014—106th Ave., N, Largo, FL 34644-5602. (813) 595-8963.

TITUSVILLE CHRISTIAN WRITER'S GROUP. Meets at Park Avenue Baptist Church, Titusville, Florida. Membership 14. Open to new members. No annual dues. Monthly meetings, third Tuesday. Occasional workshops. Contact Nancy Otto Boffo, 2625 Riviera Drive, Titusville, FL 32780, (407) 267-7604, or Flora Reigada, 2641 Applewood Drive, Titusville, FL 32780. (407) 383-9995.

Georgia

NORTHEAST GEORGIA WRITERS. Meets at Community Foundation Building, 422 Brenau Avenue, Georgia. Membership 24. Open to new members. Annual dues $20. Monthly meetings: first Wednesdays at 2 P.M. Two annual seminars. Contact Elouise Whitten, President, Secretary, Newsletter Editor, 660 Crestview Terrace, Gainesville, GA 30501. (404) 532-3007.

Idaho

IDAHO CHRISTIAN WRITERS ASSOCIATION. Meets in Dayspring Foursquare Church, Idaho. Membership 35. Open to new members. Annual dues $8 (not mandatory). Contact Sheri Stone, P.O. Box 1754, Post Falls, ID 83854. (208) 667-9730.

THE WRITING ACADEMY. Meets in New Harmony, Indiana. Membership 60. Open to new members. Annual dues. Year-round writing program and annual seminar in August. Contact Rev. Benny Boling, President, 10111 Seneca Drive, Boise, ID 83709. (208) 362-6263.

Illinois

JUVENILE FORUM. Membership 14. Open to new members. No annual dues. Contact David R. Collins, 3403 45th Street, Moline, IL 61265. (309) 762-8985.

PRESBYTERIAN WRITERS GUILD. Meets annually at the General Assembly of the Presbyterian Church, USA. Membership 142. Open to new members. Annual dues $20. Contact Dr. Dale Robb, President, 2003 South Anderson, Urbana, IL 61801. (217) 367-4990.

TRUE VINE CHRISTIAN FELLOWSHIP. Membership 8. Open to new members. No annual dues. Contact Faith Logan, 813 S 13th Street, Springfield, IL 62703.

Indiana

CHRISTIAN WRITERS. Meeting place varies. Membership 11. Open to new members. Monthly meetings and newsletter. Dues are freewill offering. Contact Aileen Karg, 1004 Cottage Avenue, Crawfordsville, IN 47933. (317) 362-9186.

CREATIVE WRITERS CLUB. Meets at Marion Public Library. Membership 18. Open to new members. Annual dues $7.50. Monthly meetings except June, July, August, and December. Contact Mary M. Cain, President, 631 Candlewood Drive, Marion, IN 46952. (317) 662-6222.

FORT WAYNE CHRISTIAN WRITERS CLUB. Meets in First Church of the Nazarene, Fort Wayne, Indiana. Membership 20. Open to new members. Annual dues $12. Monthly meetings. Contact Linda R. Wade, 739 West Fourth Street, Fort Wayne, IN 46808. (219) 422-2272.

Iowa

CEDAR RAPIDS CHRISTIAN WRITER'S CRITIQUE GROUP. Meeting place varies. Membership 12. Open to new members. No annual dues. Monthly meetings. Contact Helen Hunter, 1132—21st Street, SE, Cedar Rapids, IA 52403. (319) 362-4777.

SOUTHWEST IOWA WRITERS. Meets at Mall of Bluffs, Council Bluffs, Iowa. Open to new members. Annual dues $15. Monthly meetings. Contact D. Barrett, 16 Susan Lane, Council Bluffs, IA 51503. (712) 366-1918.

Kansas

CHRISTIAN WRITERS GROUP. Membership 5 to 10. Open to new members. No annual dues. Monthly meetings, second Tuesdays. Contact Marilyn Phemister, 206 East 10th Street, Larned, KS 67550-2616. (316) 285-6217.

CREATIVE WRITERS CLUB. Meeting place varies. Open to new members. Love offering at each meeting. Monthly meetings. Contact Fern Ruth, Recording Secretary, P.O. Box 417, North Newton, KS 67117.

LAMPLIGHTERS CHRISTIAN WRITERS CLUB. Has branch clubs in Wichita and Newton. Open to new members. One-day workshops, *Lamplighters Family of Writers* Newsletter, next large conference in planning stages. Call for help to start clubs in your area. Contact Sharon Stanhope, Box 415, Benton, KS 67017-0415. (316) 778-1043, or Aggie Villanueva, 15503 Midland Drive, Shawnee, KS 66217. (913) 268-4480.

LEARNERS CHRISTIAN WRITING CLUB. Meets at the Lincoln Library, Medicine Lodge, Kansas. Open to new members. Annual dues $10. Monthly meetings, third Thursdays. Contact Ruth E. Montgomery, 905 Goodview, P.O. Box 308, Medicine Lodge, KS 67104. (316) 886-9863.

PITTSBURG CHRISTIAN WRITERS FELLOWSHIP. Meets in Pittsburg, Kansas. Membership 12. Open to new members. Annual dues $10. Contact Anita Heistand, Rt. 2 Box 484, Galena, KS 66739. (316) 856-5157.

Kentucky

JACKSON CHRISTIAN WRITERS' CLUB. Meets at Kentucky Mountain Bible College, Van Cleve, Kentucky. Membership 10. Open to new members. No annual dues. Meets once per six weeks. Contact Donna J. Woodring, Box 10, Vancleve, KY 41385-0010. (606) 666-5000.

Louisiana

LOUISIANA CHRISTIAN WRITERS' CLUB. New group. Open to new members. Monthly meetings. Annual conference in October. Newsletter. Contact Don Aycock, P.O. Box 12765, Lake Charles, LA 70612.

Maryland

ANNAPOLIS FELLOWSHIP OF CHRISTIAN WRITERS. Meets at Evangelical Presbyterian Church of Annapolis. Open to new members. Annual dues $10. Monthly meetings. Contact Marilyn Anderes, 14107 Tollison Drive, Bowie, MD 20720. (301) 805-5550. Co-leader Jeri Sweany, P.O. Box 411, Annapolis, MD 21404. (410) 267-0924.

Massachusetts

CHRISTIANS IN THE ARTS NETWORKING. Networking, newsletter ($15 per year), and database. Contact Richard DeVeau, 9 Court Street 2nd Floor, P.O. Box 242, Arlington, MA 02174-0003. (617) 646-1541.

WESTERN MASSACHUSETTS CHRISTIAN WRITERS. Meets at Springfield Church of the Nazarene, Springfield, Massachusetts. Membership 60. Open to new members. Monthly meetings: first Mondays. Monthly newsletter $10 per year. Contact Barbara A. Robidoux, 127 Gelinas Drive, Chicopee, MA 01020. (413) 594-6567.

Michigan

CHRISTIAN WRITERS FELLOWSHIP. Meets at Covenant Alliance Church, Beverly Hills, Michigan. Membership 65. Open to new members. No annual dues. Monthly meetings, fourth Thursdays except in November and December. Contact Mae Hoover, 28045 Tyler, Southfield, MI 48034. (313) 356-0906.

Minnesota

MINNESOTA CHRISTIAN WRITERS GUILD. Meets at Woodale Church, Eden Prairie, Minnesota. Membership 100. Open to new members. Annual dues $25. Monthly meetings September through May. Spring and fall seminars. Contact Joan Webb, 7749 Cayenne Plaza, W, Woodbury, MN 55125. (612) 738-8745.

Missouri

CHRISTIAN WRITERS WORKSHOP. Meets at Rockhill Baptist Church, 9125 Manchester, St. Louis, MO. Membership 8. Open to new members. Annual dues $10. Monthly meetings: fourth Wednesdays. Contact Celeste Rhea, 7527 Flora Avenue, Maplewood, MO 63143. (341) 645-5460.

SPRINGFIELD WRITERS CLUB. Meets at Evangel College, Springfield, Missouri. Membership 20. Open to new members. Annual dues $12. Contact Mr. Owen Wilkie, 4909 Old Wire Road, Brookline, MO 65619. (417) 882-5185.

Montana

MONTANA CHRISTIAN WRITERS. Open to new members. No annual dues. Monthly meetings. Contact Margaret Wilkison, 2007 Sweetgrass Road, Helena, MT 59601. (406) 442-9939.

Nevada

HEAVENLY HOPE CHRISTIAN WRITING GROUP. Membership 5. Open to new members. No annual dues. Bimonthly meetings. Contact Cheryl L. William, 5275 Plainview Avenue, Las Vegas, NV 89122. (702) 454-5729.

RENO AREA CHRISTIAN WRITERS. Membership 6. Open to new members. No annual dues. Contact June L. Varnum, 1940 Kim Way, Sparks, NV 89431. (702) 358-2310.

New Jersey

NEW JERSEY CHRISTIAN WRITERS FELLOWSHIP. Meets at Scotch Plains Baptist Church, 333 Park Avenue, Scotch Plains, NJ 07076. Membership 10. Open to new members. Dues $1 donation per meeting. Money is used for postage to send out notices of meetings and literature for club use. Contact Fran Pasch, 165 Norwood Avenue, Plainsfield, NJ 07060. (908) 755-2075.

NEW JERSEY SOCIETY OF CHRISTIAN WRITERS. Meets at Fairton Christian Center, Fairton, New Jersey. Membership 10. New group. Open to new members. Annual dues $15. Monthly meetings September to May. One-day seminar in the autumn, usually October. Contact Mary Ann Diorio, P.O. Box 748, Millville, NJ 08332. (609) 327-1231.

SOUTH JERSEY CHRISTIAN WRITERS FELLOWSHIP. Open to new members. Monthly meetings. Contact Sandi Cleary, 1200 Mill Road, Northfield, NJ 08225. (609) 646-6786.

New Mexico

SOUTHWEST CHRISTIAN WRITERS ASSOCIATION. Meets at First Presbyterian Church, 865 North Dustin, Farmington, NM. Membership 39. Open to new members. Annual dues $15. Monthly meetings. Southwest Christian Writers Annual Seminar. Contact Kathy Cordell, 91 Rd. 3450, Flora Vista, NM 87415. (505) 334-0617.

New York

NEW YORK CHRISTIAN WRITERS GROUP. Meeting place varies. Membership 20. Open to new members. Donations to defer expenses. Monthly meetings. Contact Sharita Hunt, c/o Calvary Baptist Church, 123 West 57th Street, New York, NY 10019. (212) 975-0170.

SYRACUSE CHRISTIAN WRITERS' GUILD. Meets at Elmcreek Elementary School, Liverpool, New York. Membership 60. Open to new members. Annual dues $20. Monthly meetings. Annual seminar in May. Contact Jeri Doner, President, 917 Whiting Road, Jordon, NY 13080. (315) 689-6389.

North Carolina

FORSYTH FELLOWSHIP OF CHRISTIAN WRITERS. Twin City Baptist Church. Membership 10 to 20. Open to new members. Annual dues $10. Contact Catherine Jackson, 113D Westgate Circle, Winston-Salem, NC 27106. (919) 765-3028.

Ohio

COLUMBUS CHRISTIAN WRITERS. Meets at Columbus Metropolitan Library/Hilltonis, Ohio. Membership 25. Open to new members. No annual dues. Monthly meetings, second Saturdays. Fall writers' conference in October. Contact Brenda Custodio, 3732 Shoreline Drive, Columbus, OH 43232. (614) 837-8825.

DAYTON CHRISTIAN SCRIBES. Meets at Kettering College of Medical Arts, Ohio. Membership 35 to 40. Open to new members. Annual dues $15. Monthly meetings: second Thursday of each month. Contact Lois Pecce, 613, Dayton, OH 45459-0613. (513) 433-6470.

GREATER CINCINNATI CHRISTIAN WRITERS' FELLOWSHIP. Meets at Vineyard Christian Fellowship, 1391 East Crescentville Road, Cincinnati, OH. Membership 15. Open to new members. No annual dues. Monthly meetings, second Thursdays. Contact Teresa Cleary, 9749 Winston Road, Cincinnati, OH 45231. (513) 521-1913.

LEBANON CHRISTIAN WRITERS GROUP. Meets at a local restaurant. Membership 20. Open to new members. No annual dues. Monthly meetings, last Tuesdays. Contact Carol Hamlin, 1988 Kirby Road, Lebanon, OH 45036. (513) 932-6101.

MARION AREA CHRISTIAN WRITERS. Meets at First Church of the Nazarene, Marion, Ohio. Open to new members. Annual dues $5. Monthly meetings, third Saturdays. Annual seminar. Contact Irene Sprague, 603 Henry Street, Marion, OH 43302. (614) 387-3047.

NORTHWEST OHIO WRITERS. Membership 30. Open to new members. Annual dues $6. Bimonthly meetings. Saturday seminar in September usually with an editor as speaker. Held in Findlay, Ohio. Contact Betty Steele Everette, 2309 Riviera, Defiance, OH 43512. (419) 784-1421.

STATELINE CHRISTIAN WRITERS CLUB. Meets at the Richardson Bretz Building, Celina, Ohio. Membership 16. Open to new members. Annual dues $5. Monthly meetings: third Saturdays, March through November. Contact Shirley Knox, 54106 Club Island Road, Celina, OH 45822. (419) 268-2040.

Oklahoma

TULSA CHRISTIAN WRITERS. Meets at Helmerich Library, Tulsa, Oklahoma. Membership 65. Open to new members. Annual dues $15. Monthly meetings. Annual conference: Professionalism in Writing. Contact Vicki Musser, 800 West Memphis, Broken Arrow, OK 74012. (918) 251-2706.

Oregon

NEWBERG WRITERS GROUP. Meets in Newberry, Oregon. Open to new members. No annual dues. Monthly meetings, second Mondays. Contact Gail Denham, 12324 NE Honey Lane, Newberg, OR 97132. (503) 538-4691.

OREGON ASSOCIATION OF CHRISTIAN WRITERS. Meets in Portland in October; Salem in February; Eugene in May. Membership 300. Open to new members. Meets quarterly. Annual dues $25. Quarterly meetings. Three-day hands-on coaching conference in July. Contact Joseph Ryan, President, 15190 SE 122nd Avenue, Portland, OR 97015.

THE RIGHT TO WRITE. Membership 7. Not open to new members. Dues $5 per meeting. Contact Marion Duckworth, 2495 Maple Avenue, NE, Salem, OR 97303. (503) 364-9570.

SMITH ROCK CHRISTIAN WRITERS. Meeting place varies. Membership 8. Open to new members. No annual dues. Biweekly meetings. Spring and fall seminars. Contact Josephine Manes, 2135 NE O'Neil Way, Redmond, OR 97756. (503) 548-8872.

WORDSMITHS. Meets at Rockwood Church of God, 133 NE 192nd Street, Portland, OR 97230. Membership 6. Open to new members. No annual dues. Meets monthly, usually third Wednesday at 10 A.M. Contact Susan Thorgerson Maas, 27526 SE Carl Street, Gresham, OR 97080. (503) 663-7834.

Pennsylvania

THE FIRST WORD. Meets in Sewickly, Pennsylvania, weekly on Wednesday evenings. Membership 15. Open to new members. No annual dues. Contact Shirley Stevens, 326 B Glaser Avenue, Pittsburgh, PA 15202. (412) 761-2618.

GREATER PHILADELPHIA CHRISTIAN WRITERS' FELLOWSHIP. Meets at Belmont Baptist Church, Broomall, Pennsylvania. Membership 50. Meets monthly September through April. Open to new members. Spring Conference, Writers Day of Renewal in March. Contact Marlene Bagnull, 316 Blanchard Road, Drexel Hill, PA 45231. (215) 626-6833.

HARRISBURG AREA CHRISTIAN WRITERS' FELLOWSHIP. Meets at 4500 Creekview Drive, Mechanicsburg, PA. Membership 50. Open to new members. Dues are free will offering. Contact Georgia Burkett, 220 Dock Street, Middletown, PA 17057. (717) 944-4427.

MONTROSE WRITERS GROUP. Meets at Victorian Restaurant. Monthly meetings. Sponsors annual conference: Montrose Christian Writer's Conference. Contact Patti Souder, 35 Lake Avenue, Montrose, PA 18801. (717) 278-4815.

YORK WRITERS. Meets at Greens at Westgate Clubhouse, 1801 Kenneth Road, York, PA. Membership 20. Open to new members. Annual dues $10. Monthly meetings: fourth Mondays except in December, July, and August. Quarterly newsletter: free to members, $2 for nonmembers. YMCA Writers Conference in January. Contact Rita Atwell-Holler, 100 Greenwood Road, South, York, PA 17404. (717) 792-0228.

South Carolina

CHRISTIAN WRITERS GROUP. Membership 10. Open to new members. No annual dues. Monthly meetings. Contact Nancy Parker, 150-12C Oak Ridge Place, Greenville, SC 29615. (803) 281-0876.

SPARTANBURG WRITERS GROUP. Membership 6. No annual dues. Monthly meetings. Contact Linda Gilden, 105 Pheasant Road, Spartanburg, SC 20302.

Tennessee

CHATTANOOGA BIBLE INSTITUTE CHRISTIAN WRITERS WORKSHOP. Meets at Chattanooga Bible Institute. Membership 10. Open to new members. Annual dues $12. Monthly meetings, second Mondays. Contact Barbara Tucker, 1902 Duncan Avenue, Chattanooga, TN 37404. (615) 624-1346.

Texas

INSPIRATIONAL WRITERS ALIVE! Membership 65+. Open to new members. Annual dues $15. Monthly meetings, first Thursdays. Texas Christian Writers Forum in August. Contact Maxine E. Holder, Director, 3606 Longwood Drive, Pasadena, TX 77503. (713) 477-3716.

INSPIRATIONAL WRITERS ALIVE! Meets at Second Baptist Church, Amarillo, Texas. Newly formed. Open to new members. Annual dues $15. Monthly meetings, first Thursdays. Texas Christian Writers Forum in August. Contact Helen Luecke, 2921 South Dallas, Amarillo, TX 79103. (806) 376-9671.

PRESTONWOOD CHRISTIAN WRITERS GUILD. Meets at Prestonwood Baptist Church, Dallas, Texas. Membership 120. Open to new members. Biweekly meetings: Critique on first Monday, lecture/program on third Monday. Annual Southwest Christian Writers Conference in October. Contact Jan Winebrenner, 2709 Winding Hollow, Plano, TX 75093. (214) 867-1119.

RED CLAY WRITERS. Meets at 115 West Houston Street, Marshall, TX. Membership 15. Open to new members. Annual dues $15. Contact Ernestine Finigan, Newsletter Editor, P.O. Box 8513, Marshall, TX 75670. (903) 935-3047.

Washington

ADVENTIST WRITERS ASSOCIATION OF WESTERN WASHINGTON. Meeting place varies. Membership 25. Meets four times per year as members desire. Annual dues $10. Five-day writing class in mid to late June. Contact Marion Forschler, President, 18115-116th Avenue, SE, Renton, WA 98058. (206) 235-1435.

CHRISTIAN WRITERS. Meeting place varies. Membership 10. Open to new members. No annual dues. Bimonthly meetings. Contact Dolores Walker, 904 Ankeny, Walla Walla, WA 99362. (509) 529-2974.

NORTHWEST CHRISTIAN WRITERS ASSOCIATION. Meets at Westminster Chapel, Bellevue, Washington. Membership 100+. Open to new members. Annual dues $15. Board governed. Nonprofit status. Monthly meetings. Workshops. Contact Linda Wagner, President, P.O. Box 801, Lake Stevens, WA 98258. (206) 334-7049.

SOUTH KING COUNTY CHRISTIAN WRITERS. Meets at Midway Community Covenant Church. Membership 15. Open to new members. No annual dues. Monthly meetings.

Contact Carolyn Bishop Robinett, 1717 S 268th Street, Kent, WA 98032. (206) 839-4732.

WASHINGTON CHRISTIAN WRITERS FELLOWSHIP. Meets at Shoreline Christian Church in Seattle. Open to new members. Monthly meetings, 3rd Saturdays. Dues are a monthly meeting fee. Several annual workshops. Contact Elaine Colvin, Box 11337, Bainbridge Island, WA 98110. (206) 842-9103.

WENATCHEE CHRISTIAN WRITERS' FELLOWSHIP. Meets at Columbia Bank, East Wenatchee, Washington. Membership 25. Meets monthly. Open to new members. Dues: a free will offering. Contact Shirley R. Pease, 1585 1st Street, SE, East Wenatchee, WA 98802. (509) 884-2610.

WRITERS INFORMATION NETWORK. Open to new members. Annual dues $15 in the United States, $20 foreign. National organization with bimonthly newsletter. Several annual workshops as announced. Contact Elaine Wright Colvin, P.O. Box 11337, Bainbridge Island, WA 98110. (206) 842-9103.

Wisconsin

WISCONSIN FELLOWSHIP OF CHRISTIAN WRITERS. Meets at Randolph Park Church of the Nazarene. Membership 7. Open to new members. Annual dues $10. Monthly meetings. Contact Jean M. Wuttke, 949 East High Street, Milton, WI 53563. (608) 868-3523.

WORD & PEN CHRISTIAN WRITERS CLUB. Meeting place varies. Membership 13. Open to new members. Annual dues $10. Monthly meetings except in December. Contact Beth Ziarnik, 1865 Indian Point Road, Oshkosh, WI 54901. (414) 235-0664.

Canada

ALBERTA CHRISTIAN WRITERS FELLOWSHIP. Meeting place varies. Membership 70. Open to new members. Annual dues $30. Meets twice a year: spring and fall. Contact Sophie Stark, RR 2, Rocky Mountain House, AB, TOM 1TO Canada. (403) 845-6655.

CHRISTIAN WRITER'S CLUB. Meets at 505-45 Westmont N, Waterloo, ON. Open to new members. Annual dues $15. Monthly meetings. Contact Mrs. Pat Breithaupt, 33 Scott Street, Waterloo, ON, Canada. (519) 886-4509.

STRATHROY WRITERS CLUB. Meets at Strathroy Public Library. Membership 9. Open to new members. No annual dues. Monthly meetings. Contact Jean Thompson, 498 Saulsbury Street, Strathroy, ON, N7G 2B6 Canada.

SWAN VALLEY WRITERS GUILD. Meeting place in Swan River. Membership 8. Open to new members. Annual dues $10. Monthly meetings September to June. Contact Marlene Hohne, Box 273, Minitonas, MB, R0L 1G0 Canada. (204) 525-4652.

WRITERS CHALLENGE AND SUPPORT GROUP. Meets at Langley Arts Council Centre. Membership 22. Open to new members. Annual dues $20. Meets 1 to 2 times monthly. Contact K. Christy Bowler, Box 56040, Valley Center PO, Langley, BC, V3A 8B3 Canada. (604) 857-2696.

Religious Press Associations

Membership in a press association gives you professional status with other professionals in religious publishing. It gives you access to happenings and events that other journalists and writers don't have. It provides you with contacts, information, and fellowship that you'd never have otherwise. If this sounds interesting to you, query the organizations listed below that seem to fit your needs.

AMERICAN JEWISH PRESS ASSOCIATION, 11312 Old Club Road, Rockville, MD 20852-4537. L. Malcolm Rodman, executive director.

ASSOCIATED CHURCH PRESS, P.O. Box 162, Ada, MI 49301. John Stapert, executive director.

CANADIAN CHURCH PRESS, 12-35 Waterman Avenue, London, ON, Canada N6C 5T2. Esther Barnes, President.

CATHOLIC PRESS ASSOCIATION, 119 North Park Avenue, Rockville Centre, New York, NY 11570. Owen McGovern, executive director.

EVANGELICAL CHRISTIAN PUBLISHERS ASSOCIATION, 3225 South Hardy, Suite 101, Tempe, AZ 85282.

EVANGELICAL PRESS ASSOCIATION, 485 Panorama Road, Earlysville, VA 22936. Ronald E. Wilson, executive director.

CORRESPONDENCE COURSES

by Mary Harwell Sayler

Even if you attend workshops, conferences, and local writing groups often, correspondence study provides the benefit of one-on-one instruction in the privacy and comfort of your home. You set the pace and choose the course of study that best suits you, and usually you have a working writer as your instructor.

Correspondence programs are helpful, too, if you have published in one field of writing but want help in changing to another. Or maybe you've discovered a weak spot in your fiction, nonfiction, or poetry writing and need professional instruction in correcting it so you'll be able to market your work.

Regardless of the specific writing help you need, find out more about the reputable study programs listed below by sending a SASE to each and requesting information. When the materials arrive, read them carefully to determine which meet your particular needs.

If you're unsure which course to follow, you may want a program that covers all the bases. If you know the area of study that interests you most, concentrate on that. Or, if you feel confident about your writing ability, but don't know how to go about free-lancing, look for individual study units that will help you learn how to market your work.

Mary Harwell Sayler of DeLand, Florida, is Director and instructor for The Word Center. Guideposts Book Club will soon reprint *Candle,* one of her novels.

Correspondence Courses

PERSONALIZED STUDY PROGRAM. Thirty-three individual units that let you study the specific areas of your writing interests. Mary Harwell Sayler, director, instructs in Essential (the basics) Nonfiction and Poetry Units; Irene Brand instructs in Fiction. Write The Word Center, P.O. Box 730, DeLand, FL 32721-0730.

CHRISTIAN WRITERS' GUILD, "DISCOVER YOUR POSSIBILITIES IN WRITING." Forty-eight-lesson complete study course that covers all aspects of writing. Norman B. Rohrer, Director, instructs students. Write: Christian Writers' Guild, 260 Fern Lane, Hume Lake, CA 93628-9999.

CHRISTIAN WRITERS INSTITUTE. Offers five courses in three divisions. Write: Christian Writers Institute, Registrar, Box 952248, Lake Mary, FL 32795-2246.

INSTITUTE OF CHILDREN'S LITERATURE. A secular organization, but you can request a

Christian instructor. Write: Institute of Children's Literature, 93 Long Ride Road, West Redding, CT 06896-0811.

WRITER'S DIGEST SCHOOL OF WRITING. A secular organization that allows you to request a Christian instructor. Write: 1507 Dana Avenue, Cincinnati, OH 45207.

OTHER HELPS FOR WRITERS

by William Gentz and Sandra Brooks

Audiocassette Learning Programs

Marlene Bagnull, 14 instructional tapes on every aspect of the writing life. $5.95 each plus shipping and handling. One free with every 4 tapes purchased. Marlene Bagnull, 316 Blanchard Road, Drexel Hill, PA 19026.

B. J. Bassett, *How to Be a Published Writer: A Home Study Course.* Published through Fruition Publications, Incorporated, Box 103, Blawenburg, NJ 08504. Tape, 2 sides, notebook 60 pages. $30 plus $3 shipping and handling.

THE WORD CENTER. Eighteen tapes on a broad range of topics by experts in their field. $7.95. For a complete list and description of tapes contact Mary Sayler, The Word Center, P.O. Box 730, Deland, FL 32721-0730.

Donna Goodrich covers all the basics for beginning writers in 4 tapes 1.5 hours each. Complete set of audiocassette tapes comes with 48 pages of handouts. Great for your writers' groups to study together. Permission to copy handouts for your group. Individual tapes $8 shipping and handling included. Complete set with handouts $30 shipping and handling included. Order from Donna Goodrich, 648 Pima Street, Mesa, AZ 85210.

MOODY WRITE-TO-PUBLISH CONFERENCE TAPES. Available by mail. Request list and order blank from MBN Cassette Ministry, 820 North LaSalle Drive, Chicago, IL 60610 or call (312) 329-8010.

Videocassette Learning Programs

THE FREELANCE WRITER IN THE 1990'S. Dennis Hensley, 6824 Kanata Court, Fort Wayne, IN 46815. (219) 485-9891.

Computer Programs

ENHANCING FICTIONAL CHARACTERS, AK Images, Box 62, Selma, IN 47383. $28.95 plus $3 shipping and handling.

WRITE-PRO, 43 Linden Circle, Scarborough, NY 10510. (800) 755-1124 or (914) 762-1255. $79.95 ($99.95 for Macintosh version) plus $5 shipping and handling.

WRITER'S TOOLKIT, System Compatibility Corporation, 401 North Wabash, Suite 600, Chicago, IL 60611. (800) 333-1395. $129.

Help by Phone

WRITERS' HELPLINE gives writing tips and latest market and agent news 24 hours per day, seven days per week anywhere in the country with a touchtone telephone. Cost is $2 per minute for writers 18 or older. Messages are no longer than three minutes. Dial 1 (900) 988-1838, ext. 549. Direct questions to Marion Vuilleumier at Craigville Press, Box 86, Centerville, MA 02632.

Consultation

WORD ARTISTS, P.O. Box 680, Roy, WA 98580. Gloria Chisholm, editor of *Parents of Teenagers*, former editor with *Aglow Publications;* Michelle Cresse, writing instructor, speaker, conference director.

SUSAN TITUS ENTERPRISES, 3133 Puente Street, Fullerton, CA 92635. (714) 990-1532.

Writers Magazines and Newsletters

Christian Publications:

CA NEWS, Christians in the Arts Networking, Incorporated, Richard DeVeau, 9 Court Street 2nd Floor, P.O. Box 242, Arlington, MA 02174-0003.

CHRISTIAN AUTHOR NEWSLETTER, 177 East Crystal Lake Avenue, Lake Mary, FL 32746. Steven Strang, publisher; Dottie McBroom, editor.

THE CHRISTIAN COMMUNICATOR, Joy Publishing, P.O. Box 827, San Juan Capistrano, CA 92675. Susan Titus-Osborn, editor.

CHRISTIAN WRITERS IN TOUCH, 5400 West 8th Avenue, Lakewood, CO 80214. Chris Adams, editor.

COLORADO CHRISTIAN WRITER, Box 3303, Lyons, CO 80540. Debbie Barker, editor.

CROSS & QUILL, THE CHRISTIAN WRITERS NEWSLETTER, official newsletter for Christian Writers Fellowship International, Rt. 3 Box 1635, Clinton, SC 29325. Sandra Brooks, editor.

EXCHANGE, A NEWSLETTER FOR WRITERS THAT ARE CHRISTIAN, # 104-15 Torrance Road, Scarborough, ON, M1J 3K2 Canada. Audrey Dorsch, editor.

LAMPLIGHTERS FAMILY OF WRITERS, 15503 Midland Drive, Shawnee, KS 66217. Aggie Villanueva, editor.

OF THE MAKING OF BOOKS, Route 7, Raven's Ridge, 12C, Boone, NC 28607. Quarterly bulletin on the book publishing industry. Stephen Griffith, editor.

SOUTHWESTERN WRITERS NEWSLETTER, P.O. Box 331509, Fort Worth, TX 76163-1509. Edna L. Crenshaw, editor. Correspondence and subscriptions to Tillie Read.

WRITERS ANCHOR, 100 Greenwood Road, York, PA 17404. Rita Atwell Holler, editor.

WRITER'S CONNECTION, 1601 Saratoga-Sunnyvale Road, Suite 180, Cupertino, CA 95014. Jan Stiles, editor.

WRITERS INFORMATION NETWORK, Box 11337, Bainbridge Island, WA 98110. Elaine Colvin, editor.

Secular Publications:

AUTHORSHIP, 1450 South Havana, Suite 424, Aurora, CO 80012. Bimonthly publication of the National Writers Club.

BYLINE MAGAZINE, Box 130596, Edmond, OK 73013. Editor, Kathryn Fanning.

CANADIAN WRITER'S JOURNAL, Box 6618, Depot 1, Victoria, BC, V8P 5N7 Canada. Gordon M. Smart.

FREELANCE WRITER'S REPORT, Cassell Communications, P.O. Box 9844, Fort Lauderdale, FL 33310. Dana Cassell, editor.

WOMEN WHO WRITE NEWSLETTER, The Eleanor Press, 16216 Freyman Road, Cygnet, OH 43413.

THE WRITER, 120 Boylston Street, Boston, MA 02116-4615. Sylvia Burack, editor.

WRITER'S DIGEST, 1507 Dana Avenue, Cincinnati, OH 45207. Tom Clark, senior editor.

WRITER'S JOURNAL, Box 9148 N., St. Paul, MN 55109.

WRITER'S WORLD, Mar-Jon Publications, 204 East 19th Street, Big Stone Gap, VA 24219.

Books for Religious Writers

Books are among a writer's best friends. Most of the books in the list below are published with the religious writer in mind. A few titles are out of print, but you need to be aware of them. You may find them in a few bookstores or secondhand bookstores. Ask for them at your church or public library.

Anderson, Margaret J., *The Christian Writer's Handbook.* New York: Harper and Row, revised edition, 1983. 228 pages, $9.95. The classic in how-to books for Christian writers, now revised and enlarged.

Aycock, Don M., and Leonard George Goss, *Inside Religious Publishing: A Look Behind the Scenes.* Grand Rapids, Mich.: Zondervan, 1991. A collection of articles by well-known writers in the religious publishing industry.

Aycock, Don M., and Leonard George Goss, *Writing Religiously: A Guide to Writing Nonfiction Religious Books.* Milford, Mich.: Mott Media, 1984. 260 pages, $13.95. Direction to potential writers on how to successfully write, market, promote, and distribute their religiously oriented books.

Bagnull, Marlene, *Write His Answer.* San Juan Capistrano, Calif.: Joy Publishing, 1990. 96 pages, $6.95. Encouragement for Christian writers. An excellent resource for writers desiring growth in their craft and their relationship with Jesus Christ.

Berg, Viola, *Pathways for the Poet.* Milford, Mich.: Mott Media, 1977. 234 pages, $12.95. An accomplished poet with more than 1,600 published poems provides this resource tool with emphasis on religiously oriented poetry writing.

Berg, Viola, *Poet's Treasury,* Redeemer Books, 1992, $19.95. A sequel to Pathways for the Poet with guidance for writers of Christian poetry.

Bohrer, Dick, How-to workbooks in four different areas: (1) *Be an Editor Yourself,* (2) *21 Ways to Write Fiction for Christian Kids,* (3) *How to Write What You Think,* (4) *How to Write Features Like a Pro.* Order directly from Glory Press, P.O. Box 4247, Lynchburg, VA 24502.

Ceynar, Marvin E., *Writing for the Religious Market.* Lima, Ohio: CSS Publishing Company, 1986. 30 pages, $2.25. A small book with much of the basic information, especially for a beginner in the religious field.

Dorsch, Audrey, *Canadian Christian Publishing Guide.* Scarborough, Ontario: Exchange Publishing, 1992. 88 pages, $8. Guide to the Canadian Christian marketplace.

Gentz, William H., *Writing to Inspire.* Cincinnati, Ohio: Writer's Digest Books, 1982, 1987. 319 pages, $14.95. Constructive insights and valuable tips from 30 leading writers on all aspects of religiously oriented writing.

Goodrich, Donna, and Mary Lou Klingler, and Jan Potter, *100 Plus Motivational Moments for Writers and Speakers.* A collection of more than 100 devotionals by writers, for writers.

Hensley, Dennis E., and Holly Miller, *The Freelancer: The Writer's Guide to Success.* Indianapolis: Poetic Press, 1984. $6.95. A general guide to free-lancing, but highlighting inspirational writings by this popular speaker and leader at Christian writers' conferences and workshops.

Hensley, Dennis E., and Rose A. Adkins, *Writing for Religious and Other Specialty Markets.* Nashville, Tenn.: Broadman Press, 1987. 200 pages, $8.95. Detailed help to those attempting to reach specialty markets, particularly in the religious field.

Herr, Ethel, *An Introduction to Christian Writing.* Wheaton, Ill.: Tyndale House, 1983. 318 pages, $8.95. Written in a textbook style, this book gives basic instruction on the whole gamut of things a Christian writer needs to know.

Hudson, Bob, and Shelley Townsend, *A Christian Writer's Manual of Style.* Grand Rapids, Mich.: Zondervan, 1988. 208 pages, $12.95. A standard reference book for anyone involved in Christian publishing.

Klug, Ron, *How to Keep a Spiritual Journal.* Nashville, Tenn.: Thomas Nelson, Incorporated. $4.95. Directions on journal-keeping, a practice that many religious writers feel helps with writing from experience.

McDonald, E. L., *Stories for Speakers and Writers.* Baker Book House, $6.95.

Miller, Holly, *How to Earn More Than Pennies for Your Thoughts: A Christian Writer's Guidebook.* Anderson, Ind.: Warner Press, 1990. An articulate exposition on the why's and how's of the writing life. $19.95.

Polking, Kirk, ed., *Writing A to Z.* Cincinnati, Ohio: Writer's Digest Books, 1990. 545 pages, $25. Terms, procedures, and facts of the writing business defined, explained, and put within reach.

Ricks, Chip, and Marilyn Marsh, *How to Write for Christian Magazines.* Nashville, Tenn.: Broadman Press, 1985. 250 pages, $7.50. All the basic information needed to excel in the field, plus 25 model articles.

Simcox, Carroll E., compiler, *4,400 Quotations for Christian Communicators.* Grand Rapids, Mich.: Baker Book House. 407 pp., $17.95. Contains humorous, thoughtful, and profound quotations from the Bible, classics of antiquity, and current bestseller lists.

Stuart, Sally E., *Christian Writers' Market Guide.* San Juan Capistrano, Calif.: Joy Publishing, $18.95. A guide to the Christian marketplace, arranged topically, updated annually by the author.

Stuart, Sally E., and Woody Young, *Copyright Not Copycat.* San Juan Capistrano, Calif.: Joy Publishing, 1987. $9.95. Detailed information about this most important subject for writers.

Wirt, Sherwood E., *Getting Into Print.* Nashville, Tenn.: Thomas Nelson, Incorporated, 1977. 132 pages, $2.95. Basic insights broaden your horizons about Christian writing.

Wirt, Sherwood E., *The Making of a Writer.* Minneapolis, Minn.: Augsburg Publishing, 1987. 160 pages, $8.95. America's best-known teacher of Christian writing shows how a writer comes to be and how he or she keeps going.

Yancey, Philip, *Open Windows.* Westchester, Ill.: Crossway Books, 1982. 216 pages, $9.95. A new standard for journalism written from a Christian perspective; a unique book integrating faith and the art of writing.

Zinsser, William, *Spiritual Quests: The Art and Craft of Religious Writing.* Boston, Mass.: Houghton Mifflin Company, 1988. $8.95.

SEVEN

Minding Your Writing Business

Writing is a business—your business. The more experienced you become in the publishing field, the more you'll realize your need for business acumen. We designed the five sections in this chapter to assist you with this need. The writers in this chapter are experienced in the field they are writing about. We are grateful to them for sharing their expertise with our readers. You'll find their advice invaluable as you "mind your writing business."

COMPUTERS: THE HIGH TECH MUSE

by Aggie Villanueva

Whatever happened to the days when all a writer needed was zeal, pen, and muse? They're gone. Today the writer also needs computer, printer, and word processing program. It's said that writers are not technically inclined. The good news is, there is no need to be. Still not interested? Then brace yourself for the bad news: There is little choice. In religious writing fields, computers are no longer a luxury, they're quickly becoming a necessity. More and more publishers, like Abingdon Press, the publisher of this book, want material submitted in hardcopy (a printed copy of your manuscript) *and* on floppy disk. It's hard to accommodate those requests without a computer.

The good news is computers save time and work for both writer and publisher. The bad news is computers cost money, something underpaid writers have in short supply.

The good news is computers are rapidly decreasing in price at the same time that they're becoming more powerful and user friendly. The bad news is . . . well, I can't think of any more bad news. Everything about computing is promising and exciting.

After the travail of saving up to buy a computer system and learning to operate it, writers tend to forget the "labor pains" and rave about the new "baby." These accolades on how computers can transform the writing life may sound superfluous, but to writers serious about succeeding, the benefits of owning and operating a computer far outweigh the cost. Let's look at a few ways computing can revolutionize your daily production.

In the beginning, word processing meant endless manipulation of thought and re-thought without ever retyping, as if that weren't miraculous enough. These digitized file cabinets of paperless organization had capability for saving several copies of every word we wrote. Margins and other formatting chores were easy to permanently set; thus, secretarial chores were done in a fraction of the time.

211

Today's word processing programs have progressed much farther. They produce manuscripts with a professional look, always a plus with editors. A good program comes with several typefaces (called fonts), some more attractive and easier to read than pica, elite, or courier.

Besides paperless organization and word manipulation, today's programs automate repetitive chores. For instance, imagine every time you need your editor's address you just type the code letter, press a function key, and it appears. Instant business letter heading!

What about this? Start a new manuscript with everything already formatted according to editorial specifications: margins, typeface (or font), and paragraph spacing indents. Take it a step farther and preset your computer to insert your name, address, social security number, phone number, approximate word count, rights offered, title, and by-line in as few as two keystrokes. That's called a macro. Macros can be preset to do any repetitive chore.

Word processors can function as a database (an organized collection of related information) for marketing or bookkeeping chores. They can create an index, table of contents, combine text from two different manuscripts, automatically insert headings and numbers on each page, search for and replace errant words, check your spelling and grammar, supply a thesaurus, sort lists alphabetically or numerically, count words, and some will, believe it or not, draw pictures.

Computers even teach you how to use their programs in the privacy of your home via "tutorial" disks included with most programs. They can publish Teen Night flyers for the job you volunteered for at church or at school, furnish layouts and printing for newsletters, or print invitations to Aunt Carrie's birthday party. That's called desktop publishing.

It's best to purchase a sophisticated word processing program because it does several chores in one. In addition to recording and manipulating text, it checks your grammar and spelling. Scores of other programs enhance these capabilities still more. For instance, grammar checkers included with word processing programs usually have only basic capability. More advanced programs are available. They take grammar checking as far as technologically possible with today's equipment and programs.

In addition to power-packed grammar checkers, you can add a separate thesaurus and dictionaries with definitions. CD ROM (Compact Disk: Read Only Memory) capability provides an entire encyclopedia with screen images as clear as your television set. They can play Beethoven's *Moonlight Sonata* and bring the world's great art right into your living room. E-mail electronically sends your manuscripts to the editor via telephone line. That's really good news when a deadline pushs you into a corner. Your telephone line can also serve as an "on-line" connector with the world's public libraries and other information services. The potential is staggering!

Investigate "on-line" style guide manuals and programs that teach fiction and non-fiction writing skills. Personal information managers schedule deadlines and appointments, popping the information onto the screen at the appropriate time. Choose from dozens of Bible study programs, a boon to Christian writers, each of which has enough capability to fill an entire chapter.

This list of features almost makes computers sound like a cure-all. In truth, they can handle any writing-related chore, save huge chunks of time, and add capabilities far beyond those of writers who do not use computers.

We hope we have dispelled many long-held myths about computers. You don't have to be a technological genius. Anyone can use today's computers. Though the initial investment seems steep, the cost when compared to other business ventures is minimal.

And writing *is* a business. If you didn't believe that somewhere deep in your aesthetic soul, you wouldn't be reading this book.

Want more understanding and help with computers? Try one or more of these magazines:

CHRISTIAN COMPUTING MAGAZINE, P.O. Box 439, 814 North Scott, Belton, MO 64012. Promoting computer use in ministry, this magazine keeps readers informed about products while teaching basic and advanced computer skills. $15 per year.

CHURCH BYTES, 562 Brightleaf Square, #9, 905 West Main Street, Durham, NC 27701. A newsletter on how churches and laypeople make use of computers. Also contains product reviews and instructional material. $18 per year.

COMPUTE, 324 West Wendover Avenue, Suite 200, Greensboro, NC 27408. A secular periodical aimed at beginning and advanced home office uses (translate that "users of cheaper, but higher quality products"). Good instructional material. $19.95 per year.

PC NOVICE, P.O. Box 85350, Lincoln, NE 68501-9807. Contains product information and instructional material for beginners. $24 per year.

Aggie Villanueva of Shawnee, Kansas, is a contributing editor for *Christian Computing Magazine.* She is author of two biblical novels, *Chase the Wind* and *Rightfully Mine* (Thomas Nelson Publishers).

KEEPING TRACK OF IT ALL

by Marlene Bagnull

Filing and recordkeeping systems are not just a necessary evil! They are tools that enable us to be the best stewards of our creativity and time. Although we may feel this is *not* an area where God has gifted us, we can set up workable and efficient systems that enable us to expand the effectiveness of our writing ministries.

What are the basic filing and recordkeeping systems writers need? I believe they logically fall into five categories: musings, markets, manuscript, money, and more.

Musings

Learning to capture and file our ideas is a good antidote for writer's block. But ideas are fleeting. They will be quickly scattered and lost, like fallen leaves in a brisk autumn gust of wind, if we do not write them down almost immediately. I've scribbled ideas on the back of homework papers, on napkins, on envelopes, or whatever I could find and grab. But capturing my ideas isn't enough, if I can't find or decipher them later.

James Dobson says, "Creativity is linked to retrievability." This reminds me of my need to write more legibly and to transcribe those shorthand notes before they get too cold. It also reaffirms what I already know—time spent filing my ideas is not wasted time.

When I first started writing, I filed my ideas in a notebook with pockets by the type of manuscript I felt they would become—devotions, poems, Bible studies, articles, and so on. As my idea bank grew, I graduated to a file cabinet where my ideas are now sorted by topics and subtopics. I also have a file with a bright pink label that says "Priority Ideas to Develop."

Some of our best ideas are likely to be captured in our journals. But again, how are we going to find them when we need them? Highlighting entries we feel we may later develop into manuscripts is one method. Making notes in the margin of our journals is another method.

Markets

The book you are now reading is the first place to turn for information about prospective publishers. Its indexes and detailed descriptions make it an invaluable resource, but it is *not* meant to replace firsthand information. Before submitting any manuscript, you need to request the guidelines for writers (date them when you receive them), a list of upcoming themes (if any), and a sample copy (or catalog if you're considering a book proposal). File this material so you can refer to it frequently. Because I find it most helpful to market my work by the type of magazine (i.e., children's magazines, take-home papers, family living magazines, etc.), I file my guidelines and samples by these groupings.

Editors and editorial needs change frequently. That's why it's important to subscribe to many of the writing magazines and newsletters listed in chapter 6. Sandra Brooks, coauthor of this book, writes the "MarketLines" column in the *Cross & Quill*. Sally Stuart, author of *Christian Writers' Market Guide*, writes "Pen Tips" for *The Christian Communicator*. You can keep this book up-to-date by subscribing to these newsletters and penciling in changes.

Manuscripts

It works best for me to file manuscripts by the stage they are presently in: under consideration, in process, to be written, and never placed. In each of these groups I may file individual manuscripts alphabetically or by subject matter.

I also have two files for off-the-press work. One is an alphabetical file of the original manuscript with the editorial changes noted. I file the tearsheets alphabetically in polyvu, top-loading sheet protectors in my published works binders. When a manuscript is reprinted, I slip the reprint behind the earlier tearsheet. I note the places and dates each manuscript has been reprinted on a post-it that I stick to the top of each sheet protector. This enables me to flip through my binders and immediately see where each manuscript has been published. I have a separate binder of seasonal off-press manuscripts, again alphabetically arranged.

Manuscript Acceptance Log

Using ledger paper, or a database if you prefer, keep a log of each year's acceptances with the following information:

Date accepted
Title of the manuscript
Publisher
Rights purchased
Estimated payment (for pay-on-publication markets)
Date paid
Amount paid

Date scheduled for publication (if known)

Actual date of publication

Off press

Thank you sent (It's appropriate to drop a short note of appreciation to the editor.
   At the same time, you may want to submit another manuscript or query letter.)

Editorial changes noted

Date resubmitted as a reprint (if you did not sell all rights)

Manuscript Inventory Log

My mentor, Ann Sirna, says a manuscript (if its subject matter is of general interest) has not earned its keep until it has sold at least ten times. A manuscript inventory log will help you to be a good steward of your off-the-press work that you are free to resubmit for possible reprinting in non-overlapping markets.

Note: Before submitting a manuscript for reprinting, make certain you did not sell all rights and that the date of publication is past. You may receive something off the press several months before the actual publication date. Also be sure to learn from the changes the editor made by carefully comparing the off-press work with your original manuscript. Incorporate those changes you feel strengthened your manuscript as well as any other changes you want to make. If you are using a computer, I suggest you add the dollar sign symbol to the front of the file name to aid in locating your sold manuscripts on disk.

Using ledger paper, or a computer database, set up an inventory log with the following information:

Length

Title

Seasonal (note what season)

First publisher and date

Subsequent publishers and dates

Sheets of ledger paper aid in organizing my inventory by type of manuscript: fillers, family living articles, personal experience stories, poetry, Christian education articles, and so forth. Because I have a large inventory of seasonal manuscripts, I also group these separately.

Who Has What?

Keeping track of what manuscript is where is an essential recordkeeping task since mistakes made can be costly to both your income and reputation. Although I've been using a computer for many years for word processing, I still am not sold on databases. My Double Reference Submission System continues to give me an excellent way of keeping on top of submissions, acceptances, returns, and editorial needs. I have a 3 × 5 card for every periodical or book publisher to whom I submit my work and for every manuscript I write.

PERIODICAL INDEX CARD

Front

Name of Magazine
Editor's name—Note when on a first name basis
Address
Miscellaneous
    Current needs and date
    Overstocked and date
    Editor wants to see more of my work and date

Back

SALES

Date Sold	Title	*Type	Length	Rights Sold
		*Fiction		
		Article		
		Poem		
		Testimony		
		Personal experience story		
		Interview		
		Filler		

Second card staple to first

SUBMISSIONS

Date	Title	Decision

Circle manuscript purchased.
Highlight if editor suggests a rewrite or asks you to resubmit later.
Important—Draw a line when a new editor takes over since earlier submissions that were not accepted can be resubmitted to him/her.

Periodical index cards are filed alphabetically by type of magazine (take-home papers, women's magazines, teen magazines, etc.). I also have cards for book publishers and file them separately. In the other drawer of my two-drawer 3 × 5 file, I file my manuscript index cards. You can use a second box or the back of the same box you use for the periodical index cards.

MANUSCRIPT INDEX CARD

Front

Title   Rights Offered
Type of manuscript   # of Words
Date written
File Name - Very important if you're using a computer. Be sure to make a
back-up on a floppy disk and to assign a number to each floppy so you can
locate the three letter extension to help group your manuscripts. For example:
. art for article, . poe for poem, . fam for family living, etc.

Keep front of card empty to list:
Sales   Publication Date   Amount Paid

Back

SUBMISSIONS

Date
Submitted   To   Decision

Highlight if editor suggests a rewrite or asks you to resubmit.

Circle sales.

I file my manuscript index cards alphabetically according to their status:

Under consideration
Queries
Manuscript returns to be submitted
To rewrite
Being held—Editor has asked to hold for possible publication.
Accepted but not yet published
Off press—First rights manuscripts to prepare for resubmission as a reprint.
Reprints circulating
Reprints not circulating
All rights sold—published manuscripts I am not free to reprint because I sold all
   rights.

I suggest you shuffle through these cards periodically to make certain your manuscript hasn't gotten buried, but be patient. I double or even triple the time an editor
says he or she reports in before making contact with him or her.

Money

Keeping track of your writing earnings and expenses saves you time, stress, and money when income tax season rolls around. For years I used ledger paper and my adding machine, convinced that the financial software programs were too complicated and difficult to learn. I was wrong! *Quicken* (available in every computer store) really is user friendly and has proved to be a great time saver. I'm sure other programs are equally good; I'm just not familiar with them.

Whether or not you use a computer, I recommend that you set up a separate checking account for your writing income and expenses. Train yourself to deposit everything you receive and to pay everything by check (and get a receipt). See "Dealing with Taxes" later in this chapter for information on the expenses you can claim. Begin keeping track of these expenses now whether or not you have made any sales. It's a step of faith that helps you to view yourself as a professional. And who knows? Perhaps this will be the year when you will earn so much you'll really need those deductions.

More

You'll also want to set up alphabetical files for correspondence, contracts, writing resources, and so on. A tickler file to keep you on top of approaching deadlines, upcoming conferences, seasonal submissions, and other dates is also helpful.

Whatever filing systems you set up, keep them simple and file regularly. A file drawer full of neatly arranged dividers and folders won't help you if everything that belongs in it is buried in a stack of to-be-filed papers.

In the beginning, a portable file box with hanging files might be all you need. If you do a lot of writing and speaking, I encourage you to purchase a fireproof filing cabinet and a separate fireproof media chest to store back-up diskettes and tapes safely.

Setting up and maintaining effective filing and recordkeeping systems is hard work, but it is worth the effort. If you're a beginning writer, don't wait to set up your systems. Let them grow with you. If you've been writing for a long time, evaluate whether your systems are really working for you. Ask yourself how long it takes you to find something. If you can't put your finger on that letter you thought you answered, or the quotation you wanted to use in your latest article, chances are you need to do either some ridding out or some reorganizing.

It takes time to mind your writing business, but it's time well spent. And maybe, through increased efficiency, you'll sell enough manuscripts to employ a secretary-bookkeeper!

Marlene Bagnull of Drexel Hill, Pennsylvania, free-lance writer and writing instructor, has sold more than 900 pieces to periodicals and written three published books.

USING AGENTS

by Connie Soth

Dealing with agents, for general publishers, is a professional fact of life. Agents are screeners who stand between editors and unsuitable manuscripts or talent scouts who bring promising authors to the editors' attention. And while not perfect, as no mortal is, agents serve both author and publisher acceptably.

Many publishers who deal exclusively with religious books, however, exert widespread and ingrained resistance to authors who use agents. Some editors today still insist that they work better with an author without an agent's "interference." What do they mean by this?

Some publishers have misunderstood or mistrusted agents for many reasons. For example, when agents attempt to get a better contract for their clients, publishers may assume that the agents want to corrupt innocent authors with visions of big money, a promise the company cannot fulfill. And, candidly, some agents by being hard-nosed and adversarial prove publishers' worst fears and kill chances for friendly negotiations.

Some religious publishers, not being perfect either, have neglected to live out their avowed spiritual creed when contract time arrives. Many an unagented author, intimidated by a book contract, reports having signed it unread, "because I was just so glad to get my book published," and because the editor declared, "this is our standard contract," implying that no changes were needed or even possible.

In religious publishing, many editors perhaps from lack of experience or professionalism think of the agent as a distracting "third voice" intruding on the "family feeling" religious companies want between author and editor for the rewrite process.

The Changing Scene

Ideally, publisher and agent can function as governors for each other, if both act from enlightened consciences. Reports of change have been trickling in from various parts of the country. Some editors now assert they can work through agents, content that they will take care of business matters and negotiate contracts fairly, leaving all creative matters to the editor and author team.

Some publishers have gone farther. They make a habit of explaining the contract point by point, advising the unagented author to get an outside opinion before signing the contract. And they work willingly with agents who can see both sides—the publisher's as well as the author's.

Agents? Some are alive and well and taking care of their clients, but it would be less than honest to say all is well for all agents.

For economic reasons, there are many ex-agents. One financial pothole has been the industry-wide prejudice against agents charging reading fees. Only recently has this begun to wane, as agents have put their business on a practical basis. Some agents now issue a printed fee schedule on request, along with a project evaluation the prospective client or author must complete and return to them. Others simply state by letter to inquirers their fees and percentages. Some agents now adopt the idea of reading the manuscript for a previously agreed amount, specifying that if the agent takes the author as a client that fee will be used for the author's benefit. If the agent decides not to handle the property, the author receives a comprehensive, written critique to use as a guide for revision. That way, each gets something of value, even if the contract goes no farther. It is up to the author to get all the details on how the agent works before becoming involved.

Another hole in the road to publication is deep and longstanding. Widespread policy in the religious book industry of granting very small, sometimes *no* advances to authors, of clinging to outmoded contract forms, of keeping poor records of royalties to be paid, and of using arcane distribution systems have left authors—and by echo effect their agents—working very hard and long for skimpy returns. Moreover, some religious publishers have thought authors should be content to satisfy their personal yearning "to get out the Word"—and not expect commensurate payment for their work. Neither the author nor the agent can subsist on such airy-fairyness.

Agents who finally conclude they can't make a living in agenting have become free-lance editorial consultants, in-house authors' advocates, marketing reps, and acquisitions editors. All these positions, as one ex-agent says, "are jobs where I can still help authors."

The Ideal Agent

From your viewpoint, the agent must possess sterling qualities. One director of religious books for a large publisher wishes there were no more agents for religious book authors, saying, "It would simplify my job enormously if there were none." His list of an agent's qualifications includes knowing the market, the competition, the current trends, the history of previous religious books, and having a realistic view of the various markets each publisher is best at reaching.

One free-lance editor who does consultation and critique of manuscripts considered by publishers stresses the need for partnership in publishing between author and editor, with the agent as "groundbreaker and business consultant." She senses "trends favoring the development of agenting for the religious writer."

Finding an Agent

These days, the recluse writer is more myth than reality. To be a successful, published author of a religious, inspirational book you should:

- Go to writers' conferences. They give the author a picture of what is wanted by publishers and a chance to meet and talk with editors. Even more pertinent, authors can meet agents who, more often these days, frequent conferences looking for the "hidden gems" among authors they might otherwise never meet. Some of these agents offer workshops to writers on how to approach and choose an agent.
- Attend a secular conference, such as those given each year in my area by Pacific Northwest Writers, Willamette Writers, and Oregon Writers Colony. They often include workshops and panels for writers wanting to break into the religious markets. Secular conferences have a different atmosphere, too, valuable for authors who want to work "out in the world."
- Gather background material about agents and how they work, where to find them, and how to use one. LANA (*Literary Agents of North America*) is one important source of agents who list religious writing as a specialty. LMP (*Literary Marketplace*) lists a wide variety of companies, people, awards, and services as well as agents. A new reference book, the *1992 Guide to Literary Agents & Art/Photo Reps,* promises to be the "first annual" listing of this information/directory. The first two books are available, for reference only, in public and college libraries. The latter book is published by Writer's Digest Books.
- Join a critique group for writers, choosing carefully one that is led by a writer well versed in the ups and downs of publishing, preferably a published author. (See the list of writers' groups in chapter 6.) Such a group is part of the indispensable "writers' network" where one may well learn agents' names and addresses.
- Join writers' associations, both secular and religious, also part of the "writers' network," important investments for those who understand writing as a business.
- Talk with published authors. Find out their experience with agents, how they found one or why they don't use one.
- Check through the list of agents at the end of this section. Some specialize in

religious, inspirational literature; others range farther, into both religious and secular writings. The list of agents is growing, as religious publishers and editors become convinced of the value of working through an agent and authors become more dependent on agents as their advocates and business representatives.

Etiquette for Agent-Hunting Authors

How should an author approach an agent? Begin with the following basic rules:

- Educate yourself first. Study books and articles in writers' magazines about agents. Ask a reference librarian for sources.
- Write as carefully crafted a query letter to an agent as to an editor, including a SASE.
- Never send a whole manuscript *until* requested by the agent to do so. Unsolicited manuscripts are the bane of agents' existence.
- Include a brief biographical sketch, your published writing history, your qualifications and specific markets for your book.
- Make yourself a list of services you hope to get from an agent so your time and the agent's will not be wasted. Compare this list with what the agent offers.

Once your working relationship with an agent is affirmed, there are a few more tips to be remembered.

- Let the agent be the agent. He or she is your representative and needs to know you will not also be doing what you have engaged the agent to do for you.
- Follow any instructions your agent gives you, promptly.
- Be patient as your agent works to get you a publisher or pursues additional means of getting your work out.
- If termination of the agent agreement from your side becomes necessary, be kind—and have a contingency plan.

Above all, give your agent something to work with. Cultivate and advertise your own abilities and experience. Let the world know about you and your book wherever you have contacts. In the long run, promotion of your book will be a cooperative endeavor, with you and your agent doing most of the promoting. You are the author. It is your book; you will need to help sell yourself. Now is not the time to be shy, modest, and retiring.

Religious book authors who find this pressure to sell as well as to write disturbing are out of tune with religious publishing today. Competition for publication is fierce; your ministry of writing is perfectly fine, but it must be supported and supplemented by your willingness to take on public speaking and visibility. Developing those skills, with the guidance of your agent, is vital. Authors who accept this truth will find that the best way to achieve it and still have time to write is with the agent's expert help. Giving your agent something to work with, to talk about with publishers, and letting him or her know you trust a professional's judgment will leave you free to think, to dream, to get those words unique to you down on paper.

Literary Agents for Religious, Inspirational Works

The following agents and agencies have indicated that they are interested in handling religious, inspirational materials and welcome inquiries from writers about specific kinds of writing:

ALIVE COMMUNICATIONS, P.O. Box 49068, Colorado Springs, CO 80949. (719) 260-7080. Fax: (719) 260-8223. S. Rickly Christian, president.

ASSOCIATION OF AUTHOR'S REPRESENTATIVES, 10 Astor Plaza, 3rd Floor, New York, NY 10003. Request flyer about the organization and a list of member agents.

AUTHOR AID ASSOCIATES, 340 East 52nd Street, New York, NY 10022. (212) 908-9179 or (212) 758-4213. Arthur Orrmont, editorial director.

BRANDENBURGH & ASSOCIATES LITERARY AGENCY, 24555 Corte Jaramillo, Murrieta, CA 92562. Donald C. Brandenburgh.

PEMA BROWNE, LTD., Pine Road, HCR, Box 104B, Neversink, NY 12765. (914) 985-2936. Fax: (914) 985-7635. Perry Browne.

CREATIVE CONCEPTS LITERARY AGENCY, P.O. Box 10261, Harrisburg, PA 17105. (717) 432-5054. Fax: (717) 432-0417. Michele Glance Serwach, director.

LOIS CURLEY ENTERPRISES, 7887 Dunbrook Road, San Diego, CA 92126. (619) 689-1100. Fax: (619) 689-1194. Lois Curley.

THE CURTIS BRUCE AGENCY, 3015 Evergreen Drive, Suite A, Plover, WI 54467. Fax: (715) 345-2630.

THE DOROTHY DEERING LITERARY AGENCY, 1507 Oakmont Drive, Suite A., Acworth, GA 30102. (404) 591-2051. Fax: (404) 591-0369. Dorothy Deering or Kelly Boatman.

THE ETHAN ELLENBURG LITERARY AGENCY, 548 Broadway, #5E, New York, NY 10012. (212) 431-4554. Fax: (212) 941-4652. Ethan Ellenberg.

GOOD NEWS LITERARY SERVICE, P.O. Box 4498, Visalia, CA 93278. (209) 636-0232. Fax: (209) 636-0232. Cynthia Ann Wachner. Interested in new or handicapped writers.

HOLUB & ASSOCIATES, 24 Old Colony Road, North Stanington, CT 06359. (203) 535-0689. William Holub. Primary interest—Roman Catholic readership.

MARCH MEDIA INC., 7003 Chadwick Drive, #256, Brentwood, TN 37027. (615) 370-3148. Etta G. Wilson. Only children's and gift books.

MILLS HOUSE, 443 Pinehurst Avenue, Unit One, Los Gatos, CA 95032. (408) 879-9644. Fax: (408) 879-9645. Roy M. Carlisle.

BK NELSON LITERARY AGENCY, 84 Woodland Road, Pleasantville, NY 10570. (914) 741-1324. Fax: (914) 741-1324. Check Warren, Bonita Nelson, or John Benson.

QUICKSILVER BOOKS—LITERARY AGENTS, 50 Wilson Street, Hartsdale, NY 10530. (914) 946-8748. Bob Silverstein, president.

RISING SUN LITERARY GROUP, 1507 Oakmont Drive, Acworth, GA 30102. (404) 591-3397. Fax: (404) 591-0369. Lynn Watson.

THE SHEPARD AGENCY, Suite 3, Pawling Savings Bank Building, Southeast Plaza, Brewster, NY 10509. (914) 279-2900 or (914) 279-3236. Fax: (914) 279-3239. Lance or Jean Shepard.

STEPHEN GRIFFITH, Route 7, Raven's Ridge, 12C, Boone, NC 28607.

Connie Soth of Beaverton, Oregon, author, researcher, columnist, and teacher of writers, employed an agent for her book, *Insomnia, God's Night School.*

DEALING WITH TAXES

by Albertine Phaneuf Wicher

Writing, if pursued for profit by the free-lancer or self-employed, constitutes a business, and the income from this business must be reported on the writer's tax return, usually on Schedule C, "Profit or Loss from Business."

Because Schedule C allows you to report losses as well as profits, the IRS sets guidelines for filing this writer-friendly schedule. Currently, you are expected to show a profit from your writing in three out of five consecutive years.

In theory, you may file Schedule C without any writing income from the beginning, but many tax services will not allow this, probably because of the increased risk of audit. Realistically, after a year of zero income, could you count on three years of profits within the following four years?

With some writing income, however, you may show a loss the first time you file Schedule C. If the word "audit" scares you, claim your expenses only *up to* your income. Remember that you must declare all your income, but may absorb some expenses. An established writer having an off-year will no doubt be more aggressive than a beginner.

If you have never filed Schedule C, you won't find it in your tax package. For a copy, get in touch with your local IRS or call 1-800-TAX-FORM. Also ask for Schedule SE, "Computation of Social Security Self-Employment Tax." If your profit from writing is greater than $400, you must file Schedule SE along with Schedule C.

Once you file Schedule C, copies of both Schedules C and SE will arrive in your tax package—usually in early January. Each year get a copy of IRS Publication 17, "Your Federal Income Tax." This helpful freebie lists the new rules on page 1 and has a handy index on the back. Form 1040, the long form, must be filed with Schedule C.

Learn about the tax rules that affect your business—selling manuscripts. Whether or not you do your own taxes, understand what goes into your return. Your signature makes you responsible for its accuracy.

Generally, expenses related directly to writing—such as the categories of expenses listed below—are deductible.

Advertising: Photos for newspapers, brochures, bookjackets, business cards, and imprinted stationery.

Bank service charges: Fees for a separate checking account. Traveler's checks for business trips. Safe deposit box if you store contracts or returns in it.

Cars: Actual expenses or standard mileage—this rate changes yearly. The 1992 rates are 28 cents per mile business, 12 cents for charitable work. Tolls and parking lot fees for either business or charity. (Ask for receipts.)

Depreciation: Expense or "write-off" limit for 1992 is $10,000. If you bought some expensive equipment such as a computer, copier, or desk—something that's expected to last more than a year—consult a tax expert. Or study IRS publications, do the calculations, and have an IRS expert check them. Get IRS publication 534, "Depreciation."

Interest: Interest on a business item is part of the purchase price; hence, deductible.

Legal and professional services: Fees to an accountant, lawyer, the copyright office, Legal Aid, or Small Claims Court.

Office expense: Postage, copying, faxing, equipment, furniture. Expensive research books that are part of your library. A substantial library may be depreciated.

Rent on business property: Rent on an office outside your home. If you claim a home office, only a portion of the rent.

Repairs: Of typewriter, computer system, copier, etc. Include only 1/3 the cost of a 3-year maintenance contract.

Supplies: Stationery, pens, files, tapes, computer or typewriter ribbons, etc. Equipment, the smaller items.

Taxes: Sales tax on business items is part of the purchase price; hence, deductible.

Travel and entertainment: Fares to conferences or for research. Meals and entertainment are only 80 percent deductible—even if you accept the per diem, which varies yearly among cities. A $25 limit on business gifts; small items such as pens don't count. Accurate records are a must. The per diem reduces, but does not eliminate record-keeping; keep records to show the business purpose of your trip, the time and place. Get IRS publication 463, "Entertainment and Gift Expenses."

Utilities and telephone: Entire bill for a separate phone. Otherwise only identifiable business calls. Portion of the electric bill for running equipment—$4 to $8 per month based on 20 hours per week.

Other: Dues to writers' organizations and those related to your work. Subscriptions to professional journals and magazines. Books used for writing or current projects. Educational expenses to maintain or improve skills such as attending writers' conferences, seminars, or lectures. Get IRS publication 334, *Tax Guide for Small Business.*

When you file Schedule C, enter only *your* name, even if your return is joint. Writers usually value their inventory at "cost" and operate on a "cash" basis—income is recorded when received and expenses when paid.

If you don't claim a home office, list *only* your direct expenses on Schedule C and report your profit or loss on Form 1040. If your net profit is over $500, consider making estimated tax payments or increasing them.

The rules for a home office were eased in 1990. Before claiming expenses for a home office, decide if it is deductible and if you want to claim it. To meet IRS standards, your office must be essential to your business and used exclusively for it, but you need only use it for a "substantial amount of time." Its costs, however, cannot exceed the net profit from your writing.

If you think you meet these standards, fill out Form 8829, "Expenses for Business Use of Your Home." This new form takes you line-by-line through the calculations of your allowable deduction, which you subtract from your tentative profit reported on Schedule C.

Your business percentage or basic home office deduction rate depends on how much of your living space your office uses—10 percent, 25 percent, more? Even if you don't file form 8829, fill it in to know what your percentage is and to set income goals. Or make up a situation to get the feel for it. For example, a writer with $2,600 in gross income and $1,000 in direct expenses would pay tax on only $1,600. Same writer with a home office allowance of $1,100 would pay tax on only $500. Read the instructions because some losses can be carried forward and used another year.

IRS publication 587, "Business Use of Your Home," includes samples of Schedule C and Form 8829 filled in.

General warning: A home office depreciation taken today could complicate the eventual sale of the house, because only the business part can be depreciated, giving the house and office different cost bases. In addition, the tax on the profit realized on a business asset cannot be postponed. One solution: Don't claim a home office the year of the sale and hope that ends the matter. Seniors might complicate the $125,000 exemption at the time of the sale.

Despite this warning, if you do claim a home office, take all the write-offs; the IRS will assume you did. Depending on your age, the tax savings over the years could be considerable.

If you rent your home and maintain a home office, fill in Form 8829 to obtain your business percentage. List a portion of your rent as "Other Expenses" and proceed as does the home owner.

For general information, call the IRS, 1-800-424-1040. When the question is on complex topics such as home office, travel, or depreciation, you may be referred to a Taxpayer Service Specialist who will either give you an immediate answer or a written one within 10 days.

Do your own Schedule C, even if you use a tax expert. Tax rules are so complex and those for writers so specific, that some experts have trouble keeping up. Learning about the tax laws that affect writers will enhance your self-image as a writer and put dollars in your pocket.

Albertine Wicher is the author of *Minding Your Business: A Tax Guide for Authors*. A new edition of the book is in production. In the meantime, readers who have questions directly related to writers and taxes can write to Mrs. Wicher at 1624 Briar Hill Road, Gladwyne, PA 19035. Enclose SASE.

SELF-PUBLISHING

by William Gentz and Sandra Brooks

The purpose of *Religious Writers Marketplace* is to bring authors and publishers together. In the light of that, does "self-publishing" deserve a place in this book? We believe it does; therefore, we have discussed this route for authors in the last three editions. We still believe that self-publishing is a highly respectable course and an option for any writer.

Most of the procedures considered here are based on the article in the last three editions written by Jane Mall of Corpus Christi, Texas. In addition, we want to call your attention to the increasing possibility of self-publishing for authors who become adept at computer technology and verge into what has become known as "desktop publishing," which we won't attempt to discuss here.

If you are considering self-publishing, be warned first of all that we are not discussing either "vanity publishing" or what is commonly known as "subsidy publishing." In the former case, the author is required by the publisher to pay all the costs of publishing and is usually left with stacks of unsalable books. Subsidy publishers (sometimes called cooperative publishers) are those who ask the author to cooperate in paying "some" of the costs and in carrying out "some" of the distribution usually done by the publisher. We have not knowingly listed vanity or subsidy publishers in this book, even though there are many in the religious field.

What then should an author know about "self-publishing"? Don't approach self-publishing as a last-ditch effort, or as a way to get even with shortsighted publishers who returned your book manuscript, or as a way to become wealthy. Think of it as an announcement to the world that you are a serious writer with a marketable product.

With this in mind, consider these few important points before making the decision to self-publish.

1. Research the subject. There are several good books to guide you on all that is involved:

The Complete Guide to Self-Publishing by Tom and Marilyn Ross, Writers Digest Books, Cincinnati, OH (2nd edition), $16.95.

The Self-Publishing Manual, by Dan Poynter, Para Publishing, P.O. Box 4232, Santa Barbara, CA 93140 (1989, 5th edition), $19.95.

The Publish-It-Yourself Handbook, by Bill Henderson, Pushcart Press, P.O. Box 845, Yonkers, NY 10701, $11.95.

You can also receive excellent information on self-publishing from the National Writers Press, 1450 South Havana, Suite 424, Aurora, CO 80012. This is a subsidiary of the National Writers Club at the same address.

Other helpful organizations are Midwest Data Management, 221 North Market Street, Winamac, IN 46996; Longwood Publishing, 1310 Alberta Street, Longwood, FL 32750.

2. Consider the value of the product you wish to self-publish. Are you convinced of its worth and marketability? One way to confirm your belief is to submit your manuscript to at least three publishers. Perhaps these publishers will give some hints on how to improve the manuscript. Or you can hire a professional critiquer. If you don't know one, ask a professional writer whose judgment you trust to recommend one, or ask faculty members at writers' conferences to recommend one to you. After you have a professional diagnosis, carefully and prayerfully evaluate whether or not self-publishing is right for you and your manuscript.

3. As a self-publisher, you will be responsible for all aspects of editing, publishing, and marketing your book. If you have experience in advertising, marketing, and public relations, that will be a big plus. If these areas don't appeal to you, perhaps you would be wise to forget self-publishing.

4. Consider the investment of time and money involved in a self-publishing venture. If you can't successfully distribute your book, you may end up with a garage or basement full of copies. You'll also be responsible for obtaining the copyright, ISBN number, and naming your publishing venture. These steps are outlined in the books just listed. Consider them carefully and prayerfully before going out on the self-publishing limb.

Is self-publishing a good idea? Perhaps. Mark Twain, Walt Whitman, and Edgar Allan Poe, among others, all published themselves at one time. *The Living Bible* began as a self-publishing venture on the kitchen tables of Ken Taylor and Virginia Muir (Tyndale House Publishers). *The Christian Mother Goose Books* began when Marjorie Decker couldn't find an established publisher willing to gamble on Christian nursery rhymes (Christian Mother Goose Publishing). If you can successfully publish and market your book, it will be a true accomplishment. You may not become as wealthy or famous as Ken Taylor, Virginia Muir, or Marjorie Decker, but you will have made an important statement. You will have announced to the world that you are a serious writer, that you believe in what you are doing, and that an audience for your work does exist. And who knows? Your self-publishing venture could be a miracle in the making!

Don Poynter, author of *The Self-Publishing Manual* lists ten reasons you "must" self-publish your book. He summarizes these ten reasons with this quotation: "A self-published book has a better chance of success because it is under the control of someone who cares—the author."

A FINAL NOTE

To stay abreast of up-to-the-minute market changes, check the "MarketLines" column of *The Cross & Quill, The Christian Writers Newsletter,* official publication of Christian Writers Fellowship International. For subscription information see "Writers Magazines and Newsletters" in chapter 6.

INDEXES

We planned these indexes to help you gain maximum benefit from the information in this book.

Index I is an alphabetical list of periodicals and publications described in chapters 2 and 4. In addition, it lists publications described in chapters 5 through 7.

Index II is an alphabetical list of publishers, imprints, and organizations.

Index III combines the periodical and publisher lists and organizes them by denomination or faith group sponsorship. Thus, you can easily find entries under a particular religious group's name. An index of Jewish periodicals and publishers would be largely redundant, because they are listed almost exclusively in chapter 4. Special-interest areas for the Jewish market are included under the cross-denominational subject headings in Index IV.

Index IV will probably be used most often. Both periodicals and publishers are listed, grouped by subject, audience, or genre. Keep in mind while using this index that many publishers other than those listed under the headings use similar material. The entries chosen are listed specifically because the publisher or editor mentioned these interests on the questionnaires returned to the authors and editors of *Religious Writers Marketplace*.

Please note that in each index, periodical names appear in italics, publishers' names appear in roman type.

INDEX I
PERIODICALS AND PUBLICATIONS

INDEX II
PUBLISHERS, IMPRINTS, AND ORGANIZATIONS

INDEX III
DENOMINATIONS AND FAITH GROUPS

Adventist

Church/State, 36; Guide, 52; Kid's Stuff, 60; Liberty, 62; Signs/Times, 87; Vibrant Life, 94; Pacific, 125; Review/Herald, 130.

Assemblies of God

Advance, 14; At Ease, 18; Beginner/Paper, 20; HiCall, 53; High Adventure, 53; Junior Trails, 59; Live, 63; Pentecostal Evangel, 74; Sunday School Counselor, Take Five, 88; Woman's Touch, 97; Youth Leader, 100; Gospel Pub., 116.

Baptist

Baptist Beacon, Baptist Herald, Baptist Leader, 19; Canadian Baptist, 25; Co-Laborer, 40; Evangelical Baptist, 48; Fellowship Link, 50; Gospel Tidings, 51; Heartbeat, 52; Messenger, 68; The Standard, 86, Teenage Chr., 89; Judson, 119.

Baptist, Southern

Biblical Illustrator, 22; Chr. Single, 35; Church Media Library, 38; Discipleship Training, 45; Exaltation, 49; Home Life, 54; Living with Preschoolers/Children/Teenagers, 64-65; Pioneer, 75; Search, Sr. Musician, 83; Southwestern Journal/Theology, 85; Student, 87; Young Musicians, 99; Broadman, 108; Holman, 118; New Hope, 123.

Brethren Church

Brethren Life, 24; YouthGuide, 100.

Catholic

America, American Benedictine, 16; Annals/de Beaupre, 17; B.C. Catholic, 20; Bible Today, 21; Biblical Archaeology, 22; Canadian Cath., 26; Canadian Messenger, Caravan, Catechist, 27; Cath./Quarterly, Cath. Digest, Cath./Media, Cath. Library, 28; Cath. Near East, Cath. Register, Cath./Circle, 29; Columbia, Commonweal, Compass, 40; Conscience, 41; Creation Social, Crisis, Critic, 43; Family, 50; Liguorian, Listening, 63; Miraculous Medal, 68; Modern Liturgy, Momentum, 69; My Friend, New Covenant, 70; Oblates, Other Side, 71; Our Family, Our Sunday, 72; Parish Family, 73; PIME, 74; Positive Approach, 75; Praying, 76; Pro Ecclesia, 78; Queen/Hearts, 80; Religion Teacher's, St. Anthony, 81; St. Joseph's, Salt, 82; Sisters, Social Justice, 85; Spiritual Life, 86; Theol. Studies, 90; Today's Cath., 91; US Cath., 93; You!, 98; Youth Update, 101; Alba, 105; Ave Maria, 106; Bosco, 108; Cath. U., Chr. Classics, 109; Cistercian, 110; Crossroad, 112; Dimension, 113; Ignatius, 118; Liguori, 120; Liturgical, Loyola, 121; More, 122; Novalis, Orbis, 24; Our Sunday, Pastoral, Paulist, 125; Regnery, Resource, Resurrection, 128; St. Anthony, St. Bede's, 129; St. Mary's, St. Paul, 130; Sheed, 131; Tabor, 132.

Christian Church

Axios, 19; Canadian Disciple, 26; R-A-D-A-R, 80; Standard, 86; Straight, 87; Chalice Press, 109; College Press, 111; Standard, 131.

Christian Missionary Alliance

Christian Pub., 110.

Church of Christ

College Press, 111.

Church of God

Bible Advocate, 21; Church Herald/Holiness, 37; Church/God Evangel, 38; Leader, 61; Pathway I.D., 73; Pentecostal Messenger, 74; Vital Christianity, 95; Youth/Chr. Ed., 100; Warner Press, 134.

Covenant Church

Covenant Companion, 43.

Episcopal/Anglican Church

Anglican, Anglican Review, 17; Cathedral Age, 28; Episcopal Life, 47; Journal/Women's Min., 59; Plumbline, 75; Sewanee/Review, 83; Trinity News, 92; Witness, 96; Alban, 105, Cowley, 112; Forward, 115; Morehouse, 122.

Evangelical Free

Beacon, 20; Evangelical Beacon, 48; Pursuit, 79.

Evangelical Orthodox

Again, 15.

Foursquare World Advance

Foursquare World, 51.

Friends

Quaker Life, 79; Barclay, 107; Friends United, 115.

Jewish

See Jewish periodical lists on pages 138-48; publishers of Judaica on pages 149-58; publishers of other Jewish interest in chapter 5.

Lutheran

Canada Lutheran, 25; Canadian Lutheran, 27; Esprit, 47; Lutheran, Lutheran Forum, 65; Lutheran Journal, Lutheran Layman, Lutheran Witness, 66; Parish Teacher, 73; Pro Ecclesia, 78; Teachers Interaction, 89; Word/World, 97; Augsburg Fortress, 105; Concordia, 111.

Mennonite

Builder, 24; Christian Living, 33; Mennonite Brethren, Mennonite/Review, 67; On/Line, 71; Partners, 73; Purpose, 79; Story Friends, 86; Story Mates, 87; With, 96; YouthGuide, 100; Herald, 117; Kindred, 119.

Methodist, A.M.E.

A.M.E. Recorder, AME Review, 16.

Methodist, Free

Evangel, 48; Light/Life, 62; Missionary Tidings, 69; Power/Light, 76.

Methodist, United

Christian Social Action, 35; Circuit Rider, 39; Interpreter, 56; Leader/Today, 61; Magazine/Chr. Youth, 66; Mature Years, 67; Methodist History, 68; New World Outlook, 70; Quarterly Review, 80; UM Reporter, 93; Abingdon, 104; Dimensions/Living, 113; Kingswood, 119.

Missionary Church

Emphasis/Faith, 47; Ministry Today, 68; Bethel, 107.

Nazarene

Discoveries, 46; Herald/Holiness, 53; Journal/Camping, 56; Level C, 61; Power/Light, 76; Standard, 86; Teens Today, 90; Together Time, 92; Wonder Time, 97; Beacon Hill, 107.

Presbyterian

American Presby., 17; Asso. Reformed, 18; Horizons, 54; Presby. Outlook, Presby. Survey, 77; Westminster/John Knox, 135.

Quaker. See Friends.

Reformed Church

Chr. Renewal, 34; Church Herald, 37; Clarion, 39; Reformed Worship, 80; Inheritance, 118; Kregel, 119; Still Waters, 132.

Salvation Army

Edge, 46; Sally Ann, 82; War Cry, 95; Young Salvationist, Young Soldier, 99.

Unitarian, Universalist

Church/State, 36; Beacon, 107.

United Church

Fellowship, 50; United Church Observer, 92; United Church Pub., 133.

United Church of Christ

Pilgrim, 126.

Wesleyan Church

Asbury, 18; CLCL, 39; Discoveries, 46; Power/Light, 76; Vista, 94; Wesleyan Advocate, 95; Beacon Hill, 107.

INDEX IV
SUBJECTS

Academics
Brethren Life, 24; Abingdon, 104; Augsburg Fortress, 105; Baker, Barbour, 106; Cambridge, 108; Companion, 111; Cornell, 112; Greenwood, 116; Kingswood, 119; Princeton, 127; Scarecrow, 130; Trinity, 133; University, 134; Westminster, 135; Yale, 136; Zondervan, 136; JEWISH: American Jewish History, 138; Studies in Biblio, 147; Cornell, Fortress, 151; Harper, Hebrew Union, 152; Indiana, 153; Schocken, 155; S.P.I., Temple, 156; U/Alabama, U/Chicago, University Press, 157; Wayne State, 158.

Activity Books
Shining Star, Standard, 131.

African-American Studies
A.M.E. Recorder, AME/Review, 16; Augsburg Fortress, 105; Judson, 119; Winston, 135.

Agents
finding an agent, 220; list of, 222; need for, 218-20.

AIDS Ministry
Forward, 115; Sheed, 131.

Archaeology
Biblical Archaeology, Biblical Illustrator, 22; Princeton, 127.

Arts/Literature
Anglican Journal, 17; Breakthrough!, 23; Canada Lutheran, 25; Canadian Baptist, Canadian Cath., 26; Chr. Renewal, 34; Compass, 40; Faith Today, 49; Loyola, 121; Yale, 136.

Athletes, Athletics
Sharing/Victory, 84; Sports Spectrum, 86.

Audiovisuals
Alban, American Cath., 105; Ave Maria, 106; Brown-ROA, 108; Companion, 111; Friendship, 115; NavPress, Nelson, 123; Resurrection, 128; St. Anthony, 129; Star Song, 132; Trinity, Tyndale, 133; Word, 135; Zondervan, 136.

Bible, Biblical Studies
Baptist Beacon, 19; Bible Advocate, Bible Review, Bible Today, 21; Biblical Illustrator, Biblical Literacy, 22; Cath. Biblical Quarterly, 28; Clarion, 39; Currents, Discipleship Journal, 45; Edge, 46; Evangelical Baptist, 48; Fellowship, 50; Journal/Biblical Literature, 56; Our Family, 72; Sally Ann, 82; USQR, 93; Abingdon, Aglow, 104; Augsburg Fortress, 105; Alba, AMG, 105; Beacon Hill, 107; Bridge, Broadman, 108; Chalice, Chr. Classics, 109; College, Concordia, 111; Credo, 112; Crossway, 113; Gospel Pub., Harper, 116; Hendrickson, Hensley, 117; Holman, Honor, Inheritance, InterVarsity, 118; Kindred, Kregel, 119; Liguori, 120; Loizeaux, 121; Nelson, 123; Novalis, Old Rugged, 124; Our Sunday, Pastoral, Paulist, 125; Pillar, 126; Regal, 127; Revell, 129; Shaw, 130; Star Song, Trinity, 132; Tyndale, United Church, 133; University, Victory, 134; Westminster, Word, 135; Zondervan, 136; JEWISH: Bloch, 150; Hebrew Pub., 152; Jewish Pub., 153.

Biography
Lifeglow, 62; Young/Alive, 98; Beacon Hill, 107; Broadman, 108; Chr. Classics, 109; Chr. Lit., Christopher, 110; Companion, 111; Friends United, 115; Hensley, 117; Ignatius, Inheritance, 118; Kindred, Kregel, 119; Lion, 121; Loyola, 121; Mott Media, 122; Nelson, 123; Our Sunday, 125; Pilgrim, 126; Princeton, 127; Rainbow, 127; Regina, Regnery, 128; Star Song, Still Waters, 132; United Church, 133; Warner, 134; Westminster, Winston, Word, 135; Zondervan, 136; JEWISH: Biblio, 150; Sepher-Hermon, 155.

Books for Writers, 209-10.

Business
Bookstore Journal, 22; CBMC Contact, 29; Progress, 78; Voice, 95, Honor, 118; Moody, 122; Starburst, 132.

Calendars
Beacon, 107; Group, 116; Neibauer, Nelson, 123; Tyndale, 133; Warner, 134.

Camping
Journal/Chr. Camping, 56; Young/Alive, 98.

Canada
Anglican Journal, Anglican/Review, Annals/de Beaupre, 17; Baptist Beacon, 19; B.C. Cath., Beacon, 20; Breakthrough!, 23; Canada Lutheran, Canadian Baptist, 25; Canadian Cath., Canadian Disciple, 26; Canadian Lutheran, Canadian Messenger, 27; Caravan, 27; Cath. Register, 29; Chr. Courier, 30; Chr. Info, 32; Chr. Librarian, 33; Chr. Renewal, 34; Christianweek, 35; Church Business, 36; Clarion, 39; Compass, 40; Currents, 45; Edge, 46; Esprit, 47; Evangelical Baptist, 48; Faith Today, 49; Fellowship Link, Fellowship, 50; Hymn Society, 55; Mennonite Brethren, 67; Our Family, 72; Sally Ann, 82; United Church Observer, 92; Young Soldier, 99; Credo, 112; Inheritance, 118; Kindred, 119; Novalis, 124; Still Waters, 132; United Church, 133; JEWISH: CCAR, 150.

Cartoons, Cartoon Articles, Comics
marketing of, 164-66; Baptist Leader, 19; Breakthrough!, 23; Brio, 24; Canadian Disciple, 26; Canadian Lutheran, 27; Chr. Courier (Canada), 30; Church Teachers, 38; Clubhouse, 39; Counselor, 42; Crusader, 44; Discoveries, Door, Edge, 46; Faith Today, 49; Fellowship Link, 50; Home Life, Home Times, 54; Lutheran Journal, 66; Mature Years, Mennonite Brethren Herald, 67; Power/Light, Praying, 76; R-A-D-A-R, Reformed Worship, 80; With, 96; Women Alive!, 97; Young Soldier, 99; Your Church, YouthGuide, 100.

Challenged: Physically, Mentally
Attention Please!, 19; Lifeglow, 62; Networks, 70; Young/Alive, 98.

Charismatic
Advocate, 15; Charisma, 30; Church Herald/Holiness, 37; Helping Hand, 52; Messenger, 68; Pentecostal Evangel, Pentecostal Messenger,

74; *Preacher's,* 77; *Women Alive!,* 97; Aglow, 104; Bridge, 108; Chosen, 109; Gospel Pub., Harrison, 116; New Leaf, 124; Servant, 130.

Children

marketing techniques, 170-71; *Attention Please!,* 19; *Beginner/Paper,* 20; *Bible Time,* 21; *Bread/God's Children,* 23; *Clubhouse,* 39; *Counselor,* 42; *Discoveries,* 46; *Faith 'n Stuff,* 49; *God's World,* 51; *High Adventure,* 53; *Junior Trails,* 59; *Keys/Kids,* 60; *Listen,* 63; *My Friend,* 70; *On/Line,* 71; *Partners,* 73; *Pioneer, Pockets,* 75; *Primary Days,* 78; *R-A-D-A-R,* 80; *Shining Star,* 84; *Story Friends,* 86; *Story Mates,* 87; *Together Time,* 92; *Wonder Time,* 97; *Young Musicians, Young Soldier,* 99; Abingdon, 104; Alba, 105; Baker, Barbour, 106; Chariot, 109; Chr. Ed., 110; Concordia, 111; Credo, 112; Eerdmans, 114; Friendship, 115; Gospel Pub., 116; Harvest House, Herald, 117; InterVarsity, 118; Bob Jones, Kindred, 119; Lion, Meriwether, 121; Moody, Morehouse, Mott Media, 122; Nelson, New Hope, 123; Paulist, 125; Pilgrim, 126; Questar, Rainbow, 127; Regina, 128; St. Paul, 130; Shining Star, Standard, 131; Still Waters, 132; Tyndale, 133; Victor, 134; Winston, Word, 135; Zondervan, 136; JEWISH: *Noah's Ark,* 146; *Shofar,* 147; Board, CCAR, 150; Heb. Pub., Holiday, 152; Kar-Ben, Pelican, 154; UAHC, 157.

Christian Living

Baptist Beacon, 19; *B.C. Cath., Beacon,* 20; *Bible Advocate,* 21; *Breathrough!,* 23; *Canada Lutheran, Canadian Baptist,* 25; *Canadian Cath., Canadian Disciple,* 26; *Canadian Lutheran, Canadian Messenger,* 27; *Chr. Courier* (Canada), 30; *Chr. Info,* 32; *Chr. Renewal,* 34; *Clarion,* 39; *Currents,* 45; *Edge,* 46; *Esprit,* 47; *Evangelical Baptist,* 48; *Fellowship Link, Fellowship,* 50; *Mennonite Brethren,* 67; *Our Family,* 72; Chr. Pub., 110; Dimensions/Living, 113; Moody, 122; Questar, 127; Resurrection, 128.

Church School. See Education.

Clergy. See Ministry.

Clubs. See Writers Groups, Clubs.

Columns, Departments. See also Syndicates.

Advent Chr., 14; *Advocate,* 15; *AME/Review, America,* 16; *Asbury, At Ease,* 18; *Better Tomorrow,* 20; *Bible-Science News,* 21; *Bookstore Journal,* 22; *Campus Life,* 25; *Catechist,* 27; *Cath./Circle, CBMC,* 29; *Chapter One, Chr. Computing,* 30; *Chr. Drama, Chr. Educators,* 31; *Christianity Today,* 32; *Chr. School, Chr. Single,* 35; *Church/Synagogue Libraries,* 36; *Church Educator,* 37; *Church Teachers,* 38; *Church Worship, CLCL,* 39; *Cornerstone,* 42; *Crisis,* 43; *Door, Edge,* 46; *Episcopal Life,* 47; *Evangel, Evangelical Baptist, Evangelism,* 48; *Family,* 50; *Home Times,* 54; *Journal/Camping,* 56; *Leader,* 61; *Light/Life,* 62; *Living Church, Living Family, Living/Preschoolers/Children/Teenagers, Lookout,* 64-65; *Magazine/Chr. Youth,* 66; *Mature Years, Mennonite Brethren,* 67; *Momentum, Moody,* 69; *Networks,* 70; *Other Side,* 71; *Our Sunday, Parent Care,* 72; *Plumbline, Positive Approach,* 75; *Priest,* 77; *Progress,* 78; *Queen/Hearts,* 80; *Shining Star,* 84; *Standard, The* 86; *Teachers/Focus,* 89; *Today's/Life, Today's/Teacher,* 91; *Trinity News,* 92; *Virtue, Vision, Vista,* 94; *Women Alive!, Word/World,* 97; *Your Church,* 100.

Commentaries

Loizeaux, 121; More, 122.

Computers

writer's need for, 211-13; *Chr. Computing,* 30.

Conferences. See Writers Conferences.

Congregational Life

Abingdon, 104; Alban, Augsburg Fortress, 105; CSS, 113; Judson, 119; Morehouse, 122; Neibauer, 123; Tabor, 132.

Contests, 182-84.

Cookbooks

Starburst, 132; JEWISH: Decalogue, 151.

Coping. See Recovery, Coping.

Crafts. See Games, Puzzles, Crafts, Quizzes.

Crossover Markets, 184-85.

Cults

SCP Journal, 83; AMG, 105.

Current Issues, Social Concerns

Advent/Witness, 14; *Advocate, Again, Alive,* 15; *AME/Review, A.B.S. Record,* 16; *Anglican,* 17; *Asbury, Asso. Reformed, At Ease,* 18; *Axios, Baptist Herald,* 19; *Better Tomorrow,* 20; *Bible Advocate, Bible-Science News,* 21; *Bread/God's Children,* 23; *Brethren Life, Brigade Leader,* 24; *Cathedral Age,* 28; *Cath. Near East,* 31; *Cath./Circle, CBMC,* 29; *Charisma,* 32; *Chr. Century,* 30; *Chr. Educators,* 31; *Chr. Home/School, Christianity Today,* 32; *Chr. Living, Chr. Medical/Dental,* 33; *Chr. Reader,* 34; *Chr. Social Action, Chr. Standard,* 35; *Church/State,* 36; *Church/Evangel, Churchwoman,* 38; *CLCL,* 39; *Commonweal,* 40; *Conqueror, Conscience,* 41; *Cornerstone,* 42; *Covenant Companion, Crisis,* 43; *CSSR,* 44; *Door,* 46; *Emphasis, Episcopal Life,* 47; *Evangelism,* 48; *Family, Focus/Family,* 50; *Gospel Tidings,* 51; *Helping Hand,* 52; *Herald/Holiness, HiCall, High Adventure,* 53; *Home Life, Horizons,* 54; *I.D.,* 55; *InterVarsity, Issues/Answers,* 56; *Journal/Feminist Studies,* 57; *Journal/Women's Min.,* 59; *Light/Life,* 62; *Live,* 63; *Living Church,* 64; *Lookout,* 65; *Magazine/Chr. Youth,* 66; *Mature Years,* 67; *Ministry Today,* 68; *Moody,* 69; *Other Side,* 71; *Our Sunday,* 72; *Pathway I.D.,* 73; *Pentecostal Evangel, Pentecostal Messenger, Perspectives/Science, PIME,* 74; *Plumbline,* 75; *Presby. Survey,* 77; *Pulpit Helps,* 79; *St. Joseph's Messenger,* 82; *SCP, Search, Seek,* 83; *Sharing/Practice,* 84; *Social Justice,* 85; *Standard,* 86; *Student, Student Leadership,* 87; *Teenage Chr.,* 89; *Theo./Public Policy, Theo. Today,* 90; *Trinity News,* 92; *U.M. Reporter,* 93; *Vision,* 94; *War Cry, Wesleyan Advocate,* 95; *With, Witness, Woman/Power,* 96; *Woman's Touch, Women Alive!, Word/World,* 97; *World Vision, You!,* 98; *Young Salvationist,* 99; Abingdon, 104; Alba, AMG, 105; Barclay, Beacon, 107; Chalice, Chr. Classics, 109; Christopher, 110; College, 111; Crossway, Dimension, 113; Eerdmans, 114; Friendship, 115; Harper, 116; Judson, 119; Krieger, 120; Lion, Liturgical, Loyola, 121; Moody, 122; NavPress, Nelson, 123; Orbis, 124; Paulist, 125; Pilgrim, 126; Prescott, 127; Resurrection, 128; Revell, Review, 129; Star Song, 132; United Church, 133; University, Victory, 134; Westminster, Winston, Word, 135.

Curriculum

techniques for writing, 171-72; Christian publishers, 172-76; Jewish publishers, 172; publishers associations, 176; Accent, 104; Broadman, 108; Chr. Ed., 110; Concordia, 111; Friends United, 115; Group, 116; Harvest, Hensley, 117; Kindred, 119;

(Curriculum, *continued*)
Meriwether, 121; Morehouse, Mott Media, 122; Novalis, 124; Pacific, 125; Sheed, 131; Star Song, 132; Warner, 134; Cokesbury, 173; JEWISH: A.R.E., Behrman, 149.

Devotions, Meditations

marketing techniques, 180-82; list of devotional guides, 181-82; *Advent. Chr.*, 14; *Advocate*, 15; *Asbury, Asso. Reformed, At Ease*, 18; *Baptist Beacon*, 19; *Better Tomorrow*, 20; *Breakaway*, 23; *Brethren Life, Broken Streets*, 24; *Canadian Cath., Canadian Disciple*, 26; *Canadian Lutheran, Canadian Messenger*, 27; *Cath. Digest*, 28; *Cath./Circle*, 29; *Chr. Century*, 30; *Chr. Info*, 32; *Chr. Medical*, 33; *Chr. Reader, Chr. Renewal*, 34; *Chr. Single, Chr. Standard*, 35; *Church Herald/Holiness*, 37; *Church/God/Evangel, Churchwoman*, 38; *Clarion*, 39; *Connecting Point, Conqueror*, 41; *Cornerstone*, 42; *Covenant Companion, Creation Social Science*, 43; *Currents*, 45; *Edge*, 46; *Emphasis/Faith, Esprit*, 47; *Evangel, Evangelical Baptist*, 48; *Fellowship*, 50; *Gospel Tidings*, 51; *Guide, Helping Hand*, 52; *Herald/Holiness*, 53; *Horizons*, 54; *Inspirer*, 55; *Journal/Pastoral Care*, 58; *Journal/Women' Min.*, 59; *Just/Us*, 60; *Leadership*, 61; *Lifeglow*, 62; *Live*, 63; *Living Church, Living with Preschoolers/Children/Teenagers, Lookout*, 64-65; *Lutheran Witness*, 66; *Mennonite Brethren, Message/Open Bible*, 67; *Messenger, Ministry Today*, 68; *Missionary Tidings*, 69; *New Covenant*, 70; *Other Side*, 71; *Our Family, Parent Care*, 72; *Pentecostal Messenger*, 74; *Positive Approach*, 75; *Prayer Line, Praying*, 76; *Presby. Survey*, 77; *Pulpit Helps, Quaker Life*, 79; *Queen/Hearts*, 80; *Review/Religious*, 81; *Salt/Light*, 82; *Seek*, 83; *Sharing/Practice*, 84; *Spice*, 85; *Standard*, 86; *Today's/Life, Together*, 91; *Vision*, 94; *War Cry, Wesleyan Advocate*, 95; *Women Alive!*, 97; Alba, Augsburg Fortress, 105; Barclay, Beacon Hill, Bethel, 107; Bridge, Broadman, Brown-ROA, 108; Chosen, 109; Chr. Lit., 110; Dimensions/Living, 113; Evergreen, 114; Forward, 115; Harper, Harrison, 116; Honor, Ignatius, 118; Kindred, Kregel, 119; Liguori, 120; Morehouse, 122; Orbis, 124; Our Sunday, Pacific, 125; Questar, Regal, 127; Regina, Resurrection, 128; Revell, Review, 129; Servant, 130; Victor, Warner, 134.

Disabled. See Challenged: Physically, Mentally.

Drama

marketing techniques, 185-86; publishers list, 186; radio and TV, 186-87; video and film, 187-88; *Canada Lutheran, Canadian Baptist*, 25; *Chr. Courier* (Canada), 30; *Chr. Drama*, 31; *Currents*, 45; *Fellowship Link*, 50; *Power/Living*, 76; CSS, 113; Lillenas, 120; Meriwether, 121; Russell, 129; Sheer Joy!, Standard, 131.

Drugs

Forward Movement, 115.

Ecumenism

Alive Now!, 15; *Canadian Disciple*, 26; *Chr. Century*, 30; *Compass*, 40; *Cross Currents*, 44; *Journal/Ecumenical Studies*, 57; Friendship, 115; Paulist, 125; JEWISH: *Journal/Ecumenical*, 144.

Education

Anglican Journal, 17; *Attention Please!, Baptist Leader*, 19; *B.C. Cath.*, 20; *Breathrough!* 23; *Builder*, 24; *Canadian Baptist*, 25; *Canadian Cath.*, 26; *Canadian Lutheran, Canadian Messenger, Caravan*, 27; *Chr. Courier* (Canada), 30; *Chr. Educators*, 31; *Chr. Renewal*, 34; *Chr. School*, 35; *Church Business*, 36; *Church Educator*, 37; *Church Teachers*, 38; *Clarion*, 39; *Compass*, 40; *Evangelical Baptist*, 48; *Faith Today*, 49; *Fellowship*, 50; *Key/Chr. Ed.*, 60; *Leader, Leader/Today*, 61; *Liturgy*, 63; *Momentum*, 69; *Our Family*, 72; *Parish Teacher*, 73; *Shining Star*, 84; *Teachers/Focus, Teachers Interaction*, 89; *Today's/Teacher*, 91; *United Church Observer*, 92; *Vision*, 94; *Youth/Chr. Ed., YouthGuide, Youth Leader*, 100; *Youthworker, Youthworker Update*, 101; Accent, 104; Augsburg Fortress, 105; Beacon Hill, 107; Bridge, 108; Chr. Ed., 110; Cowley, 112; Educational Min., 114; Group, 116; Krieger, 120; Religious Ed., 128; St. Mary's, 130; Shining Star, Standard, 131; JEWISH: *Agenda*, 138; A.R.E., 149; Board, 150.

Environment

Anglican Journal, 17; *Canada Lutheran, Canadian Baptist*, 25; *Canadian Disciple*, 26; *Canadian Lutheran*, 27; *Chr. Courier* (Canada), 30; *Church Business*, 36; *Churchwoman*, 38; *Clarion*, 39; *Compass*, 40; *Currents*, 45; *Egg*, 46; *Esprit*, 47; *Evangelical Baptist*, 48; *Fellowship Link*, 50; *Our Family*, 72; *Sally Ann*, 82; *United Church Observer*, 92.

Ethics

Christianity Today, 32; *Compass*, 40; *Egg*, 46; *Harvard Review*, 52; *Journal/Nursing*, 57; *Journal/Ethics*, 58; *Theo./Public Policy*, 90; Abingdon, 104; Augsburg Fortress, 105; Herald, 117; Pilgrim, 126; Sheed, 131; Westminster, 135.

Evangelism

Anglican Journal, 17; *Baptist Beacon*, 19; *Beacon*, 20; *Canada Lutheran, Canadian Baptist*, 25; *Canadian Cath. Review, Canadian Disciple*, 26; *Canadian Lutheran*, 27; *CBMC*, 29; *Chr. Info*, 32; *Clarion*, 39; *Currents*, 45; *Esprit*, 47; *Evangelical Baptist, Evangelism*, 48; *Evangelizing/Child, Faith Today*, 49; *Fellowship Link, Fellowship*, 50; *Our Family*, 72; *World Vision*, 98; Bridge, 108; Evangelical Training, 114; Gospel Pub., 116; Herald, 117; New Leaf, 124.

Family. See Marriage, Family, Parenting.

Feminism. See Women/Women's Studies.

Fiction

Alive!, Alive Now!, 15; *Annals/de Beaupre*, 17; *Attention Please*, 19; *Better Tomorrow*, 20; *Canadian Messenger*, 27; *Chapter One, Charisma*, 30; *Chr. Drama*, 31; *Chr. Living*, 33; *Chr. School, Chr. Single*, 35; *Church Herald*, 37; *Conqueror*, 41; *Cornerstone*, 42; *Critic*, 43; *Evangel*, 48; *Family*, 50; *Helping Hand*, 52; *Home Life, Home Times, Horizons*, 54; *Light/Life*, 62; *Liguorian, Live*, 63; *Living with Preschoolers/Children/Teenagers, Lookout*, 64-65; *Lutheran Journal*, 66; *Mature Years*, 67; *Miraculous Medal*, 68; *Moody*, 69; *Other Side*, 71; *Praying*, 76; *Queen/Hearts*, 80; *St. Anthony*, 81; *St. Joseph's*, 82; *Seek*, 83; *Standard*, 86; *Sunday Digest*, 88; *US Cath.*, 93; *Virtue*, 94; *Vital Christianity, Wesleyan Advocate*, 95; Baker, Barbour, 106; Bethel, 107; Bridge, 108; Chariot, 109; Chr. Pub., 110; College, Companion, 111; Crossway, 113; Evergreen, 114; Friends United, 115; Gospel Pub., Harper, 116; Harvest, Hensley, 117; Bob Jones, Kindred, 119; Libra, 120; Lion, 121; Moody, 122; NavPress, Nelson, 123; Old Rugged, 124; Prescott, 127; Revell, 129; Servant, Shaw, 130; Standard, 131; Starburst, Star Song, 132; Victor, Victory, 134; Word, 135; JEWISH: *Jewish Currents, Jewish News*, 142; Holiday, 152.

Fillers

Advocate, Alive!, 15; *Asbury, At Ease*, 18; *Baptist Leader*, 19; *Better Tomorrow*, 20; *Bible Advocate*, 21; *Brio, Broken Streets*, 24; *Campus Life*, 25; *Cathedral Age, Cath. Digest*, 28; *Chapter One, Chr. Century*, 30; *Chr. Courier* (U.S.), 31; *Chr. Medical*, 33; *Chr. Parenting, Chr. Reader*, 34; *Chr. School, Chr. Single*, 35; *Churchman's*, 37; *Church Teachers*, 38; *Clubhouse*, 39; *Conqueror*, 41; *Covenant Companion, Creation Social Science*, 43; *Door*, 46; *Evangelical Beacon*, 48; *Family, Focus/Family*, 50; *Gospel Tidings*, 51; *Guideposts, Helping Hand*, 52; *HiCall, High Adventure*, 53; *Home Times, Horizons*, 54; *Hymn Society, Insight, Inspirer*, 55; *Journal/Chr. Camping*, 56; *Joyful*

Israel
138-58; *Israel Horizons*, 141.

Justice, Peace Issues
Chr. Social Action, 35; *Churchwoman*, 38; *Egg*, 46; *Momentum*, 69; *Salt*, 82; *Social Justice*, 85; *United Church Observer*, 92; Friendship, 115; Herald, 117; Judson, 119; Orbis, 124; United Church, 133.

Laity
Alban, Augsburg Fortress, 105.

Large Print
Walker, 134.

Leadership
Advance, 14; *Advocate*, 15; *America*, 16; *Baptist Beacon, Baptist Leader*, 19; *Beacon*, 20; *Biblical Illustrator*, 22; *Breakthrough!*, 23; *Brigade Leader, Builder*, 24; *Canada Lutheran*, 25; *Canadian Cath.*, 26; *Canadian Lutheran, Caravan*, 27; *Church Business*, 36; *Church Educator*, 37; *CLCL*, 39; *Discipleship Training*, 45; *Esprit*, 47; *Evangelical Baptist*, 48; *Faith Today*, 49; *Group*, 51; *Insight*, 55; *Journal/Chr. Camping*, 56; *Kids' Stuff*, 60; *Leader, Leader/Today, Leadership*, 61; *Mennonite Brethren*, 67; *Pioneer Clubs*, 75; *Reformed Worship*, 80; *Student Leadership*, 87; *Sunday School Counselor*, 88; *Teachers/Focus*, 89; *United Church Observer*, 92; *World Vision*, 98; *Youth/Chr. Ed., YouthGuide, Youth Leader*, 100; *Youthworker*, 101.

Libraries
Cath. Library World, 28; *Chr. Librarian*, 33; *Church/Synagogue Libraries*, 36; *Church Media Library*, 38; *Librarians World*, 62. JEWISH: *Church and Synagogue*, 139.

Liturgy. See also Worship.
Liturgy, 63; *Modern Liturgy*, 69; *US Cath.*, 93; Cowley, 112; CSS, 113; Novalis, 124; Pastoral, Paulist, 125; St. Anthony, 129; Scarecrow, 130.

Local Congregation
writing for, 160-61.

Marriage, Family, Parenting
Annals/de Beaupre, 17; *Baptist Beacon*, 19; *B.C. Cath., Beacon*, 20; *Breakthrough!*, 23; *Canadian Baptist*, 25; *Canadian Cath.*, 26; *Canadian Lutheran, Canadian Messenger*, 27; *Chr. Parenting*, 30; *Chr. Home*, 32; *Chr. Parenting*, 34; *Columbia*, 40; *Esprit*, 47; *Evangelical Baptist*, 48; *Family, Fellowship, Focus/Family*, 50; *Home Life*, 54; *Lifeglow*, 62; *Living Family, Living with Preschoolers/Children/Teenagers*, 64-65; *Mennonite Brethren*, 67; *Our Family, Parents/Teenagers*, 72; *Parish Family*, 73; *St. Anthony*, 81; *Spice*, 85; *United Church Observer*, 92; *US Cath.*, 93; *Virtue*, 94; Abingdon, 104; Alba, AMG, Augsburg Fortress, 105; Bosco, Bridge, 108; Chariot, Chr. Classics, 109; Christopher, 110; Concordia, 111; Crossway, CSS, 113; Focus, 114; Harper, Harrison, 116; Hensley, 117; Honor, Ignatius, 118; Life Cycle, 120; Lion, 121; Moody, Morehouse, 122; NavPress, Nelson, 123; Novalis, Old Rugged, 124; Pacific, Paulist, 125; Pillar, 126; Prescott, Questar, Rainbow, 127; Resurrection, 128; Revell, Review, 129; St. Paul, Servant, Shaw, 130; Tyndale, 133; Victor, Victory, Warner, 134; Wellness, Westminster, Word, 135.

Media
Anglican Journal, 17; *Canada Lutheran*, 25; *Cath. Family Media Guide*, 28; *Chr. Courier* (Canada), 30; *Compass*, 40; *Currents*, 45; *Edge*, 46.

Medicine. See Healing, Health, Fitness.

Meditations. See Devotions, Meditations.

Men
Brigade Leader, 24; *CBMC*, 29; *Listening*, 63; *Voice*, 95.

Mental Health. See Psychology.

Ministry
Advance, 14; *A.M.E. Recorder, American/Review*, 16; *Bible Review*, 21; *Biblical Archaeology*, 22; *Calvin/Journal*, 25; *Cathedral Age*, 28; *Chr. Century*, 30; *Chr. Ministry*, 33; *Chr. Standard*, 35; *Church Business*, 36; *Church Educator*, 37; *Church Worship, Circuit Rider, Clergy Journal*, 39; *Congregational Journal*, 41; *Horizons/Theology*, 54; *Hymn Society*, 55; *Journal/Pastoral, Journal/Health*, 58; *Just/Us*, 60; *Leadership*, 61; *Lutheran Forum*, 65; *Mennonite Quarterly*, 67; *Missiology*, 68; *Pastoral Life*, 73; *Positive Approach*, 75; *Preacher's, Preaching, Priest*, 77; *Pro Ecclesia*, 78; *Pulpit Helps*, 79; *Quarterly Review, Reformed Worship*, 80; *Sharing/Practice*, 84; *Southwestern Journal/Theo., Spice*, 85; *Theo. Studies*, 90; *Your Church*, 100; Abingdon, 104; Alban, Augsburg Fortress, 105; Evan. Training, 114; Harper, 116; Paulist, 125; Religious Ed., 128; St. Anthony, St. Bede's, 129; Sheed, 131; Tabor, 132; Warner, 134; Zondervan, 136.

Missions, Missionaries
Anglican Journal, 17; *B.C. Cath., Beacon*, 20; *Canada Lutheran*, 25; *Canadian Disciple*, 26; *Canadian Lutheran, Canadian Messenger*, 27; *CBMC*, 29; *Chr. Medical*, 33; *Chr. Renewal*, 34; *Clarion*, 39; *Co-Laborer*, 40; *Evangelical Baptist*, 48; *Fellowship Link, Fellowship*, 50; *Heartbeat*, 52; *Mennonite Brethren*, 67; *Missiology*, 68; *Missionary Tidings, Mission Frontiers*, 69; *New World Outlook*, 70; *Our Family*, 72; *PIME*, 74; *Pioneer*, 75; *Wherever*, 96; Friendship, 115; Herald, 117; New Hope, 123; Orbis, 124; Paulist, 125.

Monastic Studies
Cistercian, 110; Liturgical, 121; St. Bede's, 129.

Music
books about writing, 179; marketing techniques, 177-78; organizations, 179; periodicals, 178-79; seminars, 179; *American Organist*, 16; *Creator*, 43; *Exaltation*, 49; *Hymn Society*, 55; *Reformed Worship*, 80; *Religious Broadcasting*, 81; *Senior Musician*, 83; *Young Musicians*, 99; Nelson, 123; Resurrection, 128; Russell, 129.

Newspapers
writing for, 168-69; news services, 169.

Nonprofit Organizations
writing for, 162-63.

Parenting. *See Marriage, Family, Parenting.*

Pastors. *See Ministry.*

Peace, Peacemaking. *See Justice, Peace Issues; Global Issues, Concerns.*

Philosophy

Harvard/Review, 52; Cornell, 112; Open Court, 124; Paulist, 125; Princeton, 127; St. Bede's, 129; Trinity Fdtn., 132; Trinity Press, 133; Yale, 136.

Picture Books

Abingdon, 104; Alba House, Augsburg Fortress, 105; Barbour, 106; Chariot, 109; Concordia, 111; Eerdmans, 114; Friendship, 115; Gibson, 167; Harvest House, 117; Herald, 117; InterVarsity, 118; Bob Jones, 119; Liguori, 120; Lion, Meriwether, 121; Moody, Morehouse, 122; Multnomah, Nelson, New Hope, 123; Pacific, 125; Regina, 128; Standard, 131; Tyndale, 133; Victor, 134; Winston-Derek, Word, 135.

Plays. *See Drama.*

Poetry

marketing techniques, 163-64; *Advocate, Alive Now!,* 15; *America,* 16; *Anglican, Anglican/Review, Annals/de Beaupre,* 17; *At Ease,* 18; *Axios,* 19; *Better Tomorrow,* 20; *Bible Advocate,* 21; *Breakthrough!,* 23; *Brethren Life, Broken Streets,* 24; *Chapter One, Chr. Century,* 30; *Chr. Drama, Chr. Educators,* 31; *Chr. Info,* 32; *Chr. Living,* 33; *Chr. Renewal,* 34; *Chr. Single,* 35; *Christmas, Church/State,* 36; *Churchman's,* 37; *Church Worship,* 39; *Co-Laborer, Commonweal,* 40; *Connecting Point, Conqueror, Conscience,* 41; *Cornerstone,* 42; *Covenant Companion, Creation Social Science, Critic,* 43; *Cross Currents,* 44; *Decision,* 45; *Edge,* 46; *Esprit,* 47; *Evangel,* 48; *Family, Fellowship Link,* 50; *Helping Hand, Herald/Holiness,* 53; *Home Life, Home Times, Horizons,* 54; *Inspirer,* 55; *Journal/Feminist,* 57; *Journal/Pastoral Care,* 58; *Journal/Women's Ministries,* 59; *Leader, Level C,* 61; *Light/Life,* 62; *Liguorian, Liturgy, Live,* 63; *Living Church, Living with Preschoolers/Children/Teenagers,* 64-65; *Lutheran Journal,* 66; *Mature Years, Mennonite Brethren,* 67; *Miraculous Medal,* 68; *Networks,* 70; *Oblates, Other Side,* 71; *Pentecostal Messenger,* 74; *Plumbline,* 75; *Purpose, Quaker Life,* 79; *Queen/Hearts,* 80; *St. Joseph's, Salt/Light,* 82; *Sharing/Healing, Sharing/Practice,* 84; *Sisters, Spice,* 85; *Standard,* 86; *Sunday Digest,* 88; *Theol. Today, Time/Singing,* 90; *U.M. Reporter,* 93; *Virtue, Vision,* 94; *Vital Christianity, Weavings, Wesleyan Advocate,* 95; *Witness,* 96; Christopher, 110; Companion, 111; Dimension, 113; Harper, 116; St. Anthony, 129; United Church, 133; Westminster, Winston, 135; Yale, 136; JEWISH: *Jewish Currents, Jewish Frontier,* 142; *Wellsprings,* 148.

Politics, Patriotism

America, 16; *Anglican Journal,* 17; *Breakthrough!,* 23; *Chr. Courier* (Canada), 30; *Chr. Renewal,* 34; *Church/State,* 36; *Compass,* 40; *Faith Today,* 49; *Home Times,* 54; *Liberty,* 62; *Miraculous Medal,* 68.

Prayer

Congregational Journal, 41; *Parish Family,* 73; *Prayer Line, Praying,* 76; *Spiritual Life,* 86; *US Cath.,* 93; Augsburg Fortress, 105; Barclay, 107; Chosen, 109; Christian Lit., Christopher, 110; Companion, 111; Harrison, 116; Hensley, 117; Liguori, 120; New Hope, 123; New Leaf, 124; Pastoral, 125; Regal, 127; Regina, Resurrection, 128; Review, St. Anthony, 129; Servant, 130; Victor, Victory House, 134.

Preaching

Advance, 14; *Preacher's, Preaching,* 77; Abingdon, 104; Augsburg Fortress, 105; Chalice, 109; Pilgrim, 126.

Press Associations, 169, 205.

Profiles. *See Interviews, Profiles.*

Prophecy

Baptist Beacon, 19; Gospel Pub., 116; New Leaf, 124.

Psychology

Journal/Nursing, 57; *Journal/Christianity, Journal/Theol.,* 58; *Psy./Living,* 78; *St. Anthony,* 81; Open Court, 124; Yale, 136.

Puzzles. *See Games, Puzzles, Crafts, Quizzes.*

Quizzes. *See Games, Puzzles, Crafts, Quizzes.*

Radio, Television, writing for. *See Drama.*

Recovery, Coping

Alba, 105; Chosen, 109; College, Compcare, 111; Harper, 116; NavPress, Nelson, 123; Pacific, 125; Prescott, 127; Revell, Review, 129; St. Paul, Servant, 130; Triumph, Tyndale, 133; Victor, Victory House, 134; Westminster, Word, 135.

Record Keeping, for writers, 213-18.

Reference

Abingdon, 104; Baker, Barbour, 106; College, Companion, 111; Credo, 112; Dimension, 113; Harper, 116; Hendrickson, 117; Holman, InterVarsity, 118; Kregel, 119; Morehouse, More, 122; Nelson, 123; Orbis, 124; Our Sunday, Pastoral, 125; Scarecrow, 130; Star Song, Still Waters, 132; Tyndale, 133; University, Victor, 134; Zondervan, 136.

Regional Publications, writing for, 161-62.

Resources for Writers. *See Writers.*

Reviews

AME Church, 16; *Anglican Journal, Anglican/Review,* 17; *Builder,* 24; *Canada Lutheran,* 25; *Canadian Cath.,* 26; *Chr. Century,* 30; *Chr. Info,* 32; *Chr. Librarian,* 33; *Chr. Renewal, Chr. Retailing,* 34; *Christianweek,* 35; *Church Teachers,* 38; *Clarion,* 39; *Compass,* 40; *Congregational Journal,* 41; *Cornerstone,* 42; *Discipleship Journal,* 45; *Edge,* 46; *Esprit,* 47; *Evangelical Baptist,* 48; *Horizons,* 54; *Journal/Ecumenical,* 57; *Journal/Christianity,* 58; *Living Church,* 64; *Momentum,* 69; *Presby. Outlook, Priest,* 77; *USQR,* 93; *Word/World,* 97.

Scholars

Abingdon, 104; Augsburg Fortress, 105; Beacon, 107; Cambridge, 108; Cath. U., 109; Cornell, 112; Greenwood, Harper, 116; Hendrickson, 117; Kingswood, 119; Krieger, 120; Liturgical, 121; Morehouse, 122; Open Court, Orbis, 124; Penn State,

World Issues. See Global Issues, Concerns.

World Religions

Worship. See also Liturgy.

Writers Audio/Video Cassette Tape Training, 207.

Writers Conferences, 190-96.

Writers Consultation Services and Other Helps, 207-8.

Writers Correspondence Courses, 206-7.

Writers Groups, Clubs, 196-205.

Writers Magazines, Newsletters, 208-9.

Writers Training Books, 209-11.

Youth